The
BOOKER T. WASHINGTON
Papers

The

BOOKER T. WASHINGTON
Papers

VOLUME 12

1912–14

Louis R. Harlan
and
Raymond W. Smock
EDITORS

University of Illinois Press
URBANA · CHICAGO · LONDON

The BOOKER T. WASHINGTON *Papers*
is supported by
The National Endowment for the Humanities
The National Historical Publications and Records Commission
The University of Maryland

Library of Congress Cataloging in Publication Data

Washington, Booker T.   1856–1915.
    The Booker T. Washington papers.

    Vol. 12   edited by L. R. Harlan and R. W. Smock.
    Includes bibliographies and indexes.
    CONTENTS: v. 1. The autobiographical writings.
    —v. 2. 1860–89.–[etc.]—v. 12. 1912–14.
    1. Washington, Booker T., 1856–1915.
    2. Afro-Americans—History—1863–1877—Sources.
    3. Afro-Americans—History—1877–1964—Sources.
    4. Afro-Americans—Correspondence.   I.   Harlan,
    Louis R.   II.   Smock, Raymond W.
    E185.97.W274   305.8'96073'0924 [B]   75–186345
    ISBN 0–252–00974–6 (v. 12)   AACR1

*To J. Saunders Redding
and the late Oliver W. Holmes
for their fostering interest in this project*

CONTENTS

CONTENTS

CONTENTS

CONTENTS

Contents

INTRODUCTION

IN THE PERIOD COVERED BY this volume, from September 1912 through March 1914, Washington's declining personal vigor could be seen in his face but not in his actions, as he continued his heavy schedule of speaking, fund-raising, close supervision of Tuskegee Institute, and race leadership.

The election of the Democrat Woodrow Wilson to the presidency virtually forced Washington's retirement as a patronage broker, but he continued to have some political influence. On the eve of Wilson's inauguration, he expressed the belief that Wilson would be a friend to blacks.

The Democrats, however, lost no time in dismantling the political arm of the Tuskegee Machine. Washington stood by while one political lieutenant after another was removed from office, beginning with William H. Lewis only three days after the inauguration. The able Charles W. Anderson was among the last to fall, and he returned to office in the New York state government. Of all the Washington lieutenants, only Judge Robert H. Terrell received reappointment by Wilson. This was apparently because Terrell's ability and circumspection had made a favorable impression on many Democrats in Washington, D.C., and because Washington persuaded Bishop Alexander Walters, a black Wilson supporter, to intervene on Terrell's behalf.

Despite the loss of its political arm, the Tuskegee Machine remained powerful. Washington was able to secure positions in the English department of Howard University for his protegés Alain L. Locke and G. David Houston. He wrested the festivities of the fiftieth anniversary of emancipation from a rival group and awarded it to the National Negro Business League. He secured friends at Lincoln University by aiding the school to secure a Carnegie science hall. His lieutenant

Charles Anderson had enough influence in New York to wage a successful campaign to defeat for election one of the judges who had voted to dismiss the assault charges against Henry A. Ulrich, Washington's assailant in 1911. Washington employed an agent to spy upon and try to frustrate Chief Sam, leader of a back-to-Africa movement.

As Washington dropped out of politics and was free of the constraints he had felt as a presidential adviser, he began to speak more publicly and forthrightly about racial inequities. At the Black Belt Fair in Demopolis, Alabama, in September 1912, and again in *The Independent* about a week later, he dealt with the gross inequalities in public school expenditures for the two races. In November 1912, only a few days after the presidential election, he published in *The Century* his most comprehensive and direct criticism of American racial injustice, "Is the Negro Having a Fair Chance?" He answered simply, "No," but then proceeded to elaborate the job discrimination in the North, and the Jim Crow transportation and unequal educational opportunities of the South. Washington sent marked copies of this article in 1913 to nearly every railroad official in the country, and followed this in 1914 by urging all black organizations to observe Railroad Day by complaining to their local railroad officials about racial discrimination on their lines and in the railroad waiting rooms.

In other ways also, Washington made clear a change of emphasis in race relations. He expressed to Oswald Garrison Villard his disappointment at the segregation of federal office buildings under the Wilson administration, and Villard used his statement in a letter of complaint to Wilson. He urged black Georgians to resist the new Atlanta residential segregation ordinance, publicly deplored labor union exclusion of blacks from employment, opposed a rural land-segregation scheme proposed by Clarence Poe of the *Progressive Farmer,* redoubled his public letters opposing lynching, and encouraged such relatively liberal white southerners as Benjamin F. Riley, Willis D. Weatherford, and Quincy Ewing. None of this was enough to appease Villard and his allies in the NAACP, however. Villard spoke of Washington's cowardly silence in the face of injustice as proof of his unfitness as a race leader.

While Washington's utterances did have a more critical tone, he continued to give priority to the economic and educational means of black progress. He persuaded the Phelps-Stokes Fund to finance a study of black secondary and higher education and tried to persuade Anson Phelps Stokes to choose Robert E. Park to head the study, but Stokes preferred Thomas Jesse Jones. When Oswald Garrison Villard proposed to organize an association of black schools to meet at the NAACP offices, however, Washington refused to attend and discouraged every black educator he could from attending. Washington continued his direction of the Jeanes Fund and cultivated the friendship of Julius Rosenwald, who later expanded his interest in Tuskegee into a concern for the black public schools.

At home in Tuskegee, Washington fended off threats of George Washington Carver to resign, began the publication of the *Negro Year Book,* under the editorship of Monroe N. Work, in 1912 and of *The Negro Farmer,* edited by Isaac Fisher, in 1913, cultivated the good will of the new governor of Alabama, Emmet O'Neal, and began in 1912 a Tuskegee Five Year Fund, by which large donors agreed to give the school a set amount each year for five years, to relieve Washington of continuous pressure to raise money.

In the fall of 1912 Washington took his first real vacation in at least a decade, a leisurely fishing trip to Coden, Ala., on Mobile Bay. His son Booker T. Washington, Jr., got married suddenly on New Year's Eve, 1913, to Nettie Hancock, a Houston teacher whom he had known at Fisk. Despite these signs of the changing times, there was little to indicate that only a little more than a year later Washington would be dead.

The editors appreciate the help in the preparation of this volume by Sadie M. Harlan, Susan M. Valenza, and Nan E. Woodruff. Marlene Merrill informed us of two errors related to Oberlin College in an earlier volume, which we note in the errata section herein.

We are grateful to the National Endowment for the Humanities, the National Historical Publications and Records Commission, and the University of Maryland for their support of this project.

ERRATA

VOLUME 2, p. 291, John Mercer Langston enrolled at Oberlin in 1844, not 1834.

VOLUME 2, p. 364, James Monroe Trotter was recorder of deeds from 1887 to 1889, not from 1885 to 1887.

VOLUME 2, p. 411, the Oberlin College Archives have no record that Blanche Kelso Bruce was ever enrolled there.

VOLUME 11, p. 398, the missing endnote for Charles William Anderson to Emmett Jay Scott, Dec. 5, 1911, should be: TLS   Con. 435   BTW Papers   DLC.

SYMBOLS AND ABBREVIATIONS

Sᴛᴀɴᴅᴀʀᴅ ᴀʙʙʀᴇᴠɪᴀᴛɪᴏɴs for dates, months, and states are used by the editors only in footnotes and endnotes; textual abbreviations are reproduced as found.

DOCUMENT SYMBOLS

1. A — autograph; written in author's hand
   H — handwritten by other than signator
   P — printed
   T — typed

2. C — postcard
   D — document
   E — endorsement
   L — letter
   M — manuscript
   W — wire (telegram)

3. c — carbon
   d — draft
   f — fragment
   p — letterpress
   t — transcript or copy made at much later date

4. I — initialed by author
   r — representation; signed or initialed in author's name
   S — signed by author

Among the more common endnote abbreviations are: ALS — autograph letter, signed by author; TLpI — typed letter, letterpress copy, initialed by author.

REPOSITORY SYMBOLS

Symbols used for repositories are the standard ones used in *Symbols of American Libraries in the National Union Catalog of the Library of Congress,* 10th ed. (Washington, D.C., 1969).

ATT Tuskegee Institute, Tuskegee, Ala.
DHU Howard University, Washington, D.C.
DLC Library of Congress, Washington, D.C.
MH Harvard University, Cambridge, Mass.
MdBMC Morgan State College, Baltimore, Md.
NN New York Public Library, NYC
NNC Columbia University, NYC
NcD Duke University, Durham, N.C.

OTHER ABBREVIATIONS

BTW Booker T. Washington
Con. Container
NAACP National Association for the Advancement of Colored People
NNBL National Negro Business League

Documents, 1912–14

From Charles Sanderson Medbury[1]

Des Moines, Iowa, September 3, 1912

My dear Dr. Washington: I am a stranger to you though I have met you personally in several public assemblies and have even had the opportunity of introducing you a time or two in gatherings honored by your presence and address.

I need not at this time speak of my profound interest not only in you personally but in the wonderful contribution of your life. For years your word and work have been an inspiration to me and in sixteen years of student pastoral relationships I have referred to you almost countless times as an inspiration to the young. I am deeply appreciative, too, of the worth of your race and have studied its problems to some extent. I am in close touch with certain of the school life among the negro people in the South having particular acquaintance with Pres. J. B. Lehman of the School at Edwards, Mississippi, for which institution I delivered the Commencement Address some three years ago. I am stating all this that you may know something of my spirit in relation to you personally and something of my interest in the great problems with which you yourself have had so much to do.

My writing you today is the outgrowth of an experience a few days ago at Oskaloosa, Iowa, where I was booked for a series of addresses in the month that I give each year to the Chautauqua work. During my presence in Oskaloosa Senator Vardaman came to the community and delivered his address on "The Impending Crisis." Without doubt you are familiar with this address and know of its wholly inadequate grasp of the problem with which the Senator deals and of its great injustice to the negro people. The day following Senator Vardaman I gave my own time very largely to a reply to his address and there was a tense interest on the part of the people. I hope sincerely that the result was for good.

But Dr. Washington, there are one or two points in which you can be of very great service to me. I am here in a college community, being Chaplain of Drake University with its enrollment of nearly two thousand students. I am *constantly* speaking in Commencements and from the platform in other phases of work and I am tremendously interested in "the race problem" as it is termed. May I ask you, therefore, to put me in touch with literature that will in the first place

3

indicate the intellectual capabilities of the negro race. You know doubtless that Senator Vardaman maintains that the negro's mental life stops practically at the age of puberty. Of course this is absurd on its face and any intelligent man has many counter facts at hand, but I would like to have a showing as to the attainments of the negro race that would simply *overwhelm* such a statement. Then again I would be pleased to have literature that speaks of *the initiative* of the negro as that would be indicated by business and professional successes where men were thrown upon their own resources. And still further I would like more material than I have as to the spiritual transformations of negro life. Senator Vardaman declares that Christianity does not transform the negro. I myself know so many noble Christian lives that such a statement seems to me nothing short of enormous in its injustice. But I would like to have at hand the record that you may have, as to the spiritual service of your people here and there in the great world's life. Of course the Senator makes much of the unspeakable crime which frequently results in the death of negroes at the hands of mobs of white men. Though it was to reflect upon my own race I felt it just to remind those who heard both him and me that lust knows no color line and that the story of the brothel life and the white slave traffic among the whites should at least make us humble in judgment of the negro.

And it is right in connection with this very matter, my dear Sir and Brother, that Senator Vardaman is bold enough to refer to you yourself in a baldly suggestive way that many of us resented as the very greatest insult. Perhaps you have learned that he alludes to the pathetic and trying incident in New York when you were assaulted and every intimation is to the effect that the story as first told was true and that you were peeking into windows in an uncertain way and that you did use endearing names when first greeted by the woman who saw you in the entry-way of the apartment building. Now I beg you to forgive me, a complete stranger, speaking of this thing but I do it out of unquestioning love and honor. I resented the Senator's word and did so before the congregation when I had the opportunity to speak, but I want to be in a position to say something more definitely than I am able to say now. The people did not know, and indeed I do not know myself, what the final adjustment of the matter was. I would like to have from you the thing that you want your friends to say. That you are absolutely without taint in the matter *is not the question with me.* I want to be able upon occasion to meet the slur of those who would hurt you and your great cause. Of course I will not exploit anything in the least but I do want to be in a position to do justice when facing such a situation as I faced just the other day. In closing let me ask you for the name of a book that someone has written bearing some such title as "The Soul of the Negro."

With the very sincerest greetings, Cordially yours,

Chas. S. Medbury

TLS Con. 460 BTW Papers DLC.

[1] Charles Sanderson Medbury (1865–1932) was minister of the University Church of Christ and chaplain of Drake University in Des Moines, Iowa, from 1904 to 1917.

To Ernest Ten Eyck Attwell

[Tuskegee, Ala.] Sept. 7, 1912

Mr. Attwell: I was in the dining room this morning between 5 and 6 o'clock, and I was surprised to see the large quantity of food which was being dumped into the swill cart. Biscuits, corn bread and light bread that had not been touched either by students or teachers was being dumped into the cart without anyone seeming to have any idea of the loss to the school on account of such action.

2d. I find that there is no system at the dinning hall by which the swill which can be used for the pigs is separated from other waste stuff. For example, I found that glasses, tin cans, meat, bread and peas were all being dumped into the same barrel without any idea as to separation or system.

3d. On examining the cow peas I found that between one-half and one-fourth were being put back into the swill without having been shelled.

I need not call your attention to the enormous waste involved in such matters as I have mentioned, and we have gotten to the point where all this must be thoroughly changed.

5

The space in and around the elevator where the tin barrels stand is thoroughly dirty and unsanitary. In the future I want it kept clean.

Booker T. Washington

TLpS Con. 623 BTW Papers DLC.

To Charles Sanderson Medbury

[Tuskegee, Ala.] September 10, 1912

Personal

My dear Mr. Medbury: Your kind letter of September 3d has been received. I regret that I shall be compelled to answer your letter more hurriedly and briefly than my heart would lead me to do, but this is a tremendously busy season with me and I have to make every minute count for the most.

Let me thank you for the interest you have taken not only in my race, but in myself personally in this matter. For the life of me I cannot see how any intelligent and Christian community can pay to hear a man like Vardaman, but that is a matter we cannot control.

By this mail I am sending you a copy of the "Story of the Negro," "The Negro in Business," and a copy of the "Negro Year Book," a publication just gotten out by one of our instructors. In these you will find, I think, a good deal of matter that will answer some of the questions which you have asked. The book which you have in mind is evidently written by Dr. Du Bois. The correct title is "The Souls of Black Folk." It is published by a firm in Chicago, and I am quite sure you can get it at any bookstore in Chicago.

Now regarding the personal side of your letter, I would state that I am somewhat puzzled to know how to reply, because any person who would be guilty of the charge made against me in connection with that New York incident would not hesitate to deny if the charges were true. I would state in the first place that I visited the point where I did visit in New York upon a perfectly legitimate mission, and while there I was assaulted by a band of ruffians. After they found out who I was and after the main leader had been locked up in the station house, two hours after he was locked up he induced the woman with whom he was living to make a false charge; that was made with a view of mitigating his punishment. They also got three or four persons who lived in the neighborhood to give false testimony against me. I being alone and almost without witnesses was at the mercy of a lot of perjurers. Notwithstanding my disadvantage, I was determined to see the matter through the courts and do my duty in having the man punished if it were possible. During the first week of November of last year the case was tried before the Court of Special Sessions. Two of the judges deciding to dismiss the man and one deciding that he ought to be punished. Everybody who understood the case and the circumstances in New York was convinced that the decision of the judges was simply a Tammany plot, the two judges who voted in favor of acquitting the man were Tammany men and the one voting to sustain my side of the case was not. Of course in the court room I had the unpleasant task of hearing all this manufactured false testimony, but I was determined to go through it and do my duty in trying to have the man punished.

I might add further that there is not the slightest foundation for any charge to the effect that I was peeping through a key hole or spoke improperly to any woman. This is something I have never done in my life.

If in my haste I have not answered the questions fully which you desire me to answer, I shall be very glad to write you again. I thank you very much for your part in overcoming the Vardaman influence in that community. I very much doubt here in the South whether Vardaman could get a hearing before the best white people.

I ought to add that the man who assaulted me was immediately re-arrested as soon as the trial which concerned me was over, and taken to New Jersey where he is now serving sentence in the penitentiary for failing to support his wife. Yours very truly,

[Booker T. Washington]

TLp Con. 460 BTW Papers DLC.

To Julius Rosenwald

[Tuskegee, Ala.] September 12, 1912

Dear Mr. Rosenwald: Enclosed I send you report covering the disposition of the last shipment of shoes, hats, etc., which you sent us. We are careful in disposing of these things to the students, to see to it that they are not used in a way to make the students dependent, but to help really worthy students who are doing all they can to help themselves.

I want to repeat to you, how deeply grateful we are for these kindnesses. Yours truly,

Booker T. Washington

TLpS Con. 76 (new series) BTW Papers DLC.

From George Woodward Wickersham

New York, Sept. 16, 1912

My dear Doctor Washington: On my return from a fortnight's vacation I find your kind note of 30th ult. I was much gratified at the outcome in Milwaukee in Mr. Lewis' case. By assenting to the resolution which was adopted I avoided an acrimonious discussion which I fear would have injured the colored men at the south more than it would have aided them. The things that really were accomplished, were first, the rebuke of the Executive Committee by the failure even to mention its report, and the complete abandonment of the effort to oust the three colored members; Secondly, the recognition that under the constitution, although it has not been contemplated that negroes should be elected to membership, it was open to do so, and requiring that in case a local committee should nominate one for membership the fact of his race should be made known. No one, I think, could object to that. And third, the express recognition of the full status in membership of the three colored men who had been already chosen.

The movement to bring about the resignation of these three gentlemen got no further than the case of Mr. Morris,[1] of St. Paul, and I think an intimate connection existed between that resignation and the candidacy for presidency of the Association of Mr. Frank B. Kellogg[2] of that city.

I am glad to see that the prevailing newspaper comment through the country, so far as I have been able to find it, has condemned the effort of the Association to oust these men from membership. The broader question of whether or not colored men should join that Association is one which will be fought out later and under better conditions than could have been done in a Presidential year. I am gratified at your approval which, believe me, I highly esteem. Faithfully yours,

Geo W Wickersham

TLS Con. 468 BTW Papers DLC.

[1] William Richard Morris, born in Fleming County, Ky., in 1859, received an A.B. (1884) and M.A. (1887) from Fisk University, where he was the only black instructor from 1884 to 1889. Moving to St. Paul, he was admitted to the Minnesota bar in 1889 and practiced law. After he was already a member of the American Bar Association, the question of membership by blacks was widely discussed. He ultimately dropped his membership.

[2] Frank Billings Kellogg (1856–1937), a corporation lawyer of St. Paul, Minn., was president of the American Bar Association in 1912–13. He was later U.S. senator (1917–23) and Secretary of State (1925–29). He won the Nobel Peace Prize for negotiating the Kellogg-Briand Pact (1928) to outlaw war, and was a judge of the Permanent Court of International Justice (1930–35).

From Alain LeRoy Locke

Camden, N.J. September 16th, 1912

Personal.

My dear Doctor Washington, I was just on the point of writing you when I received your kindly letter of the 12th inst. Saturday, the 14th, I was elected an assistant Professor at Howard, in English and Philosophy, upon the recommendation of Dean Moore, but with work in the College Dept. as well as in Teachers' College, and therefore with Dean Miller's consent. I was about to write you news of this, and to thank you for your very valuable and timely help in the Howard matter, when your letter with its still greater willingness to assist me in getting placed arrives to put me still more in your debt. I shall see to it that I myself and certain of the Howard authorities appreciate the fine disinterestedness of your willingness to assist me in locating at Howard when you were yourself able to use me at Tuskegee. I shall hope and expect to serve your very best interests at Howard and elsewhere, until I more than repay you for your deep personal interest.

I really believe that until I have an opportunity to serve a direct apprenticeship under you in your peculiar field of organized race work and propaganda, as I fervently hope someday to have opportunity, I may perhaps be very well able to justify your good wishes and expectations in the field of journalism and college teaching which is now, and partly through your kind offices, open before me.

You will be interested to know that through the Civil Service, I have also been appointed an assistant organizer of the New Jersey Emancipation Commission, in charge of the statistical side of the work, a post that I can very well keep in conjunction with the work at Howard. This, with other journalistic matters, which I plan to discuss with you at my earliest opportunity, will keep me in touch with the larger world of affairs that I wish at all costs to keep contact with.

Believe me, Doctor Washington, until I have chance to see you and thank you personally, most deeply and acceptably indebted and grateful; and if you have taken any of your officers at Tuskegee into your council, acquaint them please with my present situation, and assure them of my willingness to serve you and them always in whatever way I may be able.

With best thanks and respects, Sincerely yours,

Alain LeRoy Locke

TLS Con. 458 BTW Papers DLC.

To Robert Underwood Johnson

Tuskegee Institute, Alabama Sept. 19, 1912

Dear Dr. Johnson: Enclosed I return the proof. I have made only two slight changes.

I cannot understand why "Negro" is spelled with a small "n" and a capital letter used in spelling "Jew." The Century of course is not the only publication that makes this difference, but I have never been able to understand it. Yours very truly,

Booker T. Washington

TLS Century Collection NN. A carbon is in Con. 451, BTW Papers, DLC. Johnson docketed the letter with the statement: "Hereafter (Mr. B. E. S. approving) let us capitalize Negro when used as a racial designation. R.U.J." He also wrote on the letter: "B.E.S. I believe we went back to the small *n* at your command. RUJ."

From Charles William Anderson

[New York City] Sunday Sept 22/12

Confidential

Dear Doctor: Read & return the enclosed from Douglas Wetmore. It is perfectly exasperating to have to stand here and battle for the right, as I am doing, and have your & my friends sit around a drinking table in Washington and support and encourage your enemies.[1] Of course I will not support Wetmore and when I tell him so, he will be my bitter and active enemy, while remaining a warm friend of Tyler[,] Terrell, Lewis & Cobb. He lives in this state and not in Washington. Our friends know him to be your enemy & mine. Why should they prove false to us? We are trying to defeat Manning on the ground that no white man should control the Negro bureau. Why then take a Negro who passes for white? This man Wetmore would no sooner land in the place than he would start in to work against both you & me. It is sickening.

I am fighting Manning almost alone. All the others are ready to compromise if he will promise them some graft. Pinchback called at Nat'l headquarters Thursday, but did not wait to see Hilles & didn't protest against Manning. They are all indifferent. Tyler writes that he did suggest Myers, but Myers would not take it. Eh? He was dropped on my statement that he was incompetent.

Keep the guns trained on Manning. By the way, you will be interested to know that Hilles sent a letter yesterday enclosing two letters from H. C. Smith of Cleveland, to Mr. Granger,[2] the Ohio Taft representative, and one to Nat'l Committeeman Dougherty[3] of that state, asking that his paper be assisted. He also enclosed one from Dougherty & one from Granger, recommending that in view of the situation in Ohio among the colored people, it would be wise to help Smith's paper. I got busy at once and by an underground route, learned that Smith's paper was on the colored democratic pay roll, and that a check had been mailed to him on Friday. This cooked his goose. So you see I am doing some real work while that Washington gang is drinking with and endorsing my and your enemies.

I have Goddard[4] of Boston & his friends, working on Sen. Crane and wiring personal protests against Manning.

Return Wetmore's letter for future reference. Yours hastely,

Anderson

ALS Con. 56 BTW Papers DLC.

[1] J. Douglas Wetmore wrote E. J. Scott that he had lunched in Washington, D.C., with Ralph W. Tyler, James A. Cobb, Robert H. Terrell, and William H. Lewis, all of whom supported him for the position of manager of the Republican campaign among blacks in the East. (Sept. 21, 1912, Con. 489, BTW Papers, DLC.)

In reply to Anderson's letter BTW sympathized with the exasperation that Anderson expressed. (Sept. 25, 1912, Con. 56, BTW Papers, DLC.) E. J. Scott, on the other hand, wrote Anderson that there would be a distinct advantage in trying to work with Wetmore. (Sept. 24, 1912, Con. 56, BTW Papers, DLC.)

[2] Sherman Moorhead Granger (b. 1870) of Zanesville, a member of the Republican National Committee from 1912 to 1916.

[3] Harry Micajah Daugherty (1860–1941), Taft's Ohio chairman in 1912, was later Warren G. Harding's campaign manager in 1920 and U.S. Attorney General (1921–24). He resigned under suspicion of having accepted a bribe, but was acquitted in 1927.

[4] Julius Goddard was a black messenger at the headquarters of the Republican state committee in Boston.

To Seth Low

Tuskegee Institute, Alabama
September Twenty-sixth, Nineteen Hundred Twelve

Dear Mr. Low: I received, several days ago, your communication, the one marked personal, referring to the matter of salaries. I have given this matter some attention ever since your letter was received, and I very much fear we cannot get up a satisfactory report by the time the Trustees meet, October 3rd, but we are making an effort to do so.

I am glad that this question has been raised because it gives us a chance to thresh out the whole subject of salaries and to get some light as to what other institutions are doing.

Without attempting now to answer the question in detail, I would state that in general, there are three types of schools in the South for Negroes.

First: Missionary Schools conducted by such organizations as the American Missionary Association (Congregationalist); The Freedman's Board (Presbyterian); the Freedman's Aid and Southern Education Society (Methodist); and the Home Missionary Society representing the Baptists.

Second: Schools partly supported by the State, and partly by the general Government.

Third: Independent institutions, such as Hampton, Tuskegee, etc.

It would be rather misleading to compare the salaries paid to an officer on the grounds at Fisk University, with an officer on the grounds at the Tuskegee Institute for the reason that the two institutions are supported and managed on a wholly different basis.

Fisk University for example, is managed and supported by the American Missionary Association, with headquarters in New York. The expense in connection with the collecting and spending the money for conducting the school is largely borne by the office in New York, but the same kind of expense here at Tuskegee is shown in our reports, and is borne by the Institute.

Illustrating my point further: I happen to know that the American Missionary Association, which supports some of the best schools in the South, has three Secretaries in New York with a salary of more than $4,000 each; one Treasurer with a salary of more than $4,000; a branch office in Boston, a branch office in Chicago, and several Field Superintendents who travel constantly through the North and the South. None of the expenses connected with the support of this Association is shown in the reports of Fisk University. If they were shown, the item of salary would be swelled to a considerable extent, because one would not get a man who is big enough to collect large sums of money for the same salary that he can get a man to do the ordinary local work of running an institution.

Many of the State institutions of the South are controlled by Boards of Regents who are responsible for getting money from the Legislatures, the buying for the institution, as well as the detail management of the schools. That kind of expense in these cases is taken off the local institutions.

Our greatest competitor in the matter of salaries is the Public schools in the large cities, such as Baltimore, Washington, Cincinnati, and St. Louis. A man comes to us and remains two or three years, gets hold of our methods and the spirit of the institution, and then is offered in one of these public schools a salary which is much larger than he is being paid here. We are often led into the temptation of increasing his salary to hold him.

Enclosed I send you a communication, referring to one of our best teachers who has just left us to go to Cincinnati. We did not feel that we ought to increase his salary in view of our financial condition.

Enclosed I also send you a communication from the State Superintendent of Education in Kentucky, bearing upon the same point. We have at least, a half dozen men on our Faculty who could fill this place.

It should be borne in mind, too, that the principal officers at Tuskegee work twelve months in the year, almost with no vacation, while in the case of other institutions in the South, with few exceptions, officers and teachers work only eight, or eight and one-half, months in the year, and the salary is based on those months. I happen to know that in many cases, the individuals who teach in these schools in the winter have regular occupations at some other point in the summer.

I appreciate, however, that all of this is in general, and not in direct answer to Mr. Dole's question.[1] We are giving that matter serious attention, and will have an answer ready as soon as possible. Yours truly,

Booker T. Washington

TLS Seth Low Papers NNC. A press copy is in Con. 58, BTW Papers, DLC.

[1] In Con. 464, BTW Papers, DLC, is a draft letter to Seth Low, dated Sept. 24, 1912, which answers thirty-five questions raised by Tuskegee trustee Charles Fletcher Dole regarding administrative matters at the school.

From Gordon David Houston

Washington, D.C. Sept. 27. 1912

My dear Dr. Washington: I have learned from a thoroughly dependable source that my elevation to the professorship of English in Howard University was due largely to your recommendation of my work.[1]
I am taking this opportunity, therefore, to thank you for this favor and
for your continued interest in my career. I am ever mindful of the
fact that both my start and much of my advancement in my chosen
field are attributable to your kindness and assistance.

I need hardly to add that I appreciate the magnitude of the trust
and responsibility, which I have so recently assumed. I wish, however,
to assure you that I shall be equal to my task, and hope to justify,
both by my service and life, your continued interest in me and your
charitable commendations of my work.

With kindest regards, I am   Gratefully yours,

G. David Houston

TLS Con. 455 BTW Papers DLC.

[1] BTW noted in reply Houston's "courteous and cordial tenor" and expressed
his pleasure at being able to say a kind word. (Oct. 2, 1912, Con. 455, BTW Papers,
DLC.)

Extracts from an Address
at the Black Belt Fair

Demopolis, Alabama   September 27, 1912

At no other place in the world that I have visited, except in the
South, could one witness such a scene as is here presented. Here we
have gathered on the same grounds, in large numbers, representatives
of the best and most cultured white people, and also the masses of
our own race present in tremendous numbers. Both races have come
here for the purpose of making an exhibition at this fair of the products

of the soil, the shop and the home. The object is to stimulate pride in farming, in mechanical work and in house work. Each race is striving to see what it has accomplished in the way of industrial progress during the past year and each race is striving to be of assistance to the other. On these grounds, while there are large numbers of each race, there is peace and friendship and good order. I question whether the same scene would be witnessed in any other section of the world except in the Black Belt of the South.

One disadvantage that both races labor under here in the South is owing to the fact that the worst things that occur are widely reported throughout the world, while the best things which indicate racial progress and friendship are seldom heard of outside of the local community.

In Marengo County there are in the rough some 10,000 white people and 30,000 colored people. Here, it seems to me, there is a significant opportunity presented for you to make an exhibition to the world in making a model county, a county that will show at all times how it is possible for these two races to live together in helpful, friendly relationship to each other; how it is possible for the white man to help the colored man and the colored man to help the white man; how it is possible at all times for the white man to see that justice is meted out to the members of my own race.

To my own race I want to say that we have advantages here in the Black Belt of the South that I often fear we do not rightly appreciate. We have one of the best climates in the world; we have good soil; we can find plenty of work to do every day in the year; we are paid reasonably good wages for that work; land is comparatively cheap and any man who has the ambition to do so, can become the owner of a piece of land. Here in the Black Belt of the South white people understand the colored people and colored people understand the white people. While in other parts of the world laboring classes have to seek labor, here labor seeks us and we must understand once for all that we will not be permitted to occupy this rich territory unless we can prove to the world that we can get as much out of the soil as any other race can get out of it. Only a few years ago the American Indian was given one of the richest territories in the United States and he failed to develop that country; the result is that the white man went in and took possession.

The fall of the year is the danger season for our race. This is the season when money comes into our hands and if we are not careful, winter or spring will overtake us and we will be without anything to live on. This is the season when every member of our race in Marengo County should make up his mind to save a portion of that which he gets from his crop. He should invest it in the bank or in some property, and be sure that he does not start the next year worse off than he is now. The time is speedily coming when the colored man who cannot get enough ahead to live on during the year will not be able to get "advances" as he has been doing in the past. One difficulty with the average colored farmer consists in the fact that he tries to pursue a policy which no other businessman pursues: and that is working about half of the year. I will guarantee to say that the merchant in Marengo County keeps his store open every day in the year; the lawyer, the doctor, the banker keep their places of business open every day in the year, but the average colored farmer in this county, I wager, does not work more than 150 days out of the 365 days and still at the end of the year he wonders why he is poor. We remain poor because we try to do something that no other businessman does, and that is try to live by working half of the time. In a climate like this, the farmer can find something to do every day in the year, and I advise you, that when your cotton crop is gathered, instead of stopping work, begin at once to put in another crop; something that will bring you in some cash between the cotton raising seasons. The farmer who grows vegetables, who takes some butter, some fowls, some eggs or fruit or berries into town on Saturday, is the farmer who has some cash coming in every day in the year instead of having cash only once a year.

I said a minute ago that you have a great opportunity to make this a model county. I want to see my race become models in this county in the matter of industry and thrift. Get rid of every idle man; get rid of every criminal character. Do not shield the criminal; do not hide the man who commits crime but let the officers understand that we are just as willing to punish the criminal as the members of any other race.

I hope, too, that our good white friends will help you make this a model county in the matter of educating members of our race. When I say education, I do not mean mere book learning; I do not mean that which is going to make a dude of a person, but I mean the kind of education that will make a person respect labor, the kind of education that will make him more reliable as a laborer, a greater producer, that will make him respect himself, obey the law and become a helpful, intelligent force in the county.

In many of the Black Belt counties of the South our race is not treated fairly in the matter of education. I know one county in a Southern state where last year the Negro child had spent upon him from the public school fund, 26 cents per capita; in that same county, each white child had spent upon him over $22.00. Now, this is unfair to the Negro child; it is unfair to the white man himself. Education will do certain things for members of every race which no other force can do. If the Negro remains ignorant he is more likely to become a criminal, become costly to the county and state. The Negro, if ignorant, cannot be expected to know what the law is; cannot be expected to exercise that degree of self-control which will make him abstain from murdering, from stealing and from other criminal acts, in the same degree that the intelligent person does. The ignorant Negro boy without education, when he commits crime is treated by the same Judge, before the same Jury, under the same laws of evidence that the white boy with education, is treated before. If the average white man, who employs Negro labor would make a reckoning, he would find that a very large proportion of the colored people who labor for him do not work more than a third of the time because they are sick. The plain meaning of this is that no race can keep its body strong, clean and healthy without some education and the ignorant Negro is costly in the matter of labor to himself; is costly to the white man who employs him because he does not understand how to keep his body strong and fit for labor. Ignorance in a county like this is not only costly in the loss of time growing out of sickness, but it is costly to the white man as well as to the Negro himself in the committing of crimes.

In a certain county of the South, I happen to know that two Negro women were tried before a court because one woman had bit off the ear of the other woman. This trial meant that two or three or a dozen of the best white men in the county had to spend a whole day in listening to the sickening and little, dirty details connected with this crime. In addition to that, this trial occupied the time of Judges, lawyers, jurymen, and grandjury men for a whole day or more, and also the time of some of the best white men in the county; time that could have been given to the matter of education, or industry or moral and religious development of the county; instead of this, all their time for a whole day was given to this little sickening, dirty, criminal incident committed between two ignorant colored people. Say what one will of educating the Negro, it is very rare that the educated Negro, men like Professor Jones and others in this county, costs the county a single dollar on account of any crime that he commits.

The policy of sending ignorant and poor people to jail, to the penitentiary or to the coal mine will not remove crime. We have got to go deeper and remove the cause of crime which is, in the majority of cases, ignorance and poverty.

The Negro woman in a county like this cooks the white man's food, nurses the white man's children, but it is impossible that that Negro woman should keep herself clean, live a moral life and render intelligent and conscientious service unless she has some degree of education. Crime draws no color line; disease draws no color line. The germs of disease that have their origin in the cabin of the ignorant Negro woman will soon spread to the mansion of the white man.

I believe, too, that it will pay the white people in a county like this to give more attention to making the Negro more comfortable and happy in the country districts. No one will dispute the fact that the Negro is better off in the country than he is in the town or city, but often the best Negro families leave the country districts and go to the cities because they cannot educate their children in the poor schools of the country districts. Often they find a school in the country taught by an inefficient teacher or in a broken-down, uncomfortable log cabin or schoolhouse, and with a school term of only three or four months in the year. By reason of these conditions, some of the best Negro families leave the farm and go to the city. From a mere point of dollars and cents, it would pay, in my opinion, every land owner in Marengo County to see to it that on each one of his farms there is a good schoolhouse with a good teacher, with a school term lasting eight or nine months in the year, and that there is a good church and good minister. Again, some of the best Negro farmers get discouraged and leave the country because the land owners are not foresighted enough to build good houses for them to live in. The best type of Negro labor cannot be kept on a farm in a broken-down one-roomed cabin. I will guarantee to say that the landowner in Marengo County who furnishes the best houses for the Negro tenants is the man who gets the best and reliable class of Negro tenants.

19

On all these matters, I have spoken plainly from my heart to my race and to my white friends. I have spoken plainly because I love the South as I love no other part of the world. In Marengo County, I am glad to see that the white people, for the most part, [are] encouraging the Negro to make the most of himself; that every Negro in this county has a white friend who is willing to stand by him so long as he shows that he is trying to help himself and do the right thing. I want all the members of my race to show to the white man in this county that they appreciate his good-will and his helpful kindness by living a useful, industrious, upright life.

TMp   Con. 829   BTW Papers   DLC.

From Joseph Oswalt Thompson

Birmingham, Ala. Sept. 29—12

My Dear Dr. Washington: When his train reached Chehaw yesterday Col. Roosevelt was engaged in dictating his Atlanta Speech. When I saw you standing at your carriage I called his attention to your presence there whereupon he went to the platform, otherwise he would not have suffered interruption. I was glad to note the old time cordiality between my two most valued friends.

Have just read your great speech at Demop[o]lis. Yours seems to be an exception to the rule that "A Prophet is not without honor save in his own land" for you are as much appreciated in Alabama as in any other part of the nation. Your Friend

Jos. O. Thompson

ALS   Con. 466   BTW Papers   DLC.

An Article in the *Journal of the American Institute of Criminal Law and Criminology*

September 1912

NEGRO CRIME AND STRONG DRINK

In the agitation of the liquor question incident to the attempt to pass prohibition laws in Georgia, Alabama and other Southern States a great deal was said about the relation of strong drink to crime, particularly crime among Negroes. This is a very important subject because from two-thirds to three-fourths of the prisoners in the penitentiaries, jails and chain gangs in the South are Negroes.

During the past year I have attempted to find out definitely what relation liquor sustained to crime among my people; that is, how much of a contributing cause liquor was to their crime rate. One reason why I became especially interested in this inquiry was that the sheriff of Macon County, Alabama, the county in which Tuskegee Institute is located, told me that since prohibition had gone into effect in the county that crime had been reduced from sixty to seventy per cent. I have always tried to keep in touch with the officers of the law in my state and have frequently had occasion to ask their opinion concerning the needs of my people. After conversing with the sheriff I determined to look further into the relation of crime and liquor among the people of my race.

In order to learn if other counties in Alabama had had an experience similar to that of Macon County I sent out a circular letter to the sheriffs of various counties in Alabama and to the chiefs of police and recorders of courts of the more important cities of the state.* In this letter the following questions were asked:

What in your opinion are the chief causes of Negro crime?

What effect does strong drink have in making the Negro a criminal?

Since the prohibition law has gone into effect has there been any decrease in the crimes committed by Negroes in your County, especially rape, murder and other serious offenses?

* Since the material for this article was gathered several counties in Alabama under the revised liquor law have gone back to saloons.

The sheriffs of fourteen counties, chiefs of police of the four principal cities of the state and the recorders of the police courts of Montgomery and Selma sent answers. The replies of the city magistrates concern the urban; the views of the sheriffs the rural Negro.

I will consider first what was given as the chief causes of Negro crime.

The chief of police of Mobile was of the opinion "that the chief cause of crime among the Negroes was a lack of necessary education and the excessive use of alcohol combined with the drug habit (cocaine)."

The sheriff of Mobile County in which the City of Mobile is located wrote that "The chief causes of arrest here are principally gambling and vagrancy."

The recorder of the police court of Selma wrote: "In my judgment intoxicating drinks are now and have for years been at the bottom of all the crimes of a grave nature committed by both Negroes and whites."

The recorder of the police court of Montgomery said: "In regard to your question as to the chief causes of Negro crime I am not prepared to enter into a lengthy discussion, but the impression I have gained from my experience in the court leads me to believe that the two chief causes, especially for misdemeanors, are drink and jealousy with its attendant passions."

The sheriff of Madison County in which Huntsville, a city of 10,000 inhabitants is located, wrote: "I will say that whiskey and gambling are the chief causes of crime among the Negroes. A great many misdemeanors are caused by strong drink."

The sheriff of Jefferson County in which Birmingham, the chief city of the state is located, wrote: "I can say without hesitation and the records in the criminal court will bear me out that more crimes are committed by the Negro race on account of strong drink than all other vices combined. Eighty per cent of the colored men confined in the County jail are there for crimes caused either directly or indirectly, by whiskey."

The sheriffs of the rural counties are also of the opinion that strong drink is the chief cause of crime among the Negroes. The sheriff of Randolph County wrote: "Strong drink tends to make the Negro vicious and to have less regard for themselves and for the laws of the country." The sheriffs of Autauga and Elmore Counties said that whiskey and women were the chief causes of crime among the Negroes. The sheriff of Walker County was of the opinion that "ignorance and whiskey are the chief causes of crime." He added: "Combined they make a brute of any man." The sheriff of Jackson County said: "I am of the opinion that whiskey is the chief cause of the majority of crimes committed by Negroes in this county." "We all understand," said the sheriff of Conecuh County, "that whiskey and crime go hand in hand."

The Biennial Report of the Attorney General of the State of Alabama for the years 1908–1909 gives further interesting information concerning crime. Under the heading "Relation of Intoxicating Liquors to Homicide" this report said:

"I am including a statement here showing, for the present period, the number of homicide cases disposed of in a number of the counties and the number of cases in which the evidence showed that the defendant or deceased had been drunk or drinking at the time of the killing. This statement deals with about 40 per cent of the total homicides reported for the period and with about 25 counties of the State.

"For the purpose of making this report, I addressed letters to all solicitors of the State during the past few months, requesting this information. Most of the solicitors of City and County Courts and several of the Circuit Solicitors furnished the data.

"This statement shows 236 homicide cases, of which 142 of the defendants were Negroes and 94 were whites. In 97 of the cases the defendant or the deceased was drunk or drinking at the time of the homicide. The percentage of liquor homicides in the several counties included in the statement ranges from 20 per cent to 83 per cent. It also shows that 60 per cent of the defendants were Negroes and 40 per cent were whites; that the general percentage of liquor homicides was 41 and non-liquor homicides 59.

"In my previous report, 1906–08, on this subject which included reports from 45 counties and embraced only nine months of the 24 months, during which the general prohibition laws were in effect, 368 homicide cases were recorded, showing Negro percentage 67.8 and liquor homicide percentage 53; non-liquor homicide percentage 47.

"Applying the liquor percentage thus obtained, to the total homicides for the period it appears that intoxicating liquor caused, or contributed to, the killing of 258 men in Alabama for the two years ending September 30, 1910, and in 372 homicide cases during the same period, there was no evidence of any intoxicating drink. That is, according to these statistics for the two years, 129 men were killed annually as the result of liquor and 186 men were killed annually without such influence.

"For the previous period, 1906–08, when the liquor percentage was 53, the annual liquor homicides were 174 and the annual non-liquor homicides were 154.

"One solicitor in reporting statistics on this subject, says: 'You will observe there has been nothing like as many homicides in this county since prohibition. We have far too many now, but conditions have been greatly improved within the last year or two. There had been no homicide in this county up to the 1st of October of this year, hence the grand jury which convened 19th Sept., was able to report there was no homicide for their investigation committed in our county during this year. The grand jury for the Spring term was able to make a similar report. However, the grand jury in order to influence enforcement of the prohibition law took a recess after three weeks' work and adjourned to reconvene or return to work November 21st, instant. Most all the homicides I have tried — and the same may be said of assaults with intent to murder — have been influenced by liquor.' The experience of several other prosecuting officers of the State is given to the same effect."

It might be said, however, that strong drink and crime are accompaniments of each other and may not in reality have a direct influence one upon the other. For that reason I have attempted to study the effects of prohibition. An examination of the effects of prohibition upon the crime rate of Negroes gives us information bearing upon this point. As in the forgoing I will give the facts as reported by the officials. I take up first the cities and the counties in which the larger cities are located.

The recorder of the police court of Montgomery reported that although the number of arrests for drunkenness had increased from 1922 for the year 1908–09 to 2175 for the year 1909–10 the total arrests had decreased from 5766 to 5430; also the arrests of Negroes had decreased from 3908 to 3444. "Speaking from recollection," said the recorder, "I would say that the number of Negroes charged with being drunk since prohibition has increased by possibly 20 per cent and the number of petty crimes largely traceable to drink has increased by 40 per cent. I have noticed particularly that in the last year a great number of Negroes who have been tried by me charged with minor offences testify that the last recollection they had was of taking a few drinks and that they had no recollection whatever of subsequent events until they awoke in the city prison. This is, I am quite sure, traceable or due to the inferior grade of liquor sold under prohibition."

The city of Montgomery contains about 40,000 inhabitants, about 19,500 of whom are whites and 20,500 Negroes. There are in Montgomery County in which the city of Montgomery is located 26,000 whites and 57,000 Negroes.

The recorder of the police court of Selma reported that since prohibition has gone into effect there has been little opportunity to observe the effect of prohibition upon Negro crime for "in spite of our efforts to enforce this law by making many arrests and imposing large fines and in many cases hard labor, whiskey and all kinds of intoxicating beverages have been easily had in Selma and vicinity. In most cases in the police court, where drunkenness was charged I have been informed on inquiry as to where the liquor was obtained that it was obtained from a Negro. This is not always true where it is asserted; but it is a known fact that whiskey is very generally 'boot-legged' by Negroes, probably in many instances for others. In town there has been little opportunity to make a test of the effect of prohibition. I will add that I have been informed by reliable people that during the first period of prohibition in the country districts the absence of whiskey had a most salutary influence. Men worked more and provided better for their families. It soon became known to the Negroes, however, that their liquor orders could be filled quickly in Pensacola, Florida, and other places, and I am told that they now get what they want in that way. This keeping of liquors at home by the country Negroes and their drinking at home accounts for the large decrease in drunkenness on the public roads."

The chief of police of Selma wrote: "I think that there is not much difference in the amount of crime committed by the colored race since prohibition in this state was established. I think a certain class of women use less whiskey; for formerly they were in the habit of lounging or hanging around the barrooms and sending in these places for beer and whiskey. I think that the situation is now possibly worse than formerly. More of the men were engaged in selling, taking large chances for the amount of gain to be derived from the sale."

Selma is a town of 14,000 inhabitants, 6,000 whites and 8,000

Negroes. In Dallas County in which Selma is located there are about 10,000 whites and 44,000 Negroes.

The chief of police of Mobile reported that so far as he had been able to observe prohibition had not materially affected the crime rate among the Negroes. He said: "Prohibition has little effect in decreasing crime. The Negro is still able to obtain any manner of intoxicants; liquor in large quantities being dispensed; a bottle being now purchased in place of the customary drink, probably followed by another or more than could be obtained in the legitimate barroom. And I may add that an inferior blend of liquor has been substituted; for the majority of alcoholic cases coming under observation of the police department have been bereft of all reason and are classed as "drunk and down." This condition I attribute to the quantity and quality obtained from the average blind tiger. I do not state that alcoholism is on the increase among the Negroes, but I do say that the number who fall by the wayside in a drunken stupor appears to be greater than the usual tipsy fellow who staggers along the thoroughfare. The drug habit (cocaine) is in my opinion a greater evil among the Negroes than the whiskey habit, notwithstanding as a rule it is invariably a combination of both. While there is no increase of crime among the Negroes the situation is apparently unchanged since the institution and operation of the prohibition law."

The sheriff of Mobile County said: "In our county the Negroes are very temperate. Very few cases of drunkenness are reported and in proportion to the population consisting of all other nationalities it is my opinion that less drunkenness occurs amongst the Negroes than amongst the others. The prohibition law has had a good effect upon them." Mobile City has a population of 51,500, of whom about 25,000 are whites and 20,000[1] are Negroes. The County of Mobile has a population of 80,000 about 46,000 of whom are whites and 34,000 Negroes.

The sheriff of Madison County, in which as above mentioned the city of Huntsville is located, said that "Since the prohibition law went into effect crime has decreased among your race wonderfully in this county, especially felony. There has not been a case of assault to rape by a colored man on a white woman in this county for four years. There is now but one colored man in jail charged with a felony." Madison County has a population of 47,000, about 20,000 of whom are Negroes.

Let us now turn from these inconclusive facts to what the strictly rural counties have to show. The sheriff of Autauga County, in which there are about 9,000 whites and 11,000 Negroes, reported that crime has increased "from one-third to at least one-fourth. Prohibition has made the Negroes worse in my county. They now send off and get large quantities of whiskey and we have blind tigers all over the county. When we had places where they could go and buy whiskey lawfully these places were policed."

The sheriff of Walker County reported that since prohibition had gone into effect there was very little if any difference in the crime rate among the Negroes. This county contains about 30,000 whites and 7,000 Negroes.

The sheriff of Elmore County, in which there are 15,000 whites and 13,000 Negroes, said: "If the prohibition law were enforced, Negro crime would be reduced."

In Randolph County, which contains 19,000 whites and 6,000 Negroes, according to the sheriff, the effects on Negro crime have been as follows: "It seems that in the policed places it has done some good in checking dissipation, but outside of the policed places the Negro and those of other races who are so inclined to disobey the law have almost absolute control of the liquor traffic and if there is any improvement among them I fail to see it; that is among the classes I have mentioned."

In Bullock County, where there are about 26,000 Negroes and 4,000 whites, the conditions, according to the sheriff, were worse than before prohibition went into effect. The chief cause, however, according to his letter was that the law was not enforced.

The sheriff of Jackson County reported that "Crimes of all nature have decreased materially in this section since the prohibition law has gone into effect, and I feel satisfied that the prohibition law has had more to do with, than anything else, the decrease of crime among the colored race." Jackson County has a population of about 29,000 whites and 4,000 Negroes.

The sheriff of Blount County, in which there are about 20,000 whites and 1,100 Negroes, wrote that "The Negro race in this county is above the average. We have no criminals here. We have not had a Negro criminal in jail in 18 months. I do not think that prohibition has decreased crime here, for we do not have any to decrease."

The sheriff of Bibb County sent a very interesting letter in which he said: "This county has been under local option for the past twenty-five years and the law for the sale of whiskey has been rigidly enforced. For that reason, therefore, no relative deduction could be drawn by me as to the increase or decrease of crime on that account. Your race in this county is far above the average in honesty and integrity and as a rule live in perfect harmony with the whites." Bibb County contains 15,000 whites and 7,700 Negroes.

The sheriff of Conecuh County, which contains 11,000 whites and 10,000 Negroes, said that "We have had prohibition in this county twenty-six years, and it has been in operation too long for me to give you an intelligent answer as to its effect on crime here. We all understand that whiskey and crime go hand in hand whether it is sold legally or otherwise. There have been but two cases of rape by a colored man on a white woman in the history of this county — the first in 1859 and the second in 1866. In both cases the offenders were legally executed."

Although the data presented above is inconclusive, yet when all the facts are considered, strong drink, I believe, is one of the chief causes of Negro crime in the South. It appears that where prohibition has really prohibited the Negroes from securing liquor their crime rate has been decreased. On the other hand, it appears that where the prohibition law did not prevent the Negroes from securing whiskey there has been no decrease in the crime rate, in fact the introduction of a cheaper grade of liquor has apparently had a tendency to increase the crime rate. In every instance, however, where the prohibition law has been rigidly enforced and the Negroes have been unable to get liquor, there has been a decrease in the crime rate.

This is the case in Macon County, Alabama, where I live. In this county there are about 22,000 Negroes and 4,000 whites. The sheriff of my county recently reported that he had only one deputy and did not have enough work to keep him busy. Sentiment has a great deal to do with the enforcement of the prohibition law and indirectly with the increase or decrease of the crime rate. In my own county there is a healthy sentiment both among the whites and the Negroes in favor of prohibition. There is published in the county a Negro farm paper, the influence of which has been very helpful in aiding the prohibition effort. Another thing that has helped has been the attitude of the Negro ministers. All the Negro ministers in the county are organized into an undenominational association. This association has given its support to the enforcement of the prohibition law and has even gone so far as to organize a Law and Order League to work in co-operation with the officers of the law. Although this League as such has not accomplished much, yet the moral effect on the people of the county has been very salutary.

A further proof that prohibition when enforced does cause a decrease in crime is shown by the reports that came from Atlanta, Georgia, and Birmingham, Alabama. During the first two months that prohibition was in effect in those cities there was a remarkable decrease in crime. At the end of the first month in Birmingham Judge N. B. Feagin reported to the mayor that "the decrease in arrests averaged about as follows: In comparing January, 1908, under prohibition, with January 1907, with saloons, aggregate arrests decrease 33⅓; for assault with intent to murder 22 per cent; gambling 17 per cent; drunkenness, 80 per cent; disorderly conduct, 35 per cent; grand larceny, 33 per cent; vagrancy, 40 per cent; wife beating, 70 per cent."

The Birmingham News, in commenting upon the first effects of prohibition said: "For ten years Birmingham has not enjoyed so orderly a period as it has since the 1st of January (1908). The moral improvement of the city has been marked since prohibition went into effect. The newspapers are no longer giving space to shootings, murders and cutting scrapes, personal altercations and other disorders as they formerly did for the reason that the regard for law and order in this community is very much more in evidence since the removal of the whiskey traffic.["]

In Atlanta there was a more extraordinary decrease in crime than in Birmingham. During the month of January, 1907, 1,653 cases were put on the docket of the recorder's court. During the month of January, 1908, there were but 768 cases on the docket, a decrease of considerably more than 50 per cent. During January, 1907, there were 341 cases of drunkenness tried, but in 1908 only 64, a decrease of more than 80 per cent.

A further confirmation of the fact that prohibition tends to reduce crime is shown by the statement of Chief Justice Walter Clark of the State of North Carolina, who says that since prohibition has gone into effect in the state the general crime rate has been reduced 50 per cent. Murder in the first degree has decreased 32 per cent; burglary, 20 per cent; attacks with deadly weapons, 30 per cent; larceny, 40 per cent; manslaughter, 35 per cent; murder in the second degree, 21 per cent; minor crimes from 25 to 55 per cent. Justice Clark, I understand, has prepared a five years' comparison which shows that some crimes have decreased more than 60 per cent since the saloons have been abolished. According to his report in five years there had been only two lynchings in the state of North Carolina and none in the last two years.

Journal of the American Institute of Criminal Law and Criminology, 3 (Sept. 1912), 384–92.

¹ Possibly a typographical error for 26,000.

From Charles William Anderson

New York, N.Y. October 3, 1912

Personal

My dear Doctor: The Advisory Committee has been enlarged. I wrote Tyler fully about the matter, explaining to him that Mr. Hilles had requested me to send in five names, and asked him to make some suggestions. He at once sent me back the names of Waters, Jones¹ of Cincinnati and Jackson² of Chicago. I included them in my recommendation, with the exception of Jackson, for whom I substituted Cummings, as I felt that Illinois would naturally belong to the Western headquarters, and assumed that Mr. Hilles wanted me to suggest names for the East, only. I passed over the modesty which impelled Tyler, on being asked for suggestions, to name the majority of the committee. Last Saturday Lewis and Tyler came over to see me, and I thought I discovered, during my talk with them, that Tyler was anxious to bring about Jackson's selection. They both suggested that the committee be enlarged, and after threshing it out and calling on Mr. Karger,³ it was enlarged, and a plan of campaign mapped out. Mr. Hilles approved of it all and the committee was named and a meeting of it called for Saturday, October 5th, at the National headquarters. The Colored National headquarters will be opened in the Colored Republican Club, #76 West 131st St. It was agreed that all matters pertaining to the colored vote shall be submitted to this committee, who in turn shall make a concrete recommendation to the National Committee. The Committee is named as follows: Gilchrist

Stewart and Fred R. Moore, New York; J. Solomon Gaines[4] (selected by Lewis) Boston; Phil Waters, W.Va.; Harry S. Cummings, Maryland; J. J. Jones,[5] Ohio; Major R. R. Jackson, Illinois and Bush of Little Rock, Ark. We were allowed a stenographer and two clerks for our headquarters. Lewis at once named one clerk (a society friend, of Boston) and Tyler named the other — (his son, Ralph, Jr.). This left Moore and Stewart, and the New York friends, with only the stenographer to name, and as you know, stenographers must be selected for ability, which shuts out an opportunity to take care of any of our political friends. However, I mean to have this force considerably enlarged before long. Mr. H. authorized the Committee to incur expenses to the extent of $2,000. I insisted that each bureau of the National Committee, such as Press, Speakers, etc., etc., be at once notified that all matters concerning colored voters should be referred to this Advisory Committee, and that the person who had handled colored matters be at once directed to "knock off." We are getting out literature. Have Mr. Scott help us all he can, for now that we have eliminated Manning, it is up to us to make good.

The Roosevelt story was explained by me just as you have explained it. When it was mentioned here, I stated, that in my opinion, you had accidentally encountered him, as I happened to know that Chehaw was the station at which persons traveling over the Southern must change for Tuskegee.

W. H. Ellis, the Duke of Abyssinia, phoned me the other day, informing me that Wetmore had told him that my relentless enmity had again defeated his aspirations, and that while Lewis, Cobb, Terrell and Tyler were all for him for chief of the negro bureau, I had knocked him out.

Thanks for the considerate courtesy which prompted you to send me the "Man farthest down." I will read it with much interest, and am confident that I will gain much pleasure and information from it. Yours truly,

Charles W. Anderson

TLS Con. 56 BTW Papers DLC.

[1] Joseph Lawrence Jones, born in 1868, graduated from Gaines High School in Cincinnati in 1886 and from Sheldon Business College in 1909. After teaching in Kentucky, Texas, and Ohio for five years, Jones was deputy recorder of Hamilton County (1890–95) and deputy county clerk (1895–1904). He also was principal of the Douglass Night School in Cincinnati (1897–1904). In 1902 Jones founded the Central Regalia Co. to provide for the growing needs of black fraternal organiza-

tions. He himself held high office in several black fraternal orders and was a vice-president of the National Negro Press Association, editor of the *Fraternal Monitor,* and member of the NNBL.

[2] Robert R. Jackson, born in Chicago in 1870, attended the Chicago public schools and entered the postal service in 1888. In the same year he joined the Illinois National Guard, rising to the rank of major of infantry during the Spanish-American War. In 1909 he left the postal service for work as a fraternal journalist. He also entered Republican politics, serving in the Illinois Senate from 1912 to 1916 and as a Chicago alderman for many years after 1918. He was a member of the influential Appomattox Club, the Knights of Pythias, and many other fraternal orders.

[3] Gustav J. Karger (1866–1924), born in Berlin, Germany, grew up in Cincinnati, Ohio, where he was a reporter for several newspapers. From 1889 to 1906 he was Washington correspondent of the Scripps-McRae Press Association. In the 1908 campaign he was the personal press representative of W. H. Taft, and in the 1912 campaign he was director of the bureau of organization of the Republican National Committee.

[4] J. Solomon Gaines, a Boston waiter, had been active in the defense of W. M. Trotter during his trial in connection with the Boston Riot in 1903.

[5] Actually Joseph Lawrence Jones.

An Article in *The Continent*

October 3, 1912

RACE FRICTION IN CUBA — AND ELSEWHERE

In the Republic of Cuba there are about 600,000 negroes or persons of African descent. In the United States there are about 10,000,000 negroes. The white population of Cuba is about 1,000,000. In other words, there are about sixteen times as many negroes in the United States as there are in Cuba, while the proportion of black people to white people is about the same there as it is in the former slave states in this country.

For a period of several months past a very large proportion of the negro population of Cuba was in a state of rebellion against the government. This racial rebellion has already cost the Cuban government many hundreds of thousands of dollars, besides the loss to the country from the destruction of crops, the interruption of business and the injury to private property.

With a negro population sixteen times as large as that of Cuba why has there been no negro rebellion in the United States? It is not because the American negro has not had provocation as compared with his brothers in Cuba. The American negro has had much more reason for a resort to physical violence. Legally there is no such thing as racial discrimination. Whatever the actual practice may be in that country in other matters, as far as concerns travel, public entertainment, schools, courts, voting and holding of public office, there are no legal discriminations in favor of one race and against the other. Lynchings, which have done more than anything else to embitter the negro in this country, are practically unknown in Cuba.

A HALF CENTURY OF FREEDOM NEXT YEAR

Beginning in October, 1913, the American negro will celebrate the fiftieth anniversary of his freedom. During all these years, in which millions of American negroes have been free, why is it that they, with more provocation and more justification for violence, have not resorted to rebellion or crime in order to secure their rights? Some say that it is because the American negro is a coward. The negro has often been called a coward because he submitted to slavery, just as the American Indian has been called a brave man because he would not or could not endure slavery. The struggles of the Indians to maintain their freedom and independence have cost the United States, from 1789 to 1800 [1900], $800,000,000 and the lives of 19,000 white men and Indians.

On the other hand, the negro, outside the United States, in Africa and the West Indies, has shown himself quite as willing as the Indian to fight for freedom and independence. In the mountains of Jamaica the negro Maroons maintained their freedom for many years against the armies of the white men which were sent to conquer them. There are negroes still living in the mountains of Jamaica who never submitted to slavery. In Haiti negroes won their independence in battle against armies sent out by Napoleon Bonaparte. Negroes had as large, if not a larger, part in the war which secured the independence of Cuba as any other portion of the population.

The question then remains why the American negro has not resorted to rebellion or insurrection when he felt that he had been unjustly treated in this country. The answer is simple and not far to seek. At the very beginning of the freedom of my race in the United States there were white people who were wise enough and self-sacrific-

33

ing enough to begin at once the training of negro leaders, who were placed, if I may use the expression, as sentinels in every negro community in the South. In most cases these negro leaders were teachers and ministers. In other cases they were doctors, pharmacists, lawyers, farmers, business men or politicians. In many cases these negro leaders had caught the spirit of their teachers and went forth with a sincere desire to make the masses of the race a better and more useful people. In other cases they had, perhaps, no other ambition but that of bettering their own condition. In any case they were men who had sufficient education and sufficient knowledge of the world to see the wisdom of patience in their struggle to improve themselves and their race. Instead of imitating the Indian, they preferred to follow, so far as they were able, another race which, like the negro, has been accused of cowardice. I refer to the Jew.

NEGRO LEADERS HAVE KEPT RACIAL PEACE

As a rule the negro leaders have kept a steady hand on the masses of the colored people, and they have also kept in touch with the white race. The result is that, for the most part, we have peace between the races in this country, instead of insurrection and war as in Cuba.

As the years pass there is likely, in my opinion, to be less friction instead of more between the races. Just in proportion as the masses of the people become land owners and householders, builders of churches and schools; just in proportion as commercial relations between the two races increase, all these things will constitute a pledge of racial peace. The negro who owns a farm or conducts a store or a bank is not likely to be a leader in a rash movement of any kind. The white man who has a bank with thousands of dollars of negro deposits, who has on loan large sums of money belonging to negroes, is not likely to be a leader in a racial war.

For a long time we have felt in the United States that the money spent by the states and by individuals in the uplift of the negro race was to be considered as a mere charity. It should not be so considered. Even if it is nothing else or higher, the spending of money in the education of 10,000,000 of negroes is good business. If we had today in the South the same kind of racial bitterness and unrest as now exists in Cuba, investments would not be safe, and the whole material progress and development of the South would halt.

In the solution of most human problems education is not only cheaper than war, but it is far more permanent in its effects. The past forty-eight years has not only demonstrated the value to the South and the whole country of negro schoolhouses, but it has also proclaimed the wisdom and the patriotism of those who, for the first time in the history of the world so far as I know, have made the school the medium for the solution of a great and perplexing social problem.

The Continent, 43 (Oct. 3, 1912), 1382.

An Article in *The Independent*[1]

Oct. 3, 1912

THE NEGRO AND ILLITERACY

Perhaps the most important single fact which the census has brought to light in regard to the negro in America is contained in the figures which show the progress of the race during the last ten years in learning to read and write. At no period in their history has so large a proportion of the negro people succeeded in gaining the sort of freedom that comes with the opportunity to live by and with the printed page.

There seems to be a pretty general agreement among people thruout the world that the black man, at the time of his emancipation, was, so far as education was concerned, at the bottom. Forty-eight years ago, when Abraham Lincoln made us free, there were, perhaps, 3, certainly not more than 5, per cent. of the freedmen who were not wholly illiterate. The census figures just published show that at the present time 69.5, practically 70 per cent., of the colored people of the United States can both read and write. In 1900 there was still 44.5 per cent. of the negro population of the country who were illiterate; now there remains only a little more than 30 per cent.

Compared with the American white man, both in the Northern and the Southern States, the negro, not only in respect to general education, but in his ability to read and write, is still far behind. The figures show that in 1900, 6.2 per cent. of the white people in the United States were still unable to read and write. In 1910 this percentage was reduced to 5. In the Southern States the illiteracy among the white race has been reduced from 11 per cent. in 1900 to 8 per cent. in 1910. Still more interesting are the figures for the immigrant white population. Among the foreign whites the number which could neither read nor write was in 1900 12.9 per cent., and in 1910 12.8 per cent. These figures indicate that while the native white population has decreased its illiteracy 1.6 and the foreign white population has decreased its illiteracy only about one-tenth of 1 per cent. the illiteracy among the negro population has decreased 14 per cent.

The significance of these figures will appear, however, when they are compared with statistics showing the conditions among people in other parts of the world in somewhat the same stage of development as the black man in America. In Cuba, for example, 59 per cent. of the people cannot read and write; in Spain, 68 per cent.; in Russia, 77 per cent.; in Portugal, 79 per cent.; in Brazil, 80 per cent. Within forty-eight years the American negro has reduced his illiteracy by 67 per cent. It should be noticed, too, that the people named above are not aliens in their country.

One of the most interesting facts brought out by these figures is that the negro seems to be making greater progress in those parts of the country where he has less opportunities than in other parts of the country where he has greater opportunities. For example, illiteracy among the colored people in Delaware decreased 12.5 per cent. in the years between 1900 and 1910. In Maryland the decrease was 11.7; in West Virginia, 12 per cent.; in Kentucky, 12 per cent. In the District of Columbia, where negroes have perhaps the best public school facilities of any place in the world, the illiteracy of the race decreased 16.8 per cent. In the following four Southern States, where the public school facilities are, as a rule, poor, it appears that so far as the mere matter of learning to read and write is concerned, negroes are making more rapid progress than in any other part of the country. For example, the decrease in illiteracy between the years 1900 and 1910 was 15.7 per cent. in North Carolina; 15.19 per cent. in Georgia; 16.6 per cent. in Arkansas; and 17.3 per cent. in Alabama.

I do not mean to say that this is an entirely fair comparison, but it does show that the one way to inspire the negro with an ambition and a determination to get an education is to let him know that some one in the community is opposed to letting him have it.

It is a great thing for the people who have been slaves to have gained possession for themselves, in so short a time, of one of the fundamental tools of civilization. We should not, however, be deceived by figures which indicate that a little more than two-thirds of the negro population are able to read and write. Races, like individuals, may be able to read and write and be little better off than they were before, so far as concerns the fundamental things of life. Few people understand the enormous handicap under which the negro labors in his efforts to get an education of any kind, and few people also appreciate the sacrifices which the progress thus far made has cost the masses of the negro people. I do not believe that the best white people of the South realize how little of the school funds, which is supposed to be distributed equally among the races according to the number of children of school age, ever reaches the negro schools, and I am sure they do not realize to what extent the money which is actually expended upon negro education in many parts of the South is wasted.

In Elizabeth City County, Virginia, for example, there are 2,200 white children of school age and 2,300 colored children of school age. These negro children have had twenty teachers to give them instruction during the past year, while the white children have had forty-nine teachers. The negro children have had school buildings costing $5,000, while the white children have had school buildings which cost $62,000. The salaries of the twenty negro teachers amounted to $4,000, while the salaries of the forty-nine white teachers amounted to $23,000.

Much has been said from time to time about the schools in the South for the higher education of the negro. Few people either in the North or the South realize, however, to what extent these institutions, which are supposed to be for the higher education of the negro race, are merely doing the work which should be done by the public schools. Of 189 schools of which we have statistics, in which negroes are supposed to get higher education, nearly 57 per cent. of the pupils are in the elementary grades and only 5 per cent. are getting what is commonly called a college education.

Not only is the negro not getting a college education to any such extent as most people believe, but in too many cases he is not getting anything in the schools that is worthy of the name of education. I can best give an idea of the conditions that prevail in some part of the South in the words of one of the recent reports made by the Superintendent of Schools for South Carolina.

In his last annual report the State Superintendent of Education in that State speaks thus concerning the deplorable condition of the negro public schools.

"The education of the negro in South Carolina is in the hands of the white race. The white trustees apportion the funds, select the teachers and receive the reports. The county superintendent has the supervision of these schools in his hands. We have expended this year $348,834.60 in the support of negro schools. I never visit one of these schools without feeling that we are wasting a large part of this money and are neglecting a great opportunity. The negro school houses are miserable beyond all description. They are usually without comfort, equipment, proper lighting or sanitation. Nearly all of the negroes of school age in the district are crowded into these miserable structures during the short time which the school runs. Most of the teachers are absolutely untrained and have been given certificates by the county board not because they have passed the examination, but because it is necessary to have some kind of a negro teacher. Among the negro rural schools which I have visited, I have found only one in which the highest class knew the multiplication table. In South Carolina we have simply turned over a portion of the school fund to the negro schools, and expect the most ignorant teachers of the State, without any suggestion or directions, to adapt to the special needs of the negro schools a course of study and text books designed primarily for the white children.

"The negro tenant is now, and will be for years to come, the tenant farmer of South Carolina. His welfare and the prosperity of the white race depend largely upon his efficiency as a farmer. I believe that the time has now come for us to attack the negro school problem with a serious intention of adapting the schools to the special needs of the negro farmer in an endeavor to teach him agriculture, to encourage manual training, cooking, sewing, personal cleanliness and hygienic conditions in his home, along with the elements of a common school education. The schools should endeavor to set for him a better standard of living, and increase those ever-present and insistant wants which enter about a well-kept home, and thus secure for him a better existence and for the land owner a more constant labor supply. This problem has not yet been solved, and the 'well done' of the whole South awaits the county superintendent and trustees who will attack it vigorously."

Notwithstanding these difficulties, the negro, as the census figures I have quoted show, is making progress. He is learning, like the Jew, to make education a part of his religion. More and more every year the schoolhouse is taking its place alongside of his church as the center of thought and interest.

Every year the amount of money contributed by the negro to his own education thru churches and other organizations grows larger. A fair estimate makes the sum of these contributions by negroes to negro education since emancipation not less than fifty million dollars. There is to my mind no better evidence of the fact that the money which has been put into negro education in the South has, in spite of all the deficiencies of the negro schools, been well invested than the fact that thru this education the negro is learning to help himself.

There has been and there still is prejudice against negro education in the South, but every year the number of thinking men in the Southern States who realize that the only practical solution of the negro problem of the South is the education of the negro race is increasing.

Let me add in conclusion that in my opinion, there is at the present time no place in this country where money could be invested to such advantage as in assisting the members of both races in the South who are seeking to inspire and direct the movement, which has already begun to build up, not a single school here and there or a single college, but a practical, adequate and efficient system of negro education in the Southern States.

The Independent, 73 (Oct. 3, 1912), 766–68.

[1] An earlier version of the article was sent to *The Independent* on May 29, 1912. A typescript is in Con. 457, BTW Papers, DLC.

To Robert Ezra Park

Astor House, New York City. October 6, 1912

Dear Dr. Park: I think a plan is now maturing by which we can carry out at the school what we have discussed several times. I have won the chief officer of the Stokes Fund over to this plan, and he says that he feels quite sure he can carry it through the Stokes Fund Board.

In brief, I have asked the Stokes Fund people to appropriate enough money to enable you to make a thorough investigation and report covering the work of all the Negro schools in the South including high schools up through colleges and universities. The plan is to ask you to make such an investigation and report on these schools as the Carnegie Fund people made with reference to the medical schools in the United States. If you have not seen the Carnegie Fund report on medical schools, I advise that you get it at once and read it. Perhaps Dr. Kenney has a copy of it.

If you are agreeable to the plan, I want to send in an application to the Stokes Fund trustees as soon as I reach Tuskegee, and this application should be an outline of what is proposed to be done, and I am writing to ask you to begin on the preparation of an application.

As you know, there is nothing more needed in the South than to state exactly to the public what these schools are doing, especially the supposed industrial schools. A lot of them are doing fake work, others are trying to do good work but do not know how. We want to try to get the truth to help the schools and for the sake of the public. Of course such a report will create a great stir, but in the end great good will be done as in the case of the medical schools.

The Stokes Fund people asked me what in my opinion would be the cost. I told them that in the rough I thought you ought to have a salary of $3,000 a year and three or four thousand dollars allowed for traveling expenses, and clerical assistance. This seemed to strike them as reasonable. I feel that you cannot do a better thing just now for the cause than to undertake this work. Mr. Stokes, the head of the fund, thinks that the work ought to be done perhaps within two years, but I am not sure whether it may not take a little longer time. At any rate, I am anxious to hear from you on the subject, and hope you will begin the preparation of the application. The Stokes Fund board has a meeting early in November. They want the whole matter before them at that time.

Some very fine reviews are appearing in many of the most important newspapers in the North of "The Man Farthest Down." I hope that you are seeing them. The New York Times gives it the foremost place in its book reviews for this week and devotes nearly two columns to it.[1] Yours very truly,

[Booker T. Washington]

TLc   Con. 61   BTW Papers   DLC.

[1] *New York Times Book Review,* Oct. 6, 1912, 552.

To Warren Logan

New York City. October 6, 1912

Dear Mr. Logan: You will remember that sometime ago I wrote you about the possibility of my wanting to purchase a few acres of land on the back side of the farm.

I am writing about the same matter again, and I wish you would take it up with the proper ones.

I find that the constant daily strain on Mrs. Washington on the grounds is too much for her, and I want to arrange for a place on the back side of the farm where she can go for a day or two if necessary each week and be quiet and away from the hurry and bustle of the school, and with this in view I am writing to ask you to arrange for me to purchase about three acres of land on the other side of the Chehaw branch. This land is so located that in my opinion it will not interfere in any way with any of the plans of the school, and as you know is quite remote from the center of the school.

I do not care for this matter to be spoken of at present at Tuskegee. Yours very truly,

[Booker T. Washington]

TLc   Con. 631   BTW Papers   DLC.

To Theodore Roosevelt

Grand Rapids, Mich. October 16, 1912

My dear Col. Roosevelt: I sent a telegram of sympathy to you on Monday night as soon as I heard of the assault on you,[1] but I fear you might not have received it, so I am writing again to express the deep sense of shame and humiliation which I feel over the fact that anyone would have tried to do you bodily harm, and also to express the deep sense of gratitude for myself and my race over the fact that you are on the road to recovery and that your life will be spared for many years in service to the nation. Yours very truly,

[Booker T. Washington]

TLc Con. 61 BTW Papers DLC.

[1] When Roosevelt was going from his hotel to deliver a speech in Milwaukee on Oct. 14, 1912, an objector to a third term shot him in the chest. Roosevelt insisted on making a brief speech before going to the hospital, where the bullet was removed from his right lung. He rested on his laurels in the final two weeks of the presidential campaign. (Pringle, *Roosevelt*, 568–70.)

To Hollis Burke Frissell

Detroit, Mich. October 21, 1912

My dear Dr. Frissell: I have been spending three days in Detroit, and I am convinced that Detroit is a place to which both Hampton and Tuskegee ought to devote serious attention. The amount of wealth that is piling up here is something almost fabulous, and the people are now getting to the point where they feel that they ought to give, and I believe that with careful cultivation both institutions can receive large sums from Detroit annually. During my three days here I have merely been skimming the surface. I do not know, of course, what your plans for the winter are, but I think if you and the quartette could spend say a week or ten days here in Detroit and vicinity it would be worth while. Yours very truly,

[Booker T. Washington]

TLc Con. 58 BTW Papers DLC.

From the United Press Association

New York Oct 22—12

We believe Nationwide agitation resulting action pugilistic Jack Johnson due primarily thoughtlessness of public failing recognize better element colored race condemns Johnson severely as whites we believe statement from you would do much to restore sane public thought   would greatly appreciate 500 words telegraphed statement to be used exactly prepared by you

United Press Ass

TWSr Con. 467 BTW Papers DLC.

A Statement on Jack Johnson for the United Press Association[1]

[Tuskegee, Ala.] October 23, 1912

Please Rush!
Replying to your telegram, please publish the following statement exactly as submitted:

Jack Johnson's case will be settled in due time in the courts. Until the court has spoken, I do not care to either defend or condemn him. I can only say at this time, that this is another illustration of the almost irreparable injury that a wrong action on the part of a single individual may do to a whole race. It shows the folly of those persons who think that they alone will be held responsible for the evil that they do. Especially is this true in the case of the Negro in the United States today. No one can do so much injury to the Negro race as the Negro himself. This will seem to many persons unjust, but no one can doubt that it is true.

What makes the situation seem a little worse in this case, is the fact that it was the white man, not the black man who has given Jack Johnson the kind of prominence he has enjoyed up to now and put him, in other words, in a position where he has been able to bring humiliation upon the whole race of which he is a member.

I do not believe it is necessary for me to say that the honest, sober element of the Negro people of the United States is as severe in condemnation of the kind of immorality with which Jack Johnson is at present charged as any other portion of the community.

In making this statement, I do not mean to, as I have said at the beginning, say how far Jack Johnson is or is not guilty of the charges that have been made against him. That is a question for the court to decide.

Booker T. Washington

TWpSr Con. 467 BTW Papers DLC.

¹ Prepared by E. J. Scott and Robert E. Park while BTW was away from Tuskegee. (BTW to Scott, Oct. 24, 1912, Con. 619, BTW Papers, DLC.)

To Anson Phelps Stokes, Jr.

[Tuskegee, Ala., Nov. 1, 1912]¹

Dear Mr. Stokes: Referring again to the conversation I had with you some weeks ago, I am now writing to put before the Stokes Fund Board of Trustees a matter of the greatest importance in developing the colored schools in the South.

Speaking somewhat in the rough, there are 600 schools in the South that can be classed as above the ordinary public schools. These include high schools, industrial schools, colleges, universities and professional schools. These schools are divided into three classes. First, those supported in part or in whole by state or municipal governments. Second, those supported by various missionary organizations in the North and South, mainly church schools. Third, those controlled by an independent board of trustees.

It would be a matter of the greatest help to have these schools thoroughly examined with a view of letting the public know just what they are doing. This has never been done. For example, there are many so-called industrial schools that have the reputation of giving industrial training, but in fact the work is a mere sham. There are not a few institutions with the name "college" and "university" that are in fact mere local schools pretending to do college work when in reality the majority of their students are in the primary or public school grades with no college work whatever being done. In other cases there are colleges and universities which have an industrial department attached to them that pretend to do industrial work, but in reality very little industrial work is being done.

The people at the head of these various institutions in many cases are honest, well-meaning persons, but do not know how to go about their jobs. There is another class of people at the head of these institutions who are not honest in intention or in work.

My idea is, that if your Board will provide the means, it would help these schools more than any one single thing that has ever occurred to have them thoroughly examined and let the public know just what they are doing much in the same way that the medical schools were recently examined under the auspices of the Carnegie Fund. When once the facts are found out and made known to the public, I believe that that would constitute the basis for the re-organization and classification of these schools, and with that done the education of my race in the South would be placed upon an entirely different basis and the public could know just what is being done.

I think it would require from two to three years to have this work done well. The person in charge I think would have to be paid a salary of about $3,000 a year, and with an allowance of $2,000 a year for traveling expenses, clerk hire and other incidental expenses. I do not think it ought to go beyond this figure.

I strongly recommend to take charge of this work, Robert E. Park, Ph.D., of Wollaston, Mass. Dr. Park is a thoroughly trained investigator. He is a graduate of Harvard and has studied for several years in Germany and other European states. Aside from this, he has traveled extensively through the South and knows Southern conditions among white people and colored people. In addition to his other training, he has had valuable experience of a newspaper reporter and magazine writer. He was recently offered a position under The North American Civil League for Immigrants.[2] In this position he was to have direction of the educational work of the League in the states of New York and New Jersey.

I very much hope your Board will agree to undertake this work, and that an arrangement can be made for the investigation to begin at once. I think Dr. Park would be ready to proceed as soon as he is authorized *and advised as to whatever is agreed on.*

[Booker T. Washington]

TLf Copy   Con. 464   BTW Papers   DLC.

45

¹ A draft, with a few minor differences, dated Nov. 1, 1912, is in Con. 464, BTW Papers, DLC.

² The North American Civic League for Immigrants, founded in 1908 with headquarters in Boston, sought the assimilation and protection of immigrants.

An Invitation

[Tuskegee, Ala., ca. Nov. 2, 1912]

You are cordially invited to attend
A Candy Pulling and Sweet Potato Party
Saturday Evening, November 2, 1912
At Mr. Callanan's place on the Chehaw Dirt Road
Vehicles to convey the party will be ready
To leave the Court Yard (Boys' Trades Building)
At seven-thirty P.M.

BOOKER T. WASHINGTON, Principal.

TLSr Con. 618 BTW Papers DLC.

From James Carroll Napier

Nashville, Tenn. Nov. 3d 12

Dear Mr. Washington: I am writing you today not because I owe you a letter for I think you have forgotten to reply to my last one but because I have not heard from you in a good long while and I feel as though I would like now to have at least a line from you.

For the past twenty days I have been making a very strenuous canvass of Middle and West Tennessee. I find our people almost a unit for Mr. Taft and the republican ticket. We have great hope of the re-election of Gov. Hooper¹ and of carrying the State for Mr. Taft. The irreparable split in the Democratic party brightens the prospects of Republican victory in Tenn. We have made a hard fight whether we come out victorious or not.

There has never been a campaign where the negro in Tennessee

46

formed so important a factor in every political faction as he does today. Our meetings have been largely attended by the whites and they have at all times given us respectful and considerate hearing. I spoke to a large audience yesterday at Pulaski in the opera house. They gave me a good reception and during my stay many references were made by the people to your visit there and the great good that your advice and words of wisdom had wrought in that community. I was told that but for your visit of two years ago the opera house would not have been open to us as it was yesterday.

I was out at Fisk University to church this morning. I saw Booker and talked with him. He looks well and more fleshy than I ever saw him before. He seems steady and is developing into a manly and scholarly looking young man. I never saw him look so well as he now looks.

I leave for Washington on Tuesday night next and hope that the first time you pass through Washington you will let me know and, if possible stop off and make us a visit. Very truly and sincerely yours,

J. C. Napier

ALS Con. 461 BTW Papers DLC.

[1] Ben Walter Hooper (1870–1957), an east Tennessee Republican, was governor of the state from 1911 to 1915. He was elected with the support of dry Democrats, after they had passed a state prohibition law over the veto of the Democratic governor.

From Anson Phelps Stokes, Jr.

New Haven, Conn., November 6, 1912

My dear Dr. Washington: I am under real obligations to you for your two letters of November 1st. I hope that we can be of some service to your school this year, but I cannot at this time make any promises.

I am tremendously impressed with the opportunities for the survey of Southern negro schools and colleges, but I find differences in opinion among those who are interested in it, and especially as to the best person to undertake the work. Dr. Frissell is strongly of the opinion that Mr. Jones of the Census Bureau who was formerly at Hampton would be the ablest man you could get. I would like your judgment of his capacity in comparison with that of Dr. Park. Sincerely yours,

Anson Phelps Stokes

TLS Con. 464 BTW Papers DLC.

To Emmett Jay Scott

[Tuskegee, Ala.] November Seventh, Nineteen Hundred Twelve

Mr. Scott: I think you had better take up seriously as soon as you can, the matter of my visit to Oregon and Washington.

I want to reduce my stay in those states to the smallest possible compass. Impress upon the gentleman who is arranging the trip with the idea that I can speak two or three times a day.

I also hope you will take up the matter of arranging for my meetings going and coming.

B. T. W.

TLI Con. 837 BTW Papers DLC.

To James Carroll Napier

[Tuskegee, Ala.] November Seventh, Nineteen Hundred Twelve

My dear Mr. Napier: I value your kind letter which you wrote me from Nashville very much. I passed through Washington a few days ago and spent several hours there, but I did not go to your house for the reason that I heard that both you and Mrs. Napier were in Nashville.

Well, the fight is all over. Matters have come out just about as I had expected. The fact is the Republican party was completely split and divided its votes between Mr. Roosevelt and Mr. Taft, while the Democrats remained solid for their ticket. Whether the old Republican party will ever [be] able to pull itself together in an effective manner again is quite a question.

I am sincerely sorry for Mr. Taft. He, in my opinion, is a first-class, clean gentleman, meaning to do the right thing, and I believe the time will yet come when the country will appreciate his true worth. Mr. Cleveland was treated [about] the same way.

I am very glad to hear of the delightful reception which you received through Tennessee. It is remarkable how you people in Tennessee have been able to keep out bitterness on the part of the white people during this political campaign.

I thank you very much for writing me regarding Booker. The Fisk football team is coming here on the 16th and play against our students. Booker is coming with them.

Please remember both of us to Mrs. Napier. Yours very truly,

Booker T. Washington

TLpS Con. 461 BTW Papers DLC.

From Charles William Anderson

New York, N.Y. November 8, 1912

(Personal) *Private*

My dear Doctor: Your good favor of the 5th is at hand. I fully agree with the opinion expressed in the last paragraph of your letter, that there will have to be a re-adjustment. I hope you will be in this "neck of the woods" in the near future, and that we can have a long talk over the present and the future.

On your last trip to this city, I called at your office at 9:30 A.M., but you had gone. My tardiness was due to the fact that I reached home from a speaking trip at 3 o'clock in the morning, and, therefore, over-slept myself. I was sorry to have missed you, but felt you must have been compelled to take a train and could not wait longer.

The black democrats are crowing very loudly, and have already divided the offices now held by colored republicans, among themselves. Du Bois, who prepared their literature during the campaign (for pay) is talked of for Hayti. A half dozen of them are pointed for my place, and each place in Washington is claimed by a dozen candidates. And thus the merry war goes on.

I thought you might be interested to know that Stewart informs me that Moore received $2,005 for his paper during the campaign from the Nat. Com. This, of course, does not include any receipts prior to

49

the Chicago convention. He also received something over $200 from the State Committee — the other amount was from the National Committee. In other words, he received more money than was used by the Colored Advisory Committee for work among colored people all over the country. This is in strictest confidence.

Among the many curious features of this very curious campaign, is that those Taft colored republicans, who were so bitterly opposed to the Colonel and so much devoted to the President, did not move a finger in his behalf after the nomination. In this city, such men as our old friend, "the Governor,"[1] deputy assistant Dist. Atty. McDougald[2] and others, who praised the President and objurgated the Colonel, did not make a single speech during the campaign. They clamored for the President's re-nomination, and then sat down and left it to the rest of us to elect him. But that's the way of the world. The man who is first to buckle on his sword in time of peace is also first to take it off in time of war.

Hoping you are very well, and that I will see you in the near future, I remain, Faithfully yours,

Charles W. Anderson

TLS   Con. 56   BTW Papers   DLC.

[1] P. B. S. Pinchback.
[2] Cornelius W. McDougald, a black man born in Whiteville, N.C., in 1879, graduated from Lincoln University and New York University Law School and was admitted to the New York bar in 1908. He served as assistant district attorney for five years. In 1923 he was appointed special assistant attorney general of the state.

From Hopson Owen Murfee[1]

Marion, Alabama   8 November 1912

My dear Dr. Washington: I thank you for your kind letter of the fourth of November, which I have read with interest.[2]

Your generous and gracious suggestion that the Tuskegee Institute do something towards raising the sum of Fifty Thousand Dollars, which the Trustees and directors of the Marion Foundation have undertaken as a memorial to my father, has touched me deeply. I am sure that the Memorial Committee would be very grateful for any gift that the students and teachers of Tuskegee might feel inclined and able to give. Such a gift would be a very inspiring thing. It would aid not only in the work of building upon this Foundation but in that larger work in the minds and hearts of men. It is very good of you and your co-laborers at Tuskegee to wish to have some part in this memorial to my father's life and work in Alabama. Far more than the gift itself, would be the spirit which shines through it. It would be an inestimable service, I believe, towards that indissoluble union of all good men in every worthy endeavor, and in the remaking of a harmonious and mutually helpful civilization.

You know, I trust, my father's faith in you, and his esteem and appreciation of your work for the betterment of Southern life. It was a source of joy to him to feel that he had unconsciously had some part in bringing you to Alabama; and to see his own ideas in this field of education, as he wrote to General Armstrong, so admirably realized by your work at Tuskegee.

He regarded this as one of his great services to the State. In the contemplated Quarter-Centennial Celebration of the Marion Institute, and the semi-centennial of his service to the cause of education in Alabama, he had planned, as you know, to have you deliver an address; and just before his sudden and unexpected illness and death, he had begun to prepare his address for the occasion, and to introduce you. He was willing to leave to other hands the introduction of President Taft and the University Heads, but he requested especially that he be allowed to introduce you, and to make his estimate and appreciation of your work his contribution to the celebration. But death, sudden and unexpected, ended all.

Perhaps at the dedication of the Memorial Hall you will consent to deliver another address in place of the one you so kindly offered to prepare for the Quarter-Centennial Celebration which has been abandoned; and I should like to attempt to take my father's place in introducing you.

I sent you yesterday a letter of introduction to my friend and classmate, Mr. M. Lee Bonner[3] of Birmingham, and I hope that you will have an opportunity to present it soon. Very truly yours

H. O. Murfee

TLS Con. 460 BTW Papers DLC.

¹ Hopson Owen Murfee (1874–1943), formerly a physics teacher at Marion Institute, Marion, Ala., succeeded his father, James Thomas Murfee, as president of the institute. He served from 1906 to 1918.

² BTW had offered to raise a small sum of money from Tuskegee faculty and teachers as a contribution toward the $50,000 memorial to James Thomas Murfee. "Of course," BTW wrote, "it is very fitting, it seems to me, that we should do something, since without his wise suggestion to General Armstrong in regard to my coming here, I question whether the Tuskegee Institute would be in its existence, certainly not in its present form." He asked if Murfee thought it would be appropriate for Tuskegee to contribute and added: "we want to be careful to help and not hinder." (Nov. 4, 1912, Con. 460, BTW Papers, DLC.)

³ A white lawyer in Birmingham.

To Anson Phelps Stokes, Jr.

[Tuskegee, Ala.] November 9, 1912

My dear Mr. Stokes: Your kind letter of recent date has been received, and I am very glad to know that you are still so thoroughly interested in the plan of the survey of Negro schools.

I very much hope that your board can see its way clear, also, to make a donation for either one or both of the objects that I asked for covering work at Tuskegee.

Now in regard to the person to have charge of the survey. I would state that Dr. Park is, in my opinion, by far the best qualified white man in any part of the country to have charge of this work. While I did not say it to you, I ought to add now that Dr. Park first suggested the necessity for such work to me and later has talked it over with me and several others. Dr. Jones is a good man and has very valuable qualifications for certain kinds of work, especially that of dealing with statistics, but what we need just now is a broader and more comprehensive study than a professional statistician would be likely to give us. Dr. Park, in my opinion, has a wider vision of the whole Southern field than is true of Dr. Jones. He has traveled extensively with me through nearly every Southern state, he knows by first hand examination something of conditions, and he has had this matter in mind for a number of years, and I believe would do a better job than a person who has not had his mind on it for so long a time. It would be Dr. Park's plan to secure the assistance, in gathering facts, of such men as W. T. B. Williams of the Hampton Institute, M. N. Work of

Tuskegee, and other persons who have been so placed as to have unusual knowledge of conditions. In addition, Dr. Park has the knack of meeting all classes of people in a way to get from them valuable information and at the same time not offend them. Yours very truly,

Booker T. Washington

TLpS Con. 464 BTW Papers DLC.

From Anson Phelps Stokes, Jr.

New Haven, Conn., November 12, 1912

My dear Mr. Washington: I have just received your very important letter of November 9th. I am quite clear about the importance of the survey of negro schools. In fact, as I told you, I talked the plan over with Dr. Dillard before you came to see me and was delighted to find that you had independently come to the same conclusion regarding the importance of the proposed work.

I am in a somewhat awkward position regarding the selection of an individual to undertake this work. I have not met Dr. Park but have met Dr. Jones and am impressed with the rare qualifications of the latter for exactly such an undertaking. He is Welsh by birth which gives him a certain intellectual detachment from the problem, has studied at a Southern white university, was afterwards for six years connected with Hampton and has later been identified with the Census Bureau. If it had not been for the cutting down of the congressional appropriation for the census last year he would have undertaken a very similar survey for the Department of Education. The mere fact that Dr. Jones is at present connected with the Bureau of Education and that they would in all probability allow him to continue to occupy his office there, would be an important consideration. I do not wish, however, to reach a definite decision in favor of Dr. Jones until I have tried to have a chance to talk with Dr. Park. I am therefore telegraphing you as follows:

"Have interviewed Jones. Would like to see Park if possible before reaching final conclusion. Please telegraph present address."

I am going to consult with several persons as to the relative qualification of the two men. I hope that we may be able to give Tuskegee some assistance but cannot pledge any particular amount until I have consulted with the Board. Very truly yours,

Anson Phelps Stokes

TLS Con. 464 BTW Papers DLC.

From Whitefield McKinlay, Francis James Grimké, and Archibald Henry Grimké

Washington, D.C., Nov. 18, 1912

Dear Dr. Washington: We have talked together relative to your plan to raise funds for the Douglass home, and we agree that it is very good as far as it goes. It does not seem to us however that you will be able to raise the necessary sum by that means alone, to lift the mortgage of $4000. on the estate. And if the estate is to be saved to the race the mortgage ought to be cancelled at an early date. We had hoped that you would have raised that sum long ago as you yourself were once confident of doing. We wish now most earnestly to remind you of your promise in this regard, and to make to you as serious an appeal as it is possible to make, that you raise the sum of $4000. or $5000. for the home and so save it for the race; and that should you fail to raise it from the Colored people next October, and we think you will fail, then that you get it from the Whites as you more than once hinted that you could and would if the Colored people did not give it. Can't you interest Mr. Carnegie or Mr. Rosenwald or some philanthropic woman in such a Memorial with its high educational value to the race? And if you can will you please do so at the earliest possible day? We ask this of you because we have always believed that you can do it and believe it still, and because you undertook to do it, we believe also, for the sake of Mr. Douglass and for the love you bear the race.

Pray Dr. Washington, if you mean to fulfill your promise, please do so quickly, for we are in sore need of help, and if you no longer feel that you can do it, we beg you to tell us so frankly and put an end mercifully to our expectations. Cordially yours,

W McKinlay
Francis J. Grimké
Archibald H. Grimké

TLS Con. 58 BTW Papers DLC.

Extracts from an Address at the Opening of the Mound Bayou Cotton-Oil Mill[1]

Mound Bayou, Mississippi   Nov. 25th, 1912

I count it a great privilege to be permitted to take part in the formal opening of the Mound Bayou Oil Mill and Manufacturing Company. The opening of this Oil Mill marks a unique and distinct step in the progress of the Negroes of America. It represents, in my opinion, the largest and most serious undertaking in a purely commercial and manufacturing enterprise in the history of our race.

I congratulate Charles Banks and his board of directors and the stockholders on account of the success that they have attained to in bringing this enterprise to its present degree of completeness. Mr. Banks and those who have stood by him in this movement are entitled to the lasting praise of the people of this country.

In the same spirit I wish to congratulate the white people of the state of Mississippi and at the same time to thank them for the encouragement and assistance which they have given to this enterprise. Further than this, I wish to congratulate and thank the white people of Mississippi because of the fact that they have been liberal and far-sighted enough to encourage the building up in the heart of the state of this distinctive and unique Negro town, a town that is a credit to the people who live in Mound Bayou, to the Negro race in Mississippi, and to every white man in this commonwealth. I need not add in this presence that just in the degree that the Negro in this state is given an opportunity to become prosperous, intelligent, happy and contented, in the same degree will the white man prosper, and [in] the same degree will peace and good order be maintained between black

55

and white citizens. Whatever the Negro has done at Mound Bayou in building up this community and in the construction of this cotton oil mill, the white man shares in the credit and in the profit.

At this late date it requires no argument to demonstrate the fact that white people and black people in this state are here to remain for all time and in my opinion side by side, and the building up of an enterprise of this kind in the commonwealth of Mississippi does not mean that it is anything which will threaten or jeopardize the white man's civilization or power, but it means that which will enhance the white man's prosperity and civilization, for if one race goes down the other in the same degree goes down. If one race goes up, the other in the same degree goes up. It is far more valuable to every white man in Mississippi to have a community of prosperous, intelligent, law abiding colored people that is willing to cooperate in every forward movement of the state than it is to have a community of black people steeped in ignorance, crime and poverty, and so again I congratulate Mr. Isaiah T. Montgomery, the founder of this town, and his co-workers because from the very beginning of this settlement they have had the good sense and the farsightedness to keep in close and sympathetic touch with the best white people in the state of Mississippi.

I congratulate Charles Banks and his fellow officers, I. T. Montgomery, J. W. Francis, A. A. Cosey, who have served through all these years without a dollar's worth of remuneration, and who intend to continue to so serve until the Oil Mill is well under way for operation.

Back of this enterprise which we formally open and dedicate today, I know that there is struggle, disappointment and heartache which the outside world little knows about or can little appreciate. I am proud of the fact that the National Negro Business League has had some influence in the starting and bringing to completion this magnificent enterprise. From the very beginning of our organization, Chas. Banks has been one of the leading spirits in keeping it alive and making the National Negro Business League powerful and useful.

I said in the beginning that this is a unique enterprise, marking a distinctive step in the development of our race. Here only 49 years after our freedom as a race, the black people have gathered and invested nearly $100,000 in this manufacturing enterprise. I am told that only about $20,000 is needed to free it from debt and put it thoroughly upon its feet. I shall be disappointed if there are not scores of prosperous and thrifty colored men throughout this region who will be glad to invest additional money in this promising business concern. Mr. Banks ought to have no difficulty in raising speedily from our own race all the money needed to put this business in first class shape. Money invested in this plant will not only bring in steady return in the way of dividends, but it will result in affording employment for a large number of the educated men and women of our race. I repeat then, that this oil mill should have the liberal financial support of that class of our people who have money to invest.

I am glad that this oil mill, the first in the history of our race, is located in the heart of the South where it will be a perpetual demonstration of the fact that our people can not only make progress, but whenever they make progress along legitimate and helpful lines that the white man is willing to stand back of them and encourage them right here in the heart of the South.

I am glad, too, that the city of Mound Bayou and this cotton seed oil mill are located in the midst of a rich and promising farming district. I have studied the life and opportunities of black people in this country and somewhat in other countries, and after making such study I am more and more convinced every day that the black man has his best chance on the soil as a farmer, that he is more free from competition, more free from temptations which beset him on every side in a city life. I want to urge, then, that every black farmer in this large audience today may feel that this cotton oil mill is a part of his life, and that if it fails he will be largely responsible for the failure, if it succeeds he will share in the glory of its success.

What Negro farmer in this audience would have dared to have ventured to have thought forty years ago that so soon after our freedom that we should be engaged today in formally opening and dedicating a cotton oil mill conceived by Negro brains, erected by Negro hands and in its completion made possible through Negro courage and energy. When we can witness right in our midst such evidences of progress, what may we not expect for the future. And in the midst of such surroundings there ought not to be a man or woman within the hearing of my voice who should feel in any degree discouraged as to the future of our race. Let me impress [upon] them, the opportunity that is before our people in this section of the South for making progress as tillers and owners of the soil. You are now occupying one of the richest farming districts that the world has discovered. You can occupy this soil for all time on one condition, and that is that through your brains, through your skilled hands that you prove to the world that you can get as much out of an acre of land as the people of any other race can get out of that acre. But the very minute the world discovers that a man of some other race or color or religion can get more out of an acre than the black man can get out of an acre in this delta district, from that moment forward the black man will begin to lose his hold as a farmer.

Sometimes we make the mistake of dwelling so much upon our disadvantages that we overlook our advantages as a race. Here as farmers you have the advantage of living in a beautiful climate. You have the advantage of living on a rich soil. You have the advantage of living in a climate and on a soil where something can be grown every month in the year. You have the opportunity of being surrounded by a class of white people whom you understand and who understand you and who in all the fundamental things of our civilization want to see you make progress.

Many Negro farmers in the South stand in their own light because they do not realize that farming is a business just the same as any other commercial enterprise. They make the mistake of trying to do business as farmers on a different scale from that of other business men. For example, a man who is engaged in the grocery business or banking business or who is a lawyer or doctor does business excepting Sunday, every day in the year, every week and every month in the year, but I will guarantee to say that the average farmer in this district does not work more than 150 days out of 365, and then when he fails and gets into debt and comes out with nothing to his credit he wonders why he is poor and the merchant is prosperous. The reason is that the farmer is trying to do business by working less than half of the year while the merchant is working all the year. We must get out of the old habit of stopping work in the fall of the year as soon as the cotton crop has been gathered until it becomes time to plant another crop in the spring. In our climate and on our soil we can work just as the other classes of business men do, every day in the year, and when this lesson is learned and applied by our people throughout this section we will be more prosperous and the farmer will in a large degree share in our prosperity. Instead of stopping work because this happens to be the month of November when your cotton crop is largely gathered, you should go home and begin work anew. There are certain vegetables and other crops which you can grow on your farms every month in the year. The women should go home from this meeting and begin anew to raise poultry, to have more pigs, more cows, more milk, more butter, more vegetables, and in proportion, as this is true the money that is gotten from the sale of cotton in these counties will remain in the counties instead of being sent to the far west or elsewhere to be used in purchasing the very food products which you can raise here on your farms. Just in proportion as you carry out this idea you will have money to invest in this cotton oil mill.

Every white man and black man in this section should be interested in this cotton oil mill for the further reason that every bushel of cotton seed which is turned into oil and exported from this community will result in bringing you many hundreds of dollars back into the South which will be distributed among all classes of people. This cotton oil mill should not only be a matter of interest to the farmer, but equally so to the professional man, the lawyer, the doctor, the minister, the teacher because in proportion as such enterprises as this prosper and give employment to the common masses of our people, in the same degree will the professional classes of our race have a foundation on which to rest their prosperity. In proportion as an enterprise like this prospers, the church, the Sunday school, the missionary society, the minister prosper. An enterprise of this character means, too, the very highest degree of encouragement and help to higher education, to the college, the university, because all these higher institutions depend for their support and success upon the prosperity of the ordinary common masses of our people.

I am glad to see gathered here today not only thousands of our own race, but I am glad to note the presence of many white people who by their presence and words have come here to show the black people of Mississippi that they mean to stand by them in everything that promotes their prosperity and happiness. There is a great deal of academic discussion about the relations between white people and black people in the South, but when we get down beneath the surface of this discussion and get into the individual communities it is found that every Negro has a white friend and every white man has his Negro friend, and that in nine cases out of ten in our Southern communities, as is proven here, that the relations between white people and black people are peaceful and happy. This is true notwithstanding the fact that in too many cases there are examples of injustice, brutal violence and outrage against the black man.

As we go on year by year demonstrating our ability to make good and law abiding citizens and our ability to create something that the white man wants and respects, in the same degree will our relations be further cemented in the direction of peace and prosperity.

Again and again I congratulate Charles Banks and his co-workers. I congratulate every white and black citizen of Mississippi on the launching of this great manufacturing enterprise, the greatest of its kind in the history of our race. I congratulate you because it is located in the heart of the black belt of the South where black people and white people are side by side to work out their destiny and prove to the world that it is possible for two races different in color to live together, each promoting the happiness and welfare of the other.

TM   Con. 64   BTW Papers   DLC.

¹ BTW was the principal speaker before a crowd of 15,000, which included not only local blacks but the passengers of special trains from Memphis, Jackson, and New Orleans. He spoke from a platform of cotton bales and pulled the cord that blew the first whistle of the mill. It was the largest cotton-oil mill in the state and symbolized the effort of this all-black town to establish the technological basis for economic self-sufficiency. The occasion was accompanied by "a County fair, with race track, exhibits of all kinds, every home open, a special dinner served in the Bank of Mound Bayou for the White visitors, and all the airs of a proud city." (Memphis *Commercial Appeal,* Nov. 27, 1912, Clipping, Con. 67, BTW Papers, DLC. See also Meier, "BTW and the Town of Mound Bayou," 396–401.)

From James Carroll Napier

TREASURY DEPARTMENT [Washington, D.C.] November 27, 1912

Dear Mr. Washington: I cannot describe the high appreciation and enjoyment of each one in attendance upon the *'Possum dinner* on Thursday night, Nov. 21st, last, made possible by your thoughtful and generous magnanimity. The menu, the opossum and the potatoes, were fine indeed. They would have proven savory and tasteful to any American, but to the "Black Cabinet" they were simply superb, highly delicious, incomparable. And then there were the post-prandial speeches. These were fine and of a high order in which reference was made more than once to your great worth and the generous spirit which prompted you to make the occasion possible. I cannot describe it. To have anything like a proper comprehension of it and of its pleasures one must have been present to see and taste and hear for himself.

I have read with a great deal of pleasure and gratification your article, "Is the Negro having a fair chance?" in the November number of the Century Magazine. It is the clearest cut statement of our case in equity that has at any time been made. You go into the details of our grievances in the coolest, calmest manner of any person who has ever undertaken to handle the subject. If this article could be gotten into the hands of and read by the southern people it would doubtless have a telling effect in opening their eyes to the inconveniences and injustices which we are so constantly forced to endure. If we could get the things that you plead for, viz: schools, representation, proper treatment on railroads, exemption from lynch law, justice in the courts, and credit for our real worth to a community, I am sure the restless spirit which prompts so many of us to be continually on the move from one part of the country to another would be overcome. We would then settle down and show the truth of the claim made by those who hold that our people are the greatest asset of the South. The eyes of those who force these conditions would soon be opened to the great injury they do us, themselves, and their own section of the country.

With best wishes for a pleasant and a restful Thanksgiving, I remain, Very truly and sincerely yours,

J. C. Napier

TLS Con. 461 BTW Papers DLC.

From P. L. Carmouche[1]

Detroit Michigan, November 30th, 1912

(Personal)

My dear Mr. Washington: I have carefully read and re-read your Article in The Century Magazine of this month. With my temperment and full knowledge combined, as to conditions existing in this supposed land of "equality and freedom," I want to say to you Mr. Washington, that I made the mistake of my life in *not* going to France when I left that *"cursed South land,"* instead of coming to Michigan as I did. I want to further say, that, in leaveing the South, I did *not* do so in order to *desert* our people — the colored people — but I wanted to get away from a condition existing there, which, In my Judgement, is *far worse* than *death* to me and to our people. A thousand pities that the millions among us — I mean colored persons — are yet blind in considering their horrid plight.

If I would leave the United States to-day, it would be to desert a condition existing in this Country which is a mockery to our Christianity and a shame to civilization. The few "oppertunities" given — in the form as it were of *charity* to us, should not be considered in any sense compensation for the injustices perpitrated against us. As for me, I do not thank, nor do I make, in words nor deeds, excuses to *no liveing man* for our "oppertunities" and presence in America. I claim for my self and our people, all the same things the "white man" claims for himself. He of course, deprives us as much as he possibly can now. But; Oh; could I be liveing when his — the white mans, day of retribution is at hand.

Notwithstanding the facts that we are improveing or moveing forward in certain directions   Yet, the Colored persons who do not see that we are being driven — as it were — to a position where death would be preferable, is blind indeed to the "things" which daily surrounds us in America. There is no denying the facts, that, Among the Millions of whites in this country, our friends are vastly in the minority, thus, all of those *grave* questions pertaining to the "black man's" rights, are obscured in our modern modes of life. *Theory* in certain things is very useful, but, it *canot* be *applied* in the *solution* of our *presence in America*. When I lived South, I could not see then, nor can I see now, the things I would wish to see done for the wellfare of our people. Thousands of colored persons like my-self, who see and feel so keenly the growing injustices perpitrated against us, *dare* to fully express our oppinions of it publicly.

Privately, I do not hesitate to say to you: As for me, the history of Tussaint L'Ouverture, of San Domingo or Muratte and Robestpierre of France, would — if we had a sufficient number of colored men to back it — suit me in every particular, in the settlement of the "Negro" Question in America. *Deal* with the *"Negro" question* as you will or may, sooner or later — those who lives there, will see a repetition of Hayti or France enacted in America, in order to *properly settle* that question. It is folly to suppose that our presence here to-day is welcome or appreciated, to the contrary notwithstanding our worth as laborers, I have long since, cast aside, such thoughts.

If it would not be for the horror of it, there are a sufficient number of *whites* who would do to the *"Negro"* to day, worse than what was done to the *Indians*. Why? Just because of the very fact that, the "Negro" has proven himself to be the "white mans" eaqual, if not his superior. Yes: Just because of that fact and no other, is the reason and why he — the "Negro" — is not *now welcome*. The "Negroes" ability to prove to "his former master?" that he was not the "thing" they supposed him to be, makes all the differences, it galls and pricks them to the quick, thus the friction and hating of him.

As the great head of Tuskegee I do not so very much blame you to do all you can to protest it, by useing the most temperate expressions in connection with those *most damnable outrages perpetrated* against us — the most patriotic citizen this country ever had and ever will have — but, re[me]mber: in doing so, my opinion is, you create a confusion or false impression as to real conditions — most especially in the South towards our people — when making the comparisons or excuses of "our oppertunities" with those "Negroes" of other countries. These "oppertunities" so much spoken and writen of, should not be "pitted" or used as "bouquets" to throw to the "white man," when the *facts still* remain that, he — the *"white man"* — is the "assassinator's" of all our hopes and aspirations.

In that same Century Magazine, in which your article — "Is The Negro Having a Fair Chance?" — appears, we find on page 153 this subject: *"If Lincoln Could return."* The *author* of that article, draws as it were, *the real "picture" as it should appear to the minds of every Colored persons in America.*

Yes! If Lincoln, and other heroes, "black and white" could return; Would they not want to do the "things" over, but, do it better? I would want to see it done in a more complete way than what was done during 1861–65. I would want to see it *settled forever* and *ever* on a *baises* of *Justice, equality,* and *humaine liberty,* in the *real sense* of the *words.* As it now stands, those who *died* in that conflict for the *Salvation* of the *"Negroes,"* died in order that this country be, in *reality,* the home of the free and the land of the *braves; realy died in Vain.* Now Sir; what I did and encouraged our people to do, in our war with Spain in 98, Is what I would not attempt to do again, *Not Unless* it was for the *complete* and *perminent* rights, liberties, oppertunites, and freedom of the Colored Citizens of America or U.S. Yes, those of us who feels so keenly the uneaqual conditions and uncivilized tratment given, in a supposed Christian country, dare to express publicly, our oppinions of it.[2]

With my best wishes to you Mrs Washington the family and Tuskegee. Im respectfully yours

P. L. Carmouche

ALS Con. 451 BTW Papers DLC.

[1] P. L. Carmouche, a blacksmith of Donaldsonville, La., began correspondence with BTW in 1900, when his nephew was enrolled at Tuskegee Institute. An ardent opponent of lily white Republicans, Carmouche secured BTW's endorsement for naval officer of the Port of New Orleans in 1902 and a letter of introduction to the President. Failing to win the appointment, Carmouche moved in 1903 to Detroit, where he established a blacksmith shop. He continued to correspond with BTW, expressing his satisfaction with the relative lack of racial discrimination in the North, and endorsing BTW's role as a presidential adviser. (Carmouche to BTW, Jan. 6, 1900, Con. 169, Mar. 7, 1903, Con. 252, July 4, 1904, Con. 286, and June 20, 1908, Con. 367, BTW Papers, DLC.)

[2] Carmouche wrote BTW again a week later predicting a black revolution in America along French or Haitian lines. He also expressed concern about lynching and about segregation in the District of Columbia. (Dec. 6, 1912, Con. 451, BTW Papers, DLC.)

An Article in *The Century*

November 1912

IS THE NEGRO HAVING A
FAIR CHANCE?

If I were asked the simple, direct question, "Does the negro in America have a fair chance?" it would be easy to answer simply, "No," and then refer to instances with which every one is familiar to justify this reply. Such a statement would, however, be misleading to any one who was not intimately acquainted with the actual situation. For that reason I have chosen to make my answer not less candid and direct, I hope, but a little more circumstantial.

The Negro Treated Better in America than Elsewhere

Although I have never visited either Africa or the West Indies to see for myself the condition of the people in these countries, I have had opportunities from time to time, outside of the knowledge I have gained from books, to get some insight into actual conditions there. But I do not intend to assert or even suggest that the condition of the American negro is satisfactory, nor that he has in all things a fair chance. Nevertheless, from all that I can learn I believe I am safe in saying that nowhere are there ten millions of black people who have greater opportunities or are making greater progress than the negroes in America.

I know that few native Africans will agree with me in this statement. For example, we had at Tuskegee a student from the Gold Coast who came to America to study in our Bible Training School and incidentally to learn something of our methods of study and work. He did not approve at all of our course of study. There was not enough theology, and too much work to suit him. As far as he was concerned, he could not see any value in learning to work, and he thought it was a pretty poor sort of country in which the people had to devote so much time to labor. "In my country," he said, "everything grows of itself. We do not have to work. We can devote all our time to the larger life."

Little Immigration of Negroes

In the last ten years the official records show that 37,000 negroes have left other countries to take residence in the United States. I can find no evidence to show that any considerable number of black people have given up residence in America.

The striking fact is, that negroes from other countries are constantly coming into the United States, and few are going out. This seems in part to answer the question as to whether the negro is having a fair chance in America as compared with any other country in which negroes live in any large numbers.

By far the largest number of negro immigrants come from the West Indies. Even Haiti, a free negro republic, furnishes a considerable number of immigrants every year. In all my experience and observation, however, I cannot recall a single instance in which a negro has left the United States to become a citizen of the Haitian Republic.

On the other hand, not a few leaders of thought and action among the negroes in the United States are those who have given up citizenship in the little Black Republic in order to live under the Stars and Stripes. The majority of the colored people who come from the West Indies do so because of the economic opportunities which the United States offers them. Another large group, however, comes to get education. Here at the Tuskegee Institute in Alabama we usually have not far from one hundred students from South America and the various West Indian Islands. In the matter of opportunity to secure the old-fashioned, abstract book education several of the West Indian Islands give negroes a better chance than is afforded them in most of our Southern States, but for industrial and technical education they are compelled to come to the United States.

In the matter of political and civil rights, including protection of life and property and even-handed justice in the courts, negroes in the West Indies have the advantage of negroes in the United States. In the island of Jamaica, for example, there are about 15,000 white people and 600,000 black people, but of the "race problem," in regard to which there is much agitation in this country, one hears almost nothing there. Jamaica has neither mobs, race riots, lynchings, nor burnings, such as disgrace our civilization. In that country there is likewise no bitterness between white man and black man. One reason for this is that the laws are conceived and executed with exact and absolute justice, without regard to race or color.

UNEQUAL LAWS THE CAUSE OF RACIAL TROUBLE IN AMERICA

Reduced to its lowest terms, the fact is that a large part of our racial troubles in the United States grow out of some attempt to pass and execute a law that will make and keep one man superior to another, whether he is intrinsically superior or not. No greater harm can be done to any group of people than to let them feel that a statutory enactment can keep them superior to anybody else. No greater injury can be done to any youth than to let him feel that because he belongs to this or that race, or because of his color, he will be advanced in life regardless of his own merits or efforts.

In what I have said I do not mean to suggest that in the West Indian Islands there is any more social intermingling between whites

66

and blacks than there is in the United States. The trouble in most parts of the United States is that mere civil and legal privileges are confused with social intermingling. The fact that two men ride in the same railway coach does not mean in any country in the world that they are socially equal.

The facts seem to show, however, that after the West Indian negro has carefully weighed his civil and political privileges against the economic and other advantages to be found in the United States, he decided that, all things considered, he has a better chance in the United States than at home. The negro in Haiti votes, but votes have not made that country happy; or have not even made it free, in any true sense of the word. There is one other fact I might add to this comparison: nearly all the negro church organizations in the United States have mission churches in the islands, as they have also in Africa.

Does the negro in our country have a fair chance as compared with the native black man in Africa, the home of the negro? In the midst of the preparation of this article, I met Bishop Isaiah B. Scott of the Methodist Episcopal Church, one of the strongest and most intelligent colored men that I know. Bishop Scott has spent the greater part of his life in the Southern States, but during the last seven years he has lived in Liberia and traveled extensively on the west coast of Africa, where he has come into contact with all classes of European white people. In answer to my question, Bishop Scott dictated the following sentence, which he authorized me to use:

"The fairest white man that I have met in dealing with the colored man is the American white man. He understands the colored man better because of his contact with him, and he has more respect for the colored man who has accomplished something."

Basing my conclusions largely on conversations which I have had with native Africans, with negro missionaries, and with negro diplomatic officials who have lived in Africa, especially on the west coast and in South Africa, I am led to the conclusion that, all things considered, the negro in the United States has a better chance than he has in Africa.

THE NEGRO AS A DEPENDENT RACE

In certain directions the negro has had greater opportunities in the States in which he served as a slave than he has had in the States in which he has been for a century or more a free man. This statement is borne out by the fact that in the South the negro rarely has to seek labor, but, on the other hand, labor seeks him. In all my experience in the Southern States, I have rarely seen a negro man or woman seeking labor who did not find it. In the South the negro has business opportunities that he does not have elsewhere. While in social matters the lines are strictly drawn, the negro is less handicapped in business in the South than any other part of the country. He is sought after as a depositor in banks. If he wishes to borrow money, he gets it from the local bank just as quickly as the white man with the same business standing. If the negro is in the grocery business or in the dry-goods trade, or if he operates a drug store, he gets his goods from the whole-sale dealer just as readily and on as good terms as his white competitor. If the Southern white man has a dwelling-house, a store-house, factory, school, or court-house to erect, it is natural for him to employ a colored man as builder or contractor to perform that work. What is said to be the finest school building in the city of New Orleans was erected by a colored contractor. In the North a colored man who ran a large grocery store would be looked upon as a curiosity. The Southern white man frequently buys his groceries from a negro merchant.

Fortunately, the greater part of the colored people in the South have remained as farmers on the soil. The late census shows that eighty per cent. of Southern negroes live on the land.

There are few cases where a black man cannot buy and own a farm in the South. It is as a farmer in the Southern States that the masses of my race have economically and industrially the largest opportunity. No one stops to ask before purchasing a bale of cotton or a bushel of corn if it has been produced by a white hand or a black hand.

The negro now owns, as near as I can estimate, 15,000 grocery and dry-goods stores, 300 drug stores, and 63 banks. Negroes pay taxes on between $600,000,000 and $700,000,000 of property of various kinds in the United States. Unless he had had a reasonably fair chance in the South, the negro could not have gained and held this large amount of property, and would not have been able to enter in the commerce of this country to the extent that he has.

Skilled Negro Labor Better Treated in the South than in the North

As a skilled laborer, the negro has a better opportunity in the South than in the North. I think it will be found generally true in the South as elsewhere that wherever the negro is strong in numbers and in skill he gets on well with the trades-unions. In these cases the unions seek to get him in, or they leave him alone, and in the latter case do not seek to control him. In the Southern States, where the race enters in large numbers in the trades, the trades-unions have not had any appreciable effect in hindering the progress of the negro as a skilled laborer or as a worker in special industries, such as coal-mining, iron-mining, etc. In border cities, like St. Louis, Washington, and Baltimore, however, the negro rarely finds work in such industries as brick-laying and carpentry. One of the saddest examples of this fact that I ever witnessed was in the City of Washington, where on the campus of Howard University, a negro institution, a large brick building was in process of erection. Every man laying brick on this building was white, every man carrying a hod was a negro. The white man, in this instance, was willing to erect a building in which negroes could study Latin, but was not willing to give negroes a chance to lay the bricks in its walls.

Let us consider for a moment the negro in the professions in the Southern States. Aside from school teaching and preaching, into which the racial question enters in only a slight degree, there remain law and medicine. All told, there are not more than 700 colored lawyers in the Southern States, while there are perhaps more than 3000 doctors, dentists, and pharmacists. With few exceptions, colored lawyers feel, as they tell me, that they do not have a fair chance before a white jury when a white lawyer is on the other side of the case. Even in communities where negro lawyers are not discriminated against by juries, their clients feel that there is danger in intrusting cases to a colored lawyer. Mainly for these two reasons, colored lawyers are not numerous in the South; yet, in cases where colored lawyers combine legal practice with trading and real estate, they have in several instances been highly successful.

The Difficulty of Obtaining Uniform Treatment

Here again, however, it is difficult to generalize. People speak of the "race question" in the South, overlooking the fact that each one of the 1300 counties in the Southern States is a law unto itself. The result is that there are almost as many race problems as there are counties. The negro may have a fair chance in one county, and have no chance at all in the adjoining county. The Hon. Josiah T. Settle, for example, has practised both criminal and civil law for thirty years in Memphis. He tells me that he meets with no discrimination on account of his color either from judges, lawyers, or juries. There are other communities, like New Orleans and Little Rock, where negro lawyers are accorded the same fair treatment, and, I ought to add, that, almost without exception, negro lawyers tell me they are treated fairly by white judges and white lawyers.

The professional man who is making the greatest success in the South is the negro doctor, and I should include the pharmacists and dentists with the physicians and surgeons. Except in a few cities, white doctors are always willing to consult with negro doctors.

The young negro physician in the South soon finds himself with a large and paying practice, and, as a rule, he makes use of this opportunity to improve the health conditions of his race in the community. Some of the most prosperous men of my race in the South are negro doctors. Again, the very fact that a negro cannot buy soda-water in a white drug store makes an opportunity for the colored drug store, which often becomes a sort of social center for the colored population.

From an economic point of view, the negro in the North, when compared with the white man, does not have a fair chance. This is the feeling not only of the colored people themselves, but of almost every one who has examined into the conditions under which colored men work. But here also one is likely to form a wrong opinion. There is, to begin with, this general difference between the North and the South, that whereas in the South there is, as I have already suggested, a job looking for every idle man, in the North, on the contrary, there are frequently two or three idle men looking for every job. In some of the large cities of the North there are organizations to secure employment for colored people. For a number of years I have kept in pretty close touch with those at the head of these organizations, and they tell me that in many cases they have been led to believe that the negro has a harder time in finding employment than is actually true. The reason is that those who are out of employment seek these organizations. Those who have steady work, in positions which they have held for years, do not seek them.

As a matter of fact, I have been surprised to find how large a number of colored people there are in Boston, New York, Philadelphia, and Chicago who hold responsible positions in factories, stores, banks, and other places. In regard to these people one hears very little. There is a colored man, for example, in Cleveland who has been for years private secretary to a railway president. In St. Paul there is a colored man who holds a similar position; in Baltimore there is still another colored private secretary to a railway president.

The Shifting of Occupations

In recent years there has been a great shifting of employment between the races. A few years ago all the rough work in the mines, on the railway, and elsewhere was performed by Irish immigrants. Now this work is done by Poles, Hungarians, and Italians. In cities like New York, Chicago, and Pittsburg one finds to-day fewer colored people employed as hotel waiters, barbers, and porters than twenty years ago. In New York, however, many colored men are employed in the streets and in the subways. In Pittsburg thousands of colored men are employed in the iron mills. In Chicago negroes are employed very largely in the packing-houses. Twenty years ago in these cities there were almost no colored people in these industries. In addition to the changes I have mentioned, many colored people have gone into businesses of various kinds on their own account. It should be remembered, also, that, while in some trades and in some places discrimination is made against the negro, in other trades and in other places this discrimination works in his favor. The case in point is the Pullman-car service. I question whether any white man, however efficient, could secure a job as a Pullman-car porter.

Better Opportunity for Education in the North

In the North, as a rule, the negro has the same opportunities for education as his white neighbor. When it comes to making use of this education, however, he is frequently driven to a choice between becoming an agitator, who makes his living out of the troubles of his race, or emigrating to the Southern States, where the opportunities for educated colored men are large. One of the greatest sources of bitterness and despondency among colored people in the North grows out of their inability to find a use for their education after they have obtained it. Again, they are seldom sure of just what they may or may not do. If one is a stranger in a city, he does not know in what hotel he will be permitted to stay; he is not certain what seat he may occupy in the theater, or whether he will be able to obtain a meal in a restaurant.

THE UNCERTAINTY OF TREATMENT OF
THE RACE IN THE NORTH

The uncertainty, the constant fear and expectation of rebuff which the colored man experiences in the North, is often more humiliating and more wearing than the frank and impersonal discrimination which he meets in the South. This is all the more true because the colored youth in most of the Northern States, educated as they are in the same schools with white youths, taught by the same teachers, and inspired by the same ideals of American citizenship, are not prepared for the discrimination that meets them when they leave school.

Despite all this, it cannot be denied that the negro has advantages in the North which are denied him in the South. They are the opportunity to vote and to take part, to some extent, in making and administering the laws by which he is governed, the opportunity to obtain an education, and, what is of still greater importance, fair and unbiased treatment in the courts, the protection of the law.

I have touched upon conditions North and South, which, whether they affect the negro favorably or adversely, are for the most part so firmly entrenched in custom, prejudice, and human nature that they must perhaps be left to the slow changes of time. There are certain conditions in the South, however, in regard to which colored people feel perhaps more keenly because they believe if they were generally understood they would be remedied. Very frequently the negro people suffer injury and wrong in the South because they have or believe they have no way of making their grievances known. Not only are they not represented in the legislatures, but it is sometimes hard to get a hearing even in the press. On one of my educational campaigns in the South I was accompanied by a colored newspaper man. He was an enterprising sort of chap and at every public meeting we held he would manage in some way to address the audience on the subject of his paper. On one occasion, after appealing to the colored people for some time, he turned to the white portion of the audience.

"You white folks," he said, "ought to read our colored papers to find out what colored people are doing. You ought to find out what they are doing and what they are thinking. You don't know anything about us," he added. "Don't you know a colored man can't get his name in a white paper unless he commits a crime?"

I do not know whether the colored newspaper man succeeded in getting any subscriptions by this speech or not, but there was much truth in his statement.

The Greatest Source of Dissatisfaction to the Negro in the South

One thing that many negroes feel keenly, although they do not say much about it to either black or white people, is the conditions of railway travel in the South.

Now and then the negro is compelled to travel. With few exceptions, the railroads are almost the only great business concerns in the South that pursue the policy of taking just as much money from the black traveler as from the white traveler without feeling that they ought, as a matter of justice and fair play, not as a matter of social equality, to give one man for his money just as much as another man. The failure of most of the roads to do justice to the negro when he travels is the source of more bitterness than any one other matter of which I have any knowledge.

It is strange that the wide-awake men who control the railroads in the Southern States do not see that, as a matter of dollars and cents, to say nothing of any higher consideration, they ought to encourage, not discourage, the patronage of nine millions of the black race in the South. This is a traveling population that is larger than the whole population of Canada, and yet, with here and there an exception, railway managers do not seem to see that there is any business advantage to them in giving this large portion of the population fair treatment.

What embitters the colored people in regard to railroad travel, I repeat, is not the separation, but the inadequacy of the accommodations. The colored people are given half of a baggage-car or half of a smoking-car. In most cases, the negro portion of the car is poorly ventilated, poorly lighted, and, above all, rarely kept clean; and then, to add to the colored man's discomfort, no matter how many colored women may be in the colored end of the car, nor how clean or how well educated these colored women may be, this car is made the headquarters for the newsboy. He spreads out his papers, his magazines, his candy, and his cigars over two or three seats. White men are constantly coming into the car and almost invariably light cigars while in the colored coach, so that these women are required to ride in what is virtually a smoking-car.

On some of the roads colored men and colored women are forced to use the same toilet-room. This is not true of every Southern railway. There are some railways in the South, notably the Western Railway of Alabama, which make a special effort to see that the colored people are given every facility in the day coaches that the white people have, and the colored people show in many ways that they appreciate this consideration.

Here is an experience of R. S. Lovinggood,[1] a colored man of Austin, Texas. I know Mr. Lovinggood well. He is neither a bitter nor a foolish man. I will venture to say that there is not a single white man in Austin, Texas, where he lives, who will say that Professor Lovinggood is anything but a conservative, sensible man.

"At one time," he said to me, in speaking of some of his traveling experiences, "I got off at a station almost starved. I begged the keeper of the restaurant to sell me a lunch in a paper and hand it out of the window. He refused, and I had to ride a hundred miles farther before I could get a sandwich.

"At another time I went to a station to purchase my ticket. I was there thirty minutes before the ticket-office was opened. When it did finally open I at once appeared at the window. While the ticket-agent served the white people at one window, I remained there beating the other until the train pulled out. I was compelled to jump aboard the train without my ticket and wire back to get my trunk expressed. Considering the temper of the people, the separate coach law may be the wisest plan for the South, but the statement that the two races have equal accommodations is all bosh. I pay the same money, but I cannot have a chair or a lavatory and rarely a through car. I must crawl out at all times of night, and in all kinds of weather, in order to catch another dirty 'Jim Crow' coach to make my connections. I do not ask to ride with white people. I do ask for equal accommodations for the same money."

Lack of a "Square Deal" in Education
in the South

In the matter of education, the negro in the South has not had what Colonel Roosevelt calls a "square deal." In the North, not only the Jew, the Slav, the Italian, many of whom are such recent arrivals that they have not yet become citizens and voters, even under the easy terms granted them by the naturalization laws of the Northern States, have all the advantages of education that are granted to every other portion of the population, but in several States an effort is now being made to give immigrant peoples special opportunities for education over and above those given to the average citizen. In some instances, night schools are started for their special benefit. Frequently schools which run nine months in the winter are continued throughout the summer, whenever a sufficient number of people can be induced to attend them. Sometimes, as for example, in New York State, where large numbers of men are employed in digging the Erie Canal and in excavating the Croton Aqueduct, camp schools are started where the men employed on these public works in the day may have an opportunity to learn the English language at night. In some cases a special kind of text-book, written in two or three different languages, has been prepared for use in these immigrant schools, and frequently teachers are especially employed who can teach in the native languages if necessary.

While in the North all this effort is being made to provide education for these foreign peoples, many of whom are merely sojourners in this country, and will return in a few months to their homes in Europe, it is only natural that the negro in the South should feel that he is unfairly treated when he has, as is often true in the country districts, either no school at all, or one with a term of no more than four or five months, taught in the wreck of a log-cabin and by a teacher who is paid about half the price of a first-class convict.

This is no mere rhetorical statement. If a negro steals or commits a murderous assault of some kind, he will be tried and imprisoned, and then, if he is classed as a first-class convict, he will be rented out at the rate of $46 per month for twelve months in the year. The negro who does not commit a crime, but prepares himself to serve the State as a first-grade teacher, will receive from the State for that service perhaps $30 per month for a period of not more than six months.

Taking the Southern States as a whole about $10.23 per capita is spent in educating the average white boy or girl, and the sum of $2.82 per capita in educating the average black child.

Let me take as an illustration one of our Southern farming communities, where the colored population largely outnumbers the white. In Wilcox County, Alabama, there are nearly 11,000 black children and 2000 white children of school age. Last year $3569 of the public school fund went for the education of the black children in that county, and $30,294 for the education of the white children, this notwithstanding that there are five times as many negro children as white. In other words, there was expended for the education of each negro child in Wilcox County thirty-three cents, and for each white child $15. In the six counties surrounding and touching Wilcox County there are 55,000 negro children of school age. There was appropriated for their education last year from the public school fund $40,000, while for the 19,622 white children in the same counties there was appropriated from the public fund $199,000.

There are few, if any, intelligent white people in the South or anywhere else who will claim that the negro is receiving justice in these counties in the matter of the public school fund. Especially will this seem true when it is borne in mind that the negro is the main dependence for producing the farm products which constitute the chief wealth of that part of Alabama. I say this because I know there are thousands of fair-minded and liberal white men in the South who do not know what is actually going on in their own States.

In the State of Georgia, negroes represent forty-two per cent. of the farmers of the State, and are largely employed as farm laborers on the plantations. Notwithstanding this fact, Georgia has two agricultural colleges and eleven district agricultural high schools for whites, supported at an annual cost to the State of $140,000, while there is only one school where negroes have a chance to study agriculture, and to the support of this the State contributes only $8000 a year. When one hears it said that the negro farmer of Georgia is incompetent and inefficient as compared with the white farmer of Minnesota or Wisconsin, can any one say that this is fair to the negro?

Not a few Southern white men see what is needed and are not afraid to say so. A. A. Gunby[2] of Louisiana recently said: "Every one competent to speak and honest enough to be candid knows that education benefits and improves the negro. It makes him a better neighbor and workman, no matter what you put him at."

Every one agrees that a public library in a city tends to make better citizens, keeping people usefully employed instead of spending their time in idleness or in committing crime. Is it fair, as is true of most of the large cities of the South, to take the negro's money in the form of taxes to support a public library, and then to make no provision for the negro using any library? I am glad to say that some of the cities, for instance, Louisville, Kentucky, and Jacksonville, Florida, have already provided library facilities for their black citizens or are preparing to do so.

One excuse that is frequently made in the South for not giving the negro a fair share of the moneys expended for education is that the negro is poor and does not contribute by his taxes sufficient to support the schools that now exist. True, the negro is poor; but in the North that would be a reason for giving him more opportunities for education, not fewer, because it is recognized that one of the greatest hindrances to progress is ignorance. As far as I know, only two men have ever given thorough consideration to the question as to the amount the negro contributes directly or indirectly toward his own education. Both of these are Southern white men. One of them is W. N. Sheats, former Superintendent of Education for the State of Florida. The other is Charles L. Coon, Superintendent of Schools at Wilson, North Carolina, and formerly connected with the Department of Education for that State.

The Negro Pays More than His Share
to Education in the South

In his annual report for 1900, Mr. Sheats made a thorough analysis of the sources of the school fund in Florida, and of the way in which it is distributed between the white and negro schools. In referring to the figures which he obtained, he said:

A glance at the foregoing statistics indicates that the section of the State designated as "Middle Florida" is considerably behind all the rest in all stages of educational progress. The usual plea is that this is due to the intolerable burden of negro education, and a general discouragement and inactivity is ascribed to this cause. The following figures are given to show that the education of the negroes of Middle Florida does not cost the white people of that section one cent. Without discussing the American principle that it is the duty of all property to educate every citizen as a means of protection to the State, and with no reference to what taxes that citizen may pay, it is the purpose of this paragraph to show that the backwardness of education of the white people is in no degree due to the presence of the negro, but that the presence of the negro has been actually contributing to the sustenance of the white schools.

Mr. Sheats shows that the amount paid for negro schools from negro taxes or from a division of other funds to which negroes contribute indirectly with the whites, amounted to $23,984. The actual cost of negro schools, including their pro rata for administration expenses, was $19,467.

"If this is a fair calculation," Mr. Sheats concludes, "the schools for negroes are not only no burden on the white citizens, but $4525 for negro schools contributed from other sources was in some way diverted to the white schools. A further loss to the negro schools is due to the fact that so few polls are collected from negroes by county officials."

Mr. Coon, in an address on "Public Taxation and Negro Schools" before the 1909 Conference for Education in the South, at Atlanta, Georgia, said:

The South is spending $32,068,851 on her public schools, both white and black, but what part of this sum is devoted to negro public schools, which must serve at least forty per cent. of her school population? It is not possible to answer this question with absolute accuracy, but it is possible from the several State reports to find out the whole amount spent for teachers, and in all the States, except Arkansas, what was spent for white and negro teachers separately. The aggregate amount now being spent for public teachers of both races in these eleven States is $23,856,914, or 74.4 per cent. of the whole amount expended. Of this sum not more than $3,818,705 was paid to negro teachers, or twelve per cent. of the total expenditures.

He also brought out the fact that in Virginia, if, in addition to the direct taxes paid by negroes, they had received their proportion of the taxes on corporate property and other special taxes, such as fertilizers, liquor, etc., there would have been expended on the negro schools $18,077 more than was expended; that is, they would have received $507,305 instead of $489,228. In North Carolina there would have been expended $26,539 more than was expended, the negroes receiving $429,197 instead of $402,658. In Georgia there would have been expended on the negro schools $141,682 more than was expended.

In other words, Superintendent Coon seems to prove that negro schools in the States referred to are not only no burden to the white tax-payers, but that the colored people do not get back all the money for their schools that they themselves pay in taxes. In each case there is a considerable amount taken from the negroes' taxes and spent somewhere else or for other purposes.

Convict Labor a Great Evil
in the South

It would help mightily toward the higher civilization for both races if more white people would apply their religion to the negro in their community, and ask themselves how they would like to be treated if they were in the negro's place. For example, no white man in America would feel that he was being treated with justice if every time he had a case in court, whether civil or criminal, every member of the jury was of some other race. Yet this is true of the negro in nearly all of the Southern States. There are few white lawyers or judges who will not admit privately that it is almost impossible for a negro to get justice when he has a case against a white man and all the members of the jury are white. In these circumstances, when a negro fails to receive justice, the injury to him is temporary, but the injury to the character of the white man on the jury is permanent.

In Alabama eighty-five per cent. of the convicts are negroes. The official records show that last year Alabama had turned into its treasury $1,085,854 from the labor of its convicts. At least $900,000 of this came from negro convicts, who were for the most part rented to the coal-mining companies in the northern part of the State. The result of this policy has been to get as many able-bodied convicts as possible into the mines, so that contractors might increase their profits. Alabama, of course, is not the only State that has yielded to the temptation to make money out of human misery. The point is, however, that while $900,000 is turned into the State treasury from negro-convict labor, to say nothing of negro taxes, there came out of the State treasury, to pay negro teachers, only $357,585.

I speak of this matter as much in the interest of the white man as of the black. Whenever and wherever the white man, acting as a court officer, feels that he cannot render absolute justice because of public sentiment, that white man is not free. Injustice in the courts makes slaves of two races in the South, the white and the black.

The Ballot to the Intelligent Negro

No influence could ever make me desire to go back to the conditions of Reconstruction days to secure the ballot for the negro. That was an order of things that was bad for the negro and bad for the white man. In most Southern States it is absolutely necessary that some restriction be placed upon the use of the ballot. The actual methods by which this restriction was brought about have been widely advertised, and there is no necessity for me discussing them here. At the time these measures were passed I urged that, whatever law went upon the statute-book in regard to the use of the ballot, it should apply with absolute impartiality to both races. This policy I advocate again in justice to both white man and negro.

Let me illustrate what I mean. In a certain county of Virginia, where the county board had charge of registering those who were to be voters, a colored man, a graduate of Harvard University, who had long been a resident of the county, a quiet, unassuming man, went before the board to register. He was refused on the ground that he was not intelligent enough to vote. Before this colored man left the room a white man came in who was so intoxicated that he could scarcely tell where he lived. This white man was registered, and by a board of intelligent white man who had taken an oath to deal justly in administering the law.

Will any one say that there is wisdom or statesmanship in such a policy as that. In my opinion it is a fatal mistake to teach the young black man and the young white man that the dominance of the white race in the South rests upon any other basis than absolute justice to the weaker man. It is a mistake to cultivate in the mind of any individual or group of individuals the feeling and belief that their happiness rests upon the misery of some one else, or that their intelligence is measured by the ignorance of some one else; or their wealth by the poverty of some one else. I do not advocate that the negro make politics or the holding of office an important thing in his life. I do urge, in the interest of fair play for everybody, that a negro who prepares himself in property, in intelligence, and in character to cast a ballot, and desires to do so, should have the opportunity.

In these pages I have spoken plainly regarding the South because I love the South as I love no other part of our country, and I want to see her white people equal to any white people on the globe in material wealth, in education, and in intelligence. I am certain, however, that none of these things can be secured and permanently maintained except they are founded on justice.

The Crime of Lynching

In most parts of the United States the colored people feel that they suffer more than others as the result of the lynching habit. When he was Governor of Alabama, I heard Governor Jelks say in a public speech that he knew of five cases during his administration of innocent colored people having been lynched. If that many innocent people were known to the governor to have been lynched, it is safe to say that there were other innocent persons lynched whom the governor did not know about. What is true of Alabama in this respect is true of other States. In short, it is safe to say that a large proportion of the colored people lynched are innocent.

A lynching-bee usually has it origin in a report that some crime has been committed. The story flies from mouth to mouth. Excitement spreads. Few take the time to get the facts. A mob forms and fills itself with bad whisky. Some one is captured. In case rape is charged, the culprit is frequently taken before the person said to have been assaulted. In the excitement of the moment, it is natural that the victim should say that the first person brought before her is guilty. Then comes more excitement and more whisky. Then comes the hanging, the shooting, or burning of the body.

Not a few cases have occurred where white people have blackened their faces and committed a crime, knowing that some negro would be suspected and mobbed for it. In other cases it is known that where negroes have committed crimes, innocent men have been lynched and the guilty ones have escaped and gone on committing more crimes.

Within the last twelve months there have been seventy-one cases of lynching, nearly all of colored people. Only seventeen were charged with the crime of rape. Perhaps they are wrong to do so, but colored people in the South do not feel that innocence offers them security against lynching. They do feel, however, that the lynching habit tends to give greater security to the criminal, white or black. When ten millions of people feel that they are not sure of being fairly tried in the court of justice, when charged with crime, is it not natural that they should feel that they have not had a fair chance?

I am aware of the fact that in what I have said in regard to the hardships of the negro in this country I throw myself open to the criticism of doing what I have all my life condemned and everywhere sought to avoid; namely, laying over-emphasis on matters in which the negro race in America has been badly treated, and thereby overlooking those matters in which the negro has been better treated in America than anywhere else in the world.

Despite all any one has said or can say in regard to the injustice and unfair treatment of the people of my race at the hands of the white men in this country, I venture to say that there is no example in history of the people of one race who have had the assistance, the direction, and the sympathy of another race in all its efforts to rise to such an extent as the negro in the United States.

Notwithstanding all the defects in our system of dealing with him, the negro in this country owns more property, lives in better houses, is in a larger measure encouraged in business, wears better clothes, eats better food, has more school-houses and churches, more teachers and ministers, than any similar group of negroes anywhere else in the world.

What has been accomplished in the past years, however, is merely an indication of what can be done in the future.

As white and black learn day by day to adjust, in a spirit of justice and fair play, those interests which are individual and racial, and to see and feel the importance of those fundamental interests which are common, so will both races grow and prosper. In the long run no individual and no race can succeed which sets itself at war against the common good.

The Century, 85 (Nov. 1912), 46–55.

1 Reuben S. Lovinggood was president of a black school, Samuel Houston College in Austin, Tex., from 1903 to 1917.

2 A. A. Gunby, a lawyer of Monroe, La., was a champion of better public schools in that state and a member of the Louisiana Education Association.

From Robert Ezra Park

Wollaston, Mass. December 3, 1912

My dear Mr Washington: I read with interest Mr Hollander's[1] letter in regard to the proposed investigation of the results of education at Tuskegee as shown in our students. I think such a systematic investigation would be a fine thing but I do not see where the science comes in.

It strikes me a good deal as if Mr Bebbington should take the interesting facts he has secured, while working over the schools accounts, and write a thesis on the subject. Such information as this report would bring out, it seems to me, is for the trustees or other persons personally interested in the school.

On the other hand a study of what becomes of Tuskegee students, compared with the results of education in white schools or other Negro schools, would have some point and would be a good thing. This, however, is just what the Stokes Fund proposes to do.

I have just had a letter from Mr Stokes which I enclose. It seems to me that now that the investigation is assured we should proceed to take the next step. The next step seems to me to be the endowment of the research work at Tuskegee. I was impressed, in talking with Mr Stokes, with the fact that the reason I did not get the job, or was not going to get it, was because I did not seem to him to represent science. Perhaps also, there was a distrust of the ability of any one connected with a Negro school to do scientific work. This suggests the advisability of my making some connection with Chicago University. Mr Thomas[2] has proposed it. Then, when I wanted to do sociological work from Tuskegee, I would have a title and the backing of the University.

There are some other matters in this connection that I should like to talk over with you. I am very truly

Robert E. Park

TLS Con. 462 BTW Papers DLC.

[1] Jacob Harry Hollander (1871–1940), an economist, was a professor at Johns Hopkins University beginning in 1904. Hollander proposed a study of the "economic usefulness" of those who had attended Tuskegee Institute. He wrote to Julius Rosenwald that such a study should be conducted scientifically and the statistical results carefully analyzed. (Nov. 5, 1912, Con. 456, BTW Papers, DLC.)

[2] William Isaac Thomas (1863–1947) was chairman of the sociology department of the University of Chicago and co-author with Florian Znaniecki of the monumental work, *The Polish Peasant in Europe and America* (2 vols., 1918–20). Thomas met Park at the International Congress of the Friends of Africa at Tuskegee in the spring of 1912, where they were both on the program. He invited Park to lecture at Chicago during the summer session, and this led to a permanent position for Park in the department.

To Naoichi Masaoka[1]

[Tuskegee, Ala.] December 5, 1912

My dear Sir: I have read with much interest your letter of October 16th, 1912, touching the book you are now engaged in writing concerning America and Americans, the Beikoku-jin, as you call us.

When that book is published I shall certainly hope to read it, or some portion of it, in an English translation. I believe that many others beside myself will be interested in learning what a Japanese man of affairs and a student, like yourself, finds worthy of study and observation in this country. I have had the good fortune to meet a good many people who have come from other parts of the world to visit this country and study our institutions and have had some opportunity to hear or read their comments upon conditions in general in America and in particular upon the relations between the races, a matter which naturally concerns me most.

I have never yet had an opportunity, however, to get a glimpse of America as it looks through the eyes of a member of the Japanese race, whose point of view we are inclined in America to believe is totally different from our own. For this and for other more personal reasons, let me add, there is no people whose opinion of our country I should more desire to know.

Speaking for the masses of my own race in this country I think I am safe in saying that there is no other race living outside of America whose fortunes the Negro people of this country have followed with greater interest or admiration. The wonderful progress of the Japanese people and their sudden rise to the position of one of the great nations of the world has nowhere been studied with greater interest or enthusiasm than by the Negroes of America.

In conclusion let me say that I am quite certain that in no other race and in no other part of the world have the Japanese people a larger number of admirers and well wishers than among the black people of the United States.

Wishing you every success in your important literary undertaking, I remain: Very truly yours,

Booker T. Washington

TLpSr Con. 461 BTW Papers DLC. Signature initialed by E. J. Scott.

¹ Naoichi Masaoka was chief managing editor of the Tokyo *Yamato Shimbun,* one of the oldest newspapers in Japan. He had visited the United States twice, in 1905 on the staff of the Japanese foreign minister and in 1909 on a Japanese commercial commission. He professed "America-worship," and asked BTW to write a brief introductory article to be included in his forthcoming book. (Oct. 16, 1912, Con. 461, BTW Papers, DLC.)

From Charles William Anderson

New York, N.Y. December 6, 1912

PERSONAL.

My dear Doctor: Replying to your kind favor of the 27th ult., I beg to say that I am working on those figures with assiduity. They will tell a strange and interesting story when completed. Unless the democratic managers be as politically obtuse as a trilobite, they cannot fail to realize that the colored vote cast for their ticket was a negligible one. I am making these investigations with great care.

I met Prof. Spingarn at the dinner given to Bishop Walters last Wednesday night. In the course of conversation, he expressed the opinion that Mr. Villard would not be very close to President Wilson, and added that he happened to know that Mr. V. was looked upon as a dangerous radical by the President's friends. He said that Mr. Walter Page would probably be "in right" at court. I pass this on for what it is worth.

While I would not say this to any other living man than yourself, folks hereabouts are saying that the Walters' dinner was really an "Anderson dinner." Like other statements of this character, this one, while not true, has some elements of truth in it. The fact is, that I happened to receive, perhaps, a little more applause than any of the other speakers, which, in my judgment, was due to a plain statement made by me during the course of what I had to say. I reminded those present that the honors and responsibility of political leadership in this State now devolved upon the Bishop, and after explaining the vexations attached to it, I called their attention to the fact that a political leader is ofttimes required to secure a transfer for some colored man in a deparment, or a slight increase of salary. If he happens to fail to secure them, he will surely be damned, if he succeeds he (may or may not) be thanked. There the matter ends so far as the recipient of the favor is concerned, but it does not end with the colored leader. The officer who granted this favor is in nine cases out of ten a prominent political leader, and during the summer will follow the practice of all leaders hereabouts by giving a popular excursion for his district. This colored leader will be sent five tickets at five dollars a piece, and if he has any red blood in his veins, he will buy them. This performance will be repeated during the winter on the occasion of this officer's annual ball. Hence, you see the colored leader will be spending from twenty-five to fifty dollars for the privilege of doing a favor for some colored clerk, who has re-paid him with thanks only, and sometimes not even with thanks. After calling their attention to the various demands made upon a political leader's pocket-book, I reminded them that I desire to say of my service here, that such as it was, it had been rendered to each member of the race according to his or her necessities, and in no single instance had I ever demanded, received or accepted a single dollar, or other valuable consideration for myself. This statement evoked tremendous applause, not so much because of any attempt at rhetoric on my part, but because most of my hearers knew that there were not many men in the room who could truthfully say the same thing. There were a number of leaders and ex-leaders there, every man of whom, had been paid for every service he had ever rendered to any member of the race. So you see that our folks are already beginning to realize that there has been a change, and that they may not be able hereafter to have strong influences brought to bear in their behalf unless they dig down into their pockets to pay for it. But enough of this.

I hope to see you in the near future, and until then believe me, Yours faithfully,

C. W. A.

TLI Con. 56 BTW Papers DLC.

To Walter Hines Page

[New York City] December 7th, 1912

My dear Mr. Page: Would [you] like to publish an article from me under the title, "What I am trying to do," or "How I am trying to help the colored race?" My idea would be to write a direct, straight out from the shoulder article showing what my ideas of getting the colored people on their feet are, and also indicating how the white people ought to cooperate in this work.

We have now reached the point in the South where in my opinion, we can talk out pretty plainly. I think those who have not lived in the heart of the South in recent years do not realize how far we have gone and how fast we have gone in the direction of securing an opportunity for free speech; in a word, all the people are beginning to think more and feel less, in my opinion. Yours very truly,

[Booker T. Washington]

TLc   Con. 57   BTW Papers   DLC.

Ralph Waldo Tyler to Emmett Jay Scott

Washington, D.C., Dec. 11, 1912

My dear Emmett: Here is a matter I wish you would take up with the Doctor, and see if something can be done along the line suggested.

Cannot some help be gotten from the Carnegie fund for publicity for The Bee? I am not familiar with the purposes of that fund, but thought the Doctor and yourself would be. "After the deluge," when "our crowd" are out of office and scattered, the anti-Washington crowd here will be sure to secure the influence of The Bee. In fact their lines are already laid. Knowing that the average Negro newspaper is always pressed each week to raise the wind to fly its next week's issue it will be no great taxing problem to secure the columns of The Bee, to propagate their ideas and to antagonize the Doctor, by the guarantee of a small weekly bonus. Of all places this is the one city in which the Doctor should have a publicity medium, for in no other city are there settled so many Negroes — 127,000, who are as intelligent, agitative and troublesome as in this city. And Negroes throughout the country, just as whites throughout the country, keep their eyes on Washington, and are influenced more or less by happenings here. Only by keeping The Bee in line, which has been a most strenuous and nerve-racking responsibility, have we kept the anti-crowd in check, and prevented them from reaching the public with venomous attacks. With proper help, The Bee might be made the most powerful Negro newspaper in the country for weal or woe — the most widely quoted. With some help it can be maintained as a dam — if nothing else, to the purposes of the Du Bois crowd, who are more considerable in numbers here than any place in the country — more resourceful and more aggressive. Chase has never suggested anything to me regarding this matter — I am just taking it up on my own initiative, and only from a desire to see the Doctor and his policies are supported. Some time ago I suggested the matter to the Doctor, in a general way, and he said he would look into it at some time. I presume, especially as it was not even near-urgent at that time, he forgot the suggestion. I dont want to appear as an alarmist, but knowing conditions here as I do, having kept my finger on the pulse more constantly than most of the followers, I am prepared to say that there will be something doing just as soon as we, "our crowd" here quit the game. Chase must raise $50 or $60 every week to assure publication. He knows this and it is never a question, with him, from where it comes, but *will it come*. When he finds we can bring no more grist to his mill, and that the other fellows will, he will accept theirs, and make his organ grind for them. I dont know whether or not anything can be done, in the line of suggestion, but if there can, I urge that it be taken up soon, for in a very brief period we here will be gone — all except Judge and Cobb. The former is a delightful, care-free opportunist who will set his sails to catch each passing breeze. He is an asset, when one of a crowd, but a liability when left to stand alone. Cobb is loyal, and has the fighting blood, but one man cant stand off an army. And besides the newspaper business is foreign to him. Wish you and yours a Merry Christmas and a Happy New Year. Sincerely,

Tyler

TLS Con. 466 BTW Papers DLC.

To Charles Dewey Hilles

[New York City] December 13, 1912

My dear Mr. Hilles: The friends of Mr. Fred R. Moore of this city are very anxious that he shall receive the appointment of Minister to Liberia, vice William D. Crum, deceased. As you know, Mr. Moore is a man of high character and fine abilities, and one who has rendered much real service to the cause and candidates of our party. In my judgment, he would make a thoroughly unexceptionable Minister. The Liberians, I am sure, would be pleased to receive him, for he has advocated their cause in season and out in the columns of his newspaper, for years. I, therefore, beg to recommend him most unreservedly for this appointment. Yours very truly,

[Booker T. Washington]

TL Copy Con. 58 BTW Papers DLC.

From Gilchrist Stewart

Washington, D.C., Dec. 16, 1912

My dear Dr. Washington: Just before leaving New York yesterday, a friend of mine in Cincinnati, sent me a little printed circular[1] or page rather, a proof sheet which he said had been sent to him to publish, purporting to give an account of the work of the Constitution League in the Jack Johnson case and myself as their representative and then drew a comparison between my supposed attitude and your supposed utterances.

This annoyed me very much because, while I am a member of the Constitution League and National Association For The Advancement Of Colored People, and a number of other so-called radical movements, and I enjoy that kind of work, I would not countenance, nor would I enter into any movement or any attacks that had for their object criticising you or condemning you.

In fact, upon a number of occasions where this spirit has been evinced at some of our little gatherings, I have condemned in no uncertain terms, its spirit and have said that aside from the merits of the case, I could not support any such criticism because I consider you one of my friends, that you were my former teacher, and that the little success that I have achieved in life, I owe more to Tuskegee than to any other source.

Upon receipt of this information, I called up Mr. Milholland at the Manhattan Hotel and he informed me that he did not send it out, nor did Dr. Sinclair in Philadelphia, but that Mr. Trotter of Boston had sent it out.

Mr. Milholland not only disdained any responsibility for it, but stated that he agreed with me, that it is a very bad thing to do, and laid the blame on Trotter. I have written Mr. Trotter to never again use my name in connection with any criticism of you and if this is published in any colored newspapers at all, while I do not ordinarily care what newspapers or people say about me, yet I shall answer this very vigorously.

I thought it was due to our friendly relations that you should know that this matter was gotten up and sent out while I was in Chicago and it was only yesterday that I heard anything about it. I do not know if it has been extensively sent. I have written Trotter about it.

I am leaving for Chicago on the 6:45 train. My address there for the next four or five days will be 3256 Rhodes Avenue. Yours sincerely,

Gilchrist Stewart

TLS Con. 464 BTW Papers DLC.

¹ The enclosed press release dated at Philadelphia, Nov. 23, 1912, stated: "While Booker T. Washington and others like him who are gratifying the enemies of the Race was keeping himself busy by denouncing 'Jack' Johnson before he had even been condemned by the courts, the Constitution League quietly dispatched Mr. Gilchrist Stewart to Chicago with orders to investigate the case thoroughly and report his findings as soon as possible." The circular quoted from Stewart's report finding the charges against Johnson unfounded. (Con. 464, BTW Papers, DLC.)

To Gilchrist Stewart

[Tuskegee, Ala.] December 19, 1912

Personal.

My dear Mr. Stewart: I thank you for taking the time to write me at such length with respect to the printed circular sent out by Trotter, of Boston. I am not surprised to learn that this circular has animated [emanated] from him. Your action in writing, however, and misrepresenting your own attitude is also sincerely appreciated.

With all good wishes for the holiday season, I am   Very truly yours,

Booker T. Washington

P.S. — With your permission, I shall be very glad to make use of what you have written in some newspapers where the publication to which you refer was made. Shall do so unless I hear from you to the contrary.

B. T. W.

TLpS Con. 464 BTW Papers DLC. Last sentence of postscript in BTW's hand.

To Roger Nash Baldwin

[Tuskegee, Ala.] December 20, 1912

Dear Mr. Baldwin: I have read with interest your letter of November 22, concerning plans for a report on Juvenile Courts and Juvenile Probation. In answer to the questions which you sent me, I beg to say that I consider among the more important of the problems connected with delinquent and neglected colored children: how to secure proper home influences and how to counteract the bad surroundings outside of the home to which most of the colored children in the cities are subject to. There is also the problem of how to secure the co-operation of the parents with the probation officers.

Another problem is to get hold of the child before it is arrested. I am not very well acquainted with the working of the Juvenile Courts, but my impression is that the attention of the probation officers is in the majority of cases not called to the colored child until it has committed an offense.

I think it is important that the probation law should be made applicable to white and colored alike. In my own state, Alabama, a judge may send the white child to a reformatory without it having committed any offense, simply on the ground that it has shown signs of delinquency. On the other hand a colored child, to be sent to a reformatory, must have first committed an offense, been arrested and sentenced.

My impression is that the colored people in cities are generally not well acquainted with the purposes of the Juvenile Courts and the function of the Probation Officers. I think, therefore, that an effort should be made to acquaint and interest the colored people in the work of the Juvenile Courts and to secure the co-operation of the colored ministers and other influential persons. Sincerely yours,

[Booker T. Washington]

TLp Con. 472 BTW Papers DLC.

To Julius Rosenwald

[Tuskegee, Ala.] December Twenty-fourth, Nineteen Hundred Twelve

Dear Mr. Rosenwald: I have a rather vague and hazy thought which may or may not amount to something — it is this: I see that President-elect Wilson is to speak in Chicago about January 11th. I have been wondering if it might not be worth while for us to try to arrange for a small side meeting for Tuskegee at which the Governor might consent to say a few words. My idea would be to have the audience composed of a small number of selected people.

I had a talk a few days ago with Mr. Walter H. Page, who is one of Governor Wilson's nearest friends, and who was largely instrumental in bringing about his nomination; and Mr. Page said the Governor had definitely declined to make any additional engagements, but I have the feeling if I saw him and explained to him the nature of the engagement, which would really be in connection with his regular Chicago engagement, that the Governor might consent to appear at such a meeting.

Of course, I would not think of urging the matter unless it met with the approval of yourself and Mr. Crane.[1] I think the chances are about even between success and failure as to getting his consent.

I would very much like to have your opinion regarding the whole matter. Yours very truly,

Booker T. Washington

TLpS Con. 56 BTW Papers DLC.

¹ Charles Richard Crane (1858–1939), president of the Crane Co., manu-facturers of iron pipe and plumbing fixtures, was vice-chairman of the finance committee for Woodrow Wilson's 1912 presidential campaign.

From Emmett Jay Scott

[Tuskegee, Ala.] December 27, 1912

Mr. Washington: I do not know whether you are disposed to pay any further attention to F. H. Murray of Washington, but his last on-slaught in the Guardian was so vicious, that I feel like mentioning the matter at any rate.

I still feel that we should make one more effort to have Tyler, or some of our strong friends there, like Terrell or Lewis for whom you have done so much, muzzle this fellow before the administration changes.

I have no doubt but what, if they talk up the matter with Mr. Hilles in the right way, that some result could be secured.

E J Scott

TLS   Con. 620   BTW Papers   DLC.

To George Washington Carver

[Tuskegee, Ala., Dec. 27, 1912]

Mr. Carver: I confess that I am very much puzzled as to what the school ought to do in regard to spending more money in fitting up a laboratory for you. We have gone some distance in this matter. In fact, we have gone as far as our finances would permit. I am aware of the fact that you were promised that this laboratory would be gradually fitted up according to your wishes, and that $400. was authorized to be spent in the near future in this direction.

In writing you as I am I have to consider my duty to the public, the trustees as well as to yourself. Since making you the promise that was made, I confess that after the conditions which were brought to the surface in regard to the poultry yard, I am greatly puzzled and my confidence is somewhat shaken. You will recall that several years ago we began the policy of doing everything you asked to be done in the way of fitting up the poultry yard. Hundreds of dollars were spent in this direction to bring things to the point where you said you wished them brought. Several of our officers and some of our trustees felt that we were spending too much money on the poultry yard, but in the face of these doubts and criticisms, I stood by you and furnished what you wanted. Just at the time when I felt that the school was in a position to reap the benefit of some of the funds put into the poultry yard, much to the disappointment of all of us it developed that either you did not know what was going on at the poultry yard, or if you did know, you did not have the strength to report the facts, or there was deception practiced on the part of somebody. The plain facts are that for months it was reported that there were at the poultry yard an average of about 3,600 head of poultry, when as a matter of fact there were on the yard only about 1,275 head of poultry. Under those circumstances, you can easily see why we hesitate to spend more money in fulfilling a promise made you.

Further than this the report of the committee seems to indicate that you are not willing to work under either Mr. Bridgeforth or Mr. Lee. If this is true, I cannot see where or how the school can place you. We are not in a position to have any persons here who do not or cannot work in harness or in connection with a systematic plan of development. I confess that the situation greatly puzzles me.

In writing you in this way, I am keeping in mind the many special qualifications you possess, and the valuable time and service you have given the school.

I shall be very glad to consider carefully any suggestions you may care to make.

Booker T. Washington

TLpS Con. 630 BTW Papers DLC.

From George Washington Carver

[Tuskegee, Ala.] December 28, 1912

Mr. B. T. Washington: I have your note of the 27th, and have read and considered same carefully; and since your confidence is shaken, the only honest thing to do, as I see it, is for me to give way for those in whom you have confidence. I do not see how the committee could get the impression that I was unwilling to teach under Prof. Lee when this was arranged July 27, 1912. I was to have all the botany, and lecture on birds, as you know I am not an academic teacher, and there are only a few subjects I could teach successfully.

I wish to thank you for the privilege of serving you 17 years, and now ask that you give me at least 30 days to wind up all of my affairs, as it will take quite that long to put my department in order, get my things packed, find storage for them, and incidentally get myself located.

With continued good wishes, and with the hope that the work will continue to grow and prosper, I am, Yours truly,

G. W. Carver

TLS   Con. 630   BTW Papers   DLC.

To Julius Rosenwald

[Tuskegee, Ala.] December Thirtieth, Nineteen Hundred Twelve

Dear Mr. Rosenwald: I have your letter of December 28th regarding the matter of Governor Wilson speaking at a small select meeting for Tuskegee while in Chicago. I have just telegraphed as follows:

> Your letter regarding Governor Wilson received. Suggest that luncheon be omitted if I am to be present making it simple meeting of selected people. Shall wait before going further until hear from you as to Mr. Crane's advice in matter.

My idea is this: if you think it important that I be present at such meeting the matter of the luncheon would bring up the old question of social equality and might embarrass Governor Wilson, and would certainly furnish the newspapers with a basis for some rather sensational reports. I think the Governor would be much more inclined to accept an invitation to meet and speak to a few selected people without the luncheon than he would to attend any affair of that character. Of course, as I wrote you before, I think the chances are about even as to our succeeding or failing.

If Mr. Crane would be inclined to take the matter up with him directly, I think it would be much better than my seeing Mr. Wilson. At any rate, I shall wait to hear from you before attempting to see him or to go further in the matter.

I know Mr. Wilson personally. He is interested in our work, but just what he will be inclined to do just now, I am not sure. Of course, it may be possible to have the luncheon without my presence, and in that case, I should be just as well satisfied. Yours very truly,

Booker T. Washington

TLpS Con. 56 BTW Papers DLC.

A List of Pledges
to the Tuskegee Institute Five-Year Fund

[Tuskegee, Ala., 1912]

In order to relieve Mr. Washington of the burden of raising such large amounts annually for the Tuskegee Institute, we, the undersigned, hereby agree to contribute the amounts set opposite our names annually for five years, commencing with 1912, providing that a total amount of $50,000.00 per annum is subscribed on this basis:

Mr. Julius Rosenwald, Roman Ave. & Harvard St., Chicago, Ill.	$5,000.00
Mr. Frank Trumbull, 71 Broadway, New York, N.Y.	5,000.00
Mr. William G. Willcox, 3 S. William St., New York, N.Y.	5,000.00
Mrs. Charles E. Mason, Readville, Mass.	5,000.00
Hon. Seth Low, 30 E. 64th St., New York, N.Y.	1,000.00
Mr. W. L. Pierce, Tremont Building, Boston, Mass.	500.00
Mr. C. A. Coffin, 30 Church St., New York, N.Y.	1,000.00

Mr. George F. Baker, 2 Wall St., New York, N.Y.	1,000.00
Mr. Henry Goldman, 60 Wall St., New York, N.Y.	1,000.00
Mr. Samuel Sachs, 60 Wall St., New York, N.Y.	1,000.00
Mr. Harry Sachs, 60 Wall St., New York, N.Y.	500.00
Mr. James Speyer, 24 Pine St., New York, N.Y.	1,000.00
Mr. Jacob H. Schiff, 52 William St., New York, N.Y.	1,500.00
Mr. George Blumenthal, 10 Wall St., New York, N.Y.	500.00
Mr. Paul J. Sachs, 60 Wall St., New York, N.Y.	150.00
Mr. Jacob Wertheim, 1020 2nd Ave., New York, N.Y.	1,000.00
Mr. Mortimer Schiff, 52 William St., New York, N.Y.	500.00
Mr. Otto H. Kahn, 52 William St., New York, N.Y.	500.00
Mr. Philip Lehman, 22 William St., New York, N.Y.	1,000.00
Mr. Herbert Lehman, 16 William St., New York, N.Y.	250.00
Mr. Sig M. Lehman, 22 William St., New York, N.Y.	250.00
Mr. H. K. McHarg, 40 Wall St., New York, N.Y.	500.00
Mr. Felix Warburg, 21 Pine St., New York, N.Y.	1,000.00
Mr. Paul M. Warburg, 52 William St., New York, N.Y.	1,000.00
Mr. F. F. Patton, 351 Fourth St., New York, N.Y.	25.00
Mr. V. Everit Macy, 68 Broadway, New York, N.Y.	1,000.00
Mr. Charles R. Crane, Chicago, Ill.	1,000.00
Mr. Moses Newberg, 60 Broadway, New York, N.Y.	100.00
Mr. Charles E. Mason, 120 Franklin St., Boston, Mass.	250.00
Mr. Harold Peabody, Hyde Park, Mass.	100.00
Mr. Austin B. Mason, Devonshire St., Boston, Mass.	25.00
Mr. & Mrs. J. Dudley Clark, 50 State St., Boston, Mass.	200.00
Mr. Albert H. Loeb, °/o Sears, Roebuck & Co., Chicago, Ill.	500.00
Mr. J. G. Schmidlapp, Cincinnati, Ohio	150.00
Mr. A. F. Estabrook, 15 State St., Boston, Mass.	100.00
Mrs. Emmons Blaine, Chicago, Ill.	500.00
New York Colored Medical Society	50.00
Mr. H. L. Higginson, Boston, Mass.	500.00
Mr. Arthur Lehman, New York, N.Y.	500.00
Mr. Zenas Crane, Dalton, Mass.	1,000.00
Mr. H. M. Byllesby, Chicago, Ill.	500.00
Mr. H. Phillip Mason, Boston, Mass.	25.00
Mr. S. P. Mendell, 33 Summer St., Boston, Mass.	150.00
*Mr. William M. Crane, 79 Wall St., New York, N.Y.	25.00
Mr. E. A. Hamill, Chicago, Ill.	250.00

Mr. William M. Scott, 19th & Hamilton Sts.,	
Philadelphia, Pa.	500.00
Mr. Arthur Curtiss James, 99 John St., New York, N.Y.	1,000.00
Dr. James Douglas, 99 John St., New York, N.Y.	100.00
Mr. William Church Osborn, 71 Broadway, New York, N.Y.	250.00
Mr. & Mrs. Donald Scott, 33 E. 17th St., New York, N.Y.	150.00
Mr. S. H. Williams, Glastonbury, Conn.	25.00
Miss Ellen F. Mason, 1 Walnut St., Boston, Mass.	2,000.00
Miss Ida M. Mason, 1 Walnut St., Boston, Mass.	3,000.00
*Mr. James S. Higbee, Newark, N.J. ($50.00 a year	
for five years)	50.00
Mr. R. Fulton Cutting, 32 Nassau St., New York, N.Y.	200.00
Mr. Francis Lynde Stetson, 15 Broad St., New York,	100.00
Mr. Frank Lyman, 88 Wall St., New York, N.Y.	100.00
Mr. & Mrs. Booker T. Washington, Tuskegee Institute,	
Alabama	25.00
Miss Georgiana Lowell, Boston, Mass.	50.00
Mr. Samuel Insull, Chicago, Ill.	500.00
Mr. Cyrus McCormick, Chicago, Ill.	500.00
Redmond & Co., 33 Pine St., New York, N.Y.	100.00
Miss Mary D. Pierce, 61 Mount Vernon St., Boston, Mass.	50.00
Mr. William Skinner, Fourth Ave., & 17th St.,	
New York, N.Y.	1,000.00
Miss Alice P. Chase, 47 Baltimore St., Lynn, Mass.	50.00
Mr. John Harney, 233 W. 27th St., Los Angeles, Cal.	500.00
Mr. William P. Wharton,[1] Groton, Mass.	500.00
Mr. G. L. Stone, 58 Buckminster Road, Brookline, Mass.	50.00
Mrs. H. M. Laughlin, 1073 Beacon St., Boston, Mass.	100.00
Mr. N. W. Harris, Chicago, Ill.	1,000.00
	$54,000.00
Mr. David Pingree, Salem, Mass. (Paid in advance)	500.00
	$54,500.00

Name used under certain conditions.

TM Con. 642 BTW Papers DLC.

[1] Probably William Fisher Wharton (b. 1847), a Boston lawyer who resided in Groton.

Ralph Waldo Tyler to Emmett Jay Scott

[Washington, D.C.] Jan. 4/13

Dear Emmett: If there is any way the Doctor and you can influence Fred to cease this editorial strife with The Bee, I wish you would do so, and act hastily. This week's Age contains an attack on Chase, quite vicious — equally, if not more vicious than Chase's reply to the first attack from The Age. The fact is people do not care for the petty personal warfare between editors. They dont buy newspapers for such reading matter. The Age is the last newspaper that ought to engage in such a strife for the reason it is regarded as above it. The whole thing, from the start, was prompted by The Age's unusual championing of Bishop Walters. Now the Bishop is simply playing one newspaper against the other, and at the same time cuddling both. He comes to Washington, visits Chase, and calls with him on the Democratic National Committee and asks for Chase's support, and is willing to pay for it. *This is a fact.* The Age and The Bee have both been supporting the Doctor. It is suicidal to permit a fight between them. The result — ultimate result, will be the loss of at least one of them for the Doctor, if the fight continues. Fortune's personal fight should be no concern of The Age. Fortune, when it comes to dependableness in support of the Doctor, is not much more to be depended upon than Chase. I have heard him roast the Doctor while accepting his alms. Fortune is more brainy — that's the only difference.

Aside from the viewpoint of Doctor's interests, this fight is liable to cost Fred a nomination to Liberia. Chase will go to any extent to defeat him. Taft and Hilles both like him (Chase) for having stood firm at Chicago. I was surprised that The Age replied. I thought after it had styled Chase "ignorant and venomous," and he had come back, the war was over. But here The Age comes back this week with a column attack. Chase will no doubt reply next week — and then the newspaper — disgusting war between two editors, in which the public is not interested will go on. When will Negro newspapers realize that a mudslinging editorial column is injurious both to the papers and the race? If you have any influence at all with Fred wire him to cut out this personal fight from The Age's columns. There is no reason why The Age should be regarded as "no better than The Bee." And besides, as I said in the onset, the Doctor must be the loser, and

Bishop Walters is playing both newspapers. What has Bishop done to demand support from The Age at the expense of The Age's standing as a sane newspaper? My interest is only to maintain, if possible, harmony between newspapers that support the Doctor. The enemy is feeding this fight flame — they are applauding it and hoping for a split in the ranks. I absolutely know this. Fortune never was above purchase, neither was Chase. Fortune was never absolutely dependable without "consideration," and neither was Chase. The editorial column is or ought to be no stage on which to present a personal warfare between employes on rival newspapers.

Tyler

ALS Con. 488 BTW Papers DLC.

From Frank W. Crenshaw[1]

Mobile, Alabama 1/6, 1913

Dear Sir: I know you are greatly interested in having the crime rate among the negro race in the State of Alabama reduced. In my position as head of the peace department of Mobile, I would like to see something done in the way of caring for the Juvenile Deliquents.

I find in my work a great need for an institution to take care of negro boys whose ages range from 7 years to 16 years.

Judge Edington[2] and myself have talked the matter over, and I see only one way out, viz: institute a Detention School for the colored race, and put the boys of that age there for all misdemeanors. It could also be used for the purpose of reformation of some boys.

The most of these boys of whom I speak, are from poor ignorant parents, or are criminals themselves, turned loose upon the world to get what they can, and they feel that inasmuch as they are already classed among the lowliest of the race, they will get their living by stealing or anything else.

Only yesterday a report came to me that some one had broken in and robbed a house, I sent detectives out on the case and they picked up three little boys, one aged 7 years the other two 8 years. Each charged the other with having made the suggestion to break, or go into this house. They had associated so much with men and women of a lower class that it was with a great deal of difficulty, I was able to get their right names. They insisted on giving assumed names.

I sent for their parents and made them whip them in the presence of officers, and I warned the parents that if those boys were ever arrested again for doing wrong, I would hold them accountable. Those parents acknowledged that they were unable to do any thing with the boys.

These same boys, and many others with whom I come in contact, might grow up to be better men and women were their surroundings made better.

I believe an institution properly handled would in time be self supporting. We have some of your race here who are fully competent to take up work of this kind, and they would find a large field to work in.

I can mention the names of two, Clarence Allen[3] and Charles Peters[4] who I think would be men of honor and integrity to take up the work. After they have entered into it, I am sure they would find willing helpers among the white race.

I am kept very busy, but would be glad to co-operate with any one or more respectable colored men in the work, and lend all the assistance possible.

Kindly let me hear from you in the way of some suggestion in the matter, and I will then take it up with Allen and Peters, but it might be that you would rather take it up with them direct.

Something will have to be done some day, for instead of boys, both white and black, getting better they will get worse if allowed to grow up in ignorance and among adult criminals etc. Yours very truly,

F. W. Crenshaw
Chief of Police

TLS Con. 474 BTW Papers DLC.

[1] Frank W. Crenshaw, a former railroad engineer and undertaker, was Mobile police chief from 1913 to 1915.

[2] David Henry Edington, born in Mississippi in 1882, was judge of the Mobile police court for twenty-six years. He was also city recorder (1912–38), and was appointed judge of the thirteenth judicial circuit of Alabama in 1938.

[3] Clarence W. Allen was a Mobile undertaker.

[4] Charles W. Peters was president of a furniture company and of the Mutual Aid Association of Mobile.

To Frank W. Crenshaw

[Tuskegee, Ala.] January 10, 1913

Dear Sir: I have read with a great deal of interest your letter of January 6 and am gratified to know that you desire to do something for the colored juvenile delinquents. This is a matter in which I am also deeply interested and will be pleased to cooperate with you in whatever way I can.

I was under the impression that the State Reformatory for Colored Youths at Mount Meigs was designed to take care of just the kind of boys that you mention. If there is anything in the laws of the State of Alabama that prevents delinquent colored boys being sent there from all parts of the State, I think that at the next session of the Legislature efforts should be made to have these restrictions removed. I will take up the situation in Mobile with Dr. A. F. Owens, formerly pastor of a colored Baptist Church in your city and now connected with our Bible Training School. He did a great deal toward getting the State to take over the Reformatory at Mount Meigs and will be able to advise with you to what extent delinquent colored juveniles from Mobile might be sent there.

We keep in close touch with this reformatory, and I know that it is doing good work for the boys that are there, who, I understand, are of the ages and class that you describe in your letter.

Trusting that I will be able to further serve you in this matter, I am Very sincerely yours,

Booker T. Washington

TLpSr Con. 474 BTW Papers DLC. Signature initialed by E. J. Scott.

From F. C. Lane[1]

New York Jan. 13, 1913

Dear Sir: As editor of a publication whose sole aim is the promotion of enlightened sport without respect to race and color, I have often wondered if baseball might not offer possibilities as a factor, in the education of our great negro population. Baseball as the foremost sport of this country has attained a prominence which is truly world wide and the remarkable strides it is making in Japan and China are proof that it is not alone a white mans game.

As you probably know baseball has been used with remarkable effect by the wardens of several state penitentiaries as a humanizing influence on the convicts in their charge. It has been employed by the great city of Cleveland as a chief factor in her campaign of education among her own boys and young men, and I might cite other instances where it has exerted an enlightening influence far superior to its rank as a mere sport.

The colored man while he often has great ability as a player is barred, as you know, from the professional ranks through out the United States. In Cuba however some of the greatest players who ever trod a diamond are of negro descent. Now it occurred to me that it would be perfectly possible to organize a colored league composed of negro players in this country which I believe would open to the negro here an opportunity which he does not at present enjoy, and which would also I believe be of benefit in a variety of ways, to the negro population as a whole. The possibilities of the plan are far reaching and the organization of such a league in a semi professional way a simple matter to one who knows the game. I have no interest in such a plan save as a step in the advancement of baseball and I believe a step in the advancement [of] the negro race, but I should be pleased to foster such a movement in a general way and more than pleased to give it my unreserved support.

I am writing to you, Mr. Washington, not as one who is interested in baseball, for I know nothing of your tastes in such matters. But you are the acknowledged spokesman for your race and knowing your interest in anything which pertains to the betterment of your race I am submitting the above proposition. I should be pleased to hear from you at your convenience and assure you of my hearty co-operation in anything in my own particular field which you may suggest. Very truly yours

F C Lane

TLS Con. 472 BTW Papers DLC.

¹ F. C. Lane was editor of *The Baseball Magazine* (1911–38) and the annual *Little Red Book of Major League Baseball* (1938–46), and author of *Batting* (1925).

From Robert Curtis Ogden

New York   Jan 16th 1913

Dear Dr Washington   I have just written an official letter to Mr Scott with my resignation from membership in the Tuskegee Board of Trustees. Physical conditions have been painfully aggravated with me of late which undermine mental as well as physical conditions and make all work a sorry burden. Aside from the foregoing I am reaching the "bound of life" that makes the grasshopper a burden so that I should make room for some younger and more active man. My best wishes and earnest sympathy will always be with Tuskegee. Please remember me cordially to Mrs Washington. Very Sincerely

Robert C Ogden

ALS   Con. 66   BTW Papers   DLC.

To Kelly Miller

[Tuskegee, Ala.] January 17, 1913

My dear Professor Miller: Thank you for yours of January 4th.[1] I hope you will forgive me for what I said about Howard University. I did not mean any harm, but meant to state the truth which might in the future do some good. I believe it will.

The fact is that in too many of our institutions our young people are getting the theory while white people are getting the practice. Suppose at some time you find out who is actually running the electric plant near Howard University that supplies light to the Freedmens Hospital, and I think also to Howard University, see if it is not an educated young white man. The Negro is getting the theory of electricity while the white man is getting the practice and the money. Is not this true? Yours very truly,

Booker T. Washington

TLpS   Con. 482   BTW Papers   DLC.

[1] Miller wrote in reference to BTW's article, "Is the Negro Having a Fair Chance?" (See An Article in *The Century*, Nov. 1912, above.) Miller regarded BTW's criticism of Howard University as "unfortunate," but agreed that it was accurate. (Miller to BTW, Jan. 4, 1913, Con. 482, BTW Papers, DLC.)

To Samuel Laing Williams

[Tuskegee, Ala.] January 20th, 1913

Personal

My dear Mr. Williams: Fulfilling my promise to write you further after communicating with Mr. Lewis as to your case, I am writing to say that Mr. Lewis has gone out of his way to exert himself in your favor. As a matter of fact, he has exhausted every possibility so far as the Washington end is concerned to have you retained or reinstated.

Without going into details, Mr. Lewis finds that nothing can be done except through the initiative and leadership of the District Attorney in Chicago. If you can bring any influence to bear through U.S. senators or your local people in Chicago on Mr. Wilkerson[1] it will help, but matters are in such shape that the Attorney General does not feel warranted in going over the head of Mr. Wilkerson. If any man in the United States could influence Mr. Wickersham to take any further step, Mr. Lewis could do so, as I know Mr. Wickersham has the very highest respect for Mr. Lewis.

Mr. Lewis is also convinced, as I am, that the matter of color prejudice does not enter into the case as far as the Attorney General is concerned.

I am very sorry that matters have turned out as they have. If I can serve you further please do not fail to make any suggestion to me. Yours very truly,

Booker T. Washington

TLpS Con. 489 BTW Papers DLC.

[1] James Herbert Wilkerson (1869–1948), a prominent Chicago lawyer, was U.S. attorney for the northern district of Illinois (1911–19). He was later U.S. district judge (1922–41).

To William Henry Lewis

[Tuskegee, Ala.] January 20, 1913

Personal

My dear Mr. Lewis: Thank you very much for both of your letters. I am sorry that we failed to make connection as I came South, but your communication covers the whole ground.

I want to express the gratitude which I feel to you for the very thorough and painstaking manner in which you have gone into the Williams case. I am sure that you have exhausted every possibility of helping him. Enclosed I send you a copy of a letter which I have written Mr. Williams.[1] It is pretty hard to help a man who has no ability to help himself.

You will be interested to know that I had two very interesting interviews with the Colonel in New York a few days ago. I want you to see him at some time. After talking with him, and in this you will agree, I consider him a bigger man than I thought he was before. I told him in rather a frank and plain manner that I did not enter into the Progressive movement, and before I had time to give my reasons he exclaimed with the greatest emphasis that he considered my course the wisest one, that he should have been disappointed and chagrined if I had entered the movement, that it would have been the very worst thing that I could have done and he honored me for pursuing the course that I did pursue. He gave as an illustration how at one time he found himself embarrassed. I think it was something like this, though I may not have all the facts correct. When he was Assistant Secretary of the Navy and Mr. McKinley was President, Mr. Tracy was candidate for Mayor of New York against Seth Low. The administration was for Mr. Tracy. Mr. Roosevelt was for Mr. Low. He said that he went to President McKinley and told him rather frankly that he did not want to embarrass the administration, but he was in favor of Mr. Low. President McKinley told him that the good he could do in supporting Mr. Low would be more than counterbalanced by the stir that would be made in the country in letting it be known that he was opposed to what the administration wanted. The result was that while he voted quietly for Mr. Low he did not oppose openly Mr. Tracy. There was much in the same line. Really, I hope you will have a talk with him sometime. There is much more that I do not care to put on paper that I will tell you about when I see you. Yours very truly,

Booker T. Washington

TLpS Con. 480 BTW Papers DLC.

[1] BTW to Samuel Laing Williams, Jan. 20, 1913, above.

To Daniel Edward Howard

[Tuskegee, Ala.] January 21st, 1913

My dear President Howard: I have your letter of December 16th, and in reply I would state that my inclination is to do whatever appeals to our Liberian friends as being wise.

A few days after Dr. Crum died I was at the State Department and talked over the matter of his successor with the Secretary. The State Department, I might say to you confidentially, has the very highest opinion of Mr. Bundy,[1] and the suggestion was made that he be promoted to the ministership. That phase of the question was considered, and it was later thought that Mr. Bundy might be of greater service to Liberia by being kept in his present position than by being promoted to the ministership. Of course as soon as he was made minister the position would become *political* and he might be removed at any time, whereas remaining in his present position he would more likely be permanent. That was the final view that determined the Department to ask the President to make Mr. Fred R. Moore, editor of the New York Age, minister. Mr. Moore's name is now before the Senate, but there is slight hope that he will be confirmed before the new administration comes in.

There is nothing definite as to what policy Mr. Wilson will pursue regarding the minister after he becomes President, but I shall be glad to do all I can to carry out your wishes.

I am writing in a similar strain to Mr. Reed Paige Clark.[2]

Do not fail to call upon me when I can be of any service. Yours very truly,

Booker T. Washington

TLpS Con. 65 BTW Papers DLC.

[1] Richard Carlton Bundy was a black man born in Wilmington, Ohio, in 1870. After graduating from Case School of Applied Sciences in Cleveland, he was head of the mechanical engineering department of Wilberforce University. From 1910 to 1916 he was secretary of the U.S. legation in Monrovia, Liberia, and he continued in the diplomatic service there and in Washington until his retirement in 1924.

[2] BTW on the same date sent Reed Paige Clark a letter worded exactly the same. (Con. 65, BTW Papers, DLC.)

To F. C. Lane

[Tuskegee, Ala.] January 21, 1913

My dear Sir: I have your kind letter of some days ago. There is already, if I remember aright, an amateur baseball college league. In New York City and in Chicago, there is, I believe, also a city league made up of white and colored baseball clubs. I am sure that this is true of Chicago, but not so sure of New York; although there is a league between the colored clubs of New York.

I heard last year from some source that there was an All Nations Baseball Club, playing professional baseball through the West against local clubs, which was composed of a Japanese, an Indian, a woman first baseman, and a Negro pitcher.

I am inclined to think that a talk with Lester A. Walton, sporting and dramatic editor of the New York Age, 247 West Forty-sixth Street, New York City, would prove helpful in getting a line more directly than I am able to indicate on these various matters.

I should very much like to learn of the successful inauguration of a league in which superior Negro teams should be a part. Very truly yours,

Booker T. Washington

TLpS Con. 472 BTW Papers DLC.

To Robert Curtis Ogden

Tuskegee Institute, Alabama   Jan. 21, 1913

My dear Mr. Ogden: Your letter notifying me of your resignation from our board of trustees has been received. I scarcely know how to find words with which to express my feelings, under all the circumstances I can not find in my heart to ask you to remain yet it seems that in losing your name from our trustee board as if I was parting with a member of my own family, but I know that should the board accept your resignation we shall have in the future as in the past your full sympathy and assistance.

We shall never be able to express to you how much Tuskegee, the Negro race and the whole South owes to you.

You will always have our prayers for a long and happy life. Yours sincerely

Booker T. Washington

ALS   Robert C. Ogden Papers   DLC.

From Charles Young

Monrovia, Liberia   January 25th, 1913

My dear Dr. Washington: I have not written you since coming to Africa because things rested in the same statu quo that you knew about at the beginning of last year. Nothing was doing in the administration and everything was waiting upon the receivership which only went into effect on the 26th of November. On the 25th of that month I left Monrovia with 125 men for Captain Brown's[1] (American) relief in the interior of the country, he having been reported here at Monrovia as being without ammunition and surrounded by hostile tribesmen backed up by Mandingoes.

I had a tough time of it and only returned ten days ago with a bullet in my right arm after a four days fight.[2] I cannot use my arm for writing up to this time but must beg my friends to get this letter off to you because of its urgency.

The President of the Republic with the best of the Liberian citizens is desiring the Appointment of Mr. Richard C. Bundy as Minister Resident at this post for the following reasons:

This young man is thoroughly cognizant of Liberian affairs, he having been through the trying times of the last three years, helping in every manner possible the Liberians to adjust their affairs with foreign governments, and bringing about the materialization of the Refunding Loan Agreement. Very often, Dr. Crum being sick, the business of the office wholly devolved upon Bundy, who discharged his duties with singular tact, good sense and patience. Upon the departure of Dr. Crum, this young man fulfilled the duty of Charge d'Affaires with such credit to himself that he elicited the praise of the whole diplomatic contingent of which he was dean and received a commendatory letter from our Secretary of State to that effect.

The President of the Republic and all interested in the welfare of Liberia believe that he should be continued here as Minister and that, for the present, all United States politics should be taken away from this post until Liberia is thoroughly straightened out. If you believe as we do, anything that you may do with the incoming administration looking toward his retention here will be for the welfare of Liberia, and put the President of this Republic under a debt of gratitude to you.

I am also interested in the appointment of Mr. Bundy and will thank you for any measures you may take in his cause looking toward that end.

With the same esteem and affection for you as of old, I am, Yours sincerely,

Chas. Young,
Major U.S. Army

TLS Con. 70 BTW Papers DLC.

[1] Captain Arthur A. Brown (or Browne) of Chicago had served as a first lieutenant in Cuba during the Spanish-American War. When BTW heard that Brown was being considered for a post in Liberia, he wrote to Reed Paige Clark: "I think I ought to say to you in all frankness that Brown is not the kind of man to go to Liberia. He is a bumptious, troublesome, sensitive, foolish fellow, and he would not be in Liberia ten days before he would give you and everybody else concerned all kinds of trouble." BTW's prediction seems to have been accurate, but he apparently did not mail the letter, as an unsigned original is in his papers. (Mar. 25, 1912, Con. 916, BTW Papers, DLC.)

[2] An account of this episode from U.S. State Department reports is in Fletcher, *The Black Soldier and Officer*, 95.

To Wickliffe Rose[1]

[Tuskegee, Ala.] February 1st, 1913

Dear Dr. Rose: I am very anxious to secure, if possible, from the Peabody Fund enough money to put two colored County Supervisors in Alabama. I am sure that the cooperation and consent of the State Superintendent and County Superintendents can be secured in this matter.

In one of our counties, Tallapoosa, under the Jeanes Fund we already have a colored Supervisor who is doing excellent work, and it is very interesting to see how closely he keeps in touch with the County Superintendent and how beautifully the County Superintendent cooperates with him. There are at least two other counties in Alabama that are ready for this movement, and I am wondering if the money could not be provided from the Peabody Fund for this purpose. Yours very truly,

Booker T. Washington

TLpS   Con. 71   BTW Papers   DLC.

¹ Wickliffe Rose (1862–1931) was a Tennessee-born white man. After teaching at Peabody College, the University of Nashville, and the University of Tennessee, he became general agent of the Peabody Education Fund (1907–15), secretary of the Rockefeller Sanitary Commission (1910–15), trustee of the John F. Slater Fund (1909–23), and executive secretary of the Southern Education Board (1909–13). After 1913 he was a member of the Rockefeller Foundation, the General Education Board, the International Health Board, and the International Education Board, all Rockefeller agencies.

From Billy Boyd

Tuskegee, Ala. Feb. 2,—13

Dear sir: I am arranging to open here in Tuskegee, a first class motsion picture theatre   will be ready to open about Wensday Feb. 5. and I would like to know if I can get the use of your audatorium for two nights out of each week to show three first class reals of motsion pictures in your place for the pleasure of your student chargeing 5¢ and 10¢ admission   now I will give a percentage of my receits to the Instute or as to what ever you see fit to use it for I am resurveing the back part of my theatre here in town for the colored people but knowing that your rules does not permit your student to come away from the campus I would like to have the pemission to bring my machiene out there two night of each week showing 3 reals of good pictures and changing every night that I give a show. I would like to have Monday and Wensday nights if that will not enterfear with any of your social or meetings nights please let me hear from you at once   thanking in advance I remain   Resp. yours

Billy Boyd

P.S. I will not require any thing to be builded or moved.

ALS Con. 472 BTW Papers DLC. The letterhead contains a silhouette of a white woman and a black man caricaturing the facial features. The caption reads: "The Boyd's. And They All Laughed."

A Circular on the Fiftieth
Anniversary Celebration of Emancipation

Tuskegee Institute, Alabama   February 3, 1913

After consultation with a number of the leading men and women of our race I have taken upon myself the responsibility of asking our people to devote the week of October 19 to 26, 1913, to the celebration of the Fiftieth Anniversary of our freedom.

There is now no reason to believe that Congress will appropriate any sum for a national exposition, and if such appropriation should be made, it would not be available until July next, which is entirely too late to arrange for a national exposition that would do credit to the progress of the race.

Something has already been done, however, in several parts of the country toward carrying into effect the plan already suggested for local celebrations. In order that these various local celebrations may be carried out harmoniously and in such a way that each local celebration will contribute to a national total, the following recommendations are submitted:

1. That the third week in October, 19–26, 1913, be known as Fiftieth Anniversary Week.

2. That schools, churches and all other societies and organizations in every part of the United States where there is a considerable number of our people, unite and co-operate for the purpose of holding local celebrations, these celebrations to take the form, where that is possible, of an exposition of the progress in commercial, professional, intellectual, moral and religious directions, made by members of the race in that community.

3. Where possible these local expositions should be held in connection with existing county or state fair associations. Where this is

done it will be necessary to make the date of the celebration conform to that of the county or state fair in connection with which it is held.

4. Wherever it is feasible the county should be made the unit of the organization of the celebration, and in every case an effort should be made to obtain city, county or state aid to carry the plans of the local committee into effect.

5. In addition to the exposition referred to, an effort should be made to secure the strongest and most representative man obtainable, North or South, as principal speaker.

6. It is suggested that Sunday, October 26th, be set apart as a day for making contributions to a fund to clear off the debt upon the Frederick Douglas[s] Home in the District of Columbia, and to set aside a sufficient sum to maintain this national memorial of the colored people.

7. In conclusion, it is strongly urged that our people begin now to prepare for the Fiftieth Anniversary Week, and that this be made at once a means and an occasion for calling the attention of the world to the tremendous progress which the Negro race has made during its first fifty years of freedom in America.

It is my earnest hope and desire that the above suggestions be read before the various churches, lodges, and other organizations of our people, to the end that the Fiftieth Anniversary Week of Freedom shall be generally observed everywhere.

Booker T. Washington

PLSr Con. 468 BTW Papers DLC. An earlier draft, dated Jan. 30, 1913, is in Con. 480, BTW Papers, DLC.

From Wickliffe Rose

Washington, D.C. February 6, 1913

Dear Dr Washington: Replying to your letter of February 1 I beg to advise that I do have a small fund contributed by the Peabody Trustees for the work of county supervisors. I shall be very glad to cooperate in the development of this work in Alabama. Dr Buttrick and Superintendent Willingham are just on the point of making arrangement for a state supervisor of rural schools to devote his time to public schools for the negro race. In Virginia all these supervisors report to Jackson Davis[1] and he keeps in touch with the work, having two or three conferences a year at Hampton. It seems to me that it would be advisable to have the man appointed in Alabama keep in touch with this work in the state and make at Tuskegee an arrangement similar to that made at Hampton. It has been our custom to make all our contributions toward the salaries of supervisors through the state departments of education. If it seems to you advisable we will hold this matter open for a few weeks until the man has been appointed in Alabama, then if you could get in touch with him and Superintendent Willingham and make arrangement for county supervisors in two or three counties I should be glad to contribute toward their salaries. It has been our custom in other states to contribute about $250 toward the salary of these supervisors. I shall be glad to do the same for these supervisors in Alabama. Very sincerely yours

Wickliffe Rose

TLS Con. 71 BTW Papers DLC.

[1] Jackson Davis (1882–1947) was a graduate of William and Mary College with an M.A. from Columbia University. After serving as superintendent of schools of Henrico County, Va., from 1905 to 1909, he was state supervisor of Negro rural schools from 1909 to 1915. He discovered Virginia Randolph, the black Virginia schoolteacher who became the first Jeanes supervisor and served as the model for similar work throughout the South. Davis became a field agent of the General Education Board from 1915 to 1929.

To Ruth Standish Bowles Baldwin

[Tuskegee, Ala.] February 8, 1913

Dear Mrs. Baldwin: Sometime when you have opportunity, I am wondering if you would not give either of the following named colored doctors in New York an opportunity to talk to you about conditions in New York so far as accommodations for colored people is concerned in the hospitals.[1] There are certain conditions, especially those relating to colored women, that are almost barbarous. I was surprised and shocked at some of the things the doctors told me about their inability to get colored women into the hospitals at the proper time.

The doctors to whom I have references are, Dr. P. A. Johnson,[2] 303 W. 33d St., and Dr. H. M. Griffin,[3] 109 W. 134th St. Both Dr. John[son] and Dr. Griffin are high class men. Perhaps you already know them. Yours very truly,

Booker T. Washington

TLpS Con. 472 BTW Papers DLC.

[1] Ruth Baldwin replied that a committee of the Urban League was already investigating hospital segregation in New York City and promised BTW a report of its findings. (Feb. 15, 1913, Con. 472, BTW Papers, DLC. See also Eugene Kinckle Jones to BTW, Feb. 19, 1913, below.)

[2] Peter A. Johnson (d. 1914) worked in the tuberculosis department of the New York City Board of Health and was chief surgeon of the short-lived black McDonough Memorial Hospital in New York City. He was a board member of the Committee for Improving the Industrial Conditions of Negroes in New York City, one of the three organizations that merged to form the Urban League. He was president of the National Medical Association.

[3] H. Malachi Griffin.

To William Malone Baskervill[1]

[Tuskegee, Ala.] February 12, 1913

Dear Sir: In my opinion no two things have done more to awaken the public conscience in regard to the crime of lynching than the Atlanta riot in 1906 and the burning of a colored man by a mob at Coatesville, Pennsylvania in 1911.

The one showed that in a city where a man could be punished for beating a horse or killing birds, it was not possible to prevent a mob from burning and torturing a human being. The other showed that in one of the leading cities in the South a mob could be incited to wholesale attack upon innocent and respectable men and women, simply because they were unfortunate enough to belong to the same race as that of an outcast who had committed an infamous crime.

These two events, more than any others, so far as my observation goes, have served to convince the thinking people of both races that when a community, like an individual, by habitually giving away to unrestrained passion, loses its power of self-control, there is no limit to which it may not go.

These two events, which showed, as I have said, that we had reached a point in America where human life is so cheap, that a citizen of an unpopular race could not be sure of receiving the same protection under the law that is given the dumb brutes, have caused people North and South to pause and consider seriously their personal responsibility for these conditions. In the long run it is public opinion that prevents crimes of this kind to go unpunished, which is responsible for their commission. The matter comes home finally to the conscience of the individual man and woman.

It is to the honor of the white people and the colored people of Atlanta that immediately after the riot in 1906, the best people of both races came together in a determination that the conditions which made that outbreak possible should be changed. The result is that today there is scarcely a city in the South where there is a better understanding between the leader[s] of both races, or where more is being done to secure for the Negro substantial justice in the courts and to encourage him in every effort that is making to improve human conditions.

What has taken place in Atlanta in six years has taken place in a somewhat lesser degree all over the South, and I am convinced that this is largely responsible for the steady decrease in mob violence in the South. The number of lynchings in the United States have steadily decreased since 1892. In that year 255 persons were killed by mobs. Of these, one hundred were whites and 155 colored. This number has steadily decreased from year to year until last year there were but 64 lynchings in the whole United States. Sixty of those who met death in this way were colored; only four were white.

In nine cases out of ten the crimes which serve to unite and give an excuse for mob violence are committed by men who are without property, without homes, and without education, except what they have picked up in the city slums, in prisons, or on the chain gang. The South is spending too much money in giving the Negro this kind of education that makes criminals and not enough in the kind of schools that turn out farmers, carpenters, and blacksmiths.

Other things being equal it is true not only in America, in the South, but throughout the world that there is the least crime where there is the most education. This is true of the South and of the Negro, just as the same is true of every other race. Particularly is it true that the individuals who commit crimes of violence and crimes that are due to lack of self-control are individuals, for the most part, who are ignorant.

The steady decrease in lynchings in the Southern States is an index of the steady growth of the South in wealth, in industry, in education and in individual liberty. Very truly yours,

[Booker T. Washington]

TLc Con. 471 BTW Papers DLC.

[1] William Malone Baskervill (1888–1953) was news editor of the southern district of the Associated Press (1911–14) after earlier experience on newspapers in Nashville, Memphis, Montgomery, and Atlanta. He later was managing editor of the Atlanta *Georgian-American* (1922–26) and of the Baltimore *News* after 1926.

From Emmet O'Neal

Montgomery, Alabama   February 17, 1913

My dear Sir: Please accept my sincere thanks for the very kind expressions contained in your letter of the 31st ultimo. I believe the views that I have expressed in reference to the education of the negro but voices the sentiment of a majority of my own race. Our prosperity is indissolubly linked with the negro whom, as you stated yesterday, cultivates at least one-fourth of the tillable lands of Alabama. We have made more progress in agriculture in Alabama in the last five years than in the preceding quarter of a century. This has been largely due to the adoption of modern and scientific methods of farming. If this progress is to continue, the colored man must be trained and fitted by education to adopt similar methods. Moreover, none can deny that education tends to lessen crime and to fit every man to perform more efficiently his duties in life. The policy of my administration has been to accord to the colored man equal, exact and impartial justice and by every possible effort to aid him in becoming a more useful member of society. I believe the whole state recognizes the value of the very great work you are doing for your race.

With highest personal regards, I am, Very truly yours,

Emmet O'Neal

TLS Con. 483 BTW Papers DLC.

To Seth Low

Tuskegee Institute, Alabama   February Nineteenth, 1913

Dear Mr. Low: If you think well of the suggestion, I think it will be very helpful and appropriate in your remarks in Montgomery to commend Governor Emmet O'Neal.

He is really an exceptionally fine Southern man. I heard him speak to an audience of two thousand colored people Sunday, and neither the Governor of Massachusetts nor New York could have spoken words more liberal and fine than was true of his remarks.

Governor O'Neal stands out boldly in favor of education for the colored people as well as white people. He lets everybody know that he opposes lynching, and does all he can to enforce the law against it and to create public sentiment in favor of law and order. He has always been generously disposed toward us. Yours very truly,

Booker T. Washington

TLS   Seth Low Papers   NNC.   A press copy is in Con. 65, BTW Papers, DLC.

From Eugene Kinckle Jones[1]

New York City   Feb. 19, 1913

My dear Dr. Washington: Your letter dated Feb. 8th 1913 and addressed to Mrs. Wm. H. Baldwin, Jr., in which you called her attention to the character of accommodation at the disposal of colored women in certain New York hospitals, has been referred to me for reply. I have talked with Dr. P. A. Johnson to whom you referred in your letter, and he informed me that his chief reference was to the treatment accorded colored women in the maternity hospitals of the city. The other hospitals receiving colored women and caring for them, in the large majority of cases, do not discriminate. Dr. Johnson's experience has been the same in dealing with maternity cases as that of other physicians in the city and of our own workers. The colored women are not admitted until they are practically ready for delivery, frequently causing so long a delay that the offspring appears before the hospital is reached. I have in mind at present a case of a woman who was put off so long by the authorities of the Sloan Maternity Hospital that a policeman, who had summoned an ambulance, had to assist in delivering the child before the arrival of the ambulance physician. We will be pleased, of course, to collect all the data that we can secure on this matter and try to improve the situation.

Another embarrassing situation in connection with the hospital treatment of colored people has been experienced in seeking entrance to convalescent homes for discharged hospital patients. Dr. E. P. Roberts[2] is now making an investigation for the National League on Urban Conditions Among Negroes of the facilities for caring for Negro convalescents, for the purpose of determining whether a convalescent home especially for colored people is a necessity. Thus far, the results of his investigation point clearly to the fact that such a home is needed. I shall be pleased to keep you informed as to the progress of this investigation as well as the results of our attempt to secure more humane treatment of the maternity cases at the hands of the maternity hospitals. Very truly yours,

E. K. Jones

TLS Con. 479 BTW Papers DLC.

[1] Eugene Kinckle Jones (1885–1954) was the child of two college professors in Richmond, Va. He graduated from Virginia Union University (1906) and received an A.M. from Cornell (1908). After teaching sociology in a black college and mechanical drawing in a high school in Louisville, he became field secretary in 1911 of the organization that soon became the National Urban League. He became its chief executive officer from 1917 until 1941, except for a four-year leave of absence to serve the New Deal as an adviser in the Commerce Department. Under his leadership the Urban League concentrated on social welfare and job programs for urban blacks.

[2] Eugene P. Roberts was born in Louisburg, N.C., in 1868. He received his education at Lincoln University and his medical training at Flower Hospital Medical School in New York City. He had the largest practice of any black doctor in New York City, and worked also in the clinics of the city health department. He was one of the founders of the National League for the Protection of Colored Women and of the Committee on Urban Conditions among Negroes in New York City, two of the constituent bodies of the National Urban League. He was a board member of the Urban League until the 1930s.

To Alfred Willard French[1]

[Tuskegee, Ala.] February 24, 1913

My dear Sir: I hope you will excuse me for seeming to meddle into a thing which does not strictly concern me in a business way. As you know, I am engaged in education and not in business, but I am deeply interested in the success of the cotton seed oil mill at Mound Bayou, Mississippi.[2]

I have recently been there, and I was greatly surprised to see what a fine and up-to-date plant they have constructed. I have seen many cotton seed oil mills in the South, but I have seen none in a community of this size that compares with this.

Mr. Charles Banks, the general manager of the concern, has been at Tuskegee for several days at my request, and we have been going over matters pretty thoroughly. I find that in order to get to the point where they can operate this plant successfully they need to dispose of about $40,000 worth of bonds. If they cannot do this, the plant will prove almost useless. I am glad to say that Mr. Julius Rosenwald, president of Sears, Roebuck & Co., Chicago, whom Mr. Banks met here, has agreed on certain conditions to take $25,000 worth of these bonds. This would leave $15,000 to be disposed of. I am wondering if your firm would not agree to let all or a portion of what is due the firm be covered in the shape of bonds.

I have the greatest confidence in anything that Mr. Banks says. I have known him for years, and for the cotton seed oil mill to get a backset or for the people there to fail to carry out the plans which they have on foot would indeed prove a great calamity to our race. For these and other reasons I am urging that you consider as carefully as you can the request which I have made.

You will be surprised, I think, and pleased to know that while the concern was capitalized at $100,000, the colored people themselves have raised $85,000.

Enclosed I send you a statement which Mr. Banks has handed me. Yours very truly,

Booker T. Washington

TLpS Con. 64 BTW Papers DLC. No enclosure attached.

1 Alfred Willard French was president of the French Oil Mill Machinery Co. of Piqua, Ohio.

2 Similar letters of the same date, seeking funds for the cotton-oil mill, were sent to other capitalists in the cotton-oil industry. (BTW to D. Gamble and BTW to E. Hobart, Feb. 24, 1913, Con. 64, BTW Papers, DLC.)

From Joel Elias Spingarn

New York   February 25, 1913

My dear Dr. Washington: A report has been circulated, and has reached me through several sources, that your latest book, "The Man Lowest Down," was not written by you at all, that it [is] the work of a Mr. Parks who is or has been employed at Tuskegee, and that, as a matter of fact, you did not visit the Sicilian sulphur mines and various other places described in the book. As a contributor to Tuskegee and a friend of the Negro in all his activities and hopes, I should like to be in a position to deny these reports authoritatively, and I am therefore writing to you directly for such a statement as you may care to send me. I am sure you will understand the friendly spirit in which this letter is sent. Sincerely yours,

J. E. Spingarn

TLS   Con. 487   BTW Papers   DLC.

Louis B. Anderson to Emmett Jay Scott

Chicago, Ill., February 25, 1913

My Dear Emmett: I am breaking my silence with the announcement that the moving picture films of "A Day at Tuskegee," have been developed and an initial private exhibition of them has been given.

They came out wonderfully fine and make 3300 feet divided into three reels of 1100 feet each. The pictures are introduced with a splendid picture of Mr. Washington, and from thence on the story is told of the development of Tuskegee from the first school house of 1881 to the present time. It is a truely wonderful story shown with its varied activities and scenes numbering nearly one hundred in active physical life, the operation needing only the living voice to perfect them. You can get an idea of what an impressive, educational lesson this exhibit makes.

We are now ready for business. This week I am placing in the MOVING PICTURE WORLD, which circulates among moving picture houses, etc., of the country, a half page add, which I am enclosing. For Thursday, March 6th, at the WASHINGTON MOVING PICTURE THEATRE, a small, but very pretty, house on State Street, I am sending out invitations to the Press and prominent people in Chicago, for a private exhibition. The form of invitation I am also enclosing herewith. This invitation will be sent to big people who know Tuskegee and are interested in it, and of course, the Press. It is my purpose and wish to make the first public exhibition the following week.

I am now negotiating with Orchestra Hall, at which Mr. Washington has spoken before, for the first public exhibition. Sometime ago in a letter from Dr. Watkins,[1] he intimated that Mr. Washington could be prevailed upon to come to Chicago and be present on the evening of the first exhibition. Can that be arranged if we procure Orchestra Hall on some near date? It would be of tremendous advantage both to the School and the pictures. The mention that Mr. Washington would be present would absolutely insure a capacity house.

I am enclosing herewith a list of photographs that I noticed in the annual catalogue, '11 — '12. I should like to make some arrangement for the purchase of these in sets of, say 12 each, for lobby displays. In planning the promotion of the pictures I find that in booking, where I am able to make arrangements, it will be necessary to have advertising matter, and I have concluded that the best form of advertisement would be life size lithographs of Mr. Washington together with group pictures of the buildings and scenes indicated in the enclosed list. I take it that you have the cuts there and can furnish us with the sets desired.

Could you also furnish us with large lithographs of Mr. Washington, printing on the margin his name and the words: "Principal, Tuskegee Institute." If you can furnish us with this matter we should like to make arrangements at once so that we can make display of the initial exhibit. The Company will, of course, pay the reasonable charges for the making and shipping.

Another idea struck me as being one of financial profit to the school in connection with the exhibit of these pictures thruout the country, and that is, to have a brief history of the growth and development of Tuskegee, to be printed in small pamphlet form and also containing about a half dozen views with Mr. Washington's picture on the title page. These could be sold at 10 or 15¢ per copy by boys at the various places where the pictures are shown and net handsome revenue, which might be contributed to scholarships for needy colored youth. I make this as a suggestion to you and would like to have your expression as to what you think of it.

I should appreciate a hurried response to requests that I have made here so that we can start to booming these pictures, likewise TUSKEGEE INSTITUTE, and get back some of the coin of the realm, which we have so liberally expended in making this very big thing.

With very best wishes and hopes for an early reply, I beg to remain,
Most sincerely yours,

Louis B. Anderson

TLS Con. 469 BTW Papers DLC.

[1] W. F. Watkins, a dentist in Montgomery, Ala., was a partner with Louis B. Anderson in the Anderson-Watkins Film Co.

A News Item in the Chicago *Inter Ocean*

February 26, 1913

TUSKEGEE PLEASES
ELLA FLAGG YOUNG[1]

CHICAGO SCHOOLS SUPERINTENDENT
PRAISES CONCENTRATION SHOWN
IN WORK BY PUPILS OF THE
NEGRO SCHOOL

Special Dispatch to the *Inter Ocean*

PHILADELPHIA, Pa., Feb. 25. — Mrs. Ella Flagg Young, superintendent of schools of Chicago, has been the most prominent educator during the meetings of the National Educational association here. At the Bellevue-Stratford she is constantly surrounded by the prominent educational authorities of the country who have become enthused over her views.

Mrs. Young is especially enthusiastic over the Tuskegee institute in Alabama. She arrived here yesterday after spending four days at the great educational center of the negroes founded by Booker T. Washington, and is scheduled to deliver an address upon this institution upon her return to Chicago. She made a very close study of conditions there.

In describing her visit in company with sixty-one other visitors from Chicago and other points, she said:

"The word enthusiasm does not seem strong enough in connection with my views upon Tuskegee. I went there with the impression that I should find at least very small buildings of frame, but instead found immense and imposing brick buildings of the most modern type.

"I was more impressed when I learned that even the bricks had been made by the students, the plans drawn by them and every detail of the construction carried out by the pupils.

"There is one point in their system of education which I intend to experiment upon after my return to Chicago. That is the fact that the student bodies spend one day in the shops, factories, cooking, dressmaking departments and the following day they spend in the academic department.

ABLE TO CONCENTRATE

"In this way they are able to concentrate themselves thoroughly upon the two things. I believe it to be much superior to our system of dabbling in each thing for a short class period.

"The concentration of the Tuskegee students is wonderful. While our large body of visitors passed through the classrooms not a single student showed the slightest sign of being aware of our presence, so deeply were they wrapped in their studies. In fact I saw many things being carried on under the staff of negro teachers that many of us might well copy.

"We occupied our private car at Tuskegee and every morning were awakened by the school band, which serenaded us regularly. I took breakfast several times with Mr. and Mrs. Booker T. Washington and I found them charming people. Their home is beautiful, far more beautiful than I ever hope to have.

"When I entered the great dining hall at the school at lunch time, when 1,600 negro students were seated, I received a reception which was far more overwhelming than any I have ever received in my life. At a signal from one of the class leaders the entire student body arose as if a unit and, after giving their college yell with an enormous volume of mellow roaring, they added three rah, rahs for me. So, you see, I felt awfully flattered.

"There are more young men in the school than there are women, although the famous singing chorus, which is perhaps unequaled in the world, is led by a woman student. The orchestra is wonderfully well trained. Perhaps the things that impressed me the most were the wonderful control Mr. Washington has over the mammoth body of students and the great concentration of the students in their studies.

REPAID BY NEGRO MELODIES

"The singing of the old negro melodies, which are being preserved carefully, as many claim them to be our only real true American art, was something that it had been my ambition for many years to hear, and I was amply repaid. I cannot attempt to express or describe this singing. When we departed from there this great chorus of singers came to our train and sang until the train left.

"The strides of progress being made are wonderful. One of the principal speakers, a man who had all the marks of extreme high culture in manners and speech, afterwards told me of his early days at the school.

"Just before our arrival a new hospital, built entirely by students, had been dedicated, and I've rarely seen any hospitals in our large cities that were superior. Later we visited a school at Mount Meigs known as the Waugh school, which necessitated a trip of forty miles by automobile, but we felt amply repaid.

"The school is conducted by a former student of Booker T. Washington, a woman who was formerly a slave child."

Mrs. Young intimated that a number of changes might be made in the Chicago school system, in order to conform to certain features she saw in operation at the institute.

She was indignant at a published interview which credited her with saying that Philadelphians should beware of Chicago and that she found more sympathy shown here than in Chicago. She strongly condemned the practice of addressing pupils in high schools as Mr.

and Miss, and said modern children had no chance to look forward to wearing kid gloves, as they wore them as soon as they were able to walk. This was said during her address at the Acorn club today, where she was the guest of honor.

Chicago *Inter Ocean,* Feb. 26, 1913, 12.

¹ Ella Flagg Young (1845–1918) was superintendent of schools of Chicago (1909–15) after a long career as a teacher and school administrator. A graduate of Wellesley with a Ph.D. from the University of Chicago, Young was a leader in educational reform and woman suffrage.

From C. B. Upton

Piqua, Ohio, U.S.A. Feb. 26, –13

Dear Sir: Your favor of the 24th received, addressed to Mr. French, in reference to the Cotton Oil Mill at Mound Bayou, Miss. Mr. French being in Europe, at the present time, the writer is taking the liberty of acknowledging your letter. On his return we will be pleased to call the matter to his personal attention, which will be in two or three weeks. We will state, however, that it has always been the policy of this Company not to in any way affiliate itself financially with any oil mill interests. We have never taken any stock or purchased any bonds since we have been in business. This policy of the Company adopted a number of years ago has been very faithfully carried out with no exceptions up to this time and, therefore, we doubt very much if Mr. French would desire to make any exceptions in this case.

We appreciate the existing conditions at Mound Bayou and the struggle they have made in a financial way to make this mill a complete success and are of the opinion that if they should be enabled to raise the necessary capital to pay off their present indebtedness and give them an operating surplus, their proposition then would be well on the way to success.

The Mound Bayou Oil Mill owe us the account, which you refer to in your letter, and we have been as lenient as possible in the collection of same, with the idea of assisting them to get on their feet and take care of their indebtedness, which we have done by not forcing our claim and bringing matters to a climax. Yours truly,

THE FRENCH OIL MILL MCHY. CO.
C. B. Upton
Ass't. Manager

TLS Con. 64 BTW Papers DLC.

To Oswald Garrison Villard

[Tuskegee, Ala.] February Twenty-seventh, 1913

Dear Mr. Villard: I have your letter of recent date with enclosures, calling attention to a meeting to be held in New York City in April.[1] I fear it is not going to be possible for me to be present at the meeting.[2]

The truth of the matter is I have been under very great and unusual pressure during the past few months, and today I am leaving Tuskegee for a somewhat extended visit to the Pacific Northwest where I am seeking new friends for Tuskegee Institute, and in addition to the unusual crowded program which is before me, I have been devoting a good part of the year to attending meetings in the interest of schools outside of Tuskegee Institute.

In the same mail with your letter came another asking me to be present at a meeting in behalf of a certain school; while I have just recently attended one in Washington in behalf of a North Carolina school.

It has become necessary, because of my duty to the school here and to our Trustees, to refuse to attend the Trustees meeting of Howard University and Fisk University, the latter being an especially important meeting because they are going to elect a new president. You have no idea of the calls I have upon me in connection with other institutions, some of which I am trying to help out of trouble and others of which I am trying to strengthen, but the fact remains in one way or another, these outside calls have taken a large part of my time for the year. Yours very truly,

Booker T. Washington

TLpS Con. 63 BTW Papers DLC.

¹ Villard had written BTW enclosing an invitation to a meeting at the NAACP headquarters of "heads of all industrial or agricultural schools for colored youth patterned after Tuskegee and Hampton." The signers of the invitation were Emma Wilson, principal of Mayesville Institute, W. H. Holtzclaw, principal of Utica Normal and Industrial Institute, Leslie Pinckney Hill, principal of Manassas Industrial School, W. J. Edwards, principal of Snow Hill Normal and Industrial Institute, H. A. Hunt, principal of Fort Valley Industrial School, and William E. Benson, treasurer of Kowaliga Academic and Industrial Institute. The purpose of the meeting was to organize an association of black industrial schools and to discuss "the elimination of unworthy schools" and "the duplication of effort." (Villard to BTW, with enclosure, Feb. 1913, Con. 63, BTW Papers, DLC. See also Kellogg, *NAACP*, 85–86.)

² Villard tried again on Mar. 8, 1913, inviting a representative from Tuskegee to attend the meeting. He asked Emmett J. Scott, since BTW was absent on the West Coast, to designate someone to attend. He wrote to Scott: "It would be a mistake, I think, *not* to have Tuskegee represented on this occasion." Scott made a notation on the letter before sending it on to BTW: "You will note he is following up the matter. Chisholm c'd attend if you think wise, but having kept Holtzclaw away it may not seem wise to suggest it — EJS." (Villard to Scott [with Scott's docketing], Mar. 8, 1913, Con. 164, BTW Papers, DLC.) Earlier, at Scott's suggestion, William H. Holtzclaw had decided not to attend the conference. (Holtzclaw to Scott, Mar. 3, 1913, Con. 478, BTW Papers, DLC.)

Emmett Jay Scott to Joel Elias Spingarn

Tuskegee Institute, Alabama   March First, 1913

My dear Sir: Your letter comes after Principal Washington has gone to fill a series of lecture engagements, extending over a month, in Utah, Montana, Idaho and Washington state. In his absence I am just a bit puzzled as to how I should attempt to send a reply to your communication.

It will suggest itself to you, I am sure, that if a man would perpetrate such a fraud upon the public as the one that you indicate, that he would not hestitate to cover up that fraud by denial or falsehood. If there be those willing to accept such a report as being truthful, such persons, I am sure, would not be disposed to believe anything that such a man would say with reference to the matter, if it be in contravention of their own conviction.

It seems to me that in Principal Washington's introduction to "The Man Farthest Down," he has frankly discussed the matter of Dr. Park's association and collaboration with him in connection with this book.

There is not one single place referred to in the book as having been visited which he did not visit personally. Upon many of these excursions he was not even accompanied by Dr. Park.

I am not writing, as you understand, for public denial, as Dr. Washington's general attitude, as I think you know, is not to spend his time and strength in making explanations or denials; if he did, he would be able to do little constructive work.

The writer remembers that a report was put in circulation something to the effect that he did not write "Up From Slavery." I do not think Mr. Washington has ever denied the falsity of this report and he is not likely to do so.

The reason for the circulation of such malicious reports must be entirely obvious to you.

Thanking you for the friendly spirit in which you write, and for the interest you have always shown in Tuskegee Institute, I am: Yours very truly,

Emmett J. Scott

TLS Joel E. Spingarn Collection DHU. A press copy is in Con. 487, BTW Papers, DLC.

From Robert Ezra Park

Columbia, S.C. March 1 1913

My dear Mr Washington: I came down here last night, on my way from Denmark to Cambria Va, to have a talk with State Superintendent of Schools Swearingen and some of his assistants. I came here on the advice of Niels Christensen, who is a State Senator and, as you know, a trustee of the Port Royal School, at Beaufort.

There has been a great fight here over the school appropriation. Senator Christensen has been a leader in that fight and the legislature has finally passed the one mill tax over his veto. They did that today while I was in the senate chamber.

Swearingen is a good man. He has something of the bluster in him of the typical Southerner but he believes in education and at heart is in sympathy with every honest effort of the Negro to better himself.

He said at once that the Denmark School was the best Negro school in the state. He said that the school at Aiken — I do not recall the name — was conducted by a good and devoted woman, who was doing what she thought was right, but summed up the situation by saying that the institution was a "curse" to the state.

He spoke well of the Penn school, on St Helena, but evidently did not put it in the same class with the Denmark school. I saw the Penn school and made up my mind that it was about as near perfect as a *white woman* could make it.

They have the handsomest school building I ever saw — I refer to the new industrial building. They have a perfect little library and the classrooms and industries are evidently conducted in model style.

Where the school fails is in the fact that [it] is away beyond and above the people. They could never create or produce any thing like it and can not feel that it is theirs in any such sense as is true of Shanklin's[1] school at Beaufort.

I hav'nt time now to report on all the schools I have visited, they all have their good points and their bad. I want to make one unqualified statement however in regard to the schools I have seen and that is the people who are in charge of them, Mrs. Calhoun, Shanklin and Menafee,[2] are all right. They are doing just as well as they know how. They are doing, it seems me, all and more than all, that could be expected of them. Nothing I have yet seen has done more to convince me of the sound and wholesome character of the teaching of Tuskegee Institute than the work that these men and woman are doing. They are, each one of them, and an honor and credit to the school and I want to give them, irrespective of what I may have to say later, in regard the character of the work of the schools — I want to give them now my unqualified endorsement. They are doing their level best and where the schools they are conducting fail it [is] not due to anything for which they can be blamed.

I am dig[g]ing as deep into local conditions as I can. I hope to discover what are some of the sources of troubles in the schools I visit and to point out some radical remedies. I am learning a great deal and I hope to make my report a document of real value not merely to the schools I visit and to Tuskegee but Negro education in general.

I am mighty glad you gave me an opportunity to do this work. I am very truly,

Robert E. Park

ALS Con. 66 BTW Papers DLC.

1 Joseph Sherman Shanklin, who graduated from Tuskegee Institute in 1901, was principal of the Port Royal Agricultural School in South Carolina beginning in 1905.

2 Martin Asabee Menafee of Goldhill, Ala., graduated from Tuskegee Institute in 1900. He became treasurer of the Voorhees Normal and Industrial School, Denmark, S.C., and married its principal, Elizabeth E. Wright, of the Tuskegee class of 1894. On her death in 1906 he became principal.

To James Bertram

Fargo, N.D., March 2d, 1913

Dear Mr. Bertram: I have gone pretty fully with several of the officers of Lincoln University in Pennsylvania over the matter of their needs for a science hall, and I think I have already told you that I feel that such a building is greatly needed at Lincoln and will enable them to accomplish much more good. It is one of the old institutions, and has sent out some very fine and useful men.

My understanding is that they promise to raise $50,000 for endowment provided Mr. Carnegie will give them $50,000 for the building. If they meet this condition, I think Mr. Carnegie will be safe in making the gift.

I am just on my way to the Pacific Coast and will not be in New York again before about the 18th of April, when I shall see you and go into the matter further if necessary. Yours very truly,

[Booker T. Washington]

TLc   Con. 64   BTW Papers   DLC.

From James Carroll Napier

Washington   March 3, 1913

Dear Mr. Washington: I suppose you have seen long before this shall have reached you the account of the good fortune of Mr. Moore. His confirmation took place on Saturday and in reply to a telegram from him I advised that he come here to be sworn in this morning. He came on an early train. We went over at once to see after his matter and were told to return again this afternoon when he would be sworn in. This, of course, Mr. Moore will not object to because upon his being sworn in his salary will begin. He was informed, however, that instructions to go to Liberia would not be given him by this administration and that for such instructions he would have to look to the administration of Mr. Wilson. He seems deeply grateful to you for his appointment.

The City is brim full of people and if we have such weather tomorrow as we are having today it will certainly be a delightful occasion for the many visitors who are with us. I wish very much that I could have been with you in Nashville during your recent visit.

I am glad to see that you are saying such good things about Mr. Wilson, and trust that they may prove true. Very truly yours,

J. C. Napier

P.S. From what I gather here and there the Negro democrats will be as solicitous for your support under this administration as were the republicans under Mr. Taft. Many express themselves as believing you the all-powerful. I trust it may be true. Yours

J. C. N.

TLS Con. 483 BTW Papers DLC. Postscript in Napier's hand.

Ralph Waldo Tyler to Emmett Jay Scott

Washington, D.C. March 6, 1913

Friend Emmett: Negro Democrats have been in session here for two days, rangling, jangling, and roasting each other to a frazzle. The Bishop Walters and the Woods'[1] factions being pitted against each other. The sessions adjourned with a harmony agreement — each side watching for an opportunity to stab the other. Fred Moore has been here since Monday, returning to New York last night. He did a very untactful thing — in fact made a grave blunder. He attended the session yesterday, was called on, out of courtesy, a[nd] proceeded to roast the Woods' faction. He, so I am told, caused almost a riot, the Woods' crowd yelling, "sit down," "put him out," etc. He really had no business there in any capacity save as a newspaper man, and then should not have anything to say. At least he should not have antagonized either side. The result is the Woods' faction are declaring that he will not go to Liberia; that he won't get more than a month's salary, if that. In his speech he told them it was his policy, as editor of a Republican newspaper, to keep the two factions at war with each other.

The State Department advised him to proceed back to New York and await his commission and instructions; that the new administration would see to giving instructions.

In spite of Wilson's refusal to see office-seekers, there appears to be good reasons for believing that resignations will be called for in regular Democratic haste. The hopes of the Negro Democrats, however, were dropped to zero by Wilson's announcement. It really looks as though the brother will get very little, if little. All attended the Walters' banquet, save myself, and all now are congratulating me because I did not attend, and wishing they had not attended. It was a regular nigger Democratic assemblage. Lewis, Cobb, Judge and Napier were given seats among the isolated herd, and although it was announced as a non-partizan affair, the Bishop dwelt upon the fact that "we" might as well pack our trunks, for they wanted our places and proposed to have them. Roscoe Bruce was the only one of our crowd down to speak; he was assigned the toast "New Leaders," and proceeded to slop over. It has really been disgusting the way Bishop has groveled in the dirt with these strong-armed fakirs. Just thought you would like a bit of news, so have hastily dished the foregoing up. Sincerely,

Tyler

Taft signed Customs reorganization — consolidating Customs districts, and McKinlay goes out of office June 30 next in consequence, his office having been consolidated with Baltimore. That's one office lost to us.[2]

TLSr   Con. 466   BTW Papers   DLC.

[1] Robert N. Wood.

[2] Whitefield McKinlay, in a letter to BTW, lamented the fact that he had been put out of office by the action of a Republican president. (Mar. 12, 1913, Con. 65, BTW Papers, DLC.)

From William Henry Lewis

Washington, D.C. March 7, 1913

Dear Dr. Washington: The axe has fallen rather sooner than I expected. This morning I was sent for by the Attorney General, Mr. McReynolds,[1] whom I have known ever since I have been in the Federal service. He recognized me at once and expressed his pleasure at seeing me, and asked me for my resignation and said that while he had high appreciation of my ability etc., he would be regretfully compelled to accept it not later than April 1st. You can imagine the panic in which I was thrown. The family three thousand miles away and no means of getting them home or relocating myself in Boston, the initial expenses of beginning the practice of law there over again from the bottom being very high. I have written to Mr. James M. Beck,[2] one of the general counsel for the Standard Oil in New York, asking him if he could locate me in the offices of the law department of the company in New York, Boston or eslewhere. Of course the immediate necessity is that of securing something so as to enable me to support my family.

Knowing your many connections in New York, I wonder if through Mr. Rockefeller or Mr. Carnegie, you can assist me in any way. I realize that you have done a great deal for me and I have no manner of claim upon you in any way, but I know that you will be interested in helping to keep me from going the way of all the ex's. I have no notion of giving up the struggle if I can only get started again outside of the official line I think I shall let it alone. I am thoroughly cured of "the lure of office." I am not purposing to make any announcement of my resignation, so please treat the matter as confidential. I think I will let the Department make the announcement. Hastily yours,

William H. Lewis

TLS Con. 480 BTW Papers DLC.

[1] James Clark McReynolds (1862–1946), a Kentuckian, was U.S. Attorney General in 1913–14. In Aug. 1914 President Wilson appointed him associate justice of the U.S. Supreme Court. He served until 1941 and was one of the opponents of key New Deal legislation.

[2] Possibly James Montgomery Beck (1861–1936), a prominent lawyer in New York City in this period. In later years he was U.S. Solicitor General (1921–25), a congressman from Pennsylvania (1927–35), and a conservative publicist.

To the Editor of the New York *Age*

[Helena, Mont., ca. Mar. 7, 1913][1]

I have long cherished the idea that I might have the opportunity of visiting this part of the country. As frequently as the opportunity affords, I like to get into new territory where I can see new faces and new physical surroundings. Above all things, I like to meet and study all kinds of men. Here in the far Northwest I get a rich opportunity to do this. Not only is the opportunity rich in a chance to study men, but equally rich in an opportunity to see how the people are laying the foundation for life in a new territory.

It is hard for a person living in the East or South to appreciate what a tremendous territory the United States possesses in this part of the world. One county in Montana is as large as the whole State of Massachusetts.

The thing that most interests me is to study the character and activity of men and women who are taking up these immense tracts of land, but it will be years before all the land is occupied. There are twice as many colored people in the State of Alabama as the whole population of the State of Montana represents. One cannot be a "tenderfoot" and exist in this part of the world.

As I have ridden through the States of North Dakota and Montana my attention has been constantly attracted to the thousands of little huts along the railway. In many cases these huts are worse looking than the poorest log cabin in the South. In fact, these people do not wait, in many instances, to build a house of any kind, but tunnel into a hill and in that way make a place for their families to live in for a few months, until they can erect some semblance of a house, but the main thing is that they get hold of their land first. They settle on a few hundred acres which they get from the government or buy at a cheap rate, and in this way they make their start, suffering for many months all kinds of privations. I have heard of scores of people who 10 or 15 years ago began life in this way who to-day are prosperous, intelligent and independent farmers. In getting their start they have suffered more hardships by reason of the extreme cold and long distances than many colored families ever suffer in the South.

IRRIGATION NECESSARY

Often, too, after they get hold of their land, they are disappointed in rasing crops. Sometimes they have a crop failure every other year, but nevertheless they stick to their job. In nearly every portion of this part of the country the farmer does not depend upon rain, but upon irrigation. Irrigation is something strange to the colored man, and this makes me question whether colored people will ever settle in this part of the world in large numbers. The average Negro farmer likes for the water to come down from heaven, not from under him or from a hill, and then the average Negro farmer likes to lay off and take it easy during a shower of rain.

Everywhere that one goes, however, he is likely to meet a small group of colored people, and one becomes intensely interested in hearing their individual stories as to why they came into this country and what success they have met with. A few of them came here as long as thirty years ago when there were almost no railroads.

Perhaps most of my readers will recall that when Lewis and Clark came through this part of the country over a hundred years ago, colored men came with them, and a spot on the Northern Pacific Railroad is now marked which is said to be the grave of one of the colored men who was a cook for Lewis and Clark.

Of course the number of colored people in North Dakota and Montana is small, but they "bob up" everywhere. They have come into this country from practically every part of the United States, most of them from the South. Perhaps I may not have seen enough as yet to enable me to reach a definite decision. I still have an open mind, but I have seen enough to almost convince me that the lot of the colored man in this part of the world is not an easy one. It is very noticeable that some of our race lack something, and they seem to be in need of something which they do not find here, and that is racial solidarity, racial oneness. They lack that confidence, as a rule, in their ability to succeed and surmount obstacles which one finds all over the South. They talk more here about racial difficulties and racial discriminations than one hears in the South.

In spite of obstacles, however, at every point one finds a few members of our race who are succeeding either in the country as ranchmen or in the cities. There are a good many individuals who have accumulated considerable property.

Progressive Negroes Found

At nearly every point one finds a group of well-meaning, progressive colored people, and certainly I should be the last to criticise them harshly, for they have treated me with the utmost kindness. They have gone out of their way and put themselves to much expense to make my stay in this part of the world agreeable and instructive. In many cases they have worked side by side with the white committees that have made arrangements for the meetings where I am to speak, and I might add that I have been surprised at the tremendous audiences which have greeted me at every point.

But back to my race. Industrially and materially the Negro is not having an easy time, that is to say, he has not gotten on the ground floor of industrial activity except in a few scattered cases here and there where individuals have taken up land and have had tenacity and wisdom enough to hold on to the land. In the cities and small towns, with very rare exceptions, the Negro is a porter either in a bank, a store or barber shop, or perhaps runs an elevator in a store. He is the "odd job man," and the white people, it seems, do not expect him to occupy any other position. I ought to make one exception, and that is in the Pullman service and dining car service. Here the Negro holds his own, and in the Pullman cars and dining cars one finds him here, as all through the United States, polite, kind and attentive, going out of the way especially to serve one of his own. The white man has not been able yet to break into the Pullman car and dining car service.

Trade Unions Bar Negroes

It is just about as difficult here for a Negro to get regular work as a carpenter, brickmason, plumber or machinist as it is for a Negro in the South to get a county or State office. The trades unions seem to have made up their minds to keep the Negro out. The result is that he is continually pushed to the outer edges of the industrial world, and this fact naturally hurts him in the estimation of the white man who grows into the habit of associating all black faces with odd jobs of a menial character.

Regardless, however, of the character of the work that the individual is engaged in, almost without exception I find that our people receive a high wage. In some cities they are permitted to be hod carriers, and in that case they receive from $5 to $6 a day. For common labor and hotel labor the price received by them is much higher than in the East or South.

Another illustration will emphasize one of the Negro's difficulties. There are not enough members of his race in the towns and cities to support a first-class eating place. The white man, in one way or another, lets him know that members of his race are not welcome in white restaurants. Consequently, the black man is placed in a trying position, not being able to support restaurants of his own and not being welcome in the white man's restaurant.

So far, I have found practically no colored man engaged in business of a character that is common for our people in the South. Two things are against them in the matter of conducting commercial enterprises. First, large capital is required to begin business. Secondly, there are not enough colored people in any one community to support any large business, and the white man here has not accustomed himself to trade with the Negro. The result is that he is practically out of the commercial world. It would be hard here for colored people to realize that in a city like Montgomery, Ala., colored merchants have large dry goods stores, do business as bankers, and occupy brick business houses two and three stories high, and that they trade with both white and colored people. If the number of colored people increases, things may grow better industrially, but that is problematical.

A good many of our people, however, I am glad to say, are far-sighted enough to see that now is the time for those who mean to live in this country to accumulate something that may be handed down to their children.

VERY LITTLE DISCRIMINATION IN SCHOOLS OF NORTH DAKOTA

In North Dakota and Montana I have seen no evidence of discrimination between the races in public schools or in the higher institutions of learning. At nearly every point one learns of a few cases where either women or men have graduated at a high school or at some of the State institutions, but when one inquires what has become of these individuals who have gone through the high schools or State universities or normal schools, he is almost invariably told that the individual is either a waiter, a porter or on the Pullman cars.

The number of colored children who finish the public school and get their diploma from the high school is comparatively small. The colored children do reasonably well and are treated well in the lower grades, but when they reach the high school they find themselves rather tolerated than actually wanted; and then in many cases I find because they cannot dress as well as the white boys and girls in their classes in high school they are inclined to become discouraged and drop out before finishing the high school. In a word, the Negro children have the same opportunity to get education here that the white children have, but the difficulties begin to present themselves when the Negro seeks an opportunity to use the education which the State has given him. The result is that one often finds individuals with good book education who are engaged in the same kind of tasks that the most ordinary people follow.

From a moral point of view, in proportion to their numbers, I am led to believe that the colored people conduct themselves as well or better than is true of the same type of white people. In a country where the opportunity to degrade oneself through drink and other vicious habits is constantly about him, it is surprising to note that such few colored people yield to the temptation of drink and other vicious habits. From this point of view the white people speak well of them.

MINISTERS A HARD-WORKING SET

Wherever one finds a group of fifty or one hundred colored people in any community, there he is likely to find one to three churches, and I am glad to testify to the fact that the ministers who have come under my observation are an earnest, worthy and hard-working set, who under many difficulties and in the face of many discouragements are laboring hard to better conditions among the colored people through the medium of the church. The African Methodist Episcopal Church seems to be the leader in this respect. The most intelligent ministers and the best church buildings that I have so far seen are of this denomination, but the minister has a hard road to travel. The number of people of his race in the town is small, the church membership is small, often he can't get any large proportion of the people into his congregation, and the result is that he has to struggle from year to year on a very meagre salary, and the wonder is that they sustain themselves as well as they do. A few days ago I asked a minister who has a small congregation, not more than twenty members, in Montana, how he got his salary, how he supported his family, and it was pathetic to hear him describe the struggle that he had to go through in order to live. Bishop Parks of the A.M.E. Church, is doing fine work in these States under many disadvantages and discouragements.

From a social point of view the colored man feels lonesome. Those who have come from the South long for the large church gatherings, the camp meetings, the numerous large gatherings to which they had been accustomed. Some of them go to the white churches, but they do not feel exactly at home there. There is lacking the opportunity for them to get that strength and encouragement which can only come by close association with large numbers of their own race.

The discrimination in hotels, eating places and places of amusement in the larger cities of Montana is rather marked. I am told that most of the saloons have a sign up stating that colored patronage is not wanted.

The white man that one finds in Montana presents a curious subject for study. He is not an Eastern man, not a Southern man, but a kind of cross between the two. A large part of the white population, it seems, originally came from the State of Missouri.

The Negro here votes freely; that seems to be about the only thing he can do unhindered and untrammeled, but in some way the ballot does not seem to be able to cure the difficulties to which I have made reference.

As I write this letter I still have an open mind, and I may be led before I am through with this trip to change the opinion which I have rather hastily so far formed. One thing is sure, and that is the Negro everywhere is proud of his race and is determined to succeed if success be possible.

New York *Age,* Mar. 20, 1913, 1–2.

[1] BTW's next letter to the New York *Age* referred to this letter as sent from Helena. According to his itinerary, he was at Helena on Mar. 7. (F. A. Golder to BTW, Feb. 15, 1913, Con. 837, BTW Papers, DLC.)

To the Editor of the New York *Age*

North Yakima, Wash., March 14 [1913][1]

In my letter from Helena I discussed conditions as I had found them up to that point. I think it well for me to add this additional word as to what I found in Butte and Helena. In both of these cities one will meet some individuals who are as wide-awake and progressive as can be found anywhere in the country. In Helena especially one finds evidences of intelligence and culture among the colored people that is surprising. Their occupations, however, in most cases do not, as I have said, compare with their intelligence, but the leaders have on foot a plan to organize the people in each community throughout the State in a way that will call their attention to the business opportunities that are before the race. In both Butte and Helena, as well as at one or two other points, they have already organized Negro business leagues and are planning to have the State of Montana represented at the National League meeting to be held in Philadelphia, August 20, 21 and 22, 1913.

As one travels still further in the direction of the Pacific Coast, conditions among our people change, sometimes for the better, sometimes for the worse, but on the whole for the better. I spent three pretty busy days in Spokane and spoke nine times to various kinds of audiences. One piece of information which was given me by both white and colored people, especially by whites in Spokane, interested me very much, and that was that the 25th Infantry, a Negro regiment of the United States Army, made a better record when in camp at Fort Wright near Spokane than any soldiers that have ever camped there. One of the members of the Chamber of Commerce told me that the citizens of Spokane were practically unanimous in their regret that the colored soldiers were replaced by white ones. The members of the 25th Infantry made an exceptional record for fine and orderly conduct. It was very noticeable in Spokane that the reputation which these soldiers made had gone a long ways toward giving the white people a higher regard for the colored people in that vicinity.

WHITE CLUB WOMEN RECOGNIZE WOMEN

There was another occurrence at Spokane which interested me, and that was to find that when the Federation of Women's Clubs of that city tendered me a reception at which I spoke to them, that the colored club was invited, and I was told that it is a usual thing for the colored club to be recognized in this way.

As one goes further West he meets an increasing number of persons of our race who have taken up homesteads, or who are buying land and are succeeding in cultivating the soil. These almost without exception are doing well. One finds in a city like Spokane a few colored people who are succeeding in the professions and in business, and these men are well thought of. The principal drawback, however, to the people in the city grows out of the fact that they are barred, as I stated in my former communication, from the trades. As yet I have found no place where the trades unions give the colored man any chance at the trades. It seems to be pretty well understood in this part of the world that a colored laborer must be either a porter, a messenger, or something of that kind. About forty miles from North Yakima there is a colony of colored people who have bought land and who are doing well as farmers. One colored lady told me that she raised last year over a hundred turkeys on her ranch. Notwithstanding these farmers are succeeding from an economic point of view, I can easily discover in talking to them that they miss the churches and lodges which they were accustomed to attending in the sections where they lived before coming out here.

MANY THRIFTY SUCCESSFUL NEGROES AT SEATTLE

As I have stated, as one goes farther West in the direction of Seattle and Takoma it is noticeable that conditions as far as the Negro is concerned seem to grow better. Seattle evidently has the largest colored population of any city in either Washington or Oregon, and among them are some mighty thrifty, ambitious and successful individuals. While in Washington one meets with large numbers of white people from every Southern State; as a rule they are of a pretty high type, and many of these Southern white people are among the best and most useful friends the Negro has, but there is a disposition at every point that I have so far touched to keep the Negro out of the skilled labor trades. He can practice law or medicine or preach, but finds little opportunity to teach school or work at a trade. In many of the hotels where I have stopped it has been interesting to note that Japanese, white people and black people are employed as servants. In most of the large hotels, however, the Japanese seem to control the work, and they are mighty good hotel workers. The Negro waiter and porter in the hotel has to compete with the Japanese and it is a pretty hard job. The Japanese are steady, reliable, sober, and are always on the job.

I have visited and spoken to the faculty and students in practically all of the colleges, State universities and agricultural colleges in the States that I have traversed, and it is very noticeable that these institutions have gone further in technical and industrial education — in a word, in applying education to the needs and conditions of the people — than is true of the same type of institutions in the Eastern States. It is also noticeable that the general average of intelligence of any audience that one addresses in States like Idaho and Washington is much higher than in the old Eastern States. I have never been among a people anywhere in the world who read so much as is true of these Western people, and they read the higher grade of publications.

READ BEST PAPERS AND MAGAZINES

In proportion to the population the standard monthly magazines and high-type weekly publications have a larger circulation, I think, in the West than in the East. It is not only true that the white people are great readers, but the same is equally true of the colored people. They know what is going on in the world, and anyone who comes into this part of the United States expecting to find ignorance will soon be undeceived.

It is interesting, too, to note how, in cities like Spokane, Seattle and Tacoma, all the leading business men in the white race work together practically as one man. I have never been anywhere in the world where the Chamber of Commerce is such a center of activity and life as it is in these cities. I have never spoken to a set of business men who showed such a high degree of intelligence and enthusiasm as I have seen in the Boards of Trade and Chambers of Commerce that I have addressed.

I am glad to add that in most of the cities where there is any considerable number of colored people they also have a Negro Business League or some such organization, and are beginning to organize themselves in business and commercial directions. In several of the large cities our people have good church organizations and good church buildings. The ministers as a rule, while they have many difficulties to contend with, are of a high type, unselfish, intelligent. Tacoma,

Wash., where there is a large group of colored people, seems to harbor less prejudice than any city that I have been in. In Tacoma there seems to be practically no racial discrimination, and one finds here, as I have stated, a fine aggressive class of colored men and women. At every point that I have touched I have simply been overwhelmed with kindnesses and attentions shown me by members of my own race.

New York *Age,* Apr. 3, 1913, 1–2.

¹ The dateline in the New York *Age* is Mar. 24, but an earlier draft of the letter in Con. 607, BTW Papers, DLC, is dated Mar. 14. BTW's itinerary places him in North Yakima on Mar. 14. (F. A. Golder to BTW, Feb. 15, 1913, Con. 837, BTW Papers, DLC.)

To Oswald Garrison Villard

Portland, Oregon, March 21, 1913

My dear Mr. Villard: I have seen your letter addressed to Mr. Scott.¹ I regret the delay in answering it, but I have been kept so busy out here that I have not had time to keep closely up with my correspondence.

As I wrote you sometime ago, I fear it would be impossible for me to attend the conference on the 17th of April for the reason that I have already been kept away from the school more than I ought to be for this year, but if you could see your way clear to have the meeting held at some place other than the headquarters of the Association for the Advancement of Colored People I should be very glad to make an effort to have Tuskegee represented even if I could not be present myself. I think it would be a mistake to confuse the work which that organization is doing with education in the South. I do not think it would help matters, and in fact I feel rather sure it would hinder matters, and it would be impossible for a meeting of the character you name to be held at the headquarters of the Association without such a meeting being associated with the work of the Association. I am not undervaluing the work of the Association, but we must face conditions as they actually are in the South.

As I understand it, the Association has not the matter of education especially in mind, and I think it is better to keep the two lines of work wholly separate. Could the meeting not be held just as well at the rooms of the General Education Board, or somewhere else, for example.

Dr. Buttrick, Mr. Low and Dr. Frissell, as you know, have great influence among the Southern white people, and their influence is growing. Without having communicated with either of them on this subject, I do not hesitate to say that if it became known through the South that they were actively connected with the Association it would hurt their influence and the students they represent.

Of course you will naturally conclude, I fear, I have taken a pretty narrow view of the whole matter and am too fearful, but I am basing my statements upon actual observations and experience in the South.

I am taking the liberty of sending Major Moton and Mr. Low a copy of this letter. Yours very truly,

[Booker T. Washington]

TLc Con. 63 BTW Papers DLC. A typed copy in the Oswald Garrison Villard Papers, MH, contains some minor differences in wording.

[1] O. G. Villard to E. J. Scott, Mar. 8, 1913, Con. 164, BTW Papers, DLC. See also n. 2 of BTW to O. G. Villard, Feb. 27, 1913, above.

To Emmett Jay Scott

Portland, Oregon. March 21st, 1913

Dear Mr. Scott: Enclosed I send you a copy of my letter to Mr. Villard, also copy of one to Major Moton and Mr. Low. I think if he accepts the suggestion as to change of place I shall ask you to represent Tuskegee.

You will see that my letter cuts all of the foundation out from under the thing. Their single object was to give the public to understand through the Crisis that they are taking charge of education and had drawn Dr. Frissell and myself into their movement. If Villard consents to change the place of meeting, I see no harm that can be done, though I confess I do not have much faith in the efficacy of any organization that can be brought about in this way. My impression is that unless the meeting is held at the headquarters of the organization he will lose interest in it. I do not of course know what attitude the Hampton people will take. Yours very truly,

B. T. W.

TLI Con. 18 BTW Papers DLC.

To Robert Russa Moton

Portland, Oregon, March 21, 1913

My dear Major Moton: The enclosed copy of a letter which I have just written to Mr. Villard explains itself. If you care to, I wish you would show it to Dr. Frissell. Of course you and he may not agree with me in this matter. I am placed in rather an awkward position because these people are hiding the real purpose of their movement and everything else that they do from our friends. The conversation that Milholland and Du Bois had with Dr. Shepard[1] represents the real purpose of those two men. It is just as well to not overlook this fact or not be deceived. Of course I want to do everything I can to consistently further education.

I have seen one or two references in newspapers to the effect that Dr. Frissell is not well. I have had no way to confirm these reports. I am hoping that what I have seen is exaggerated or not true. I wish you would let me know his real condition.

I am having a great time out here. The meetings are simply tremendous. A lot of enthusiasm, but so far not much money. Yours very truly,

[Booker T. Washington]

TLc   Con. 18   BTW Papers   DLC.

[1] Probably James E. Shepard.

To William Henry Lewis

Portland, Oregon. March 21st, 1913

Personal

My dear Mr. Lewis: I know you will forgive me for my seeming tardiness in answering yours of March 7th. You will see that I am out here on the Pacific Coast where I have been for two weeks.

I am as much astounded as you by the sudden and unreasonable action taken by the Attorney General. When I came through Nashville I gave out a little interview regarding the new President which I hoped might have the effect of encouraging him to stand by the colored

people in action as well as in words.[1] It is really a shame and an outrage that you should be treated in this way.

As soon as I return east I shall do my best to serve you in the direction that you suggest. I have the feeling that your best chance is through
Senator Crane. He has large financial interests and many avenues of
serving you. If nothing else better presents itself, I have the feeling that
it might be well for you to consider associating yourself with Wilford
H. Smith in New York. I have known Smith for a number of years,
and he is really a fine, high-toned man.

I hope you will feel at liberty to call on me whenever you think I can
be of the slightest service.

I am really having a great trip in this part of the world.

I fear the President's high-sounding phrases regarding justice do not
include the Negro. Yours very truly,

[Booker T. Washington]

TLc Con. 480 BTW Papers DLC.

[1] Without quoting BTW directly, the Nashville *Banner* reported him as predicting "that the negro race would not suffer by the change in the National
Government." The newspaper report added: "He stated that in his belief the next
President of the United States is one of the best friends of negro education who
has occupied the presidential chair, and that he will favor at all times all things
that will prove beneficial to the people of his race. He said that he had known
President-elect Wilson for many years, and that he had great confidence in his
willingness to hear any just cause that might be presented in behalf of the negro.
Being Southern born, he had the knowledge of conditions in the South that would
give him a thorough understanding of things that would tend to their advancement
in the true sense." (Nashville *Banner,* Mar. 1, 1913, 2.)

Ralph Waldo Tyler to Emmett Jay Scott

Washington, D.C. March 25/13

Dear Emmett: As per the Doctor's request to advise him at once when
my services with the government would be severed, I am advising you
that my resignation was called for today to take effect upon appointment and qualification of my successor.

In this position I will be "the last of the Mohicans." Have not seen
Napier, but presume he received the same request. The policy of this
administration is to eliminate the Negro, from office. Sincerely

Tyler

ALS Con. 488 BTW Papers DLC.

From William Henry Lewis

Washington, D.C. March 27, 1913

Dear Dr. Washington: I thank you for your letter from Portland, Oregon. I am glad that you are having such a delightful trip in that part of the world. I saw your little interview in the Nashville papers. The "Washington Post" commenting upon your interview, said that "now it appears that Booker Washington is a life long democrat."

The President's inaugural, so far as justice is concerned was pitched rather high and I am eager to see how it works out. Pressure for office is pretty strong here. Ralph has just informed me that his resignation was asked for yesterday. I am not sure about the wisdom of going to New York. In the first place, Mr. Smith has not asked me to become a member of his firm. I will say this that I have the same high appreciation of him as a man and his ability as a lawyer which you yourself entertain for him and it would be an honor to be associated with him. If I were without a family I would not mind breaking up and going to New York but two things influence me in determining to remain in Boston. The first is my wife and children want to live in Cambridge, and you will agree that Boston and Cambridge would be a better place for them than New York. Secondly, I have a larger acquaintance in Boston and Massachusetts than I could possibly get in New York in many years. I do not know how much business it will bring me, but the acquaintance and popularity there of course are an asset of the highest value. Although I am not troubling myself about politics for the time being, my political future would be better there than in New York. Of course there is not the same money to be made in Boston as there is to be made in New York. If I were invited to join an established firm in New York with a large practice I should not hesitate to sever my connection with Boston and Massachusetts, but going there practically as a new man, although not exactly a stranger, to build up a practice substantially alone is a large task as you must admit, still I should be very glad to have your opinion about it. What I most need at the present time is money. It will take a couple of thousand dollars to open up suitable offices and enable me to keep going until funds begin to come in. I am working away hoping and praying. Believe me Sincerely yours,

William H. Lewis

TLS Con. 927 BTW Papers DLC.

To the Editor of the New York *Age*

[Salt Lake City, Utah, ca. Mar. 28, 1913][1]

For a long while I have been anxious to get right into the midst of the Mormons to see what kind of people they are, what they look like, what they are doing, and in what respect they are succeeding. I have been spending two of the busiest days that I have ever spent in my life in the very midst of these people. They have been mighty interesting days, and I have seen some mighty interesting people. The leaders of the Mormon church from President Smith down have gone out of their way to show me kindnesses and to make my trip here successful.

I am not going to discuss the Mormon religion as I am not a theologian; I shall have to leave that to others. I am always interested in studying and observing people regardless of their religion. One of the Mormon bishops called to see me and from him I got some mighty interesting information that ought to prove of value to our race.

In speaking of the Mormons, my readers must remember that it was only sixty-six years ago that, led by Brigham Young, 150 people came into this country when it was a wilderness. They traveled in ox carts over a thousand miles from the Missouri River. The Mormon church itself was organized in New York State only eighty-four years ago. From 150 people, hardy pioneers who entered Utah sixty-six years ago, the number has grown year by year until in Utah there are now over three hundred thousand Mormons, and they have certainly made the desert blossom as a rose. I have never been among a more intelligent, healthy, clean, progressive, moral set of people than these people are. All through Utah they have turned the desert into gardens and orchards. Wherever one finds a Mormon colony there he finds evidence of hard work and wealth.

Interesting Talks with Mormon Leaders

The Mormon leaders here told me in detail about the policy that they pursued when they first came here, and here is a great lesson for our people in the South and throughout this country. From the first the Mormons consistently and persistently pursued the policy of having their people get hold of land, to settle on the soil and become farmers. They knew that if they once got possession of the soil and taught their people how to become successful farmers that they would be laying the foundation so secure that they could not be disturbed. Several of the leaders told me that when they first came into this country that there was great temptation to exploit the gold, silver and copper mines, but they would not let their people do this, but held them to the soil. It is only within the last few years that the Mormons have begun to get wealth out of the mineral resources of the country, notwithstanding they have known all along that this wealth existed. Now that they are in possession of the soil and have taught their people how to become successful farmers they say they can afford to go into mining.

There are two parallels between the Negro and the Mormons. First, as my readers already know, the Mormons were most inhumanly persecuted almost from the first organization of their church. This was especially true in Missouri and Illinois. Hundreds of their followers were put to death. The courts gave them little protection. The mob that either killed or wounded the Mormons was seldom, if ever, punished. They were an easy mark for any inhuman brute who wanted to either kill or wound them. Joseph Smith himself, the founder of the church, was murdered in Illinois. But out of this inhuman and unjust treatment grew the strength of these people. The more they were punished the more determined they became to succeed. Without opposition and injustice, I question whether the Mormon church could now be in its present flourishing condition. They were deprived of their property as well as their lives in their early years, but the more they were persecuted the closer they banded themselves together and the more determined they were to succeed. Persecutions advertised this little sect to the world. The result was that through persecution their numbers increased instead of being diminished.

THE PROPER WAY TO STUDY GROUPS OF PEOPLE

The second parallel between the Mormon and the Negro is this. These people, I am sure, have been misrepresented before the world. I have learned by experience and observation that it is never safe to pass final judgment upon a people until one has had an opportunity to get into the real life of these people. The Negro is suffering to-day just as the Mormons are suffering and have suffered, because people from the outside have advertised the worst in connection with Mormon life and they have seldom called attention to the best in connection with the life of the Mormons. And then I have learned, too, that no person outside a race or outside a group of people can ever really know that race or that group of people until he gets into their homes and has a chance to observe their men and women and their children, has a chance to partake of their hospitality and get into their inner life. There are many people to-day who consider themselves wise on the condition of the Negro, who are really afraid to go into a Negro home, who never go into a Negro church or Sunday School, who have never met the colored people in any social circle; hence such people know little about the moral standards and activities of the colored people. The same, I am convinced, is true regarding the Mormons. The people who speak in the most disrespectful terms of these people are the ones who know least about them.

I am convinced that the Mormons are not an immoral people. No immoral people could have such strong, fine bodies as these people, nor such vigorous and alert minds as they. It has been my privilege to address schools and universities in nearly every part of America, and I say without hesitation that I have never addressed a college anywhere where the students were more alert, more responsive, more intelligent than is true of the students in these Mormon colleges. I was hardly prepared for the over-generous and rapturous reception that was given me at the State University, the students of which for the most part are Mormons, and I had the same experience in addressing the private schools and other institutions conducted by Mormons.

MEETS A DAUGHTER OF JOSEPH SMITH

I met, for example, one of the daughters of Joseph H. Smith, the successor to Brigham Young and now the head of the church. I was told that she was one of forty-nine children, but she was an intelligent, modest, fine young woman with a strong body and an alert mind. I was told that the other forty-eight children were just as healthy and strong and alert as she. Just how many wives President Joseph H. Smith has or had I do not know. I am not going into the subject of plural wives, but I am simply stating facts and giving my impressions.

These Mormons have first class schools of every character, and they are pushing the matter of technical and industrial education to a stronger degree than we are in the South among the colored people. In fact, time and time again I was told that they learned their methods for the most part from Hampton, Tuskegee and similar institutions. I was nearly taken off my feet when I went into a class in the university and the teacher showed me a large piece of pasteboard, with the pictures of our students at Tuskegee at work in the various industrial departments. They said they were taking this as their model.

The Mormons have recently begun a systematic effort to give their young people training in gymnastics with a view of strengthening their bodies. Here again the colored people, especially in the schools of the South, can learn a great lesson. Everywhere in our colored schools we ought to have systematic and constant training in gymnastics.

There are about a thousand colored people in Salt Lake City, and they are above the average in intelligence and in other respects. The colored women especially strike me as exceptionally intelligent, more so, I think, than the men. They have here an Art and Music Club which I had the privilege of addressing, composed of very intelligent women. They have two good churches with very intelligent ministers. The main weakness in the life of the colored people in this city, as in some others I have gone to, grows out of the fact that instead of having a commercial organization to promote business and industrial interests of the colored people they have a club house for which I am told they pay a rental of $150 a month, where the men are encouraged to drink and gamble. It seems that they cannot throw away their money fast enough, but in order to help it along they rent a house for $150 a month for the purpose of helping them to dispose with their money faster. I have spoken to them plainly about this mistake, and I believe that a change for the better will take place. I met several colored men who have accumulated a respectable fortune and who are in good business enterprises.

I think it will interest my readers to know that there are colored Mormons in Utah. I met several of these. Many of them came here in the old days, in fact Brigham Young brought colored people with him to this country, and they or their descendants have remained. Of course in the old days plural wives were not prohibited by law, but I have made careful inquiry and could find no case where a colored man ever had more than one wife. It seems to have been the custom in the old days that a man could not take a second or third or fourth wife without the consent of his first wife, and I was told that no colored woman in Utah would ever give her consent for her husband to take a second wife.

I met one colored man who came out here in the early days who is now 82 years of age. He is a staunch Mormon, and neither the Baptist church nor the Methodist church can get hold of him. He came here from Mississippi. He is a fine looking old fellow, a kind of colored Brigham Young. He has a farm worth $25,000, and lives in the midst of a Mormon colored colony of which he is the leader. I am told that the Mormon church treats the colored people well. I will, in my next letter, discuss the Mormons further, and call attention to their creed, and so forth.[2]

New York *Age,* Apr. 17, 1913, 1, 2.

[1] The *Star of Zion,* Apr. 17, 1913, carried the same article with the dateline: "Salt Lake City, March 28."

[2] In another letter on his western trip, BTW included the Mormon creed, which he had received from Bishop John M. Whittaker. BTW stated that while he was not a Mormon and had "no immediate intention of becoming one," he did find much in the creed that appealed to him. He went on to say that he found no evidence that polygamy was being practiced. Aside from the matter of religion, BTW was impressed with the Mormon control of land, mines, banking, and all aspects of business. "They say," he wrote, "and I think wisely, that economic progress must go hand in hand with religious progress." (New York *Age,* Apr. 24, 1913, 2. A typed copy of the letter, dated Mar. 27, 1913, is in Con. 835, BTW Papers, DLC.)

From James Carroll Napier

Washington   April 1, 1913

My dear Mr. Washington: Enclosed I am handing you a card of invitation to three lectures delivered by Mr. Du Bois at Howard University. I heard the two delivered at night and regret that I did not hear the midday one.

Each was of one hour's duration and was an interesting account, or rather recount, of prehistoric governments in Africa. He recited events, changes in governments and rulers with an alacrity which showed that he had devoted much time to committing his lecture to memory. He pronounced the names of the old emperors, kings and princes of Africa with a precision and an apparent familiarity that would lead one to think that he had lived among them himself. He had a good audience at each meeting. There was a fine occasion for him to impress some fact, some practical idea upon the minds of a large number of intelligent, ambitious and progressive young people. He seemed not to have discovered this opportunity and during his three hours failed utterly to offer a single word of advice or counsel touching the practical side of the life which these young people will soon have to face. His paramount aim seemed to be to show that he had profound learning and had made deep research. No thought of the influence he might exert in shaping the lives or activities of his hearers seems ever to have entered his mind. He simply showed *"learning."*

After it was over and Mrs. Napier and I came to compare notes we agreed that there was little or no benefit to be derived from these lectures; and that one of your speeches of an hour's length would result in greater benefit to the race and to all who might hear it than a whole month of such recitals would bring.[1]

Hoping that you have had both a profitable and pleasant trip to the West and that you have returned home in safety, I remain, Very truly yours,

J. C. Napier

TLS Con. 483 BTW Papers DLC.

[1] In regard to Du Bois's lectures, BTW replied: "I am not at all surprised to note what you write, because it is exactly in line with what I have heard from other sources in the general content of his lectures on 'The History of the Negro Race.'" BTW thanked Napier for "what you and Mrs. Napier write with reference to myself." (Apr. 4, 1913, Con. 483, BTW Papers, DLC.)

To the Editor of the New York *Age*

Portland, Ore., April 2 [1913]

The white people who amount to most in the States of Washington and Oregon are for the most part those who have gone from the New England States, the Middle States or the far South. I have been constantly surprised since entering Washington and Oregon at the number of Southern white people I have met. One of the finest and most liberal white men I have met since I left home was born in Mississippi and lived there until a few years ago. He moved into Oregon not long ago from the vicinity of Jefferson Davis's old home in

Mississippi. If there is the slightest trace of race prejudice about him I have not been able to discover it. A good many of the meetings at which I have spoken have been presided over by Southern white men.

Most of these people seem to have left the South because they felt that they were cramped and hampered there in too many ways in bringing up their families. The gentleman I have referred to from Mississippi told me frankly that he got tired and sick of the influence of such men as Vardaman and others of that kind.

Another thing that has surprised and pleased me has been the liberality of the colored people. At almost every point I have visited, without suggestion or urging they have contributed toward the work of Tuskegee Institute gladly. I was at a little dinner party given me by some colored citizens in Portland. Without any previous preparation some one suggested that a scholarship be provided for Tuskegee, and within a few minutes they raised $75.

MORE NEGROES IN ALABAMA THAN ENTIRE POPULATION OF OREGON

One does not get an idea of the strength and size of the Negro population in the South until he gets out of the South. Here in Oregon, for example, there are only about 750,000 people all told. In the single state of Alabama we have more black people by several hundred thousand than there are people altogether in Oregon. Here in Portland as in other large cities of the coast, there are quite a few colored people who are doing well in the professions, in business and in farming. Among the professional class I have met a Tuskegee graduate who has a good reputation, stands high in his profession and is succeeding. I refer to Mr. McCants Stewart,[1] who has been practicing law successfully in Portland for a good many years. He has a nice family and stands high in the profession and is looked up to in every way as a model citizen.

For one reason or another the colored people in Washington and Oregon do not seem to take advantage of the opportunities offered by the institutions of higher learning. They are reasonably well represented in the public schools but one rarely hears of a case where colored persons enter any of the classical colleges, agricultural and mechanical colleges or State universities. After careful inquiry I could discover only nine colored people who have ever graduated from any of the high schools in the State of Oregon. None it seems has ever graduated from any of the colleges of the State of Washington. Here as elsewhere there is a good deal of talk about "higher education" but it does not seem to go much further than talk. It certainly is a mistake for our people not to enter those higher institutions of learning when they can do so with so little cost. Speaking further of education in the West, in Utah I could discover only three colored persons who have ever graduated from the high school, and not a single one from any of the colleges or universities.

In Portland the colored people have a better chance at skilled labor trades than any other point I have touched. Here the labor union is not strong and the policy of the Chamber of Commerce and other organizations is not to recognize the unions.

The colored people who have been far-sighted enough to buy land years ago are almost without exception prosperous, I mean those who are engaged in some form of farming.

TELLS EDUCATOR SHE IS LONESOME

In one of my previous letters I referred to the fact that the colored people out this way seem to be somewhat "lonesome," I mean those who have come from the South. The following letter from a colored girl who is now living in Southern Oregon will illustrate this point:

Roseburg, Oregon, March 23, 1913

Mr. B. T. Washington:

Dear Sir: For fear I would not be able to see you in Roseburg, I am writing you again in the hope of getting you by mail if I fail to see you. I know it is an awful strain on you this being your first visit this way to stop over here, so I will just write as plainly as I can and explain to you what we want. I am all alone out here and it is so lonesome for me, still I can go to any church or theatre in town. I don't feel like I would if I could only get some colored people to be with. Oh, Mr. Washington I just hunger to see some more of our race out here. I get good pay considering this is such a small town; I get $25 per month and I am made welcome to anything in the house, besides Mrs. Hamilton is so nice to me; she takes me to the show quite often. But if I had some of my own folks to be with I would be happy. Judge Hamilton was in Corvallis but he arrived too late to hear you speak Wednesday. Mrs. Hamilton thinks just like I do, if we could only get about four or five girls or families here they could do so well. There have been several but they have all been the very lowest class; have gotten into trouble. Some left town and some went to jail. So you see how it has been all the while.

Respectfully, etc. etc.

White people who have formerly lived in the South seem just as glad to see colored people from the South as the members of my own race.

One will be deceived if he attempts to judge the intelligence of a man out here by his appearance. Frequently one may meet a man with his pants stuffed in his boot legs, without any collar, with his sleeves rolled up, having all the appearance of an ordinary working man, but when you ask him some questions you must not be surprised to find that while he works in a field, usually an orchard which he owns, or is in some other line of farming, he may be a graduate of Harvard, Yale, Amherst, Dartmouth, or some of the leading eastern colleges. In this part of the world family connection counts for little. Every man is valued and respected for what he really can do in the community in which he lives.

Should Not Imitate Whites

It is unfortunately true that the majority of colored people in the far western states have the kind of employment which brings them into touch with the white man at the white man's weakest point, and this means that they try to imitate the white man at these points instead of at his stronger points. The white man in this part of the country has a great many social clubs. The Negro is usually the waiter or steward in these clubs. After the white man is through with his hard day's work in his factory, his bank, his office or on his farm, he goes to these clubs for any easy hour or two. In these clubs the white man sips his beer, drinks his wine, and smokes his cigar. The Negro comes into contact with him at these points and it is very natural that the Negro should try to lead the same kind of life that he sees the white man leading. This is unfortunate. It is unfortunate that so large a proportion of our people are engaged in waiting upon somebody else instead of producing something out of the natural resources of the land.

The Negro in the South who owns 50 or 100 acres of land, has it paid for, and a little money in the bank and is educating his children, even though he may be dressed in an unfashionable manner is far more independent than a man who dresses in a flashy way and is employed in waiting on somebody else. I have found that some of the most prosperous individuals among our race are saloon keepers or men who run "clubs" for the flashy element among our people.

While I have come into contact with much that is encouraging in connection with the comparatively few colored people on the Pacific Coast, I am more convinced than ever that the Negro in the South is doing better than any group of colored people that I have found in this part of the world, and I am still further convinced that the Negro in the South has a better future than in any part of the world that I have yet visited.

New York *Age,* Apr. 10, 1913, 2.

[1] Thomas McCants Stewart, Jr.

Robert Russa Moton to Emmett Jay Scott

Hampton, Virginia   April 3, 1913

My dear Mr. Scott: The enclosed letter from Mr. Villard[1] is interesting. All the same I think Dr. Washington was wise in suggesting a change of place for the meeting.[2] In view of Du Bois' sayings and attitude I should certainly doubt the wisdom of Dr. Washington meeting in his office, but as he very well put it in his letter, though he did not mention Du Bois (wisely) that the meeting should be on common ground and disassociated from the National Association. Sincerely yours,

R. R. Moton

Dr Washington's letter *showed courage* and a great deal of it too.

R R M

TLS Con. 70 BTW Papers DLC. Postscript in Moton's hand.

[1] Villard wrote Moton and encouraged him to attend the meeting, stating that "Dr. Washington has declined for the cowardly reason that the meeting is being held in the rooms of the National Association. To meet that objection we have hired a gymnasium outside of our quarters. . . ." (Mar. 31, 1913, copy in Con. 70, BTW Papers, DLC.)
[2] See BTW to O. G. Villard, Mar. 21, 1913, above.

From Oswald Garrison Villard

New York   April 4, 1913

Dear Mr. Washington: I have your letter from Portland, Oregon of March 21st, of which you have sent a copy to Major Moton and Mr. Low. I am also sending a copy of this letter to them.

In the first place, you are under a complete misapprehension. From the first conference at which this organization[1] was formed, it took for its field the education of the colored race. We have, therefore, had the matter of education specifically in mind ever since we began, and have quietly been working on one or two phases of it. We are, therefore, only steering our proper course in doing what should have been done by Tuskegee or Hampton years ago in getting the rural industrial schools together in a strong organization[2] to standardize and systematize and weed out the unworthy, like Smallwood's.[3] It is greatly to be regretted that Tuskegee will not be represented. Major Moton expects to be present from Hampton, and most of the leading schools of this kind will be represented. Tuskegee's absence will perhaps be misunderstood, and will doubtless be regarded as hostility on your part either to our organization or to some persons in it; this will be very regrettable.

You must, of course, be your own judge of conditions in the South, but I cannot help saying to you how strongly I feel that in giving way to prejudice as much as you do in the stand you have taken in the letter before me you increase prejudice and weaken yourself. Our national organizer, Dr. Mason, whom you well know, has been holding meetings on behalf of our Association in the South with the clearest statement of our purposes, and these meetings have been attended by white people as well as black. We have a number of Southern supporters like Miss Breckinridge[4] and Miss Moffat[5] and others, and have never held a Conference without Southern speakers — we shall have at least three including Prof. Mims at our annual Conference in Philadelphia on April 23rd, 24th and 25th — and we do not find that there is any serious feeling against us as yet, as you seem to think. More than that, we have been recently called upon by the Alabama & Vicksburg Railroad, a Southern corporation, manned and officered by Southern white men, to aid them in the Supreme Court of the United States to overthrow the recent decision of the Supreme Court of Mississippi which would "Jim Crow" the Pullman cars. Does this look as though it would injure you or Tuskegee in any way to attend a meeting which, as a matter of fact, will not even be held in the rooms of the Association, but merely in a vacant space in the same building? The call, as you are aware, was not signed by me, or the Association but by six of the leading colored educators in this field who naturally look to Tuskegee for leadership, and are amazed to find it holding aloof. I have always dealt perfectly frankly with you, as you are aware, and I must say that I think your timidity is running away with you, and that, as you suggest, you are too fearful. Is it not a time for you to appeal to the undercurrent in the life of the South, to the many men and women who know that the present policies are wrong, who despise the agitators and demagogues and want to do what is right by the colored people? The other day Dr. Hammond[6] of Paine Institute of Augusta, a white man, got up in our annual meeting and stated that he sympathized with our platform, and that he had recently addressed a meeting of some of the leading ministers of Georgia and stated to them publicly that what the negro in the South needed was not less social equality, but more. From our enclosed programme you will see that Dr. Dillard does not feel that there is any reason why he should not speak to our organization.

How I wish from my point of view, which may, of course, be as narrow or as broad as yours, or narrower, that you could take to heart the lesson of my grandfather's life and know no such thing as compromise with prejudice or with evil. Then a nation of whites and blacks would rise up and call you blessed. Yours in the work,

Oswald Garrison Villard

TLS Con. 63 BTW Papers DLC.

[1] The National Association for the Advancement of Colored People.

[2] The Association of Negro Industrial and Secondary Schools.

[3] John J. Smallwood was the head of a black school, the Temperance Industrial and Collegiate Institute, in Claremont, Va. BTW for many years warned his supporters in the North against aid to Smallwood, whom he accused of "Fraud, Immorality and Unfaithfulness." (Smallwood to BTW, Dec. 26, 1896, Con. 112, BTW Papers, DLC.)

[4] Sophonisba Preston Breckinridge (1866–1934), daughter of a Kentucky congressman and Confederate colonel, graduated from Wellesley (1888), became the first woman admitted to the Kentucky bar, earned a Ph.D. (1901) and J.D. (1904) at the University of Chicago, resided at Hull House for fourteen years, and became dean of the social-work school that later was incorporated into the University of Chicago. She signed the call in 1909 for the conference that established the NAACP and was an active member in its early years.

5 Adelene Moffat (1862–1956) was born in Cincinnati of Canadian parents, but she began her career as a social worker in Sewanee, Tenn. Later she spent thirty-five years in Northampton, Mass., as a social worker.

6 John Dennis Hammond (b. 1850) was president of Paine College from 1911 to 1915.

From Charles William Anderson

New York, N.Y. April 4, 1913

PERSONAL.

My dear Doctor: I wish it were possible to induce the editors of colored newspapers to emphasize the fact that the race is in great danger of losing many of its rights and privileges through the lack of interest in the protection of our people, on the part of colored democratic leaders. Since the last election no colored democratic leader in the country has exerted himself, or lifted his voice in the advocacy or defense of the rights of the race. They have all been engaged in a mad scramble for office. As a result, jim-crow car bills, segregation bills and marriage restriction bills have whitened the legislative chambers in almost every state in the union. Here in New York there is a bill before the legislature providing against intermarriage and inflicting dire penalties on those who violate it. The penalty proposed for concubinage between the races is one so horrible that it cannot be expressed in language, even between man and man. The colored democrats have been flying at each others throats over the division of the few menial places in the legislature but have done nothing in opposition to this infamous bill.

The state Boxing Commission here has made a rule against boxing matches between white and colored pugilists and that rule is now in full force. In so far as it eliminates Johnson,[1] I have no fault to find with it, but it is certainly most unfair to the other men engaged in that sport and is a ruthless violation of justice and of decent public sentiment. I forgot to say that Johnson is barred by an excellent special law which provides against contests in this state, in which a professional shall take part. This rule has been in operation for the past six or seven months, and yet no word of condemnation has been uttered by either the Bishop[2] or Mr. Wood[3] or any one of their followers, nor has either of the newspapers made any fight against it. What is true of this state is also true of many other states of the union, and it is all due to the fact that these new leaders are concerned about the "loaves and fishes" and are wholly indifferent to the rights and privileges of their people. If the good Bishop and some of the others would bestir themselves to bring about a more just feeling on the part of congress and the senate, and to induce the sensible members of both bodies to repudiate the "fire-eaters" from the South, they would be better employed than they now seem to me to be. If we are not very careful and vigilant we will wake up some bright morning to find that many of our most precious rights have been destroyed while we were engaged in watching the strife for office.

Cannot something be done to stir up newspapers in this matter? Surely the Age ought to have enough of democratic duplicity by this time, and ought to be willing to address itself to this high and immediately necessary task. Yours truly,

Charles W. Anderson

TLS Con. 64 BTW Papers DLC.

[1] Jack Johnson.
[2] Alexander Walters.
[3] Robert N. Wood.

To Charles William Anderson

[Tuskegee, Ala.] April 5th, 1913

Dear Mr. Anderson: I have just received your letter. The fact is, I have just reached home today after my Western trip.

Before I received your letter I had already written our friend, Mr. F. R.[1] about the dunce he was making of himself in attacking Mr. Anderson.[2] It is really pathetic to see a man go off in this fool kind of way just at the time when he needs friends. Of course Mr. Moore was not wise enough to see that in attacking Mr. Anderson in this way that he was defeating his slim chance to go to Liberia. Yours very truly,

Booker T. Washington

TLpS Con. 64 BTW Papers DLC.

[1] Frederick Randolph Moore.
[2] Probably James Henry Anderson, editor of the New York *Amsterdam News*.

To Charles Allmond Wickersham

[Tuskegee, Ala.] April 5th, 1913

My dear Sir: You have been so very kind in connection with making improvements for the comfort of colored passengers that I hesitate to suggest anything else.

There is but one toilet room provided for the colored passengers. This makes it very embarrassing for women. I very much hope that you will see your way clear to have these toilet rooms provided. I know that the colored passengers would very much appreciate it. Yours very truly,

Booker T. Washington

TLpS   Con. 934   BTW Papers   DLC.

To Willis Duke Weatherford

[Tuskegee, Ala.] April 7, 1913

Dear Sir: I have your very kind letter of some days ago and thank you for writing me so fully with reference to the work for the Negro in the South which is being done under your supervision.

I confess that I was not aware that there is so much activity and interest on the part of white college students in the study of "Present Forces in Negro Progress." Their close personal investigation of conditions among the Negroes and their willingness to render service through Bible teaching, lectures on sanitation, etc., will certainly give them a better insight to real conditions, and to my mind marks the beginning of a new era in the South for both races. It is needless to say that one race cannot advance very far without the helpful influence and personal contact of the other, and I am glad that the day seems to be approaching, through the influence of the Young Men's Christian Associations, the Southern Sociological Congress and other such movements, as to bring about a better understanding of the problem of the races in this country. Your very sincerely,

Booker T. Washington

TLpS   Con. 934   BTW Papers   DLC.

To R. D. Pusey[1]

[Tuskegee, Ala.] April 7th, 1913

Dear Sir: Please excuse me for troubling you about the following matter. Our institution, as perhaps you know, does a good deal of business with your road. Whenever your special agent comes here, usually once or twice a year, to induce students to travel over your road, we encourage our students to do so. In addition we do quite a freight business with your road. Under all the circumstances I feel you will not mind my calling your attention to the fact that no smoking car is provided for colored people. This means that women often have to ride in a car where smoking is being done or have to get into a car where smoking has just ceased. Besides, the colored people feel that since they pay full fare that the colored men ought to have a smoking compartment provided for them the same as is done on most of the other Southern roads.

In addition to this, only one toilet room is provided. It is very embarrassing, as was true yesterday when I came down from Birmingham on No. 9, for men and women to have to use the same toilet room.

I hope very much you can see your way clear to look into both these matters. Yours very truly,

Booker T. Washington

TLpS Con. 930 BTW Papers DLC.

[1] R. D. Pusey was general passenger agent of the Louisville and Nashville Railroad.

To Oswald Garrison Villard

Tuskegee Institute, Alabama April 8th, 1913

Dear Mr. Villard: Your letter of April 4th has been received. I think it well for the present at least, to leave aside all mere personal considerations and elements. If it will do the cause any good I am willing to plead guilty to the charge of cowardice and timidity. If you feel quite sure that the cause of education will be advanced I shall see to it that our institution is represented by two of our workers, Mr. J. R. E.

Lee, the Head of our Academic Department, who is in constant touch with the small schools, and Dr. Robert E. Park, whose special work is to visit the smaller schools.

I think if you will take a little time and find out just what is being done in the very direction that your letter emphasizes it will prove of value. For example. Friends have supplied us with special funds by which for sometime we have had one man on the road visiting and gearing up small schools, not confining his work to those which have grown out of Tuskegee or largely manned by Tuskegee people. Dr. Robert E. Park, who is representing us is now on a trip of inspection covering practically all the Southern states. He has been at work on this trip for two months, and after he is through with this will go on another trip of the same kind lasting perhaps for two or three months. In visiting these schools his object is to in a kindly but tactful way find out their weak points and show them how to articulate their work into the life of the people around the school, to show them how to keep the school clean and attractive, also to discourage the unnecessary multiplication of schools in the same territory.

Through the generosity of the same friend we have had in training at Tuskegee for six months a man under Mr. Bebbington who will give all his time in the future to visiting these small schools with a view of helping them introduce the same standard of accounting that we employ here at Tuskegee as far as practicable. The name of this man is Mr. Chambers C. Clayton.[1] If the expense involved will not be too great, we shall perhaps have him present at the conference also. He is likely to make his first visit to the school at Ft. Valley, Ga., under Mr. Hunt[2] sometime this month. After this year Mr. Clayton will be kept on the road constantly visiting all the schools that desire his services.

Six months ago I had the enclosed circular printed and have been sending it out from time to time as the occasion seemed to demand. I do not know to what extent you will agree with the ideas emphasized in this circular.

Let me add that while both in the present and in the future we may differ as to methods, I wish you, however, to understand that I never cease to feel grateful to you for your personal kindness to me and also for your generous action from time to time toward this institution. I think we can always depend upon this, that I will be frank with you and when we can cooperate I shall be glad to do so. When I cannot agree with you, I of course will say so in the most frank and kindly way. I very much hope that this letter paves the way for at least our cooperation and united effort in reference to the forthcoming conference.[3] Your very truly,

Booker T. Washington

P.S. — Of course, I suppose you understand that we have had here for the past fifteen years, practically every college and boarding school in the South for our race represented in our annual Worker's Conference, which is a regular and fixed organization.

B.T.W.

TLS Oswald Garrison Villard Papers MH. A press copy is in Con. 55, BTW Papers, DLC. No "enclosed circular" was found with the letter.

[1] Chambers Cassius Clayton, of Columbus, Miss., graduated from Tuskegee in 1911 and was a postgraduate student in 1911–12.

[2] Henry A. Hunt (1867–1938), brother of Adella Hunt Logan of the Tuskegee faculty, was a graduate of Atlanta University. He was teaching at Biddle University until 1903, when Wallace Buttrick and others of the General Education Board supported his founding of Fort Valley High and Industrial School, of which he was principal. He received the Spingarn Medal of the NAACP in 1930. At the time of his death he was an assistant to the governor of the Federal Farm Credit Administration.

[3] Villard wired BTW: "Thanks for most satisfactory letter. Earnestly urge attendance of Lee and Park." (Apr. 11, 1913, copy in Oswald Garrison Villard Papers, MH.)

Seth Low to Oswald Garrison Villard

New York   April 9th, 1913

Dear Mr. Villard: I received from Dr. Washington a short time ago a copy of the letter to which you refer; but until I received your own letter of April 4th I did not know to what it referred. I perfectly understand your point of view, yet I am not sure that it is the one which ought to prevail with Dr. Washington. I fancy that your honored Grandfather, to whom you refer, might easily have said of President Lincoln what you say of Washington, "How pitiful it is that this big man cannot also be brave!" From my own observation Dr. Washington does not seem to me to lack any courage; but his philosophy of the situation is radically different from your own. Personally, I think there is room and need for both philosophies. To borrow a military figure, your own is a frontal attack; Dr. Washington's is a flank movement. But while both movements may be good, those who are identified with one cannot ordinarily be useful in the other; and I think that Dr. Washington represents a force of too great value to justify him in exposing himself to misunderstanding by active cooperation with those whose fundamental philosophy is so different from his own. On this point I think Dr. Washington's judgment is far more likely to be correct than either yours or mine; and, therefore, I think that he is entitled to be kindly interpreted in the stand that he takes, however much you may regret it.

With kind regards, Sincerely yours,

Seth Low

TLS   Oswald Garrison Villard Papers   MH.

From Charles Allmond Wickersham

Atlanta, Ga. April 10, 1913

Principal: Replying to yours of April 5th.

It would be quite difficult and at the expense of seating room to provide additional toilets in the coaches usually assigned to colored passengers.

You understand that partitioned coaches are usually assigned to colored passengers for the reason that the travel is not sufficiently heavy to warrant furnishing a full car; that the end which may be used today for colored passengers may be used as a smoking car for white people tomorrow, therefore, to comply with your wishes, it would be necessary to put an additional closet in each end of the coach which would necessitate in many instances the removing of the Baker Heater to obtain the additional room, which would not be advisable. Unless this was done the additional closet would take up the space of at least two seats, which at times we could not well spare. In new coaches, however, which we may purchase, it will be possible to provide for these closets by changing the design and increasing the length, and we will certainly give this feature consideration in all of our new equipment.

We are, as you have been kind enough to state, anxious to add to the comfort of all passengers of either race whenever we can consistently, and I hope that so far as our old equipment is concerned these additional closets will not be insisted upon.

With kindest regards, Yours truly,

Chas. A. Wickersham
President & General Manager

TLS Con. 934 BTW Papers DLC. Written on stationery of the Atlanta and West Point Railroad Co. and the Western Railway of Alabama.

To Robert Smalls

[Tuskegee, Ala.] April 17, 1913

Dear Gen. Smalls: I have just received a letter from the former Secretary of the Treasury, Hon. Franklin MacVeagh, expressing the deepest regret that you have been removed from office. He said he took for granted that you were going to be permitted to hold this office all your life, as should have been the case. Yours very truly,

Booker T. Washington

TLpS Con. 931 BTW Papers DLC.

To Franklin MacVeagh

[Tuskegee, Ala.] April 17th, 1913

My dear Mr. MacVeagh: I thank you very much for your generous check toward our expenses.[1]

I shall never cease to thank you for recommending Mr. Rosenwald for a member of our board of trustees. He certainly is a fine and useful man. He brought a whole train load of Chicago people to see us a few days ago.

The colored people are very much disappointed and almost embittered because of the displacement of Robert Smalls. Most of the colored people thought that he at least would be permitted to retain his position. I was in Beaufort, S.C., a short while ago, and it was most pleasing as well as interesting to see how highly he is regarded by white and colored people in Beaufort. The white people look upon him as a kind of godfather, and there is not the slightest trace of bitterness against him because of the office he has held so many years.

I might say that the colored people are beginning to feel disappointed regarding the present administration because it is removing colored people and appointing none in their places. Perhaps you have already noticed that Mr. Lewis has been retired, Mr. Tyler has been asked for his resignation, and so far no colored men have been asked to take the places of those who have been removed. Perhaps the colored people needed this lesson, however, after all. Yours very truly,

Booker T. Washington

TLpS Con. 762 BTW Papers DLC.

¹ MacVeagh sent BTW $100. (MacVeagh to BTW, April 14, 1913, Con. 762, BTW Papers, DLC.)

To Robert Heberton Terrell

[Tuskegee, Ala.] April Eighteenth, 1913

My dear Judge Terrell: I am very glad to have your letter of April 15th¹ and to have you write me in appreciation of the articles sent by me from the Northwest to various colored newspapers.

I enjoyed very much the opportunity of reaching a new class of people both white and black, and I am hopeful that some good was accomplished by my visit.

I also want you to know how much I value and appreciate your thoughtfulness in writing me with reference to whatever little support I have been to you in your public life during the past twelve years. You have justified entirely the confidence of your friends, and it seems to me that nothing could be more satisfactory than the action of the Southern Democratic lawyers who are presenting the President with an appeal for your re-appointment² even if the re-appointment should not issue; it is, nevertheless, a magnificent testimonial as to the fine record you have made during your incumbency. It is rather interesting to note that the only two colored lawyers to whom the petition was present[ed] refused to sign it. Yours very truly,

Booker T. Washington

TLpS Con. 933 BTW Papers DLC.

¹ Con. 525, BTW Papers, DLC.
² The petition was signed by 300 District of Columbia lawyers, including all the judges of the D.C. Supreme Court. Only two lawyers refused to sign according to Terrell, "our colored brothers — Horner and Richards (of the Howard law school)." (Terrell to BTW, Apr. 15, 1913, Con. 525, BTW Papers, DLC.)

To the Editor of the Philadelphia *Public Ledger*

Tuskegee Institute, Ala., April 18, 1913

OSTRACISM OF NEGRO

PREJUDICE IS CONFINED TO NORTH, SAYS
BOOKER T. WASHINGTON

Sir — I write regarding what you say in your recent editorials on "Negro Labor."¹ I do not in any degree attempt to minimize or overlook the wrongs perpetrated upon our race in many parts of the country in reference to labor, but I think some of the statements are often put before the public which are likely to be misleading.

It should be borne in mind that out of the 10,000,000 black people in the United States, 9,000,000 reside in our Southern States, and so far as I am able to discover, there is little, if any, problem in the South so far as getting an opportunity to labor is concerned, whether the labor is common or skilled. In fact my experience and observations convince me that instead of the negro having to seek work in the South, work seeks him; and I know of no section in the South where there is an able-bodied man or woman of our race who wants to work who cannot find it. The present problem among both white employers of labor and black employers of labor is to find enough colored people to perform the work. The South is guilty of a good many sins, I know, but the native Southern white man is seldom guilty of the sin of keeping a negro out of a job simply because he is black.

Many Negro Shipbuilders

A few months ago I visited the shipyard at Newport News, Va., perhaps the largest shipbuilding concern in the United States. I found here 2250 colored persons were being employed in connection with the building of ships. Many of the most skilled laborers, doing the most delicate and high-class work in the construction of the ships, were black persons. The manager of the shipyard told me that his only problem was to get more negroes who would learn the shipbuilding business and those of the kind that would stick to their jobs, and render effective service after they got the jobs.

At Tuskegee Institute, for example, we can scarcely keep men and women in school long enough for them to finish the courses of training, so great is the demand for service. If we could turn out five times as many skilled mechanics as we are now turning out, every one of them could find employment without waiting a day. One of the largest manufacturing concerns in the Birmingham district keeps a standing order with us to the effect that it will employ any one of our men whom we are ready to recommend. The Cahill Iron Works, in Chattanooga, readily takes any man from this institution who has only had a partial training in foundry work.

When the Tuskegee Institute closes the school term for a short vacation next May I will guarantee to say that there will be many large business concerns that will have their agents on the ground seeking to induce our students to go to various places in the South to labor for these concerns; this includes both common and skilled labor.

It is our experience here at Tuskegee that letters reach us even from the North, asking us to recommend laborers to work in various capacities. During the present week letters have come from Trenton, N.J., asking us to recommend a number of skilled men for a large brick making firm, and from another asking us to recommend laborers at from $2 to $2.50 per day to work in connection with a Maryland cement company.

Colored Firemen Abound

There is a good deal of talk, from time to time, about the negro being debarred from the railroad service as a fireman; not withstanding the talk, one who travels in the South, as I do constantly, sees negro firemen on the locomotives. I do not know how many negro firemen are employed on the locomotives in the Northern and Western States, but I do know that hundreds and I believe thousands are employed in this capacity throughout the South.

But my main object in sending this communication is to emphasize the fact that in this part of the country, at least, the negro can find all the work he is willing to perform, and in some cases the pay is disgracefully low, but, on the other hand, the cost of living is much lower than it is in any other part of the world.

My own belief is that the negro in the North will never solve his problem in the labor world until, in a large degree, the negro begins at the bottom and creates industries of a kind that will enable him to give employment to members of his own race. So long as a man, whether he is white or black, has to seek an occupation in an industry that somebody else has created, just so long will that individual or race be placed at a disadvantage.

BOOKER T. WASHINGTON

Philadelphia *Public Ledger,* Apr. 22, 1913, 10.

¹ An editorial in the Philadelphia *Public Ledger* stated that in the North and the South blacks "are being excluded from the fields of honest employment." The editorial concluded: "Society is coming to have less and less patience with the negro who does not conform to high standards of civilization. The economic conditions being imposed upon him tend constantly to lower his standards of living." The result, according to the *Public Ledger,* was that "the very existence of the negro masses will be a misery to themselves and a menace to the country." (Philadelphia *Public Ledger,* Apr. 16, 1913, 10.)

To James Bertram

New York, April 28th, 1913

Dear Mr. Bertram: Mr. Carnegie will perhaps recall that some years ago he gave something over $20,000.00 without condition, to erect a library at Fisk University. He has given smaller amounts from time to time.

The trustees of Fisk University have been making for several months a tremendous effort to secure $300,000.00 for endowment and for clearing the institution of debt. Toward this sum the General Education Board has offered $60,000.00. Some months ago through the efforts of Mr. Paul D. Cravath, Mr. Carnegie promised to give the last $10,000.00 toward the sum needed. The trustees have been hard at work for about two years in an effort to secure the $300,000.00. I think I am safe in saying that they have now exhausted practically all of their resources. They have now secured, as you will see by the enclosed list, practically $240,000.00, leaving out Mr. Carnegie's $10,000.00.

When I saw you a few days ago I did not understand that the $10,000.00 from Mr. Carnegie was included in the total sum, but I now find that it was.

The trustees have asked me through you to appeal to Mr. Carnegie to increase the size of his gift in view of the circumstances by which they find themselves surrounded. I know practically all the institutions in the South that work for the education of our race, but in the matter of first class college work Fisk University stands at the head. The South is full of strong, useful, level-headed men and women who have been educated at Fisk, and it would indeed prove a calamity for this institution not to secure the sum that it so much needs.

I might add that Mr. Paul D. Cravath, as you will see by the list, has been most generous in his personal gifts. This institution, as you perhaps know, was founded by Mr. Cravath's father.[1]

Anything that can be done in the direction of helping at this critical moment will be greatly appreciated. Yours very truly,

[Booker T. Washington]

TLc Con. 64 BTW Papers DLC. No list of donors was found with the letter.

[1] Erastus Milo Cravath.

An Address at the Fourth American Peace Conference

[St. Louis, Mo., May 1, 1913]

EDUCATION AND INTERNATIONAL PEACE

The schools and colleges have a great opportunity to make themselves felt in creating a public sentiment against war between nations. World peace will come largely through a gradual process of education of right public sentiment.

In many respects the same principles that bring about peace between individuals can be applied to nations, but it can not be done in a day; in fact, the most lasting and fundamental things are of slow growth.

Many now living can remember the time when in this country it was thought to be not disgraceful for a business man or a public man to get intoxicated or to be known as a common drunkard. Through education of public sentiment the individual today who is known to drink to excess is excluded from business and public office in a very large measure.

It was once true in this country when the man who carried one or two pistols and perhaps a bowie knife on his body was looked upon as a brave man. Through education of public sentiment such a man today is looked upon as a coward and a coarse specimen of humanity.

It was once true in this country as well as in other countries, that the habit of dueling was countenanced and the participants were looked upon as heroes. That day has passed. If two business men in St. Louis having some disagreement on business should get out on the streets and attempt to shoot out their differences they would be disgraced in the commercial world. There is no more reason why nations should be permitted to settle their differences by the use of shot and powder than is true of individuals.

Throughout the civilized world we have learned that it is not safe to permit the two most interested parties in a dispute to settle their differences, but the differences are settled by a disinterested party. This has all come about through education of public sentiment.

Only within the last few years in our own country, I am sorry to say, it was a common habit for individuals or groups of individuals who suspected a man of committing crime to band themselves together and lynch or burn the individual without trial before a proper tribunal. Public sentiment, I am glad to say, has been brought to bear upon the disgraceful habit of lynching until we have reduced the number of lynchings in this country to less than a third or fourth of what the number was twelve or fifteen years ago; in fact, during the last four months we have only had thirteen of these disgraceful crimes against civilization as compared with twice that number a year ago.

In another respect the schools and colleges can perform an important task in bringing about international peace. The time is at hand when in all of our schools the man of peace, of industry, of scientific attainment and generosity should be exalted in our teaching above the man of war. We must teach the youths of this country that it is just as noble for one to live for his country as it is to die for his country on the battlefield. In our schools in the present and the future we should spend less time in teaching students the names of great battle-fields, but we should point them to the great grain fields of the world. In our school books and in our class rooms we should teach the youths of the land not so much the names of the great man killers, but the names of the great man saviors.

I believe within a few years through the education of public sentiment that the name of Mr. Andrew Carnegie will be exalted as the hero of peace as much as the name of Napoleon Bonaparte as the hero of war. Mr. Carnegie has given and is giving his life and means not in devising methods of slaying men, but in devising methods for saving men and exalting peace above war.

Through the education of public sentiment, in the future the greatness of a nation will be measured not by the tons of lead and iron and armorplate which it possesses, but by its service to the world. The greatness of nations in the future will be measured not by the number of war vessels that it floats, but by the number of schools and churches and useful industries that it keeps in existence. It will be measured not by the number of men killed, but by the number of men saved and lifted up. We must cease to judge the greatness of a nation in terms of tons, but judge it in terms of service. There is no more justification why the place of a nation should be fixed by its tons of lead and iron than there is why the greatness of an individual should be gauged by the number of pistols or daggers or bowie knives that that individual carries on his body. In the future a nation will be judged, if we do our duty in creating public sentiment, not by the number of idle men enlisted as soldiers, but by the number of its producers.

War between nations is not only wasteful in the highest degree, but brutalizing. War means destruction. Peace means construction.

It is a good deal with a nation as it is with an individual. When it once gets started in the wrong direction it is not easy to stop. Within the last ten years Great Britain has increased its expenditure on its navy from $174,000,000 to $222,000,000. Germany from $47,000,000 to $110,000,000. The United States from $80,000,000 to $132,000,-000. Few sane men will dare question whether or not it would have been wiser to have spent this tremendous sum in the education and enlightenment of the people of these countries instead of investing it in iron and lead which will prove a body of death about the neck of these nations. A shot from one cannon can destroy in a single moment that which it has required years to create.

In the last analysis, the carrying of a pistol and gun on one's person or keeping them in his home does not protect an individual. I should be ashamed to live in a community where I depended for the safety of my life upon the use of lead and powder. The greatest protection that an individual can have is in his service to the community, and the same is true of nations.

Not many months ago I was in Denmark. As many of you know, in Denmark there is tremendous public sentiment in favor of complete disarmament, of getting rid of army and navy. When I asked the Danish people how, if they got rid of their army and navy, they meant to protect themselves, they replied that they meant to protect themselves through their service to the world; that they meant to supply Europe with a large part of its dairy and poultry products, and that in proportion as they let Europe understand that it was dependent upon them for a large part of the necessities of life that this would prove a greater protection than either army or navy could bring about.

A nation can not teach its youths to think in terms of destruction and oppression without brutalizing and blunting the tender conscience and sense of justice of the youths of that country. More and more we must learn to think not in terms of race or color or language or religion or of political boundaries, but in terms of humanity. Above all races and political boundaries there is humanity. That should be considered first; and in proportion as we teach the youths of this country to love all races and all nations, we are rendering the highest service which education can render to the world.

For years we have been sending our missionaries to Japan to teach them Christianity, to teach Japan our methods of industry and civilization. The Japanese have learned to believe in us, have thought that we were sincere and in earnest in our endeavor to help them. But our nation is placed in an awkward position when a few thousand of the Japanese come to our country and attempt to put into practice the very lessons of economy and industry which we have taught them, and in return for this we attempt to humiliate them and degrade them as a people. Such a course is unworthy of our civilization. I pity the white man in America who is afraid to stand up in open competition in the commercial world by the side of a few thousand Japanese.

The Great Book, in whose teachings we believe, says in effect that which is temporal passes away, but that which is spiritual remains. Let us teach the youths of America that in proportion as we cling to the higher and not lower things that our nation will be made strong, useful and influential throughout the world.

Book of the Fourth American Peace Congress, St. Louis, May 1, 2, 3, 1913 (St. Louis, 1913), 309–13.

From T. L. Trew

Cincinnati, Ohio, May 7, 1913

Dear Sir: I have been thinking about writing you for some time. I am the man who organized and taught the first colored school in Tuskegee under the Freedmans Bureau. I was just a boy, only 20 years old then, and I had not been teaching very long until my life was threatened by one, Bat Clark, an auctioneer and saloon keeper: He told me they would allow no d——d Yankey to come down there and teach their niggers. You see, I was a Union soldier and my Company was stationed there before I was mustered out of the service and I went back down there and organized the school. There was a crowd of boys come over to the school house one evening after that to mob me but I talked and bluffed them out of it; so you see a smart reporter could make quite a story out of my experience as a school teacher in Tuskegee.[1]

I met the Minister of a Colored Church in Walnut Hills and we got to talking about Tuskegee School. He told me his son was educated there and that brought it all back to me and I decided to write you as I suppose my experience there is really a part of the history of the Tuskegee School.

I am getting old and have recently suffered by having a stroke of paralysis and I have often thought I should have written you long before this.

I would give anything to meet some of my old scholars. Of course they are all grown up as I was only 20 years old then and I am 67 years old now.

I shall not give out my experience there until I hear from you.[2] Yours truly,

T L Trew

TLS Con. 935 BTW Papers DLC.

¹ In an address in 1884, BTW had mentioned this incident as having occurred fourteen years earlier. (See A Speech before the National Educational Association, July 16, 1884, above, 2:255.)

² BTW replied: "I am very glad to learn that you are the organizer of the first colored school taught under the Freedmen's Bureau at Tuskegee Alabama." He sent Trew a copy of *Up from Slavery* and several pamphlets on Tuskegee Institute, but did not respond to the suggestion that Trew's early experiences might be worthy of publication. (May 13, 1913, Con. 935, BTW Papers, DLC.)

From Mahadev Hari Modak

India, Bombay-Khandala—9.5.13

Respected Sir: I am an utter stranger to you personally, nevertheless perfectly familiar with yr name and deeds through that wonderful book, I mean yr autobiography published by Thomas Nelson & Sons, New York. No book ever impressed me so deeply in my life except perhaps the life of President Garfield. To tell you the truth I was so much enamoured of it that I at once even without getting yr permission began translating it into my own Vernacular — Marathi — for the benefit of my young friends in Schools & Colleges. I find in you an ideal example of a practical educationist. You are an object lesson in self help and philanthropy to the youths of every country, at least to those of India and I have, therefore, Ventured to hold up your life as a model to our younger generation for which you will kindly excuse. I ought to have got yr permission previously but then the impulse of the moment proved too strong for me and I at once set my pen to work. I however feel morally bound to acquaint you with the fact and crave your indulgence.¹ I read of another work from your pen. It is named "Negro in Business." But I don't know whom to write for it. I shall feel obliged if you would kindly refer me to your publishers of this Book. I shall also be happy to know the names of all the books written by yourself regarding the education of the young. Happy would be this land when the youth here were to copy you in love of labor for labor's own sake & for the independence and self reliance which the ability to do something which the world wants done, brings — to quote yr own esteemed words. I dare say a study of yr Biography will animate any reader with a love for labor and it is expressly from this motive that I am putting yr unique life before the rising generation of this ancient land.

Apologising for the trouble and wishing you and yrs long life to carry on your noble work   I beg to remain yrs ever admiringly

M. H. Modak

ALS Con. 935 BTW Papers DLC.

¹ BTW replied that he appreciated having his book translated and hoped "that much good will be accomplished by this work." (June 12, 1913, Con. 935, BTW Papers, DLC.)

To Laura J. Stern¹

[Tuskegee, Ala.] May Twelfth, 1913

Dear Madam: In further reply to your letter of April 23rd, I send you the following facts which have been compiled by our Division of Records and Research:

The Negro population of Alabama, 908,282; number of Negro voters, 213,928; convicts in Alabama, January 1, 1913, 2,400, cost of maintaining, according to the report of the State Convict Department, $1,177,590.43 for the four years, 1906 to 1910, which is a yearly average of $294,397.60.

The amount spent per capita on Negro education in Alabama, that is for public schools, normal schools, and colleges, is about $3.00. About $1.50 of this sum is paid by the State.

According to the census report of 1904 on prisoners and juvenile delinquents, 60 per cent of the prisoners committed in Alabama for that year was 25 years of age or under. This indicates that a large number are boys and girls. There were 20 committed in 1904 who were from 10 to 14 years of age, 124 who were from 15 to 19 years of age, and 34 who were 20 years of age.

From 5 to 6 per cent of the state convicts and, from 7 to 8 per cent of the county convicts are female. For the first six months of 1902 there were 2000 white persons committed to jails of the State, of whom 107 were women. During this same period there were 8,900 Negroes committed to jail, of whom 1,100 were women.

From 40 to 60 per cent of the Negro convicts are illiterate.

Dr. C. O. Boothe, Room 403, fourth floor, Alabama Penny Savings Bank, Birmingham, is making an extended study of conditions of Negro convicts, and I find that he is able to give very valuable information concerning the conditions of Negro convicts in the various mines and camps of the State where he has visited.

With regard to whether I have any suggestions to make as to changes in the treatment of convicts, I beg leave to offer the following general suggestion: That the basic object in dealing with the convicts be to promote their welfare and reformation, and the securing to their dependent families a fair proportion of their earnings. At present, the basic thought in dealing with the convicts is that they may be kept in good physical condition so that they may bring the greatest financial returns to the State. This creates a tendency to increase the number of convicts and to have as large a proportion of them as possible able-bodied. As a result, there is almost entire absence of any attempts at reformation. From various sources, I am informed that the convicts, in order to get the greatest amount of work out of them, are, in many instances badly treated. In regard to this, the accompanying clipping from the Advertiser of February 8, 1912 is enclosed.

I fear that too many of the convicts who serve out their time are sent back to the various communities of the State, in many instances, broken in health and more vicious than they were when sent to prison.

Trusting this information will be of service to you, I am: Very truly yours,

Booker T. Washington

TLpS Con. 932 BTW Papers DLC.

[1] Laura J. Stern (Mrs. S. B. Stern) of Montgomery, Ala., was chairman of a committee of the Montgomery Federation of Women's Clubs that was investigating social abuses in the state. (Stern to BTW, Apr. 23, 1913, Con. 932, BTW Papers, DLC.)

From Julius B. Ramsey, Charles H. Gibson, and Robert Robinson Taylor

[Tuskegee, Ala.] May 15, 1913

Mr. B. T. Washington: The committee appointed to inquire into the behavior of Mr. Lovette[1] and Miss Howard[2] in the dining room have gone into the matter very exhaustively and beg to report our findings as follows:

Mr. Lovette denies positively that he had come in contact with Miss Howard in any way in the dining room, either by holding her hand, by any movement of the foot, or by touching her person in any way. He was very strong in his denial of this charge.

Miss Howard admitted that occasionally Mr. Lovette had shaken her hand bidding her good morning, and usually this was done under the table. At times he had also touched her foot and she innocently had touched his foot, but she attached no significance to this. Miss Howard stated that while she had noticed these various actions of Mr. Lovette she had made no comment on them nor did she wish to say anything to him, fearing that he might misconstrue her noticing this into a belief that she had some wrong idea about these actions.

The committee feels that Mr. Lovette did not tell the truth when he denied the charges. The committee further believes that Miss Howard is perfectly innocent of this matter and that she had no idea at all of any wrong doing. In fact she expressed surprise that this had been noticed at all by anyone in the dining room. If there is any blame to be attached to anyone we think it should rest solely on Mr. Lovette and not on Miss Howard. Respectfully,

> J. B. Ramsey
> Chas. H. Gibson
> R R Taylor

Committee:
Mr. Gibson
Mr. Lee
Mr. Whittaker
Mr. Scott
Mr. J H W — J B Ramsey
9:30 a.m. Friday

TLS Con. 636 BTW Papers DLC.

¹ Albert B. Lovett.

² Carolyn G. Howard, an assistant in domestic science at Tuskegee in 1912–13.

To Mabel Delano Clapp Lord[1]

[Tuskegee, Ala.] May 17, 1913

My dear Mrs. Lord: This is a very tardy reply to yours of April 28th which came during my absence.

Of course I do not know on what you are basing your suggestion regarding myself and the Mormons. It often occurs that people put words into my mouth that I do not utter, and very often headlines in newspapers are made to misrepresent actual sentiments.

So far as I can recall I did not say a single thing either for or against mormonism. I said I knew nothing about it, or meant to say so. All I meant to do in my articles was to report what I observed. I did not attempt, except in one case, to give advice. I did say rather emphatically that in the matter of industry the colored people can learn a great lesson from the Mormons, and I also said that there was a parallel between the Mormons and the colored people growing out of the fact that both had been persecuted.

I remember you very well, and shall hope to see you when I come to Boston again. Yours very truly,

Booker T. Washington

TLpS Con. 928 BTW Papers DLC.

¹ Mabel Delano Clapp Lord, a Unitarian and wife of the Boston physician Frederick Taylor Lord, cautioned BTW about praising the Mormons. Describing herself as a person interested in the welfare of blacks and also "as a woman who is opposed to woman suffrage," she said of the Mormons: "It is not a religion based on the spirit but on the body and the work of the Mormon missionaries is a menace that we are fighting just as we fight white slavery." (Lord to BTW, Apr. 28, 1913, Con. 928, BTW Papers, DLC.) BTW also received a letter from Alice B. Coleman (Mrs. George W. Coleman), president of the Council of Women for Home Missions in New York City, warning him not to be taken in by Mormonism. (May 1, 1913, Con. 925, BTW Papers, DLC.) BTW replied: "I have written a letter to our good friend, Mrs. Frederick T. Lord, which I hope will give her a different idea of my writing on the Mormons. I am not as yet converted to the Mormon religion." (May 17, 1913, Con. 926, BTW Papers, DLC.)

To Reed Paige Clark

[Tuskegee, Ala.] May 23d, 1913

My dear Mr. Clark: I have received your letter of April 28th and am very glad to hear from you again.

I presume before this that you have heard that Mr. Moore was recalled before he started for Liberia. The whole matter of the appointment of a successor to Dr. Crum seems to be held up, and I do not think one is likely to be appointed much before Congress adjourns.

I shall use the information which you gave me regarding Mr. Bundy to the best advantage if I get a chance. It is very pleasing to know about your high opinion of him.[1]

I am very glad indeed to hear you say that real progress is being made since the loan became available, and that Liberia's salvation lies in the bond of friendship with the United States. I hope the Liberians are realizing this. I confess that I have become a little troubled about the future of Liberia since the change of policy on the part of Mr. Wilson which gets rid of what is termed "Dollar Diplomacy." I presume, however, that the loan is too far on the way to be affected now by this change of policy. I hope the Liberians will be impressed on every occasion with the fact that in the last analysis no loan is going to help them except as they produce more out of the natural resources of the country than they consume.

Mr. Scott begs to be remembered to you. Yours very truly,

[Booker T. Washington]

TLp Con. 70 BTW Papers DLC.

[1] Clark had written BTW that he believed Richard Carlton Bundy, secretary to the U.S. legation in Monrovia, should be named as the American minister to Liberia. (Apr. 28, 1913, Con. 70, BTW Papers, DLC.)

To N. Clark Smith[1]

[Tuskegee, Ala.] May 26, 1913

Captain Smith: All of us appreciate the great improvement in the band from year to year. There is one suggestion which I want to make to you. In my opinion you are losing a great opportunity by not making more of the plantation melodies in connection with the band music. In every part of the country, especially in New York, and even in foreign countries the plantation songs are being used by bands. You have an opportunity to set a pace in that matter for all the other people in the country. I do not hear very many of these melodies played from time to time when you have your concerts or when the band is playing on other occasions. It is always a safe policy to do the thing which one can do better than anybody else. You can get hold of the plantation songs, set them to music and play them better than anybody else because you have advantages over any other band leader in the country. In this way you might make a distinct and unique reputation for yourself. On the other hand, if you attempt to play the high classical music to imitate Sousa and other great band leaders, you will find that people will compare your music with theirs to your disadvantage. The whole country is seeking to see and appreciate the plantation melodies, and I urge you to take hold of them with new interest and zeal and emphasize them constantly in your concerts and playing generally. If you try to play one of the difficult pieces played by famous bands and familiar to Northern audiences, as I have said, people will compare your playing with the others to your disadvantage, but if you emphasize the kind of music which the other people know little or nothing about, and you can do it better than anybody else, there will be no chance for any such comparison, and as I have said, the band will make a unique and distinct reputation which will be of the greatest advantage to it.

If one goes to hear a Mexican band he expects to hear music suited to the atmosphere of Mexico, that is peculiar to Mexico, and consequently when one goes to hear a colored band or Southern band he expects to hear something different from a band in the North.

[Booker T. Washington]

TLp Con. 638 BTW Papers DLC.

[1] N. Clark Smith (1877–1933) was born in Leavenworth, Kan. He attended Western University (Kan.) and Guild Hall, London, and was a graduate of the Chicago Music College (1905). He was bandmaster at Tuskegee from 1907 to 1913. He arranged black spirituals and folk music and was the composer of "The Tuskegee Institute March."

To Alfred Tuckerman[1]

[Tuskegee, Ala.] May Twenty Sixth, 1913

My dear Sir: Our Treasurer has shown me your letter of May 10th, in which you inquire as to why it should be necessary for Tuskegee to appeal to the public for additional funds, and also stating that the Indians receive much less than Negroes in money and care.

Under the circumstances, I thought you would not object to my making the following report to you, covering the inquiries suggested in your letter.

The Indians from a financial standpoint are better off than any other race or class of people in this country. The 265,683 Indians in the United States own 72,535,862 acres of land, which is 273 acres for each Indian man, woman, and child. If all the land in the country were apportioned among the inhabitants there would be 20 acres per person. The value of property and funds belonging to Indians is $678,564,253 or $2,554 per capita, or about $10,000 per family. The Negroes, but lately emancipated, are by contrast poor and are struggling to rise.

The Indians are carefully looked after by the United States Government. In addition to the elaborately organized Indian Bureau at Washington, there are six thousand (6000) persons in the Indian field service, to especially look after and supervise them. This is one, director supervisor or teacher for each 44 Indians.

Some of the things that the Government does for the Indians are:

(1) Look after the health of the Indians; for this purpose there are in the field one Medical Supervisor, 100 regular and 60 contract physicians, 54 nurses, and 88 field matrons.

(2) Supervise their farming and stock raising. For the 24,489 Indians engaged in farming, there are two general supervisors, 48 expert farmers, that is, men with experience and scientific knowledge, and 210 men in subordinate farming positions.

Over $7,000,000 have been spent in irrigating lands for Indians. Congress in 1911 appropriated $1,300,000 for this purpose. For the 890,000 Negro farmers in the South, the United States Government maintains 34 Agricultural Demonstration Agents.

For the supervision of the 44,985 Indians engaged in stock raising, the Government maintains, 22 superintendents of live stock. For the

700,000 Negro farmers engaged in livestock raising, there is only one Government expert working especially among them.

(3) A system of schools is maintained by the Government for Indian children. For this purpose there are 223 day schools, 79 reservation boarding schools, and 35 boarding schools away from reservations. In these schools in 1911, there were 24,500 pupils. For the support of these schools the United States Government for 1912 appropriated $3,757,495. To assist in teaching the 1,700,000 Negro children in the South, there was received in 1911 from the United States Government $245,518.

In general the Indians are not taxed for any purpose. On the other hand the Negroes are taxed the same as other persons and in this way contribute a considerable amount for their own education, and the education of the whites. In this connection, I call your attention to the enclosed pamphlet "Public Taxation and Negro Schools."

I enclose herewith copy of my last Annual Report, giving information as to the various activities of the institution. Yours very truly,

[Booker T. Washington]

TLp   Con. 784   BTW Papers   DLC.

1 Alfred Tuckerman (b. 1848), of Newport, R.I., a Harvard graduate and a Ph.D. of Leipzig, was a chemist and bibliographer. He sent Warren Logan a donation of $10 but remarked: "I do not understand why such an appeal should be necessary after the large gifts by Mr. Kennedy [Carnegie?] and others. The Indians have received much less than the Negroes in money and care, yet they beg less, and are more ready to imitate the Whites in being self-reliant. All over the North I find Negroes despised by the Whites for their laziness and disposition to be dependent." (May 10, 1913, Con. 784, BTW Papers, DLC.)

To Benjamin Franklin Riley[1]

[Tuskegee, Ala.] May Twenty-seventh, 1913

Dear Dr. Riley: I have received your letter of recent date and thank you for writing me so promptly and so fully.

The extract which I quote on the attached slip constitutes my principal answer, not, of course, to *you* but to those who utter falsehoods. It is needless for me to go into details with you because it is not necessary. I would add that I have never been under the influence of liquor in my life and do not know what such a feeling means: in other words, I have an abhorrence for liquor used in the ordinary sense.

We have never had at any time, a white woman as teacher at this institution.

It may interest you to know that I received only a few days ago, a communication from one of the Trustees, asking me to recommend someone in the place of the man, Gordon, to whom you refer. Of course, I did not know at that time that he was engaged in the kind of business that he is.

Manning is too small and little for us to discuss. We both know him. Some years ago, when I did not know him as well as I now do, he worked on my sympathy in Boston, and I gave him a letter of introduction to a person, and this helped him to get the money for a printing press. He was then living in Tallapoosa County. As soon as he got his press he began abusing me in the paper which I had enabled him to publish. Perhaps you may not know also that the mean article which appeared in the Iconoclast regarding myself some months ago was written by Manning.

I think I may safely say this to you: anything regarding myself which is not true gives me little concern. I have enough faith in Providence and in my fellow man to believe that any falsehood that is not founded upon truth will eventually work out to a serviceable rather than a hurtful end. There is one thing I fear in the world and that is to do wrong.

Now, regarding yourself. I am constantly discussing you and the value of your work. It is a constant regret to me that I have not been able to be of more practical benefit to you in helping you carry the financial burden which rests upon you, but you have no idea of the many responsibilities that rest upon me. I am responsible for raising a large amount of money for enterprises not directly connected with Tuskegee. Many of these enterprises have grown out of my own efforts, and I am responsible for keeping them alive. They are of such a serious nature that I could not lightly throw them aside.

When a man is doing such a fine job as you are doing, words constitute little in the way of compensation. I hope, however, the time will come at sometime in the future when I can manifest my deep interest and my faith in your work in a more substantial way.

I want you always to write me or speak to me in the utmost frankness and I shall not misunderstand you. I shall be glad to have you tell me what you consider any of my faults or what you consider regarding my meanness or goodness. I shall use it all to the best advantage.

Come to see us whenever you can. Yours very truly,

Booker T. Washington

[*Enclosure*]

"If I were to try to read, much less answer, all the attacks made on me, this shop might as well be closed for any other business. I do the very best I [know] how — the very best I can; and I mean to keep on doing so until the end. If the end brings me out all right, what is said against me won't amount to anything.

"If the end brings me out wrong, ten angels swearing I was right would make no difference."
                "Speeches and Presidential Addresses"
                        By Abraham Lincoln

Blessed are ye, when men shall revile you, and persecute you, and shall say all manner of evil against you falsely, for my sake.
                        Matthew 5, 11.

TLpS Con. 930 BTW Papers DLC.

¹ Benjamin Franklin Riley (1849–1925), a Baptist clergyman born in Pineville, Ala., was typical of a class of southerners in sympathy with blacks but not particularly enlightened about their nature or needs. President of Howard College in Alabama from 1883 to 1893, and professor of English literature at the University of Georgia from 1893 to 1900, he first met BTW during the latter's tour of Texas in 1906, when Riley was head of the Texas Anti-Saloon League. Riley sought and received BTW's advice on his forthcoming book on the race question, which he entitled *The White Man's Burden* (1910). Though a negrophile, Riley presented blacks as friendly children. (See the characterization of Riley's work in Fredrickson, *Black Image in the White Mind,* 289.) BTW invited Riley to give two addresses at Tuskegee and another in New York on behalf of Tuskegee, and praised him as one "who sees the difficulties and the opportunities in the situation, and has the courage to say frankly and positively, what thousands of other white men know, but have been held back from saying heretofore...." (BTW to Riley, Feb. 20, 1911, Con. 438, BTW Papers, DLC.) Riley also wrote *The Life and Times of Booker T. Washington* (1916).

To Amanda Ferguson Johnston

[Tuskegee, Ala.] May 28th, 1913

Dear Sister: On July 31st or near that date our band is planning to give a concert in Charleston, and if the people of Malden would like for the band to do so, I shall arrange for the band to give a concert in the public square in Malden either the day before it gives the concert in Charleston, the same day or the day after. This I should like to do as a compliment to the citizens of Malden without any charge being made.

I should like for a temporary band stand to be erected in the public square that would hold 45 or 50 people. It of course could be built of rough boards. There should be chairs placed on the band stand.

Please talk to the white and colored people there, and let me know if they would like the band to come to Malden and I think I can perfect plans by which it will be there on either one of the dates I have mentioned.

I should not like for the concert to be advertised or spoken of to any extent outside of Malden, for the reason that the people in Charleston will be charged admission and the persons in charge of the concert there would naturally object to a free concert being given so near Charleston if it was advertised to any large extent outside of Malden.

Mr. John D. Stevenson[1] will be with the band, and Captain Smith is the bandmaster. I will give them full instructions about getting to and from Malden.

I suppose it will be necessary to provide them with at least one meal while in Malden.

I sent you a basket of peaches a day or two ago which I hope reached you safely.

I hope all of you are well. Your brother.

[Booker T. Washington]

TLp Con. 923 BTW Papers DLC. Docketed: "copy of this sent to Mr. Byrd Prillerman."

[1] John D. Stevenson was a bookkeeper in the Tuskegee Institute auditing department (1903–5), assistant to the cashier in the treasurer's office (1905–8), and general secretary of the school's YMCA from 1908 until after BTW's death.

From Robert Ezra Park

Wollaston, Mass. May 29, 1913

My dear Mr. Washington: I completed my inspection of the schools you asked me to visit May 18, as near as I can now remember. The last school I visited was the Topeka Industrial Institute at Topeka, Kansas. Now that the work is over and done I want to give you a few general impressions of what I learned.

With three exceptions all the fifteen schools which I visited were "Tuskegee Schools," that is to say they were either founded or built up by Tuskegee graduates. Owing to the interruption of my itinerary, in order to attend the Conference of Rural Industrial schools which met in New York City in April, I was not able to visit as many schools as I had planned to do, and there is still a number of schools of which you gave me the names that I have not yet been able to look at.

As the schools I did visit, however, were scattered all the way from Virginia to Texas I had a pretty good opportunity to get a good general notion of the condition of Negro education in different parts of the South, particularly in the rural districts. This was the more true because, in making my studies of the different institutions I visited, I did not confine my observations to the class room but went out into the surrounding country; talked with white people and colored people; interviewed, where it was convenient to do so, prominent citizens, the trustees of the schools and state and county superintendents.

As I lived for the most part in the schools themselves I had an opportunity to get pretty well acquainted with a number of the teachers, and particularly with the heads of the institutions, and I came away with the feeling that I had made the acquaintance of at least one good friend in nearly every school I visited.

I can not go into particulars here but I want to tell you, Mr Washington, that this trip has been an inspiration. In spite of all the opportunities that I have had to see and study the work and influence of Tuskegee Institute, nothing I have ever seen or learned heretofore has so convinced me of soundness and wisdom of the work you are doing as what I have learned through this intimate acquaintance with the men and women who have gone out from Tuskegee to plant these smaller schools.

Not all of these schools are successful. Some of them have fought a losing battle and are now practically bankrupt. But some of the best men who have ever gone out from Tuskegee are, in my opinion, among these apparent failures. I say apparent failures, because in spite of the fact that they have not been able to put their schools on a secure footing or make of them what they hoped to do, these men have in every case done a good work in the communities in which they have lived. They have won the respect of both races; they have set an example of industry, honesty and thrift, and they have been positively heroic in their patient and unselfish efforts to build up their schools and make them a source of light and leading to the communities by which they are surrounded.

I can understand now the enthusiasm which Mr Bedford always felt for the work of these smaller schools. I feel as strongly as ever he did that we should do everything in our power to back up and support the work they are trying to do.

I do not mean to say that these schools have not sometimes made mistakes; I certainly do not mean to say that all of them could not be greatly improved. But these people — the heads of these schools I mean — have the right spirit. They are working in the right direction and where they have failed it has been because they could not get the support they needed and deserved.

I intend to write you fully in regard to the condition and needs of each individual school but I want to set down here, once and for all, my positive conviction, in the case of the "Tuskegee Schools" — and I would not say much less of the other schools I visited — that the work they are doing is necessary and right and is profoundly appreciated by both races. The men and women who are conducting these schools, no matter how inadequately the work is done, are a real asset. They ought to be backed up to the limit.

There is one thing more that I have learned, as a result of this trip. No one can know much about the Negro race, either of its difficulties or its possibilities, until he has become acquainted with the masses of the people as they are in the black belt counties of the South. They are a strong, vigorous, kindly and industrious people; simple minded, wholesome and good as God made them. They are very different from the people of the cities. As yet they have been very little infected with either disease or vice. The boys and girls that come from the country are usually earnest and ambitious. The young folks from the cities on the other hand [are] very likely to be indifferent and frivolous, and disposed to live by their wits. I noticed the difference as soon as I entered a school where a majority of the students were drawn from the sophisticated classes in the cities.

Fortunately the great majority of the race still live in the country and if they can be educated there, where they can grow up slowly and naturally, and be kept out of the cities where they will be forced along at a pace that will make them superficial and trifling, the race problem will eventually solve itself. In my opinion the hope of the race is these people in the country districts.

One thing further I ought, perhaps, to mention here. Everywhere throughout the South the white people are beginning to think seriously about the education of the colored people. More and more I find that the superintendents of education, where they are beginning to interest themselves in the education of the Negro, are turning to the heads of these industrial schools for advice and aid in supervising and improving the character of the colored public schools. This indicates to my mind a new and extremely important service which these smaller schools, if properly supported, may be able to perform.

In nearly every one of the schools which I visited I found some sort of cooperation with the public schools already in existence. Sometimes the head of the school himself was performing the work of a county supervisor. In other instances it was some one connected with the school who was doing the work. Frequently these schools have been the centers from which the United States Farm Demonstration Work among Negro farmers was carried on. Incidentally I might add that these Farm Demonstration Agents are doing a great deal, directly and indirectly, to improve the rural public schools. In other instances, the Industrial schools have organized and maintained county school associations, or they have conducted model public schools in conjunction with the work of the secondary schools. In fact they are all doing more or less of the sort of work that Tuskegee is trying to do in the surrounding counties.

What all of the schools, primary and secondary, public and private need, in addition to funds to enable them to carry on their work in a satisfactory way, is careful and competent supervision. Most of the schools that I visited need expert advice in all depart[ment]s of their work, which in their present isolation they are not able to get. They need this expert advice in the keeping of their accounts, in the conduct of their class room work and in the industrial operations. They are facing everywhere new and difficult problems, more difficult than any one who has not studied them can well understand. They need, as we need at Tuskegee, text books, that touch the lives and experience of their pupils, and deal with the problems around them.

As fast as we succeed in solving any of these problems at Tuskegee I feel that some arrangement should be made for giving these smaller schools the benefit of our experience. The summer school has helped; the visits of our teachers from time to time has been of great value to the smaller schools.

In conclusion let me say that I have learned much every year that I have been at Tuskegee but I believe that I have learned more in the last four months than I have in any previous similar period. I am very truly

[Robert E. Park]

TL   Con. 66   BTW Papers   DLC.

To N. Clark Smith

[Tuskegee, Ala.] May Thirtieth, 1913

Captain Smith: Criticism has come to the school from several centers with regard to the piece, "I Am Afraid To Go Home In The Dark."

The Executive Council feels that the impersonation of the man staggering home drunk should be eliminated from the program, although it has no objection to the music.[1]

[Booker T. Washington]

TLp   Con. 638   BTW Papers   DLC.

[1] Bandmaster N. Clark Smith apparently ignored BTW's order, since further criticism of the drunken act, from a niece of R. C. Ogden, came to BTW's attention in Aug. 1913. He again ordered Smith to drop the act. (Alice Ida Hannaford to BTW, ca. Aug. 1913; BTW to Mrs. Foster Hannaford, Aug. 14, 1913, Con. 935, BTW Papers, DLC.) For further correspondence on the band question, see BTW to N. Clark Smith, June 5, 1913, and N. Clark Smith to BTW, June 13, 1913, below.

To N. Clark Smith

[Tuskegee, Ala.] June Fifth, 1913

Dear Capt. Smith: Let me make one or two suggestions regarding the band, and I do so for very definite reasons.

First, I advise and urge that you leave out the singing on the part of the students. The singing is disappointing and not good; it is very rare that anybody can sing and play an instrument. The singing of the students does not represent the best that we can do. It places us at a disadvantage. Please leave that out. Please leave out the greater part of the singing on the part of the students.

Second, you will note by the enclosed article from the Advertiser that the critic who heard the band in Montgomery brought out just what I tell you, and that is, the band is at its best when playing Negro airs. I hope you will stick to that very largely.

I do not think it does you or the institution any good to be advertised as the greatest colored band master. I think you are, and others think so, but it is a great deal better to let your work prove that you are the greatest than for you to say so in your printed advertisements. I think it best in the future to leave that off. It is better for the people to be disappointed by getting more than they expected. The more modest we make the advertisements the better.

I have not heard from you or any one since I wrote you regarding Malden, West Virginia. Please let me know whether you can go there on the 30th or 31st. It is only five miles from Charleston and Mr. Stevenson will know how to get there and back. I do not want to disappoint the Malden people.

I might add, that going to extremes in the matter of advertisement is not in keeping with the policy and character of the school. Modesty and conservatism win in the long run.

One other thing: the artificial song that is attempted to be created in connection with the playing of "Swing Low Sweet Chariot" did not appear to me to add a thing to the playing but rather detracted. It did not come in naturally but rather grated upon the ear. Yours very truly,

Booker T. Washington

TLpS   Con. 923   BTW Papers   DLC.

To Emmett Jay Scott

[Tuskegee, Ala.] June 6, 1913

Mr. Scott: If you can get the time, I wish you would write a letter to several colored papers with a Nashville date line describing the bad conditions that exist in the colored cars on the L. & N. road after leaving Nashville.

B. T. W.

TLI   Con. 58   BTW Papers   DLC.

To Bruce Kinney[1]

[Tuskegee, Ala.] June Sixth, 1913

My dear Sir: Referring very briefly to yours of May 30th, which I find on my return home, I would say that all I attempted to do in the series of articles which I dictated rather hastily on my journey West was to give a report of my impressions. Perhaps in my haste, in several directions I might have stated part of the truth rather than the whole truth; in any case, I was trying to be truthful and fair.

My own race has suffered so much through misrepresentation, that I naturally have a kind of fellow-feeling for any group of people that is likely to be misrepresented.

I heartily wish I could reply more fully to your interesting letter, but, as I am preparing to leave Tuskegee for an important commencement engagement very soon, I cannot at this time do so. Perhaps I may see you at sometime and talk matters over with you more fully. Yours very truly,

[Booker T. Washington]

TLp   Con. 927   BTW Papers   DLC.

[1] Bruce Kinney (b. 1865) was southwest district superintendent of missions and district secretary of the American Baptist Home Mission Society from 1907 to 1914, and general superintendent for ten states west of the Mississippi River beginning in 1914. In 1912 he published *Mormonism — the Islam of America*, which was widely distributed by the Women's Home Mission Council.

Kinney criticized BTW for his favorable utterances regarding the Mormons, and claimed that BTW had been the victim of a "deliberate plan to remove prejudice" on the part of Mormon leaders in Salt Lake City. "Why one of your race," Kinney wrote, "should hasten to their defence who have absolutely no gospel to preach to the colored man who state that he has the mark of Cain upon him and is, therefore, under the displeasure of Almighty God and is not entitled to be treated as a man in this world and cannot enter into exaltation in the world to come, I cannot understand." (May 30, 1913, Con. 927, BTW Papers, DLC.)

To William Robert Ware[1]

[Tuskegee, Ala.] June Sixth, 1913

My dear Dr. Ware: Thank you so much for yours of June 2nd.[2] I wish I had time to answer it more at length, but, nevertheless, I am always glad to hear from you.

I did not mean in anything that I said or suggested in my Atlantic article to indicate that I had sympathy with the labor unions. As a rule, they have treated my race unfairly even though they make no discrimination in the letter of the law, they do discriminate in spirit and in practice; this is true of many of them not all.

One of my points in writing the article was to put these people on record as far as possible in the favor of justice to the Negro, and it sometimes occurs that when a man goes on record in favor of justice, he is inclined to live up to his promises.

When I spoke of a "good member" of the trade unions, I simply meant good from the standpoint of those on the inside of the union, not from my standpoint. I presume an anarchist would consider a man a good anarchist who lived up to all the teachings of anarchy; that was the idea that I had in mind.

It was most generous and kind of you to offer to help circulate this article and I am very glad to take advantage of your offer. I can use to good advantage any sum you care to send in this respect. My only suggestion is that I ought to know as soon as possible what to expect in order that I may secure the extra copies as it will be difficult to secure them as the days pass on.

Only a few hours before your letter came I was wishing that there was some way by which I could distribute a number of extra copies of the magazine.

I hope you are keeping quite well. Yours very truly,

[Booker T. Washington]

TLp Con. 923 BTW Papers DLC.

[1] William Robert Ware (1832–1915), a distinguished Boston architect, was the first head of the school of architecture at Massachusetts Institute of Technology and is considered the founder of architectural education in the United States.

[2] Ware had written that there was no such thing as a "good member" of a trade union. He said: "I hope you people may be saved from this sort of humiliation. It would be deplorable if, in the very act of self-assertion, they should prove to have substituted one kind of slavery for another." (Con. 923, BTW Papers, DLC.)

To Hartwell Douglass[1]

[Tuskegee, Ala.] June 9, 1913

Dear Sir: On yesterday I had the privilege of visiting and inspecting the Alabama tuberculosis camp under the care of your Board, and I want to let you know how very much I was pleased and surprised at what I saw in the tuberculosis camp. Of course I was anxious to see just how the prisoners were being treated, the greater part of whom are colored. I was surprised at the extreme cleanliness, and then I was equally surprised and pleased to see how well the rooms were ventilated, and how bright and full of sunshine they were kept. In fact, while I have had the privilege of visiting hospitals and camps of various kinds in many parts of the country, I have never seen any one anywhere which in my opinion is better kept than is true of the one at Wetumpka.

I was greatly pleased too, to note the fine relationship that existed between the convicts and the keepers. There seemed to be nothing of the strained and stilted attitude that one finds especially in Northern prisons. I was surprised in the penitentiary proper not to see a single gun or pistol in the possession or on the person of any of the keepers. While I know nothing, except by hearsay, of the way convicts are treated in the coal mines, lumber camps, etc., I do not hesitate to say that in the tuberculosis camp I found that the prisoners were receiving better care than is true of the majority of sick persons in tuberculosis camps outside of prisons. In fact, it would be well if something of the same kind of intelligent and conscientious care could be provided for the sick who are not in prison.

The prisoners with whom I talked and to whom I made a short address, seemed to be as happy and cheerful as prisoners could possibly be under the circumstances, and I want to thank you and your co-workers for what you are doing in the fine work that is being done in this camp. Yours very truly,

[Booker T. Washington]

TLp   Con. 923   BTW Papers   DLC.

¹ Hartwell Douglass of Montgomery, Ala., born in Lowndes County, Ala., in 1865, was in the real estate and insurance business until his appointment in Apr. 1913 as president of the Board of Inspectors of Convicts in Alabama.

From N. Clark Smith

Clarendon, Ark., June 13, 1913

My dear Mr. Washington: The last letter received from you disturbed my mind very much. I am sure you have not the slightest idea of how much worry, strength, energy, and vitality is going out in handling 47 boys and looking after every detail.¹ I remember the last conversation we had in the office, and Mr. Stevenson was to look after the business affairs of the organization, and I was to look after the music; but when we get out on the road and strike unusual problems I am forced to go to the rescue and take on the same worry that you told me to dispense with.

Rains have interfered with our success in about four places, but the public is loud in its praise of our entertainment, especially the singing and the glee club. I note with much regret that you constantly nag me about the singing of the students in the band. You must remember that this is not my first trip with the band, nor is it my first experience before the public; and entertainments of this kind are best given when the master is permitted to use his own judgment as to whether the audience approves or not. I have never attempted to interfere with the singing of Tuskegee Institute, as you know, except to help out wherever it was required. The singing of the band on this tour, as in former years, is only to relieve the monotony of so much band music, but this year it has taken on a feature rather than a grating noise — you will notice by the press clippings I am sending you under separate cover that this letter is no exaggeration. I hope, however, that you will not embarrass me any more with letters of this kind, for I am on the field of battle, and the public and not individuals are pleased beyond any question. My fifteen years' experience in preparing programs for this sort of entertainment serves me as a stimulant, though I am discouraged by the way the Tuskegee authorities write me. The band at present is entertaining the public with Negro music, which as you know I have worked on for so many years. It is rather embarrassing to have authorities dictate to one about his own structure, as to its merits good or bad, when they know absolutely nothing about it. I repeat; I hope you will give me more encouragement rather than discouragement, as I do not expect it of you.

The white people invariably call for classic selections, which we give them to the best of our ability. The press speaks for itself.

Now, in regard to the advertising which refers to me as the greatest "Negro bandmaster in America," it was not designed by myself, but they are the plates made by Dr. Proctor for the Atlanta engagement, and were turned over to me for use on this trip. Please your honor, I have always tried to be honest in regard to advertising myself, and have no control over the press-agent's wording of the same.

Negro music as played by the Tuskegee band on this trip is a revelation to all the musicians who attend our concerts, and it gives me much hope and encouragement for long years of study on the subject and a final opportunity to present it properly to the public.

Hoping that my strength will improve from what it is at present, I am, Yours very respectfully,

N Clark Smith
Bandmaster

For special mention of the Glee-Club; see

Tuskaloose Times-Gazette, June 5
Jackson Daily News   "   6
Vicksburg Evening Post   "   9
Greenville News   "   11
Memphis Ap[p]eal   "   13

TLS Con. 923 BTW Papers DLC. Postscript in Smith's hand.

1 John D. Stevenson, who accompanied the band on its tour, wrote BTW: "I would like to ask that you not bother Captain Smith any more in regard to suggestions about the kind of programme to be rendered. It is only a source of irritation to him and it does very little good in regard to having him change." (June 13, 1913, Con. 923, BTW Papers, DLC.)

From George Washington Carver

[Tuskegee, Ala.] June 18—'13

Mr. B. T. Washington, I have your note of June 17th and am wondering what I have done to merit such embarrassment as this places me in.[1]

I think you will agree with me that this is not only an embarrassment and injustice to me but to the school as well and forces me to do things that the school I am sure does not want done.

1st

I received the summer schedule from Mr. J. H. Washington to the effect that I would be on for the summer as usual.

So I made no plans to pack and store my goods and look for work, in fact I refused work elsewhere, depending upon the school, and at this date, upon 13 days notice, I get word that my services are not needed.

3d

It will be impossible for anyone to go into the exp. station now and car[r]y on the work intelligently. I am just now planting the catch crops, and making dry weather tests on different crops. I have accepted in good faith and planted 10 Dif. crops from the U.S. Dept. of Agr., 4 Dif. beans from Manchuria, which must be analyzed for their oil content, (some of them are nearly ready now.) 3 new varieti[e]s of tomatoes from Maryland and two choice new cultures from white men in Ga. and Ala.

In accepting the seed I told all of the parties I would do as they wished and make them deffinite, and regular reports as to growth, fungus diseases, insect enemies, yield of crops ect. ect.

So you see in this my awkward position also the schools.

Also there is the State and Govt. Weather Service which must be looked after daily or the instruments returned.

All the correspondence relating to the station and its work must be answered and Bul. sent out. This of course would have to be done in yours or Mr. J. H. Washington's office.

Again I agreed to teach as usual in the summer school, which I would not have done had I not expected work.

4th

Now as to the matter of salary it certainly cant be that, as I can and am actually making money for the school, by mfg. goods the school is paying out cash for I can more than make my salary, e.g. the $44.00

saved in the bed bug solution is simply one transaction. (Which is only a beginning) this is nearly ½ months salary.

I have arranged with the business committee to make all of the bed bug solution, silver polish, fly poison, pastes of Dif. kinds, and as much brown paint, as the capacity of my mill will turn out, also wood stains, and soldering fluid.

Now if you still decide that I am no longer needed, I will prepare to turn over every thing just as it is, but I do not see how it is possible for me to close out every thing in 13 days. Yours very truly

G. W. Carver

ALS Con. 639 BTW Papers DLC.

¹ BTW confessed that his office had made a "serious mistake" in not notifying Carver sooner that summer work was not available. About twenty-five other teachers had received earlier notice on the matter. (June 17, 1913, Con. 639, BTW Papers, DLC.)

From George Washington Carver

[Tuskegee, Ala.] June 18—13

My dear Mr. Washington, If you do not care to consider my appeal, please give me a recommendation as I must seek employment right away.

Thanking you in advance for any courtesy you extend in the matter I am yours truly,

Geo. W. Carver

ALS Con. 639 BTW Papers DLC.

To Benjamin Jefferson Davis

[Tuskegee, Ala.] June Nineteenth, 1913

Dear Mr. Davis: I see that the city government of Atlanta has just passed a segregation act.¹ We are sure this act is wholly unconstitutional and cannot stand before any unprejudiced court. What are you all going to do about it? I advise that you hire the best lawyer you can get and fight the matter from now on. Let me know if you need any outside help and what your plans are.

As I understand it, notwithstanding the fact that you might live in a district where the colored people are in the majority; the very minute the population should decrease and your home be surrounded by a majority of white people, these white people would have to insist that you part with your property. This, of course, would be robbery and no court would up-hold, in my opinion, such a law. I should be greatly disappointed if the colored people of Atlanta do not begin to fight this unjust act and keep up the fight until victory has been attained even if it has to go to the United States Supreme Court. Yours very truly,

Booker T. Washington

TLpS Con. 925 BTW Papers DLC.

[1] The Atlanta segregation ordinance of 1913 established all-white and all-black neighborhoods, and allowed persons in mixed areas to object to a person of another color moving next door. The law was enforced in such an arbitrary fashion that the Georgia Supreme Court struck it down in 1915, but the city council replaced it with another segregation ordinance. The U.S. Supreme Court found this unconstitutional in *Buchanan* vs. *Warley* (1917). (Dittmer, *Black Georgia*, 13–14.)

To Herbert Hornell Wright

[Tuskegee, Ala.] June 20, 1913

My dear Dean Wright: You do not know how very glad I am that you have written me in the frank way you have concerning both matters referred to in your two letters.

In regard to the Carnegie allowance, I will have a personal conference with Dr. Pritchett as soon as I can see him after going to New York. If nothing can be gotten from that source, it may be that we can induce Mr. Carnegie, when he returns, to put you on his private personal list in the way he has done in several cases.

Now, in regard to the other matter. I am very glad indeed for your frank opinion.[1] It will prove of the highest service to me and I shall pass the opinion on to others. The selection of a president for Fisk is a very serious and delicate undertaking, and no mistake must be made.

I have been blaming myself ever since I spoke at the alumni dinner for not making known the fact to the alumni that Howard had conferred the LL.D. degree upon you. I presume you have received the diploma by this time.

It was a great privilege for me to have a little part in the commencement exercises, and a greater privilege to be constantly making an effort to be of service to Fisk.

Booker is now at home, and he and I both are somewhat puzzled as to what he ought to undertake for the future. We have just a little idea that it may be better for him to take a year or two of post graduate work in some institution before entering upon any active enterprise. Mrs. Washington and I shall never forget what we owe Fisk University for making him what he is. Yours very truly,

Booker T. Washington

TLpS Con. 934 BTW Papers DLC.

¹ In an undated letter ca. June 15, Wright said that he did not believe rumors circulating at Fisk that the alumni, faculty, and students favored Cornelius Wortendyke Morrow for the presidency of Fisk University and that he hoped BTW would carefully investigate the matter before coming to a decision. (Con. 934, BTW Papers, DLC.)

To Robert Robinson Taylor

[Tuskegee, Ala.] June Twentieth, 1913

Mr. Taylor: I was at the brickyard this morning and stayed in the vicinity sometime.

I found that about only half the men were at work, the others were standing idly talking or going to or returning from the woods. There seemed to be nobody in charge of these men.

I was told that Mr. Gregory¹ was in charge, but as I have stated, I remained in the vicinity sometime and could not see or hear anything of Mr. Gregory.

I fear this is the beginning of piling up a deficit at the brickyard in the same way we have piled up a deficit for some years.

Booker T. Washington

TLpS Con. 637 BTW Papers DLC.

¹ William Gregory.

From Mrs. W. F. Behr[1]

Santa Monica, California   June 23, 1913

Dear Sir: Please pardon the liberty I am taking in addressing you at this late day, but I know the following must be of vital interest to you.

For some time I have contemplated writing to you, but for various reasons have postponed doing so.[2]

The night you were so frightfully beaten in W. 63d St., New York City, and were taken bleeding to the hospital was all witnessed by me. I was in the apartment on the lower floor in the left hand side of the house at the time.

The mother of the lady you met in the hall with the dogs had been a friend of my mother in Chicago, for many years, since childhood. I happened to call on her that evening, and [heard] and know everything connected with the affair.

I went to the police station. You had just left in the ambulance. I was horrified, [hea]ring your name, knowing the good you had done, fearing the result of your injury, knowing the nature of the weapon with which you were beaten (it being a very formidable looking object, having been sent from Africa.)

I was still more horrified to hear the lie — "He called me sweetheart" which I knew was spontaneously spoken to protect the man in the case. He had no weapon when he left the house. The commotion in the hall was heard inside and a roomer who had the weapon hanging on the wall as an ornament of curiosity grabbed it, running out in his house sandals, following you down the steps and into the street. Between the two you were severely cut and beaten on the head, for no other reason whatsoever than because you were a Negro, presumably with no object other than looking for the name of a party in the reference rack which was located in the vestibule of the house.

For personal reasons I did not wish to be associated with the scandal, as it had been a sorrow to me to know that my girlhood friend was living in such an atmosphere. For the sake of befriending her, however, I promised silence, and left New York state, battling with my sense of justice to come forward in your behalf. I have been troubled quite frequently, especially since the good I have received through Christian Science has predominated, knowing there is no reality except in truth and love and the good must triumph. I have admired your progress and feel it my duty to vindicate your honor in this unmerited and hideous affair, in which I know that you were absolutely innocent.

I am writing a letter to Col. Roosevelt which may also help you.

Please do not use my name, which I am reluctantly giving. Respectfully,

Mrs. W. F. Behr

TLpSr Copy Con. 931 BTW Papers DLC. Docketed: "sent to Wilford Smith."

[1] Santa Monica city directories listed the name of George C. Behr at 1747½ Ocean Avenue, the street address given in the letter.

[2] Forwarding a copy of the letter to his lawyer, Wilford H. Smith, BTW wrote that he did not plan to use it at present. "It is interesting and encouraging to have the exact truth brought out," BTW wrote. "I think this is a genuine letter." (July 12, 1913, Con. 931, BTW Papers, DLC.)

To Jacob Henry Schiff

Union Square Hotel, New York, June 27, 1913

Dear Mr. Schiff: I am replying to yours of June 17th in regard to the schools to be helped for next year. I have been keeping a pretty close eye on the schools that you have been helping and find for the most part that they are doing very good work.

In regard to the schools that have made application since the last distribution, I would state that Camp Hill Industrial Institute at Camp Hill, Ala. is doing good work but it is a school for white people.

The National Religious Training School at Durham, North Carolina seems to be involved so heavily in debt that I fear that there is no chance for it to get out of debt and get on its feet again. Until it does get out of debt I hardly think you would care to help it.

In regard to the American Church Institute for Negroes, I would state that you are helping two schools under the auspices of that organization. Under the circumstances I do not suppose you would care to help the organization itself.

The location of Wilberforce University at Wilberforce, Ohio is such that I do not think that it comes within the class of schools that you would desire to help at present, though the institution is doing good work.

I would suggest the following changes:

I would give Wiley University, Marshall, Texas, $75.00 instead of $100.00.

I would suggest that you give Voorhees Industrial School, Denmark, South Carolina $75.00 instead of $100.00, and that $50.00 be sent to the North Louisiana Industrial School, Grambling, Louisiana, Mr. Charles P. Adams, Principal. You have not heretofore helped any school in Louisiana and it is a very needy state. Yours very truly,

[Booker T. Washington]

TLc   Con. 67   BTW Papers   DLC.

An Article in the *Atlantic Monthly*

June, 1913

THE NEGRO AND THE LABOR UNIONS

When the Negro boy from the Southern states leaves the plantation or the farm and goes up to the city, it is not work, in many cases, that he is looking for. He has labored in the field, beside his father and his mother, since he was old enough to hold a hoe, and he has never known the time when he, and every other member of the family, could not find all the work they needed and more than they wanted. The one thing of which he has always had plenty at home has been work. It is very likely that a promise that he would earn more and do less has turned his steps from the farm; but at bottom it is not the search for easier work or higher wages that brings the country boy to town; it is the natural human desire to see a little more of the place he has heard of over yonder, beyond the horizon — the City.

The thing that takes the country boy to the city, in short, is the desire to learn something, either through books and in school, or in actual contact with daily life, about the world in which he finds himself. One of the first and most surprising things the country boy learns in the city is that work is not always to be had; that it is something a man has to go out and look for. Another thing he very soon learns is that there is a great deal of difference between skilled and unskilled labor, and that the man who has learned to do some one thing well, no matter how small it may be, is looked upon with a certain respect, whether he has a white skin or a black skin; while the man who has never learned to do anything well simply does not count in the industrial world.

The average Negro learns these things, as I have said, when he comes to the city. I mention them here because in considering the relation of the Negro to the labor unions it should be remembered that the average Negro laborer in the country districts has rarely had the experience of looking for work; work has always looked for him. In the Southern states, in many instances, the employment agent who goes about the country seeking to induce laborers to leave the plantations is looked upon as a kind of criminal. Laws are made to restrict and even prohibit his operations. The result is that the average Negro who comes to the town from the plantations does not understand the necessity or advantage of a labor organization, which stands between him and his employer and aims apparently to make a monopoly of the opportunities for labor.

Another thing which is to some extent peculiar about the Negro in the Southern states, is that the average Negro is more accustomed to work for persons than for wages. When he gets a job, therefore, he is inclined to consider the source from which it comes. The Negro is himself a friendly sort of person, and it makes a great deal of difference to him whether he believes the man he is working for is his friend or his enemy. One reason for this is that he has found in the past that the friendship and confidence of a good white man, who stands well in the community, are a valuable asset in time of trouble. For this reason he does not always understand, and does not like, an organization which seems to be founded on a sort of impersonal enmity to the man by whom he is employed; just as in the Civil War all the people in the North were the enemies of all the people in the South, even when the man on the one side was the brother of the man on the other.

I have tried to suggest in what I have said why it is true, as it seems to me, that the Negro is naturally not inclined toward labor unions. But aside from this natural disposition of the Negro there is unquestionably a very widespread prejudice and distrust of labor unions among Negroes generally.

One does not have to go far to discover the reason for this. In several instances Negroes are expressly excluded from membership in the unions. In other cases individual Negroes have been refused admittance to unions where no such restrictions existed, and have been in consequence shut out from employment at their trades.

For this and other reasons, Negroes, who have been shut out, or believed they had been shut out, of employment by the unions, have been in the past very willing strike-breakers. It is another illustration of the way in which prejudice works, also, that the strikers seemed to consider it a much greater crime for a Negro, who had been denied an opportunity to work at his trade, to take the place of a striking employee than it was for a white man to do the same thing. Not only have Negro strike-breakers been savagely beaten and even murdered by strikers or their sympathizers, but in some instances every Negro, no matter what his occupation, who lived in the vicinity of the strike has found himself in danger.

Another reason why Negroes are prejudiced against the unions is that, during the past few years, several attempts have been made by the members of labor unions which do not admit Negroes to membership, to secure the discharge of Negroes employed in their trades. For example, in March, 1911, the white firemen on the Queen and Crescent Railway struck as the result of a controversy over the Negro firemen employed by the road. The white firemen, according to the press reports, wanted the Negro firemen assigned to the poorest runs. Another report stated that an effort was made to compel the railway company to get rid of the Negro firemen altogether.

Shortly after this there was a long controversy between Public Printer Donnelly and the Washington Bricklayers' Union because, so the papers said, Mr. Donnelly would not 'draw the color line' in the employment of bricklayers on a job at the Government Printing Office. It appears that an additional number of bricklayers was needed. Mr. Donnelly drew upon the Civil Service Commission for the required number of men. A colored man was certified by the Commission, whereupon the white bricklayers struck, refusing to work with a Negro. Other Negroes were hired to take the strikers' places. The labor union objected to this and threatened to demand that President Taft remove Mr. Donnelly. These are some of the reasons why Negroes generally have become prejudiced against labor unions.

On the other hand, many instances have been called to my attention in which labor unions have used their influence in behalf of Negroes. On the Georgia and Florida Railway the white and colored firemen struck for higher wages. Mobs composed of both white and black men held up trains. It was reported that the Negroes were as violent in their demonstrations as the whites. In this instance the strikers won. A recent dispatch from Key West, Florida, stated that the white carpenters in that city had struck because two Negro workmen had been unfairly discharged. The members of the white Carpenters' Union refused to return to work until the Negroes had been reinstated.

At the 1910 National Council of the American Federation of Labor, resolutions were passed urging Negroes and all other races to enter the unions connected with the Federation. Since that time I have learned of activity on the part of the Federation in organizing Negro laborers in New Orleans, Pittsburg, Pensacola, Richmond, and several other Southern cities. In spite of the impression which prevails generally among colored people that the labor unions are opposed to them, I have known several instances in which Negroes have proven enthusiastic trade-unionists, and in several cases they have taken a leading part in organization and direction, not only in the colored, but in the white unions of which they chanced to be members.

Notwithstanding these facts, some of which seem to point in one direction and some in another, there seems to be no doubt that there is prejudice against Negroes among the members of labor unions and that there is a very widespread prejudice against labor unions among Negroes. These are facts that both parties must reckon with; otherwise, whenever there is a strike, particularly among those trades which have been closed to Negroes, there will always be a considerable number of colored laborers ready and willing to take these positions, not merely from a desire to better their positions as individuals, but also for the sake of widening the race's opportunities for labor.

In such strikes, whatever disadvantages they may have in other respects, Negroes will have this advantage, that they are engaged in a struggle to maintain their right to labor as free men, which, with the right to own property, is, in my opinion, the most important privilege that was granted to black men as a result of the Civil War.

Under these circumstances the question which presents itself to black men and white men of the laboring classes is this: Shall the labor unions use their influence to deprive the black man of his opportunity to labor, and shall they, as far as possible, push the Negro into the position of a professional 'strike-breaker'; or will the labor unions, on the other hand, admitting the facts to be as they are, unite with those who want to give every man, regardless of color, race or creed, what Colonel Roosevelt calls the 'square deal' in the matters of labor, using their influence to widen rather than to narrow the Negro's present opportunities; to lessen rather than to magnify the prejudices which make it difficult for white men and black men to unite for their common good?

In order to get at the facts in reference to this matter, I recently sent a letter of inquiry to the heads of the various labor organizations in the United States, in which I asked the following three questions:

What are the rules of your union concerning the admittance of Negroes to membership?

Do Negroes, as a rule, make good union men? If not, what in your opinion is the cause?

What do you advise concerning the Negro and the Trade-Unions?

I confess that I was both interested and surprised by the number and the character of the replies which I received. They not only indicated that the labor leaders had fully considered the question of the Negro laborer, but they also showed, in many instances, a sympathy and an understanding of the difficulties under which the Negro labors that I did not expect to find. A brief summary of these letters will indicate, better than anything I can say, the actual situation.

In reply to the question, 'What are the rules of your union concerning the admittance of Negroes?' nine unions, all but two of which are concerned with transportation, stated that Negroes are barred from membership. These unions are: the International Brotherhood of Maintenance-of-Way Employees, Switchmen's Union, Brotherhood of Railroad Trainmen, Brotherhood of Locomotive Firemen and Enginemen, Brotherhood of Locomotive Engineers, Order of Railway Conductors of America, Order of Railway Telegraphers, American Wire Weavers' Protective Association, and the International Brotherhood of Boilermakers, Iron Shipbuilders and Helpers of America.

Fifty-one national labor organizations, several of which are the strongest in the country, reported that there was nothing in their constitutions prohibiting the admittance of Negroes. In fact, many of the constitutions expressly state that there shall be no discrimination because of race or color. This is the case, for example, with the Wood, Wire and Metal Lathers' Union. The constitution of the United

Brotherhood of Carpenters and Joiners contains the following statement: 'We recognize that the interests of all classes of labor are identical regardless of occupation, nationality, religion or color, for a wrong done to one is a wrong done to all.'

Mr. Samuel Gompers, President of the American Federation of Labor, replying to the question concerning the admission of Negroes to labor unions wrote: 'Realizing the necessity for the unity of the wage-earners of our country, the American Federation of Labor has upon all occasions declared that trade unions should open their portals to all wage-workers irrespective of creed, color, nationality, sex, or politics. Nothing has transpired in recent years which has called for a change in our declared policy upon this question; on the contrary, every evidence tends to confirm us in this conviction; for even if it were not a matter of principle, self-preservation would prompt the workers to organize intelligently and to make common cause.'

With two exceptions the answers to my question, 'Do Negroes in your opinion make good Union men?' were that they do.

Mr. Ralph V. Brandt, of Cleveland, secretary-treasurer of the Wood, Wire and Metal Lathers' Union, wrote: 'I regret to say I must answer "no" to this question. We have had several locals in the South,' he continues, 'where the membership was made up either exclusively of Negroes or a large majority, and we have had only two out of the entire number that have made a success. One of these locals is in Savannah, Georgia, and the other in Charleston, South Carolina, and, as it happens, both of these are among the earliest locals chartered by our organization. I have had this situation come under my personal observation in our locals in this city, of which I am a member, and I must say that the Negro lathers in Cleveland have failed absolutely in meeting the general requirements of union men.'

The letter goes into details, describing the various efforts, all of them unsuccessful, which the local unions made to induce the Negro lathers to re-affiliate. They were promised recognition in the governing board of the union and, at the suggestion of some of the colored lathers, one of their number was recognized as a contractor, but these measures also failed of their purpose.

Another letter to much the same effect was received from the secretary of the Tobacco Workers' International Union. The secretary wrote: 'Our experience has been that very few of them have turned out to be such [good union men]. They have a large Union in Richmond, Va., all colored men, and only a few of the whole membership are what I would call union men. They do not seem to grasp the significant feature of the trade-union [movement].'

Mr. B. A. Larger, general secretary of the United Garment Makers of America, said: 'I think the Negroes working in the trades do make good union men, but I do not think that the Negro waiters make good union men, as I have had some experience in trying to organize them. They would be well organized and apparently have a strong organization, but in a short time it would go to pieces. Among them there would be some good loyal members, but not sufficient [in numbers] to keep up the organization.

'I am unable,' he adds, 'to give a definite reason except, perhaps, that it might be the fault of the head waiter, who would induce some person to go into the organization and break it up. Nevertheless, it is true that they are the most difficult to organize of any class of people.'

A somewhat different light is thrown upon the situation by a letter from Mr. Jacob Fisher, general secretary of the Journeymen Barbers' International Union. This letter is so interesting that I am disposed to quote from it at considerable length. 'In my opinion,' Mr. Fisher writes, 'Negro trade-unionists make as good members as any others, and I believe that the percentage of good trade-unionists among the Negroes is just as high as of any other class of people; but the percentage of Negroes of our trade belonging to our organization is not as high as among other classes. One of the greatest obstacles we have to confront, in inducing and urging the Negroes to become members of our organization, is a general current rumor that the white barbers are trying to displace and put out of business the Negro barbers. There is no foundation whatever for the rumor, but it has become generally spread among the Negro barbers, and this feeling has been urged upon them more strongly than it would otherwise be, by Negro employers, who do everything they can, as a general rule, to keep their employees from joining our trade-union. We have tried for years to impress upon the minds of Negro barbers that their best hope for better conditions lies in becoming members of our organization. But the feeling that exists among them has been so impressed upon their minds by no one else except the Negro employer, as to make it a very difficult matter to induce individual Negro barbers to become members of our organization.'

Mr. Fisher adds that a few years ago a large percentage of the barbers were Germans. In more recent years Jews and Italians have been getting into the barber business in large numbers. Barbers of all of these nationalities are 'rapidly becoming educated' in the trade-union movement, and are active in bringing other members of the trade of their nationalities into the union. 'On the other hand,' he continues, 'the Negro barbers, while loyal to the movement and active in the affairs within the organization, do not direct their attention to the unorganized Negro barbers and use their endeavors to educate them in trade-union matters.'

The Mine Workers' Union has the largest Negro membership of any of the labor unions. Mr. John Mitchell, the former president, states that, while there are no exact statistics as to the number of Negro members in the United Mine Workers of America, it is safe to say that not less than 30,000 of the 300,000 members are Negroes. Many important offices are filled by colored members.

'The Negroes who are mining coal in the Northern states,' he adds, 'make first-class union men. In the Southern states where Negroes are employed in large numbers in the mining industry, unionism is not so strong. This, however, is in part accounted for by the fact that the mine-owners oppose strongly the organization of their workmen, and the miners are so poor that they cannot contend successfully against the corporations unless they are supported financially by the organized men in other states.'

Mr. Edwin Perry, secretary-treasurer of the United Mine Workers of America, replying to the question, 'Do Negroes make good union men?' wrote: 'I say unequivocally "yes," and point with pride to the fact that the largest local branch of our organization has at least 80 per cent colored men. It is progressive and up to date in all things. This local is located in my home state at Buxton, Iowa.

'It is possible,' he adds, 'that misguided individuals may, in some isolated instances, discriminate against the Negro, but when our attention is called to the same, we endeavor to overcome that condition by the application of intelligence and common sense. The time is not far distant when the working men and women of our country will see the necessity of mutual coöperation and the wiping out of existence of all class lines.'

Mr. John Williams of Pittsburg, president of the Amalgamated Association of Iron, Steel and Tin Workers, stated that the laws of his association provide that 'all men working in and around rolling mills are eligible to membership.' No line of demarcation is drawn. He was of the opinion that Negroes, if given the opportunity, make good union men. He also advised that Negroes should be educated in the principles and ideals for which the labor-union movement stands.

In view of the newspaper reports from time to time concerning the discrimination against Negro chauffeurs, the statement of Mr. Thomas L. Hughes, general secretary-treasurer of the International Brotherhood of Teamsters, Chauffeurs, Stablemen and Helpers, concerning Negroes in labor-unions is particularly interesting.

'I have had considerable dealing with colored men as members of our trade-union,' he writes. 'In every instance where the colored men have been organized, we find them to be loyal to our union in every shape and manner. To say that they make good union men is only putting it too lightly. We have local unions composed entirely of Negroes in certain parts of the country that are a credit to our international union.'

In many localities Negroes, Mr. Hughes asserts, belong to the same organization as white men and get on satisfactorily. In many of the large local unions, where there are both, the colored membership is large. The officers of the organization are also colored.

The secretary of the Amalgamated Meat-Cutters and Butchers' Workmen, replying to my question, 'Do Negroes make good union men?' said, 'I will say that the Negro averages up with the white man and I cannot see any difference, as it is all a matter of education. Both classes improve as they become more familiar with the work. I might say, incidentally, that one of the best and most conscientious officials we have is a Negro member of our local union in Kingston, N.Y. He is a man who not only has the entire confidence of his associates in the organization, but is held in the highest esteem by the entire community and, as an officer, stands second to none.'

The answers to the question, 'What do you advise concerning the Negro and Trade Unions?' were practically unanimous in advising that the Negro be organized and educated in the principles of trade-unionism. Even the leaders of those unions which bar out the Negro advised that he be organized. The president of the Switchmen's Union, Mr. S. E. Heberling, wrote: 'The laws of our union will not permit Negroes to join, the constitution using the term "white." However,' he adds, 'I advise that the Negroes in all trades organize to better their condition. This organization, in reference to Negroes following the occupation of switchmen, has advised the American Federation of Labor, with whom we are affiliated, to grant the Negroes charters as members of the Federal Labor Union. I hope your race will take advantage of the opportunities afforded them.'

Mr. H. B. Perham, of St. Louis, president of the Order of Railroad Telegraphers, wrote: 'The Order of Railroad Telegraphers is a white man's organization, that provision having been in its constitution since its inception twenty-six years ago. I advise the organization to help the poor man to a better standard of living, better education, resistance of injustice and the like. As the Negro, generally speaking, is poor, he needs organization.'

Mr. John J. Flynn, of Chicago, secretary and treasurer of the Brotherhood of Railroad Freight Handlers, wrote: 'I believe that a campaign of education should be started among the Negro workers of the country, this education to dwell principally on the fact that in organization there is strength and that the surest way to rise above their present condition is to become members of labor organizations that their craft calls for. In short, the best way for the Negro to improve his present condition is to become a member of a branch of the labor movement which covers his craft.'

Mr. James Wilson, general president of the Pattern Makers' League, said: 'I would advise that the Negro be taught to join the union of whatever occupation he is following, and if there is no union of that calling, that he organize one, for there is no greater educational movement in the country for all wage-earners than the trade-union movement.'

Mr. E. J. Brais, general secretary of the Journeyman Tailors' Union, wrote: 'Our opinion is and our advice would be that the Negroes should organize trade-unions by themselves under the jurisdiction, of course, of the American Federation of Labor, being governed by the same rules in all their trades as the white mechanics. We believe in that case, if they organize into separate locals in the various trades and insist upon the same scale of wages as their white brethren, it would be a source of strength to both elements.'

Mr. James Duncan, international secretary of the Granite Cutters' International Association of America, replied in substance as follows to my inquiry: 'I advise concerning Negroes and trade-unions, that they be organized the same as white people are organized, mixed with

white people, where that is advisable, but in local unions by themselves where circumstances make it advisable for white people and
Negroes being in separate organizations.'

Mr. Duncan stated that the rule did not prohibit Negroes joining
the union, but throughout the South granite-cutting was usually considered a 'white man's trade.' Because of the feeling in the South he
believed that Southern granite-cutters would not be disposed to work
at that trade with Negroes.

'This,' he added, 'is sentiment, and forms no part of the rules of our
association.'

I have quoted at some length the statements made by the labor leaders, because it seemed to me that these statements not only disclose
pretty accurately the position of the labor organizations as a whole, in
reference to the Negro, but indicate, also, the actual situation of the
Negro at the present time in the world of organized industry. In this
connection it should be remembered that the labor unions are not
primarily philanthropic organizations. They have been formed to meet
conditions as they exist in a competitive system where, under ordinary
circumstances, every individual and every class of individuals is seeking to improve its own condition at the expense, if necessary, of every
other individual and class. It is natural enough, under such conditions,
that union men should be disposed to take advantage of race prejudice
to shut out others from the advantages which they enjoy.

The leaders of the labor movement, however, see clearly that it is
not possible permanently to close, to the million or more Negro laborers
in this country, the opportunity to take the positions which they are
competent to fill. They have observed, also, that race prejudice is a
two-edged sword, and that it is not to the advantage of organized
labor to produce among the Negroes a prejudice and a fear of labor
unions such as to create in this country a race of strike-breakers. The
result has been that in every part of the United States where Negro
laborers have become strong enough in any of the trades to be able to
hold their own, the Negro has been welcomed into the unions, and the
prejudice which shut him out from these trades has disappeared.

As an illustration of this fact, I cannot do better than quote a few
paragraphs from the report of the English Industrial Commission in
1911 in regard to labor conditions in the Southern states, which gives
a very clear and, I think, accurate description of local conditions in
cities to which it refers.

Concerning the Negro labor unions in the Birmingham district, the English Industrial Commission reported: 'It is not owing to the existence of any very sympathetic feeling between the white men and the Negroes that the latter are allowed to join the union; it is simply because the white men feel that their interest demands that colored men should be organized, as far as possible, so as to prevent them from cutting down the rate of wages. Wherever a sufficient number of colored men can be organized, they are encouraged to form a union of their own, affiliated to the white man's union, but where there are not enough to form a separate union, they are allowed in the South to become members of the white man's organization.

'The building and mining industries,' the report continues, 'are the two in which the white and colored races come into the most direct competition with each other, yet it cannot be said that in either of these industries a situation exists which occasions friction. No doubt in both industries the white men would like to monopolize the skilled work for themselves, but they recognize that that is impossible and make the best of the situation. . . . The white men make it quite clear that their connection with the colored men is purely a matter of business and involves no social recognition whatever. It is in the mining industry that the relations between the two races, though working side by side, in direct competition, are smoothest. They acted together in the great strike of 1902, and in fact the good feeling between the whites and the colored men was used with great effect by the opponents of the strikers, who charged the white miners with disloyalty to their race.'

In New Orleans the Commission found a very interesting situation which is described as follows: 'It is probable that in New Orleans there is a larger number of white and Negro people in very much the same economic position than in any other American city, or anywhere else in the world. The industries of New Orleans are of a kind which employ mainly unskilled or semi-skilled labor, with the result that both white men and Negroes are found doing the same kind of work and earning the same rate of pay. . . . The various unions combine in maintaining the Dock and Cotton Council, which dominates the entire business of compressing, carting, and loading cotton. . . . By arrangement between the Dock and Cotton Council and the employers, work has to be impartially apportioned between the white compress gangs and the colored gangs.'

In the letters from which I have so far quoted the writers have been content, for the most part, simply to answer the questions asked them, and sometimes, when they have not come into contact with the racial problem involved, have been disposed to discuss the advantages of labor organizations in the abstract. More interesting are the letters which I have received from labor men who have come into close quarters with the problem, in their efforts to organize Negro labor in the face of existing conditions.

As these letters indicate better than any discussion on my own part, the way the problem works out in practice, it will be well, perhaps, to let the writers speak for themselves.

One of the most interesting letters which I received was from Mr. M. J. Keough, of Cincinnati, acting president of the International Moulders' Union. Mr. Keough wrote that one of the national officers of the Moulders' Association, who was a Southerner by birth, had been devoting a very considerable part of his time in trying to organize the Negro Moulders of the South. In Chattanooga, for example, there were between six and eight hundred moulders, whom they had been trying, with no great success, to get into the union.

'Of course you are aware,' he continues, 'that there is a certain feeling in the South against the Negro, but we have succeeded in overcoming that, and have educated our members to the fact that if the Negro moulder of Chattanooga is not brought up to the level of the white man, he, the Negro, will eventually drag the white man down to his condition. It is our purpose to continue the agitation in order to have a thorough organization of the Negro moulders of Chattanooga.

'We find there is considerable opposition on the part of the employers in Chattanooga to the Negro moulders joining the union. I might state we have a shop on strike in which practically all of the men were Negro moulders and are being supported by our organization. The employers are having these Negro moulders out on strike arrested for loitering, etc., and have put us to considerable expense in keeping our Negro members, who are on strike, out of jail. In conclusion let me state that we are very anxious that the Negro moulders should become members of our organization and enjoy all its rights and privileges.'

Another important letter in this connection was received from Mr. John P. Frey, editor of the *International Moulders' Journal*. He said: 'As I made many earnest efforts to organize Negro moulders in the

South some twelve years ago and met with almost complete failure, owing to what appeared to be the Negroes' suspicion as to the genuineness of our intentions, it is but natural that I should still be interested in the question. While a Northerner, I have spent sufficient time in the Southern states to become familiar personally with the several phases presented by the question of the Negro status, both socially and industrially.'

In his further reply to my question, Mr. Frey referred to an editorial in a recent issue of the iron-moulders' official organ. In this editorial the statement was made that the fact that there were so few Negroes in the Moulders' Union was due largely to race prejudice.

'As the years rolled by,' the editor continues, 'our members in the South realized that the question of Negro membership was an industrial one. The castings made by the Negroes were worth as much as those made by white men, but they might be sold for less in the open market because the Negro was forced to work for much smaller wages. It was not a question of social equality, but a question of competition in the industrial field. Other trade-unions in the South have faced the same problem and have been even more ready, in some instances, to take the Negro mechanic or laborer into their ranks. Not long ago the largest union in the South, No. 255, of Birmingham, Alabama, gave the question thorough consideration, with the result that it decided to take qualified Negro mechanics into membership. Their action may not have been in line with the sentiment of twenty years ago, but it was in line with justice to themselves and to the Negro who had learned the trade, for industrial competition pays no heed to questions of social equality. In our trade, the Negro has become an industrial factor in the South, and the wise policy of giving him the benefit of membership in our organization will not be of value to him alone, but to every one who works at moulding. To expect that race prejudice and social questions will be eliminated or adjusted in a generation or two, is to expect too much, but the question of the Negro moulder is neither one of race nor of social equality; it is purely one of industrial competition.'

Mr. Frey referred, also, to an article by Mr. Nick Smith, who is a Southerner by birth and training, has worked all his life as a moulder in the South, and is now organizer of his union. In this article Mr. Smith said in part: 'If we want to make the Negro a good union man, we will have to grant him the same privileges and the same treatment in the shop that is enjoyed by the white moulder. Treat the Negro square; allow him to work in our shops when he presents his union card, and we will take away from the foundryman his most effective tool, the Negro strike-breaker. Refuse the Negro this privilege and the foundryman will continue to use him to trim us with when we have trouble. The Negro is here, and here to stay, and is going to continue to work at moulding, and it is for us to say whether he shall work with us as a union moulder, or against us as a tool in the foundryman's hands and a strike-breaker. When a Negro comes to your town, do what you can to see that he gets a job, and is treated as a union man should be treated. Refuse to do this and you force him to allow the foundryman to use him as a club to beat us into submission. The I. M. U. has spent considerable money and time to get the Negro moulder educated up to the point where he is today, and the refusal of the white moulder to work with the Negro will undo all that has been accomplished. Brothers, it is up to us to think it over.'

Mr. William J. Gilthorpe of Kansas City, secretary-treasurer of the International Brotherhood of Boilermakers, Iron Shipbuilders and Helpers, said: 'Being a Southern man myself, in breeding and education, I naturally think that I am acquainted with the colored people. I served, in 1880, in New Orleans with the colored delegates to the central body, and I want to say that the colored delegates were as true and loyal to the principles of true labor movement as any delegate in that body. They make the best of union men. There is no trouble with them whatever. In answer to your question I say this: The rules of this organization do not permit them to be initiated into this order. Now I am one of those who advocate the organization of the colored men, as well as the white men. I possess a few followers, but this is a principle that is going to live, and it is going to be an established fact, in this order, sooner or later. As far as my advice goes, and humble efforts, I would say organize them in every case where they are eligible.'

Mr. Frank Duffy, general secretary of the United Brotherhood of Carpenters and Joiners, wrote: 'I wish to inform you that we do not draw the color line in our organization, as is evidenced by the fact that throughout the Southern states we have in the United Brotherhood twenty-five unions composed exclusively of colored men. We have found in our experience that where there are colored carpenters in great numbers, it is an absolute necessity both for their advancement and for the welfare of the white carpenters as well, to organize them.

We have a colored organizer in the South, Mr. J. H. Bean, who has done splendid work in getting the colored carpenters together.'

In order to find out what were the experiences and views of colored union men, I communicated with Mr. Bean and received a very interesting reply. He wrote that he had been connected with the United Brotherhood of Carpenters and Joiners of America for more than twelve years and had been a delegate to every national convention but one since 1902. Since October, 1908, he has been continually engaged as general organizer for colored carpenters in nine Southern states. 'During that time,' he added, 'I have met with some opposition from both races, until they saw that one carpenter is largely dependent upon another, and to organize our forces in the right way is not only helpful to one but to all engaged in similar work. Then their opposition ceased.'

One of the easiest things in the world, I have found, is prophecy, and there have been a good many prophecies in regard to the Negro. Some persons have said there is no future for the Negro, because, in the long run, he cannot compete with the white man, and, as a consequence, in the course of time the Negro will be crowded out of America and forced to go to some other country.

Other persons say that the future is dark for the Negro because, as soon as it appears that the black man is actually able to live and work alongside of the white man in competition for the ordinary forms of labor, racial prejudice will be so intensified that the Negro will be driven out of the country or he will be reduced to some form of industrial servitude and compelled to perform the kind of work that no white man is willing to do.

While the letters I have quoted do not tell the whole story of the Negro and the unions, they at least throw some light upon the value of the predictions to which I have just referred. They indicate, at any rate, that the Negro, as a matter of fact, can and does compete with the white laborer, wherever he has an opportunity to do so. They show also that, on the whole, the effect of this competition is not to increase but to lessen racial prejudice.

It is nevertheless true, that the prejudice of the Negro against the unions, on the one hand, and of the white man against the black, on the other, is used sometimes by the unions to shut the Negro from the opportunity of labor, sometimes by the employer to injure the work of the unions. In the long run, however, I do not believe that, in the struggle between capital and labor, either party is going to let the other use the sentiment of the community in regard to the race question to injure it in an industrial way.

When, for example, the capitalist, as has sometimes happened, says that Negro and white laborers must not unite to organize a labor union, because that would involve 'social equality,' or when, as has happened in the past, the white laborer says the Negro shall not work at such and such trades, not because he is not competent to do so, but because he is a Negro, the interest in 'social equality,' so far as it refers to those particular matters mentioned, tends to decrease.

So long as there is any honest sentiment in favor of keeping the races apart socially, I do not believe the unions or the public are willingly going to permit individuals to take a dishonest advantage of that sentiment. On the contrary, so far as the labor unions are concerned, I am convinced that these organizations can and will become an important means of doing away with the prejudice that now exists in many parts of the country against the Negro laborer. I believe that they will do this not merely, as Mr. Gompers has said, from 'principle,' but because it is to their interest to do so. At present, however, that prejudice exists and it is natural that individuals should make use of it to their own advantage. If proprietors of Negro barber shops seek to prejudice their workmen, as is reported, against the white unions, so that they may pay them less wages, it is likewise true that some white unions take advantage of the existing prejudice wholly to exclude colored men from some of the trades in which they are perfectly competent to work.

There is, in my opinion, need for a campaign of education not only among Negro artisans but among white artisans as well. With every such effort of the labor leaders to create a sentiment among white men, as well as colored, which will permit both races to work together for their common good, I am heartily in sympathy.

In spite of all that has been said to the contrary, we are making progress in the solution of this, as of other problems connected with the relations of the races in this country. To say that we are not is pretty much the same as saying that, in spite of all our efforts, the world is growing worse instead of better. Justice, fair play, and a disposition to help rather than to injure one's fellow are not only good things in themselves, but in the long run they are the only things that pay, whether in the case of an individual, a group of individuals, or a race.

It seems to me that the letters to which I have referred in this article show clearly that the leaders of the labor organizations fully realize what the masses of laboring men must inevitably come to see, namely, that the future belongs to the man, or the class of men, who seeks his own welfare, not through the injury or oppression of his fellows, but in some form of service to the community as a whole.

Atlantic Monthly, 111 (June 1913), 756–67. A typed rough draft, entitled "The Negro and the Trade Unions," is in Con. 959, BTW Papers, DLC.

An Article in the *American Magazine*

June 1913

WILLIAM HENRY LEWIS

About five years after Abraham Lincoln signed the proclamation that set four millions of my race in America free, there was born in Berkeley, Virginia, a little colored boy who became Assistant Attorney-General of the United States and, after some difficulty, a member of the National [American] Bar Association.

Shortly after his first appearance, in a Negro cabin on the outskirts of Berkeley, the little Negro boy received the name of William Henry Lewis. One of the first privileges that freedom brought to the colored people was that of having just as many names as white folk. Those of us who happen to have come along a little earlier did not, in most cases, enjoy this privilege. We were born with only one name and did not acquire the other until shortly after the Surrender. But this boy of whom I am writing was born not only under the Stars and Stripes, but also under the Proclamation, and so he was able to start out in life William Henry Lewis, instead of just plain Bill. This, in my opinion, is quite as it should be, since a man with only one name, that anyone knows anything about, is usually a man who wears only one gallus and no collar, and amounts to very little in the community.

I mention this matter of a name because I want to emphasize the fact that this boy was born in the early days of Emancipation, when all the colored people round about Berkeley and Portsmouth, where he lived, were inspired with a great hope. William Henry was the sort of boy to be touched and stimulated by the big feeling that prevailed everywhere throughout the South about this time. In fact, he is one of the "new issues," as the younger generation is sometimes called, who seems to have come as near as anyone else to justifying the expectations of those early days. I say this, not merely because he has succeeded in reaching what is, perhaps, the most responsible position ever held in the Government by a colored man, but because he has reached this position as a merited promotion after long service and has demonstrated his ability to fill his place.

It was young Lewis's fortune — comparatively rare among colored boys — to get into school at an early age. By peddling matches and by doing odd jobs he managed in one way and another to make his way through the Virginia Normal and Collegiate Institute, one of the early schools for colored youth in that part of the country. From there he went to Amherst College, Massachusetts, where he was graduated in 1892. While he was in Amherst he did two things which, aside from the color of his skin, served to mark him off from the rest of the student body. He made himself captain of the college football team, and distinguished himself as an orator and debater. He not only carried off the prizes in at least two of the most important contests, but was finally elected by his class at graduation to deliver the class-day oration, an honor of which he is still very proud.

In the early days after the war, one of the great sources of entertainment and instruction for the masses of the people, white and black, who had the good fortune to live in a town where there was a court house, was the opportunity to go to court on days when some important cases were on trial. Particularly when there was a murder case people would gather from all the surrounding country.

Mr. Lewis has told me that he received many a good thrashing for running away from home at night to attend the trial of some of the cases that were once famous in the annals of the Portsmouth courts. A murder trial is not, perhaps, the best sort of amusement for a boy, but the excitement of these murder trials, in which some of the keenest minds in the state were pitted against each other, provided a kind of stuff to kindle the imagination of an impressionable boy, and it was this early experience, more than anything else, that led young Lewis, after he had completed his course at Amherst, to go farther and try what the Harvard Law School could do toward giving him a profession and making him a lawyer.

While Lewis was at Harvard he gained an almost national reputation as a football player. It was his business, as he has explained to me, from his position in the center, to hit the opposing line, and hit it hard. He did this so well that in his day he had the reputation of being the best player who had ever played in that position. He believes that, perhaps, the most valuable portion of his training in college was obtained on the football field, where he learned, as he says, "to regard with indifference trifling insults or severe physical hurts." Mr. Lewis has been playing the game of life much as he learned to play football in Harvard. He fought his way up without fear, and has never been satisfied except to win.

Many people believe that it is much easier for a colored man to succeed in the North than in the South, because there is no "color line" in the North as there is in the South, at least, no color line that is clearly marked and officially recognized. And yet, one of the most baffling and discouraging obstacles in the way of colored people in the North is this same "color line" — all the more perplexing because it is so vague, so inconsistent and so changing. Mr. Lewis has been no exception in this respect. He has had his turn at "bucking the color line," as he sometimes calls it. I am glad to say, however, that he has not permitted himself to be discouraged or permanently soured by any of his experiences.

After leaving the university, Mr. Lewis settled in Cambridge and practiced law in Boston. He entered politics and was elected city councilman of Cambridge in 1899, 1900 and 1901. In 1902 he was elected to the State Legislature, but was defeated for reëlection the following year. In 1903 he was appointed by President Roosevelt to the position of Third Assistant United States District Attorney with headquarters at Boston. He was promoted to Second Assistant United States District Attorney in 1904, and was head of the Naturalization Bureau from 1903 to 1909.

In 1911, when he was appointed to the position he occupied until recently, that of Assistant Attorney-General of the United States, the colored men of Boston gave him a banquet at one of the leading hotels of the city. At this banquet, in reply to the congratulations showered upon him by other speakers, Mr. Lewis made a speech in which he made two references that particularly impressed me. He recalled the fact that in this same hotel in which he was at that moment an honored guest, he had once served in the capacity of a waiter; and in reference to the honor that had been conferred upon him, he declared that he had no illusions, he knew, he said, that it was not in spite of, but because of the fact that he was a Negro that he had been honored with this high office. He added that he accepted the responsibilities of the position not merely as a distinction conferred upon himself but upon the whole race which he represented.

The reason I mention this fact is because it is not always comfortable to be a colored man in this country, and the inconveniences frequently increase as individuals, either by fortune or through their own particular merits, succeed in rising to a position above the masses of their fellows.

One reason why I, with most other colored people, believe in, honor and respect Mr. Lewis is because, in the high position in which he has risen, he has neither forgotten his own path nor sought to separate himself from the race to which he belongs.

Booker T. Washington

American Magazine, 75 (June 1913), 34–37. BTW submitted the article to the *American Magazine* in Sept. 1912. See BTW to the Editor of the *American Magazine,* Sept. 13, 1912, Con. 447, BTW Papers, DLC.

From Thomas B. Patterson[1]

Downingtown Pa., Ind. School, July 2/13

My Dear Dr. Washington, I am writing you this letter in fear & trembling because of the fact that I am uncertain as to the out-come of it, but deep down in my heart I hope that it will not have been written in vain.

Inclosed you will find 2 clippings from a recent letter that I received from Mr. T. Thos. Fortune of the Age which will give you an inkling of the mission of this letter.[2] Also my authority for writing it.

I am a friend of Mr. Fortune's and have been for a number of years. I am also a great & staunch admirer of you, not because of your great work alone, but because of your friendship to me when I could not help myself. This being the case it occurred to me that it was a national calamity for the greatest Negro Educator living, or dead and the greatest living Negro Editor to be estrainged from each other when the union of two such great forces me[a]nt and means so much to our people.

Being constantly in t[o]uch with Mr. Fortune I have finally gotten his consent to approach you on this very delicate subject and I now feel that he is ready to smoke the pipe of peace and make any amends for his part in the estrangement. In your work Up from Slavery Mr. Fortune is there held up as being one of your best advisers. Is it not possible for that statement to be again true as of yore?

In all these years Mr. Fortune has not said one word to me against you altho I have plied him with question after question. He is also ready to make any advance necessary to make the dream of my life one great grand song of reality.

Men & Measures almost demand your reunion & it is the prayer of my heart that you heed the call.

Just one word & I am through. Forgive my presumption for writing this letter, but one great consuming desire compelled it.

May I have a word from you?³ Most respectfully,

Thos B Patterson

ALS Con. 930 BTW Papers DLC. Written on stationery of the Emancipation Proclamation Commission of Pennsylvania.

¹ Thomas B. Patterson, born in Columbia, S.C., in 1866, graduated from Hampton Institute in 1890. After working for the school's Hemenway Farm for several months, he moved to Philadelphia.

² Fortune had written to Patterson: "If you think *the race* needs a closer relationship, personal, between Dr. Washington and myself, and thousands of the race think so, 'do what seemeth good in thy sight' in the case. Personally, I think as much of Dr. Washington as I ever did, and appreciate and sympathize as much in the hard task he has of helping the race and leading it into the better life." (Undated enclosure in Fortune's hand, ca. June 1913, Con. 930, BTW Papers, DLC.)

³ BTW replied to Patterson: "I do not regard myself as being estranged from Mr. Fortune, and I do not know as he regards himself as being estranged from me in any matter of mutual interest. I am sure we shall be able in the future as in the past to work together." (July 11, 1913, Con. 930, BTW Papers, DLC.)

Timothy Thomas Fortune to Emmett Jay Scott

Lawrenceville, N.J., July 4, 1913

Dear Mr. Scott: Your little visit has made me feel like a new man. It was so good to have an hour with you "all by our lonesome."

The letter you mailed me in New York has not reached me as yet and if you sent the line from Philadelphia yesterday it also has yet to arrive.

Talking about letters: Did Dr. Washington ever tell you how I came to return to him all those he ever wrote me during 18 years? No! Well it was on this wise. In 1909, I think, Mrs. Fortune told me a friend of Dr. Washington had visited her and asked her *how much money* she would want for those letters, as it was feared Mr. Fortune might use them against Dr. Washington. She told the party that no money would buy them of her and that she would only release them to me or on my signed order. She refused to tell me the name of the Doctor's friend.

Well, some time after that, I happened to be at The Age office when Dr. Washington came there, in Chatham Sqr. When he went out I went with him. On the way to Park Row I told him I understood from Mrs. F that he desired the letters, and that if he did I would go to Red Bank gather up and send them to him. He said he would like to have them, so I went to Red Bank, gathered them up, and Mrs. Fortune expressed them to him.

I never betrayed a friend nor deceived an enemy.

With much love for you and yours, Yours sincerely,

T. Thos. Fortune

ALS Con. 476 BTW Papers DLC.

Emmett Jay Scott to Monroe Nathan Work

[Tuskegee, Ala., ca. July 9, 1913]

Mr. Work: Mr. Washington has raised an important question as to the ownership of the Negro Year Book. You remember, of course, that the capital for printing the Year Book was supplied out of a fund provided by Mr. Washington. You remember, that the second edition is being supplied in the main from the capital which came from the sale of the first edition of the Year Book.

As I understand it, the Year Book is copyrighted in your name. It is Mr. Washington's idea that the Year Book belongs to the Institution because of the reasons above stated and further, because of Dr. Park's cooperation in connection with the book from the very beginning.

The matter is sufficiently important to warrant a conference before you leave here on Saturday, July 19th.

I am attaching copy of letter I am sending Dr. Park in the matter.

Emmett J Scott

TLpS Con. 639 BTW Papers DLC.

To George Wesley Harris

[Tuskegee, Ala.] July 12, 1913

My dear Mr. Harris: I note what the News says in reference to the Emancipation Celebration. I am not in any way, directly or indirectly, responsible for the agitation in reference to the celebration. In fact, I think the present bitterness and discussion is deplorable and hurtful from several points of view. There is no earthly reason, in my opinion, why the forces in New York cannot get together and settle their differences in private rather than in public. I think it extremely unfortunate that such differences are aired in public press in the way they are. Such discussions make a bad impression among our white friends.

Suppose you use your influence to try to get all the forces together and get them to bury their differences for the time being and all work together in a way to make the celebration a success. Yours very truly,

Booker T. Washington

TLpS Con. 926 BTW Papers DLC.

To Frederick Randolph Moore

[Tuskegee, Ala.] July 12, 1913

Dear Mr. Moore: This week's Age presents a good appearance except for the fight on the Emancipation Committee. I cannot feel that any good is going to be gained by keeping up this fight. It places The Age in the same category with Trotter's publication and others of that character. The Age is a paper which any white man in the United States would like to have in his family, but white people are not interested in this continual scrapping. There is a great difference between fighting for a principle and a scrape.

I think your idea of making a tour through the country is a good one. I hope matters are going well with you. Yours very truly,

Booker T. Washington

TLpS Con. 65 BTW Papers DLC.

To Clinton Joseph Calloway

[Tuskegee, Ala.] July 14, 1913

Mr. C. J. Calloway: Your note regarding salary has been received. After considering the matter very carefully, I have decided to recommend that you have a salary beginning September 1st of one thousand dollars.

I fear that you have forgotten our original understanding, that was that you were to have opportunity to trade in real estate and that you were given the privilege of using the good will and name of the school as far as practicable in this respect. This I am sure you will agree has proved of great financial advantage to you. Just now matters are rather dull in real estate trading, but I am sure you will feel the benefit of real estate activity in the fall.

In regard to a vacation. I will have to leave that in the same way I do the other teachers. When the time comes that you feel you need a vacation, if you will take the matter up with me I think it can be arranged to your satisfaction. It is not the policy of the school to arrange definitely for vacations, but I think I know of no case where teachers' requests in this respect have not been granted.

In reaching this decision, I am not overlooking your long, faithful and valuable service to the school, but there comes a time in the history of all institutions and organizations when the limit of increasing salaries is reached, and we have now reached the point where we must stop for a while. You will have to bear in mind that the other teachers who have long been in the service of the school are receiving no salary whatever this summer, and others are working without salary.

I would like the whole matter closed up within the next few days.[1]

[Booker T. Washington]

TL Con. 636 BTW Papers DLC.

[1] BTW and C. J. Calloway negotiated until October the matter of salary and vacation time. BTW refused to grant Calloway an increase of $23.33 per month in salary, and also refused to commit himself to a specific vacation provision. (BTW to Calloway, Sept. 30, 1913, Con. 636, BTW Papers, DLC.) Calloway countered with a request for $100 per month salary and acquiesced in a specific vacation agreement. BTW refused Calloway's suggestion and offered him $90 per month, which he apparently accepted. (Calloway to BTW, Oct. 1, 1913, and BTW to Calloway, Oct. 3, 1913, Con. 636, BTW Papers, DLC.)

To Victor Fellner[1]

[Tuskegee, Ala.] July 15, 1913

My dear Sir: I remember our conversation on the train a few days ago. Sometime when I am in New York I shall be very glad to call to see you.

Referring again to our conversation, by this mail I am taking the liberty of sending you a copy of my most recent book, "The Man Farthest Down." In view of your wide travel in European and other countries, I am sure you will be interested in a good deal I have said in this book.

One other thing. I am wondering if the management of your hotel would object to my stopping there sometime when I wish to do so when in New York.[2] If necessary I could take my meals in my room. I should want a room with a bath. Yours very truly,

Booker T. Washington

TLpS Con. 925 BTW Papers DLC.

¹ Victor Fellner was maitre d'hôtel of the Hotel McAlpin, at Greeley Square in New York City.

² Fellner acknowledged receipt of BTW's book but did not say whether or not BTW could be accommodated at the hotel. (Fellner to BTW, Aug. 27, 1913, Con. 925, BTW Papers, DLC.)

To the Editor of the Boston *Transcript*

Tuskegee, Ala., July 15, 1913

Editor Boston Transcript: At the end of the first three months of the present year I called attention to the fact that 14 lynchings had taken place. Six months have now passed and 10 additional lynchings have occurred. For the same period a year ago there were 36 lynchings, making a reduction of 12 as compared with last year. The smaller number indicates a growing regard for law and order.

In connection with two of these lynchings the conduct of the mob, according to the newspaper reports, was exceedingly barbarous and inhuman. In one case it is stated that the mob went so far as to cut off the ears, fingers, toes and lips of the individual in order to keep them for souvenirs. In still another case it is stated that the mob dragged the victim along the streets, beat the body with a crowbar, then boiled the body in oil, then set fire to it, then strung the body up to an electric light pole in the center of the town in the glare of the electric lights and shot over a thousand bullets into the body. It is further stated that 5,000 persons, including many young white women, witnessed these acts. So far no person has been arrested.

The crimes for which individuals were lynched since I last called attention to this matter were as follows:

April 5, a Negro at Mondak, Montana, for shooting officers attempting to arrest him.

May 5, a Negro at Appling, Georgia, for firing pistol and creating disturbance.

May 12, a Negro at Hogansville, Georgia, for killing a white man.

Date unknown, a Negro at Issaquena, Mississippi, attempted murder.

Date unknown, a Negro at Springfield, Mississippi, murderous assault.

Date unknown, a Negro at Hickory, Mississippi, murderous assault.

June 4, a Negro at Beaumont, Texas, accused with two others of attacking a party of white men.

June 13, a Negro at Anadarko, Oklahoma, for murder.

June 19, a Negro at Hot Springs, Arkansas, for rape and murder.[1]

June 21, a Negro at Americus, Georgia, for shooting an officer.[2]

Out of the 36 lynchings, in only one case was the crime of rape charged against the individual that was lynched.

Booker T. Washington

TLcS Con. 929 BTW Papers DLC.

[1] Actually no rape occurred in this incident. See J. H. Henderson to BTW, Aug. 3, 1913, below.

[2] For an account of this incident see John M. Collum to BTW, July 25, 1913, below.

From James Carroll Napier

Washington, July 16th, 1913

Dear Mr. Washington: Your letter relative to life memberships has been received. I shall do the best I can and secure as many as possible, but fear that the people of Washington are not sufficiently strong yet to come up with six.

We held an enthusiastic and largely attended local league meeting at the Y.M.C.A. Building Monday night. This league is growing in numbers, in respectability and in point of its usefulness. You would have been proud to look in upon them at this meeting.

All of us hereabouts are in the dumps today on account of the *scavenger order* issued by this Administration yesterday as to the use of toilet rooms in the Departments.[1] The colored brother is beginning to realize that things *were not* as bad as they could be under republican rule.

Howard University is *"bleeding"* and I am anxious to see and talk with you about some recent developments. Mrs. Napier asks me to return and thank you for sending her the enclosed letter. Very truly yours,

J. C. Napier

ALS Con. 929 BTW Papers DLC.

¹ An unsigned statement on the issue of the segregation of washrooms for federal employees, dated July 19, 1913, is in the same container as Napier's letter and may have been enclosed with it. The statement called the segregation order "distinctly Unamerican, and the discriminatory feature of it a shocking abuse of power." The statement said that the NAACP planned to protest the order, and hinted that many black clerks might resign as a result of the insult. (Con. 929, BTW Papers, DLC.)

To Mary C. Turner¹

[Tuskegee, Ala.] July 18, 1913

My dear Madam: Your kind letter has been received. While I have absolutely no business connection with anybody or any institution at Mound Bayou, I have great confidence in the people there. The past few months have been very hard months in most parts of the South. Many banking institutions under the care of white people have failed outright. The colored banks have had, in many cases, a hard struggle to keep on their feet.

Without knowing anything of the details as to conditions at Mound Bayou, my advice to you is to be a little patient. I feel rather sure that when the new cotton crop comes in in September and October that conditions will so improve at Mound Bayou that anybody who has any money invested there will be satisfied.

I think that it will be a great mistake for persons to pay out money just now in hiring lawyers or paying court expenses. This will accomplish no good, but will detract from the amount of money which in my opinion investors will ultimately receive. Yours very truly,

Booker T. Washington

TLpS Con. 488 BTW Papers DLC.

¹ Mary C. Turner, a hairdresser in Oakland, Calif., complained to BTW that she had not received any interest on her deposit in the Mound Bayou Bank for three years. She said she was considering the possibility of turning the matter over to a lawyer. (July 8, 1913, Con. 488, BTW Papers, DLC.) Two years later she wrote to BTW again expressing her discouragement about recovering any of the $1,500 she had invested in the bank, oil mill, and town lots. (Mar. 1, 1915, Con. 946, BTW Papers, DLC.)

From Ernest Ten Eyck Attwell

Tuskegee Normal and Industrial Institute   July 18, 1913

Mr. B. T. Washington: With reference to what we are paying at present for groceries beg to advise that we are not buying at present in very large quantities. We have made contract on only one standard item of groceries, and that is flour.

I mention a few of our invoice prices, etc. as follows:

Flour, Washburn-Crosby's Gold Medal, $4.85 per bbl., Del'd.

Sugar, market prices, standing order, five barrels per week. Last invoice T. J. Henderson, (standing order) $4.20. American Standard granulated f.o.b. New Orleans, La.

Lard Compound, (Cottolene only) $.08⅝ del'd here, Fairbanks Company.

Jap Rice, $.04

Fancy Head Rice, $.05½

White Potatoes, $1.00 per bu.

Lump Starch, $.04½

Armour's Grape Juice, $4.25 del'd.

Grits, $.01¾ per lb.

Navy Beans, $2.85 per bu.

Kellogs Corn Flakes, $2.80

Sugar Cane Syrup, $.33 del'd

Prunes, $.07½

Dried Apples, $.07½

I tried the early part of last season to secure contracts on rice, sugar and things of that character but we did not find it profitable or feasible to do this and many of the houses would not bid on contracts of these commodities.

The above prices where not marked "delivered" are basis f.o.b. Montgomery, which place is the largest jobbing center nearest us.

We were particularly fortunate in the purchasing of our cottolene the past season for the reason that we were below the market from the time we placed the contract at the beginning of the school term to the present time. We were able to save ten to twelve dollars each week based on the quantity used. Very respectfully,

E. T. Attwell

TLSr   Con. 635   BTW Papers   DLC.

To Oliver Bainbridge

[Tuskegee, Ala.] July Nineteenth, 1913

Dear Sir: Your cordial letter of June 11th reached me a few days ago and in reply let me say that I should be very glad if I were able to say a word which would serve to emphasize the lesson of the Anglo-Saxon Peace Centenary, or in any way further the purposes which it is intended to promote.[1] As you know we have a good many races here in America and I happen to belong to the race which I believe I am safe in saying has known the Anglo-Saxon race longest and most intimately.

The Negro in America has known the Anglo-Saxon in peace and war; in slavery and in freedom. Black men and white men fought side by side in the war which resulted in the separation of this country from yours and in all the wars so far as I know, that have been fought upon this continent.

The Negro has had his part, also, in the more peaceful work of settling and building up the country and establishing Anglo-Saxon civilization in this part of the world. In fact, no other dark-skinned race, with which the Anglo-Saxon has come in contact in any part of the world, has so completely accepted and so thoroughly absorbed the Anglo-Saxon ideals of life and of civilization as the American Negro. Some of us count ourselves Americans, while others are proud to call themselves Englishmen, so that it is natural and proper that we should rejoice in any movement or event that serves to bring the two branches of the Anglo-Saxon race into closer sympathy and cooperation. Aside from that fact, however, it seems to me that every man, of whatever race and whatever nationality, can and should look with satisfaction upon a movement that is intended to cement the peace of the two great English speaking countries because it tends to insure the peace of nearly half the world.

Anglo-Saxon peace means not merely the peace of one hundred and fifty millions of white people but of some four hundred million other people of a darker skin in these two countries and their dependencies, whose welfare, progress and prosperity are bound up directly or indirectly with their own. About one-third the present population of the world is directly concerned, one way or another, not merely with the peace, but with the law and order and justice which England and America imposes upon its citizens and subjects. I am very truly,

Booker T. Washington

TLpSr Con. 932 BTW Papers DLC.

[1] Oliver Bainbridge had written on the stationery of *The Empire Magazine,* a London monthly. He asked BTW for a message to include in his book in progress on "the lesson of the Anglo-American Peace Centenary." (June 11, 1913, Con. 932, BTW Papers, DLC.) After the outbreak of World War I, Bainbridge wrote again, asking BTW's opinion of "this atrocious war which has sprung out of the lustful ambition of the Kaiser and drenched in blood a number of innocent and peace-loving countries." (Dec. 31, 1914, Con. 493, BTW Papers, DLC.) BTW apparently did not reply.

From Ralph Waldo Tyler

Washington, D.C. July 19th., 1913

Sir: I have just completed a week in West Virginia, and beg to submit the following report:

Monday, July 14 — Visited Wheeling, W.Va., arriving there at 12:30 noon. Letter notifying them of my coming had only been received by Mr. A. L. Jackson[1] an hour before my arrival. Original notification was sent to Prof. Hughes,[2] who is away, being in Chicago for the summer. He so advised you, stating that he would forward letter to Mr. Jackson, an officer of the League. Immediately on receipt of Mr. Hughes' letter, which you forwarded me from Tuskegee, I sent Special Delivery to Mr. Jackson, (Sunday July 13th.) advising what train I would arrive on. As before stated he received it Monday just an hour before my arrival, being his first knowledge of my coming. I spent all that afternoon going around with him in an effort to get up a meeting. Though late in beginning, succeeded in getting out an attendance of perhaps from 100 to 150 that evening at the M. E. Church. The League here has not had a meeting for two years. It was practically dead. They promised me that as soon as Mr. Hughes returns from Chicago (he is the holding over president) they will call a meeting, elect new officers and try to revive the organization. I injected enough interest in the movement, while there, to incline me to the belief that they will revive. I secured a contribution of $5 to the National League, which I am sending to the National Secretary, Mr. Scott. I have urged that Mr. A. L. Jackson, if possible, be chosen the next president of the Local League. He is a business man and full of enthusiasm and hustle. Wheeling has very few Negro business men. I succeeded also in getting the ministers and professional men there interested.

Tuesday, July 15th. Arrived in Charleston today. Found no preparations whatever had been made for my visit. Mr. James,[3] to whom you had written advising of my proposed visit, and to whom I had also written, appears to have been influenced by Dr. Gamble to throw cold water on the movement, and make impossible the organizing of a league here. Dr. Gamble, it seems, feels that he was not given the cordial reception, while at Tuskegee during the Medical Associations meeting last summer, by you due him. Mr. James, who is the only Negro business man of real prominence or consequence there is influenced by Dr. Gamble. Two previous attempts have been made to organize a league here without success. Mr. Courtney, to whom you also had written, from what I could learn, is a very inactive quantity. Although ill during the two days (15th. & 16th.) spent in Charleston, I made the rounds among the Negroes, and I am sure I made Mr. James ashamed of the part he took in preventing a meeting or any arrangements being made for my coming, and for the letter he wrote you. James is a wholesale commission merchant whose patrons are all white. I succeeded, however, in making it possible to actually organize there at some later date. However, outside of a drug store, a grocery store, an indifferent restaurant and one or two small barber shops there is no Negro business here. This state goes dry for twenty years, beginning next July, and then, I think it will be a ripe spot for labor along league lines. It is *too wet* now for good work.

Thursday July 17 — Arrived in Huntington today at 1,25 P.M., from Charleston. No arrangements had been made for my coming, and the league here has not held a meeting for two years. Letter advising of my coming had been sent to Spencer Lewis.[4] He is not an official of the Local League, and not recognized as a member. The president, Dr. White,[5] had only learned of my coming the night before my arrival. Spencer Lewis, to whom letter had been sent, not much known. Found a revival in progress at one of the Baptist Churches, a meeting at another, a K. P. meeting, and the weather simply torrid. I hustled around, however, all afternoon with Dr. Barnett[6] and succeeded in arranging for a meeting at the A.M.E. Church, with about thirty in attendance. The short notice, and the counter attractions, and the weather were against a large meeting. Dr. White, the president, promised to call a meeting of the Local League next week. While there I arranged for a regular meeting place for the organization at the A.M.E. Church. They also promised that they would do their utmost to revive the organization and make it a factor. There are 2000 Negroes here, and about 38,000 whites. Negroes are only doing moderately well — hardly that. One drug store, one small grocery store, a very large saloon and a small restaurant constitutes the business en[ter]-prises here. Dr. Barnett owns and conducts a very up-to-date hospital here, known as "The Barnett Hospital," which has perhaps twenty-five beds, a thoroughly modern operating room, and other modern hospital appliances. The city sends all Negro patients to it, and the coal mines, in the coal mining regine just below the city, send all their injured to it, which makes for its success as a business proposition. Respectfully,

R. W Tyler
National Organizer

REMARKS

My trip to all cities north of the Ohio River has convinced me that before any attempt is made to organize new leagues the old chartered leagues, all of which are either dead or dying, must first be revived in order to serve as an influencing factor for towns that have no leagues and where we hope, some day, to establish leagues. In no northern city that I have visited, outside of Wilmington, Del., Atlantic City, N.J., and Philadelphia, has the local league met in one or two years. My visits to date have also shown me the necessity of revising your list of names of people to whom to write. In many cases the people written to are inactive persons or persons whose influence is nil. Have also found that many leagues were organized without, rather than with, business men as members and officers. In Cumberland, Md., found the president a waiter in a second rate hotel, and ripe for retirement even as a waiter. In Huntington, Spencer Lewis, to whom you wrote, and who, perhaps was an officer at "last accounts" is simply a laborer. In Wheeling, the president is a school teacher. In some places the saloon keeper is too prominent in local leagues to attract membership of other business men. The leagues in the North must, in most cases, be made over, and those in the South I visited had not been seriously active.

R. W. T.

TLS Con. 851 BTW Papers DLC. Written on stationery of the National Negro Business League.

¹ Austin L. Jackson was proprietor of the Metropolitan Shaving and Bathing Parlors in Wheeling, W.Va.
² John W. Hughes, principal of the Lincoln School, a black public school.
³ Charles H. James operated a wholesale produce company in Charleston, W.Va.
⁴ Spencer J. Lewis was listed as a "helper" in the 1913–14 Huntington city directory.
⁵ Possibly Benjamin F. White, a physician in Huntington, W.Va.
⁶ Constantine C. Barnett.

From Asa Leland Duncan¹

Missoula [Mont.] July 23, 1913

Dear Sir: I have for a number of years thought of writing to you. I doubt if you remember me though I am sure that I remember you when you and I were each small children. I have watched your course through life with no little interest and read your book Up from Slavery. I lived on a plantation a part of which joined the one on which you were born. You lived on what we called the Old Burroughs place. I lived when I saw you with my Grand father, Asa Holland, down the Turnpike below where you and your people lived. You may perhaps remember my grand father, Asa Holland. He was the post-master at the Hale's Ford post office during the civil war and for a long time afterwards. The place just opposite, or nearly opposite where you were born was the place known as the Ferguson place. He was generally called Old Cy Ferguson. I recall him as a man of rather low stature, florid face, and was said to be a very hard master. I remember that he owned two slaves, one a very dark man called Jordan, and another mulatto, I think named Dennis. The reason I remember Jordan so well was that on one occasion in the winter, Jordan had run away and some one found him in the barn of my grand father. It was a cold snowy morning, and there was great excitement when they found him. Mr. Ferguson came and he was taken in to the post office and a colored boy named Giles, who belonged to my Grand father went out there to see him. Giles was much older than I and when I went out there they had this poor fellow with a rope around his waist. I was a very small child five or six years old, and I remember that when I looked in to the room and saw the rope, I was so agitated, and frightened, that I wept and told Giles to take me away. I never knew what became of Jordan after the emancipation. I think I recall seeing you several times and I will mention the incidents and would like to know if I am correct and if your memory corroborates my recollection. Miss Eliza Burroughs about the close of the War taught school at my great Uncle's, Thomas Holland. She used to ride Horseback there to teach. I think she went on Monday Morning and returned home on Friday afternoons, evenings as we call it there. And if I am not mistaken you used to go with her and take the horse back home and go for her. Some small colored boy did and I think it must have been you. Then again, I think they sent you at times to the post office in the yard of my Grand father on what we called "mail days" during the war.

If I am not mistaken once you were going to mill, the old grist mill, that was then known as Forbes' Mill down near Staunton River, on a small creek, however, and your sack of corn fell off. Of course it was impossible for you to again get it on the horse and you came back to the post office to get some one to put it back on the horse. My grand father sent his nephew, Alexander Holland to put it up for you.

I suppose that you are entirely too old now or were then too young to recall these little incidents and I should perhaps not remember them but for the fact that for years I have heard and read of you with much interest. For I can realize in some small way what you have done, the great good you have done for your race and the people of this country by your educational work.

My own life has been a very hard one especially my boyhood days and my efforts to get an education.

I was in Virginia about a year ago and My Aunt, Anne Leitch Duncan, who was Anne Leitch Holland, a daughter of Asa Holland whom I have mentioned above, told me of your visit there and of the little speech that you [gave] when you went back there several years ago. It made a strong impression on her I know for the reason that she gave me the very ideas and seemed to have remembered nearly every thing that you said.

I saw one of my old playmates, a colored man, named James Holland. He lives near where you lived when you were living there. He lives out on Gills Creek on some land which I helped to buy a number of years ago. The land belonged at one time to the Dillons. You may recall the name.

For years I have thought I would write you and learn if you remembered any of these incidents. As we both came from the same neighborhood, and probably had some acquaintances in common, I wished to learn if you recalled any of the things, people or incidents mentioned in this letter. It has been so long ago that it is all like a dream to me.

If you feel like doing so I would be glad to have a reply to this. Yours sincerely,

Asa L. Duncan

TLS Con. 934 BTW Papers DLC. Written on stationery of the Montana district court, fourth judicial district, of which Asa L. Duncan was judge.

¹ Asa Leland Duncan (b. 1857) lived for a time with his grandfather, Asa Holland, in Hale's Ford, Va., where he knew BTW. A graduate of Washington and Lee University, he moved to Missoula, Mont., where he became a lawyer and in 1912 a state district judge.

To James Carroll Napier

Lake Minniwaska, N.Y. July 23, 1913

My dear Mr. Napier: I received your letter just before leaving Tuskegee. I am sorry to learn that matters are going so badly in the departments in Washington, but I hardly see how any one can be sure of anything since the Democratic Party is only living up to the record that it has always maintained when dealing with race.

I am indeed [glad?] to learn of the fine condition of the local League in Washington. I am very grateful to all of you.

Mrs. Washington tells me that she plans to be in Washington after August. Yours very truly,

[Booker T. Washington]

TLc Con. 929 BTW Papers DLC.

From John M. Collum

Americus, Ga. July 25, 1913

Dr. Booker T. Washington, Several days ago I read in the Atlanta Constitution your letter enumerating the lynchings of the year, the recent Americus lynching being at the end of the list. In many respects this lynching was, possibly, the most disgraceful affair that has at any time occurred in any part of the whole country.

While many good people here abhor the disgraceful act, from after happenings it must be concluded that the lynchers have terrorized the whole people, or that a vast majority is in sympathy with the mob. The judge of the superior court called the grand jury together, and he and they made diligent inquiry, and yet no one would swear that he saw a single one of the mob commit an assault upon the victim. Or was there another court official entrusted with drawing the bill, who helped to block the efforts being made by the grand jury? His is an elective office.

I was not in the city on the night of the lynching, but can state these as facts:

The victim was minding a team for a colored man who was in a store. Chief Barrow ordered him to move the wagon. He explained to him that the owner would take charge of it at once and move it. He jumped from the wagon and as he did was seized by the chief. Two men went to the assistance of the chief. There was resistance and a struggle and, possibly, the prisoner was struck several times. The chief drew his pistol when the prisoner seized it and fired as he ran. As he ran men followed in pursuit, firing at him as they ran. He was captured badly wounded, and carried to jail. A mob was formed. The whole city knew it was being formed, and yet apparent indifference and inactivity on the part of the officials. Policemen arrested women for being on the streets after 9, and yet they stood about in pairs remoter from the lynching.

Rev. J. B. Lawrence,[1] Rev. J. W. Stokes, and Rev. R. L. Bivins[2] followed the lynchers into the jail, and were forcibly put out. Rev. Lawrence would return, and was finally thrown out. Bivins plead that the body be not burned; threats came from the crowd, "If you don't leave we will burn you."

But this feature of the affair makes the whole situation that we are facing the more alarming. The Governor[3] called out the local military company at about 10, and after the lynching was over, but before the

243

call, members of the military organization, with arms furnished by the government, had contributed more than the average number of shots fired by the lynchers in riddling the body with bullets.

I have been in Americus since July 1907. My home is at Putnam in Schley County, my family still residing there. We employ many colored people on our plantations. We have never had one brought before the courts. I superintended both white and colored schools for 14 years before coming here. During the time there was not a single murder in the county, and the courts would convene on Mondays twice each year, and finish all business in nearly every instance in one day. But a change has come about, even in Schley County.

Back behind all this, there is more, but it is not to be written on paper. I have written you only as a matter of information; that I knowing, and that you may know the truth, and that knowing it, as bad as it is, we may make the most of it. This is only a private letter so far as my name is concerned.

I am trusting that the like will never occur again, and yet I feel these are times demanding, from somewhere, tactful, careful, diplomatic, strong, and sensible, people to grapple with the situation.

I beg to remain, Very resp.

J. M. Collum, Princ
Third Dist A & M. Sch

TLS Con. 925 BTW Papers DLC.

[1] James B. Lawrence, rector of Calvary Episcopal Church.
[2] Robert L. Bivins, pastor of Furlow Lawn Baptist Church.
[3] Joseph M. Brown.

From J. H. Henderson

Hot Springs, Ark., Aug. 3rd 1913

Dear Dr. You will notice here, enclosed a clipping which explains the cause of this communication. This clipping is taken from The Bluff City News. Aug. 2nd '13.

There was no rape connected with the lynching [which] took place here June 19th last, of one, Will Norman, a half-wit, comparatively known by no body here but the family for whom he worked. He was the cook and "all-round man" for the family, and of course demanded nothing for his labour — but took what they gave him.

There was a little girl, the only daughter in the family. It is a fact known to the family that the little girl and Norman never did get along. Whenever they met there was a quarrel ending sometimes in blows between them. This seems unreasonable, but I am told that it is a fact. It is said that the mother and wife frequently entered her protest against the boy's staying, knowing the little girl did not like him, and that their dislike of each other was mutual, she fear[e]d that some day would bring the worst. Her protest was over-ruled because of an important financial consideration.

June 19th was the day. Norman was at his work in the kitchen, the child came, and the usual "scrap" insued between them. Norman threw the potato masher at her. Evidently the blow was stronger than he intended it to be. When he found that he had stunned the child he dragged her into a near by closet closed the door of same and left the house. It was a very hot day. The blow hardly caused her death, if it had the papers would have eagerly said so. If the truth was known the heat in that closed closet was the direct cause of death, but that is not here nor there. The fact I wish to emphasize is, that no body here mentioned rape in connection with the case, only one paper, here mentioned it indirectly, for effect, of course. I don't believe the parents of the child would give color to that idea.

Now all this I have said, may amount to nothing in the case. Norman was said to be a worthless Negro who seemed to have added absolutely nothing of good to his race.

Since it is said that there is only one rape case in this list it is to our interest as a race to show that none of those unfortunates were lynched for the crime the other people say provokes lynchings. Further, more, out of justice to Norman, I feel that it is fair to say to you that he was *not* accused of rape, and his name, though worthless, should be cleared from that awful stain. This is the truth, and yet in this case it might not be safe for me to make public the truth over my signature.

So many good white people hire worthless Negroes to work about their homes, simply to save a few dollars. As a result all three of us suffer.

Hoping you abundant success, I am yours for thruth.

J. H. Henderson,
Pastor Roanoke (1st) B.C.
Hot Springs

ALS Con. 929 BTW Papers DLC.

To Oswald Garrison Villard

Tuskegee Institute, Alabama.[1] Aug. 8, 1913

Personal.

My dear Mr. Villard: I have just had the opportunity of reading your editorial of Aug. 4,[2] and I want to thank you most sincerely for it. You express the feelings of practically of every Negro in the United States; I am glad to see that a number of daily papers in other parts of the country have written editorials based upon yours.

I see by the morning papers that a white man has been nominated as minister to Hayti,[3] this would seem to indicate that the present administration is hopeless. I am deeply disappointed in Pres. Wilson.

As a race we can never repay you for all that [you] have done and are doing. Yours Sincerely,

Booker T. Washington

ALS Oswald Garrison Villard Papers MH.

[1] Though written on BTW's stationery carrying a Tuskegee address, this letter was answered on the same day, and Villard's reply was sent to Huntington, L.I. In the meantime, however, BTW had apparently returned to Tuskegee.

[2] An unsigned editorial on "The President and the Negro" in the New York *Evening Post* objected to the appointment of an Indian as Register of the Treasury and to the demands of Senators Vardaman, Tillman, and Hoke Smith that the federal office workers be segregated. It called on President Wilson to decide whether to yield to this pressure or to adopt "fair play" to a "heavily disadvantaged race." (Aug. 4, 1913, 6.)

[3] Woodrow Wilson nominated former Missouri congressman Madison Roswell Smith, who served as minister to Haiti from Aug. 1913 to July 1914.

From Oswald Garrison Villard

New York   August 8, 1913

Dear Mr. Washington: I am much touched and gratified by your letter just received. I have had a number of letters from colored people thanking me for it, and have felt that I could trace its effect in other newspapers, as you suggest. I can tell you confidentially that I have been laboring with the President, or rather his Secretary,[1] and I hope to see him again next week. Will you give me permission to show him your letter?[2] It would help enormously.

I enclose for your *confidential* reading a letter which the National Association has prepared to send to him.[3] Under no circumstances let this get into the hands of any newspaper men. Indeed, I feel that I must ask you to destroy it after reading it, for premature publication might ruin the whole plan. Sincerely yours,

Oswald Garrison Villard

P.S. If you could send me the editorial references to my editorial in the Post, to which you refer, I should like very much to see them.

TLS   BTW Papers   ATT.   A carbon copy is in the Oswald Garrison Villard Papers, MH.

[1] Joseph Patrick Tumulty (1879–1954), a lawyer and former member of the New Jersey Assembly (1907–10), was private secretary to Woodrow Wilson during Wilson's terms as governor of New Jersey (1910–13) and as President of the United States (1913–21).

[2] Villard referred to BTW's letter of Aug. 8, 1913, above. The letter that Villard actually sent to President Wilson was BTW to Villard, Aug. 10, 1913, below.

[3] A copy of the NAACP's printed version, "A Letter to President Woodrow Wilson on Federal Race Discrimination," dated Aug. 15, 1913, is in Con. 934, BTW Papers, DLC. The letter, signed by Moorfield Storey, W. E. B. Du Bois, and Oswald Garrison Villard, described the segregation of federal employees as a "new and radical departure," and called for an end to the drawing of color lines in the federal government. The suggestion in the letter that the policy of segregation originated in "a genuine desire to aid those now discriminated against," aroused the ire of Charles W. Anderson, who condemned the letter as "special pleading put out for the purpose of befogging the real issue and obscuring the real cause of complaint." (See Anderson to BTW, Aug. 19, 1913, below.)

To Oswald Garrison Villard

Tuskegee Institute, Alabama   August 10, 1913

Personal

Dear Mr. Villard: You do not know how very glad I am to see your recent editorial on the racial discrimination in the departments at Washington. It shows a fine spirit and I am sure will do good. I am glad to note that a number of newspapers, especially those in Western New York, have already based editorials on the Evening Post editorial. They all speak in the same tone that you do.

I cannot believe that either President Wilson or Mr. Tumulty realizes what harm is being done to both races on account of the recent policy of racial discrimination in the departments. I have recently spent several days in Washington, and I have never seen the colored people so discouraged and bitter as they are at the present time. I am sure that President Wilson does not realize to what extent a lot of narrow little people in Washington are taking advantage of these orders and are overriding and persecuting the colored people in ways that the President does not know about.

I have always had great faith in President Wilson. Soon after his inauguration I gave out an interview in which I stated that I believed he would be just to the colored people.

As I have come into contact with President Wilson and read his addresses, his whole heart seems to be centered in trying to give every man a chance, especially the man who [is] down. Surely the Negro in this country is the man who needs encouragement from the hands of President Wilson.

I believe that your editorial and a good frank talk with the President and his secretary will result in changing this hurtful policy before it goes further.

The colored people are especially embittered and discouraged over the fact that an Indian was made Register of the Treasury instead of a colored man. Added to this, it seems that a white man has been nominated for Minister to Haiti instead of a black man.

I think that the President ought to know that one of the most hurtful and harmful organizations in Washington is one called the "Democratic Fair Play Association," composed of a lot of white clerks in the various departments. This organization is constantly seeking to stir up strife between the races and to embarrass the colored people. If the President or somebody else could suggest that they ought to attend to their own business in the departments and let the President run the government it would help immensely.

I think and hope that before President Wilson is in office much longer that he will domonstrate to the world that he is a firm true friend of both races. Yours very truly,

Booker T. Washington

TLS   Woodrow Wilson Papers   DLC.   Enclosed in Villard to Wilson, Aug. 18, 1913.

From Oscar Scott Lewis[1]

Tuskegee, Alabama. August 11, 1913

Dear Sir: I have been employed by one Sanford Woodruff[2] to represent him in a claim against the Tuskegee Institute for false imprisonment. This boy was arrested on the 4th, day of June, 1913, under a warrant sworn out by one John W. Whittaker, who with Mr. C. W. Hare was representing the Normal School, and charges him with assault with intent to murder Lycurgus Knight.[3] The boy was arrested and confined in the County jail for something like three weeks. His case was tried by Mr. William Varner, a J.P., by whom the papers were issued, and the case against him was dismissed. After Woodruff got out he discovered that his clothes and other things had been stolen from his room at the Institute while he was incarcerated in jail. The boy was put to considerable expense in hiring counsel, saying nothing of the humiliation of being confined in jail and the suffering caused thereby.

In my judgment the School is clearly liable, and I am taking the matter up with you to the end that it may be adjusted without litigation if you desire.

I await your prompt attention. Yours truly,

O. S. Lewis

TLS   Con. 927   BTW Papers   DLC.

[1] Oscar Scott Lewis (b. 1872) was a lawyer in Tuskegee, Ala. From 1903 to 1909 he was mayor of Tuskegee. In 1915 he became a state senator.

² Sanford Woodruff, of Birmingham, Ala., was a member of the B preparatory class at Tuskegee Institute in 1909. He was listed as a junior in the 1912–13 school catalog.

³ Lycurgus Knight, from Lineville, Ala., was a member of the C preparatory class at Tuskegee Institute in 1909. He was listed as a junior in the 1913–14 school catalog.

To Oscar Scott Lewis

[Tuskegee, Ala.] August 13, 1913

Dear Sir: Yours of August 11th relating to Sanford Woodruff has been received.

I would state that it has always been the policy of this institution never to trouble the civil authorities with cases of any kind except those which, in our opinion, are of extreme nature.

After hearing very carefully the evidence against Woodruff we felt that we would not be doing our duty unless we acquainted the officers with the facts as we saw them in his case. Mr. Hare was asked not to take any stand against Woodruff in court for the reason that we stand in the position as guardian to all our students, and we did not care to seem to be prosecuting a student. We felt that our duty was to let the county authorities know about the case and we presumed that the proper county officials would put the evidence before the court.

I repeat that we made no effort to put our side of the case before the court, but we have the evidence, and I believe that if it is not evidence that would convict, it is certainly evidence that would justify us in causing the arrest. This, of course, is only my personal opinion.

In regard to the clothing: If we can secure a list of the clothes lost, while the boy was in jail, we should be glad to replace them or reimburse him for them.

I regret very much that this case has come up, but I cannot feel that we would have been doing our duty both to the other students and to the public had we not had the boy arrested. Yours truly,

Booker T. Washington

TLpS Con. 927 BTW Papers DLC.

To Oswald Garrison Villard

Tuskegee Institute, Alabama   August 14th, 1913

Dear Mr. Villard: Your letter of August 8th was sent to Huntington and had to be forwarded here, hence it did not reach me until today.

I did not keep a copy of my letter to you, and so I am sending you the enclosed[1] which you can show the President or his secretary if it is not too late. It seems to me that perhaps the one I am enclosing is in better form than the other.

I was in Western New York when I read your editorial and did not keep the papers that had editorials based on this one, but I remember especially that strong editorials appeared in many of these papers. Yours very truly,

Booker T. Washington

You can show the enclosed letter to either the President or his Secretary.

B. T. W.

TLS   Oswald Garrison Villard Papers   MH.   Postscript in BTW's hand.

[1] BTW to Villard, Aug. 10, 1913, above.

To George Washington Carver

[Tuskegee, Ala., Aug. 14, 1913]

Mr. Carver: I have received your letter of August 7th. I thank you for informing me so frankly concerning your intentions.

I cannot agree to accept your resignation before the end of the present school year. You are under a moral promise to remain here during the coming year. In March or April of every year, as you know, I place before teachers the proposition of deciding whether they are going to remain during the coming year or not. In the past I have exempted members of the Council from making a definite promise in the way that I have teachers not members of the Council. This I have done as a matter of compliment to the members of the Council. I have always felt that the Council, knowing the policy of the school would let me know in March or April if they meant to make any change. For this reason, I have not asked them to go through the same form of making a promise that I have the subordinate teachers. Nevertheless, it seems to me that the obligation is binding.

I would suggest, also, in connection with this whole matter that before next March you decide definitely what you want to do: If you want to stay in the service of the school I should be glad to have you, if not, I think you should decide to withdraw. You cannot do justice to yourself or to the school when you are in an unsettled state of mind.

The proposition of your going or remaining has come up, as you know, a good many times in the past few years, and I think it is best for all concerned for the matter to be decided definitely by next March.

Booker T. Washington

TLpS   Con. 639   BTW Papers   DLC.

From George Washington Carver

[Tuskegee, Ala.] Aug. 14—'13

Mr. B. T. Washington, I beg to acknowledge receipt of your note of the 14th inst., and simply wish to say that the part placing me in the same group with those who desired to break their contracts is misjudging my motive.

This was wholy foreign to my mind. Two Govt. Exp. stations are likely to be established within the next year and I have been asked to consider the directorship.

I told them in the beginning that I would not be available until next year, but I thought it right and propper to at least let you know my intentions, so that some one could be prepared ready to drop right into the work I am doing should such a thing take place.

I certainly should regret to see my part of the work go backward in any way, and if necessary assist you in getting some one to fill the place propperly.

My only thought was to do unto others as I would like to have them do unto me. This has been and I trust will always be my policy.

Please do not take up your valuable time to answer this note. Very truly

G. W. Carver

ALS   Con. 639   BTW Papers   DLC.

To Asa Leland Duncan

[Tuskegee, Ala.] August 15, 1913

My dear Sir: You do not know what great pleasure it gave me to read your letter of July 23rd on my return home a few days ago. I thank you so much for thinking of me and writing me. Of course, I do not remember in detail all of the incidents referred to by you, but I remember many of them, especially the matter of the bag of corn or meal falling off the horse. My older brother, John H. Washington, I expect remembers more than I do.[1] He is here with me and is General Superintendent of Industries.

By this mail I take the liberty of sending you a copy of my book, "Up From Slavery." I shall be very glad to have your opinion concerning it after you have looked it through. I hope you will accept this book with my compliments.

If you ever come to Alabama, I very much hope you will look in upon our institution.

I hope some day to return to Hale's Ford when I can spend three or four days in the neighborhood. I keep in touch as far as I can with many of the older people in that neighborhood both white and black. Yours very truly,

Booker T. Washington

TLpS   Con. 934   BTW Papers   DLC.

[1] See John H. Washington to Asa L. Duncan, Aug. 20, 1913, below.

To William Junior Edwards

[Tuskegee, Ala.] August 15th, 1913

Dear Mr. Edwards: I have your letter of recent date, and I want to state that I *am* deeply interested, as you know, in Snow Hill and I want to see it succeed, but it seems to me that more attention should be given to suggestions which are made to you from time to time. Every one who goes to Snow Hill is disappointed in these respects:

1 — The grounds are not kept clean and attractive;

2 — The repairs are not kept up — windows are out and houses are unpainted.

3 — You do not give enough attention to the growing of the ordinary farm and garden crops.

4 — Another thing that would help the appearance of conditions at Snow Hill is to see that everything is finished up. There are too many unfinished jobs there now — it is much wiser to finish up one thing no matter how small it is before undertaking something else.

These are matters in which I would like to have you make an improvement and they should be given immediate and constant attention. You will recall that when I asked Mr. Rosenwald for $4,000.00 it was with the distinct understanding that it was to be used largely if not wholly in making repairs at Snow Hill.

We are all proud of Snow Hill and are gratified at its success in the past, but want to see it do better. I always speak a good word for Snow Hill wherever and whenever I can, but I wish to be sure that my recommendations are based upon the truth.

I think Mrs. Mason[1] will help you later on. With all good wishes, I am, Yours very truly,

Booker T. Washington

TLpSr Con. 925 BTW Papers DLC.

[1] Elizabeth Andrew Mason and her husband Charles Ellis Mason (b. 1884), of Boston, were donors to black education in the South. Charles E. Mason, a Harvard graduate (1905) and business executive, served as a trustee of Tuskegee Institute beginning in 1910. In 1913 the Masons gave Tuskegee an up-to-date medical facility, the John A. Andrew Memorial Hospital, named for Mrs. Mason's father, the Civil War governor of Massachusetts. They provided $50,000 for the building and $5,000 for furniture and equipment. (Charles E. Mason to BTW, Feb. 5, 1913, and BTW to Mason, May 15, 1913, Con. 928, BTW Papers, DLC.)

To Julius Rosenwald

[Tuskegee, Ala.] August 15, 1913

Dear Mr. Rosenwald: Our school opens on September 9th, and while I cannot find it in my heart to beg you, because of your great kindness, I hope you will not mind my saying that we could use to great advantage any old shoes or hats you might send by that time. Yours very truly,

Booker T. Washington

TLpS Con. 66 BTW Papers DLC.

To N. Clark Smith

[Tuskegee, Ala.] August 15, 1913

Captain N. Clark Smith: I shall not be here when the band returns, but I want to let you and the band know how very greatly all of us are pleased with the fine record which the band has made during the summer. I know it has been a long, hard, trying trip. I have not heard any criticism so far as the moral conduct of any one connected with the band is concerned. This pleases us a great deal.

One other thing. I advise that you arrange with Major Ramsey to take a vacation of several weeks away from the school as you need the rest. Yours very truly,

Booker T. Washington

TLpS Con. 923 BTW Papers DLC.

To Frank Trumbull

[Tuskegee, Ala.] August 15, 1913

Dear Mr. Trumbull: I am very glad to have had the privilege of reading the report from President Stevens[1] of the Chesapeake and Ohio Railroad, covering the matter of the possible strike on the railroads because of Negro labor. I certainly hope that no such action will be taken in the South.

I have the feeling that the average white railroad engineer prefers Negro firemen for two reasons:

First, Negro firemen mean fewer engineers,

Second, Negro firemen wait upon the white engineers in a way that they know no white firemen will do.

In many cases these Negro firemen not only wait upon the white men on the engine but perform personal service for them at their homes.

I am very grateful to have the information. Yours very truly,

Booker T. Washington

TLpS Con. 933 BTW Papers DLC.

[1] George Walter Stevens (1851–1920), a railroad employee beginning in 1864, became general superintendent of the Chesapeake and Ohio Railroad in 1890 and its president in 1900.

To E. B. Webster[1]

[Tuskegee, Ala.] August 15, 1913

Dear Sir: I am obliged to you for your interesting letter of July 27th and for the eloquent words in which you refer to my race. It is always a source of encouragement to me to hear from those who are giving time and thought to the welfare and improvement of the people to whom I belong. I have not been to Cuba. Perhaps it is a better country than this one, but my own impression is just the contrary. I am probably prejudiced in favor of my own country, most people are. I have traveled about a good deal and I have not as yet found any place where I thought the Negro was better off than right here where he was born. In saying this I do not overlook the fact that we have disadvantages in this country. But aside from the question whether this is a good or a bad place for the Negro, I cannot believe the race problem is going to be solved by emigration or any other artificial means.

In the first place any attempt to isolate the Negro would put him out of touch with civilization and remove from him the very stimulus he needs to spur him on to make the most of himself. This is no theory: study any isolated community, white or black, anywhere in the world and see what you find. Hayti and Liberia are examples, but there are others. I do not believe the Negro will gain in civilization by running away from civilization. On the other hand I believe civilization will gain if the Negro stays here and the best people of both races unite to solve the problem, by learning to live together in peace and harmony. The Negro learned to get on pretty comfortably all things considered, during slavery and he is rapidly learning to do the same thing in freedom. Meanwhile the race is making progress, immense progress.

But even if the Negro should go off to some other part of the world, and prosper, what reason have we to believe that the white man would stay away from him? If he went away to some inhospitable part of the world and failed the white man would possibly leave him alone, for a time, but just so sure as he was successful the white man would follow him and then we would have another race problem.

My own plan, as you know, is to settle right down where we are, take advantage of the opportunities around us and our disadvantages will have this advantage that this will spur us on to better and higher things. It seems to me the last thing that a new race like mine wants is to have rest. Let the races who have arrived rest. We want to live and in my opinion we are going to live right here in America.

I am   Very truly,

Booker T. Washington

TLpS   Con. 932   BTW Papers   DLC.

[1] E. B. Webster of Washington, D.C., was a member of a communal religious sect called the Koreshan Unity. According to Webster, the group believed that the race problem would eventually be solved by amalgamation. In the meantime, he advised BTW, blacks would be better off in Cuba than in the United States. (Webster to BTW, July 27, 1913, Con. 932, BTW Papers, DLC.)

To John Henry Washington

[Tuskegee, Ala.] August 16, 1913

Mr. J. H. Washington: The following matter I hope you will give attention to as soon as possible.

We are going backward instead of forward in the matter of the appearance of our vegetable wagons and also in the manner of putting up the vegetables. The real test of the efficiency of a department or division consists in the fact as to whether it is able to improve, stand still or go backward.

We have a great opportunity to impress both white and colored people in the direction of system, cleanliness and order through our vegetable wagons.

I want you to take hold of the whole matter and keep at it until you get all the vegetable wagons to present the very best and neatest appearance.

Secondly. We have gone backward in the matter of seeing that our vegetables are carefully and attractively put up. We should teach every student, family and person in the vicinity of the school a lesson in seeing that the vegetables are clean and orderly and are put up in an attractive way.

I am surprised to see how far back the farm department has gone in this direction. I hope you will take hold of it and put it in good shape again.

Booker T. Washington

TLpS   Con. 58   BTW Papers   DLC.

From Charles William Anderson

Saratoga Springs, N.Y. Aug. 19, 1913

My dear Doctor Washington: I hope ere this you have received my letter with enclosure, addressed to 1438 Lombard Street.

Did you see the Du Bois circular letter to President Wilson? It was undoubtedly prepared under the eye of Mr. Villard. You will notice that they complain of placing all of our folks in one bureau, whereas there has been no such action taken or contemplated. The segregation of which we complain, is, that although our people are scattered all over the buildings, they are required to go to a particular toilet room on the top floor. Again, the last paragraph of the letter states that this segregation was established by persons who desired to benefit us. This is a falsehood made out of whole cloth, and the writer of it, knew it to be one. In fact the whole communication was a piece of special pleading put out for the purpose of befogging the real issue and obscuring the real cause of complaint. Why was not something said about the number of men, holding presidential places, that have been separated from the service? On this subject the Du Bois letter is as silent as the grave. As a matter of fact, the only presidential appointee in whom Du Bois is interested, Henry Lincoln Johnson, is still in office. The letter is also silent with respect to the reflex influence of the Administration's attitude towards us. This influence is more hurtful than all of the removals, demotions, and segregation put together. It inspires our enemies all over the country to feel at liberty to run amuck at any time without fear of punishment and it notifies the oppressor that oppression is safe and protected by the highest authorities in the land. I do hope that some other organization will speak out soon and tell the true and whole story.

If we could only induce the preachers and editors to make a fight for the retention of those of our officials *against whom the various communities in which they serve are not in opposition,* I feel reasonably sure that it would save both myself and Cottrill. But perhaps that's rather too much to expect.

Did you hear that Governor Pinchback had resigned? Undoubtedly he was requested to do so. It happened on the 15th and I have been here since the 7th. I will be back on the job on September 1st. Yours very truly,

C.W.A.

TLI Con. 64 BTW Papers DLC.

An Address Before
the National Negro Business League

Academy of Music, Philadelphia,
Wednesday evening, August 20. 1913

This the fourteenth meeting of the National Negro Business League, marks also the fiftieth anniversary of our freedom as a race. It is, then, both timely and fitting that this great gathering of the representatives of the backbone and progress of our race should be held in Philadelphia. It is most appropriate that this meeting should take place after fifty years of freedom in the city where 137 years ago that immortal document, the Declaration of Independence, was issued. Whether the American Negro was meant at the time to be included within the scope and meaning of the words of the Declaration of Independence has been a debatable question. However that may be decided, we mean as a race through this and similar organizations to make ourselves such a useful and potent part of American citizenship so that in all the future no one will dare question our right to be included in any declaration that relates to any portion of the body politic.

During the fifty years of our freedom we have been subjected to some pretty severe tests. First, there were not a few who raised the question as to whether or not the American Negro could survive in a state of freedom. We answer that question by showing that when freedom came to us we were 4,000,000 in number; now we have grown to over 10,000,000 free American citizens. This means that we have a population of American Negroes that is more than twice as large as the population of Australia, one and a half times as large as the whole population of Canada, and nearly twice as large as the combined population of Norway, Sweden, Switzerland and Denmark. These facts should put an end for all time to doubt about our ability to survive in a state of freedom.

One other question was debated fifty years ago, and that was the question as to our ability to support ourselves from a physical and personal point of view. There were not a few who fifty years ago predicted that this newly freed race would become a perpetual burden upon the pocketbook of the nation. It was freely predicted that we would neither feed, clothe or shelter ourselves. Every year the American Congress is asked to appropriate between ten and twelve millions of dollars to be used largely in providing food, clothes and shelter for about 300,000 American Indians. While this is true of the American Indian (and I have nothing but the highest respect for the Indians)[1] ever since the days of Reconstruction the American Negro has not called upon Congress to appropriate a single dollar to be used in providing either clothes, shelter or food for our race. Absolutely in all these personal matters we have supported ourselves and mean to do so in all the future, and it is very seldom that in any part of this country does one find a black hand reached from a corner of a street asking for any man's personal charity. Within fifty years, then, we have proven that we can survive from a physical point of view, and we have proven that we could not only support ourselves but could contribute taxes from $700,000,000, worth of property toward the support of local, state and national government.

Within the fifty years of our freedom we have been subjected to a third test that is one of the conditions of growth and permanency under the conditions of freedom. This third test embraces our ability to combine, to work in harness in the capacity of organized human beings. There can be little civilization and little progress without the capacity and the willingness to work together in organized groups.

Fifty years ago we had almost no experience in working together as organized groups. During the past half century we have proven our ability to organize. We now have 62 banks under the control of black organizations. Fifty years ago we had few religious organizations. Now we have four great religious branches to say nothing of smaller ones having a total membership of 3,113,900 members or about 33 per cent of the race.

Our capacity to organize has been shown too in the case of the National Negro Business League with its numerous local branches, and more especially in the numerous secret and beneficial societies which have been originated and are being sustained by Negroes. A rough study indicates that we have at least 13 of these organizations with distinct aims and purposes, and which are either local, state wide or national in their scope. A study of these organizations reveals the fact that these organizations have a total membership of at least 3,000,000[2] persons or [blank] per cent of the entire Negro race.[3] These figures take no account of the fact that not a few individuals belong to many different organizations.

So much for indications of progress in the past. What about the present, and our duty in the immediate future?

First and foremost I call the attention of the race through this League to the fact that there are at least 200,000,000 acres of unused and unoccupied land in the Southern States. This means a territory as large as Australia, France, Germany, Italy and Spain. I am glad to say that we already own and occupy 20,000,000 acres, but this is only about two acres for each individual. All this means one thing, that the time has come when this Business League and other organizations should send forth a voice which can be heard everywhere and cannot be misunderstood, for a larger proportion of our race to leave the towns and cities and plant themselves in the country districts on the soil before it is too late. Verily it is true that right here in the United States the words of the prophet of old are fulfilled, when he said there was a land awaiting the occupation of the people, that was "flowing with milk and honey." In our case as a race, the milk will come from our own Jersey cows and the honey from our own well kept bees. *Forward to the land should be our motto everywhere.* Instead of owning 20,000,000 acres, we should own within the next quarter of a century 40,000,000 acres. To the man or the race who owns the soil all good things come in time. Let us leave the fleeting and often deceiving easy life of the cities and get on God's green earth. I want to see members of my race that are now in too large numbers flocking to the cities, join the great world movement "back to the land," or better still "forward to the land."

While the millions of Negroes in the South are largely an ignorant people so far as letters are concerned, they are not as a rule a degraded people. Some of the finest specimens of physical and moral manhood to be found anywhere in the world can be found among the country people of our race. ~~While they may be ignorant, they are not degraded.~~ There is a vast difference between ignorance and degradation.

In order to get ourselves planted on the soil, for a season we shall have to forbear the enjoyment of some of the things that make life inviting in the cities. In the cities it is with our race in a large measure as with others in the same relative position of civilization. There is tremendous temptation in the cities for us to get the signs of civilization instead of the substance itself. In the city the temptation is to get an automobile before we get a house, to get a dress suit before we get a bank account, to spend all that we get in for rent, food and dress and lay up little for old age or for those dependent upon us. In the city the temptation is to be dependent instead of independent, to let some one else think and plan for us instead of thinking and planning for ourselves. If any one doubts the truth of this statement, let him go through the streets of one of our Northern cities early in the morning and note the large number of colored people that are washing some one else's windows or sweeping some one else's floor. No disgrace in this, but the white man will have more respect for us in proportion as we are able to create positions for ourselves. We must learn to sacrifice today that we may enjoy tomorrow, to do without today that we may possess tomorrow.

Now as to our program for the future. We should make up our minds thoroughly that there is a permanent place in the country for us, and that we have more friends both in the North and the South than we have enemies.

We should make up our minds that we are to use material gain and prosperity not as an end but as a means toward securing and enjoying the best things in our American life.

What are our chances and what is the outlook? The large number of independent, prosperous and law-abiding black people right here in Philadelphia partly answers this question. What hundreds in Philadelphia have done others can do throughout the United States.

Remember, as I have said, that we have a race of ten millions with whom to do business and in the South especially our commercial activity is not confined to our race. In a Southern city when I was spending a half hour in a Negro bank, I noted that one-fourth of the people who came in to do business with the bank were white people. Young men, young women, there are openings in this great country of ours for Negroes to establish and maintain many additional and various kinds of business concerns.

There is a place for at least 900,000 independent, self-supporting Negro farmers. When I was recently in the far West, nothing impressed me more than to note the large number of educated white men who were beginning life as farmers. Often they started in a little hut or "dug out," and suffered privations, but they were sticking to it. Those are the people who in the future make the great kings of industry.

There are openings in the South for 1000 more saw mills and 1000 brick yards.

It is easily possible to find inviting places North and South where 4,000 more grocery stores can be opened.

We need 2000 additional dry goods stores, and 1500 shoe stores. Our race needs 1000 more good restaurants and hotels.

White women in all parts of the world are opening millinery shops. I want to see a larger number of our bright ambitious colored women do the same thing. There are opportunities for starting 1500 millinery stores.

We already have over 350 drug stores, but 1000 more could be started and would be sustained.

We already have over 60 Negro banks, but 150 additional banks should be organized. In cities like Philadelphia, New York, Baltimore,

Washington, Memphis, New Orleans, Atlanta, Charleston, Savannah and Mobile three or four banks properly organized and conducted can be supported.

Now is the time to seize hold of these golden opportunities and use them before it is too late. These great chances are at our door. Shall we use them? Too many of our well educated young men and women are content to be merely salary drawers or wage earners, depending on some one else to think and plan for them.

Activity and success in all these economic directions lay the foundation for the most enduring success in all professional directions. For our race like others must be built upon an economic foundation as well as an intellectual, moral and religious one. Work [more] and more in these directions and neither we nor our children will be dependent upon the uncertainties of seeking and holding political office for our success. I repeat we must create positions for ourselves — positions which no man can give us nor take from us.

The land, the forests, the minerals, the streams, sun and rain from which original wealth comes draw no color line.

Of the ten millions of black people in the United States, nine million at least belong to the ordinary, hard working classes. In all our planning for business success we will not, can not succeed unless we get close to these hard working masses. They are the back bone of our race. We must not feel we are not a part of them nor must we ever get above them. I beg of you that in your local leagues that you get hold of the man who works with his pick or plow and of the woman who cooks, washes, irons or sews. These will put money into your banks and support your other commercial enterprises.

Finally, as a race we must not be discouraged. There will come to us as to all races, seasons of depression and gloom. Once in a while even those in high places may seem to seek to insult and humiliate and harass us, but this can not last. "The morning cometh." Those who treat us unjustly are losing more than we are. So often the keeper of the prison is on the outside but the free man is on the inside. As I said in the beginning, we have more friends both North and South than enemies. Let us advertise our friends more and our enemies less.

We must not lose faith in our white friends, and above all this we must have constant and unvarying faith in our own race. We must have pride of race. We must be as proud of being a Negro as the Japanese is of being a Japanese. Let us go from this great meeting filled with a spirit of race pride, rejoicing in the fact that we belong to a race that has made greater progress within fifty years than any race in history, and let each dedicate himself to the task of doing his part in making the ten millions of black citizens in America an example for all the world in usefulness, law abiding habits and high character.

TMc Con. 957 BTW Papers DLC. Numerous editorial changes in BTW's hand. The speech appeared, with minor emendations, in the Indianapolis *Freeman*, Aug. 23, 1913, Clipping, Con. 987, BTW Papers, DLC.

[1] The parenthetical phrase was added in BTW's hand.
[2] This figure was left blank in the typescript. It is supplied from the version that appeared in the Indianapolis *Freeman*, Aug. 23, 1913.
[3] In the Indianapolis *Freeman* version the sentence ends after the phrase 3,000,000 persons.

John Henry Washington to Asa Leland Duncan

[Tuskegee, Ala.] August 20, 1913

Dear Sir: My brother, Dr. Booker T. Washington, sent me your letter of July 23rd, written to him, and you cannot imagine how glad I was to have an opportunity of reading it, as it brought back to my memory so many things that happened in my childhood days.

Many of the incidents mentioned in your letter refer to me, not my brother, as I was three and a half years older than he, and am the one who usually went around with the Misses Burroughs, and also who went to the mill and to the Post office, and drove the carriage to church and other places on Sunday. Perhaps my brother did go to some places with them.

I was born in '54 and my brother being about 3½ years younger, you can readily see was not very old. My Mother, with her three children, Booker, my sister Amanda, and myself belonged to the James Burroughs family, and were emancipated at the surrender and left Franklin County in 1865 for West Virginia, at a little town named Malden, near the capitol, where we made our home until coming to Alabama to start this school in 1881.

In order that you may know that I know about that section of the county, and also many of the people mentioned in your letter, I am going to take your valuable time in telling you a few things that I do remember:

I could until a few years ago call the name of almost every family that lived on the Rocky Mount and Lynchburg turnpike, from Bord's store in Bedford County up to the Booth store in Franklin County. Booth's store was located near Armstead tobacco factory.

You speak of Mr. Simon Ferguson, usually called "Old Sy," as being a hard master, but you did not put it strong enough. He was a cruel master and bad man, as I recall it. I well remember the large number of slaves he owned. The mulatto Dennis spoken of in your letter was a boy considerably larger than I, and a tough one. He used to come to our house Sunday afternoons to play marbles with me. I usually had some store bought marbles, but the most of my marbles were made of red clay rolled out as nearly round as I could make them and put in the ashes in the fire place and baked hard. Dennis would play marbles with me until nearly dark on Sundays, then grab my store marbles and run. I might say here, that in making or burning these clay marbles, I learned that in order to keep them from cracking while being burned, it was necessary to apply a very little heat at first, until they had dried out, and then gradually increasing to a red heat. This lesson was of great value to me in beginning to burn brick at our school.

The person called Jordan was named Jerry. I remember the incident mentioned in your letter when he was caught in Mr. Holland's barn after being gone a year. In fact Jerry lived in the woods more than he lived in the house, but he was very slue footed and whenever it either snowed or rained and he went out they usually could track him.

Mr. Ferguson had one daughter, named Charlotte. She was considered by all of the slaves owned by her father and the community generally as being an extraordinarily good lady, and took great interest in her slaves. She married a man by the name of Mr. Garrett, which doubtless you remember something about.

My stepfather belonged to this Mr. Ferguson but never would live on his place so he used to hire him out during slavery to a man at the Salt works in West Virginia. Just before West Virginia seceded from Virginia he brought my stepfather back home and hired him out to the Tobacco factory in Lynchburg, Va.

When Hunter made his raid in that part of Virginia, my stepfather left with the Yankees and went back to West Virginia, where he was free. After the emancipation he sent a wagon to our home in Franklin

County, Virginia for my Mother and the three children. This accounts for our being raised in West Virginia.

There was another cruel man who did not live very far from your Grandfather, by the name of Mr. Benjamin Hatcher. He had a large tobacco store or factory, and a blacksmith shop, and I used to take horses to his shop every week, passing by your Grandfather's. Mr. Hatcher's Mother was a sister of Mr. James Burroughs. She had two daughters, named Misses Fannie and Pattie.

You doubtless remember Mr. Newman's old wagon and coffin shop, which was located between your Grandfather's and Mr. Ferguson's.

I used to drive the carriage on Sunday and sometimes in the week, to take the ladies to the old Baptist church, which is located between your Grandfather's and Mr. Hatcher's store. I remember being at the church on the Sunday when the first Yankees, consisting of one company, about 100 or more, came through that section. When notice was given out in that church that the Yankees were coming and the advance guard appeared coming down the road, the preacher stopped preaching and everybody got down to praying. I never heard so many people praying at one time before or since then. The Yankees passed on by, and so far as I know did not disturb anything in that section, and did not even take any of the horses around that church, as was expected.

The Methodist church was located further down the road, below Mr. Hatcher's store, near Mr. Meadows.

I remember very distinctly the young man Giles spoken of in your letter. He used to be sent out by your Grandfather at times and we would meet up together. As I remember it there was another Holland lived on the turnpike near the bridge on Sta[u]nton river. Also I remember Mr. Powels, who lived on the same turnpike. I am not certain but think his name was Mr. Kit Powels. He had a daughter named Miss Fannie.

I think Mr. Tom Holland, who lived, as I remember it, out as you turn blackwater,[1] was related to the Burroughs family. I remember also the Dillons spoken of in your letter. There were two families of them living on the plantation adjoining the Burroughs plantation. One of them was named Mr. Bob Dillon and he had two sons. These sons shot one of our horses because he got in the corn field on Gill's creek, and I never liked them after that.

One of the Hollands, though I am not certain he is related to your

Grandfather, married Miss Laura Burroughs. I correspond with Miss Laura now. She is located a few miles out from Bedford City, Virginia, which used to be called Liberty.

I am the person who was on the way to the mill when the sack of corn fell off the horse and some one was sent from your Grandfather's house to put it on.

I have never been back in that section of the country since I left there in my childhood, though I have often wanted to travel the turnpike from Rocky Mount over into Bedford County.

A man by name, Mr. Ferdinand Price married Miss Lucinda Burroughs. The last I heard from here she was living as a widow at Salem, Virginia. One of the grandsons of one of the young Burroughs is now a very prominent lawyer in New York city. My brother has met him more than once. You know that Mr. James Burroughs had quite a large family, consisting of seven boys and six girls. Two of them were killed during the war. Gill's creek runs through the Burroughs plantation, and I have had a pleasant time in it, catching fish and going in wading.

Several years ago, when I was sent to inspect a school presided over by one of our graduates near Christiansburg, Va., I went up to Rocky Mount and stayed all night with the intention of going down to Burroughs' plantation, but at that time Gill's creek was up very high and had washed the bridge away. While in Rocky Mount I noticed by the paper that Mr. Ben Hatcher was there that night attending court and I went to the hotel to see him, but he was so thoroughly under the influence of strong drink that I could not hold an intelligent conversation with him.

I hope that you will at least find time to read this letter and that some things in it will be of interest to you.

Should you at any time be in this section of the country I hope that you will not fail to visit Tuskegee Institute.

It might be well to state to you that a large number of colored people from that section of the county, belonging to the Wrights, Fergusons, Hatchers, Hollands and others, located in West Virginia, at or near Charleston, there was a man by the name of Peter Holland who lived in that section, and also a man by name of Abner, who did the blacksmithing at Hatcher's shop. He, with all his family lived in West Virginia until he died.

To be plain about the matter, Cy Ferguson had a number of children by one of his slaves. Some of these children are now living at or near Charleston, W. Virginia and doing well, and one of them, a daughter, is married and living in Birmingham, Ala. Very truly,

[John H. Washington]

TLc   Con. 934   BTW Papers   DLC.

[1] The Blackwater River, about five miles south of the Burroughs plantation.

From Edmund Hext Dryer[1]

Birmingham, Ala. September 1, 1913

My dear Doctor: In order to believe my sincerity, it is, perhaps, unnecessary that I thank you again for your kindness in commending me to Mr. Taft when the time seemed propitious for my appointment to the position of a district judge. But now, since it is apparent that I shall never attain my ambition to become a Federal judge — the only public office to which, I explained to you, I should ever aspire — I wish you to know that I appreciate very greatly your efforts in my behalf; and am as sincerely grateful for them as I should have been had my appointment been secured. Your friend, sincerely

Edmund H Dryer

ALS   Con. 925   BTW Papers   DLC.

[1] Edmund Hext Dryer, born in Tuskegee in 1863, practiced law in Talladega, Ala. (1888–1907) and in Birmingham after 1907. He was mayor of Talladega from 1891 to 1893.

From Pinckney Benton Stewart Pinchback

Washington, D.C. Sept. 4, 1913

My dear Doctor Washington: It has been some time since I wrote you. There are several reasons why I have not written. The first and best is that I did not have anything of special interest to write about. Second I hoped to meet you in New York and have a talk with you.

I would be untruthful if I did not admit to grievous disappointment at my failure to see you on your last visit to New York while I was there. Heretofore you have rarely passed me by when in close proximity to me. Why this marked departure from your custom? I trust it is not my fault in any way.

Well, I am in *permanent* retirement. Like an old Roman I fell upon my own sword rather than submit to decapitation. I requested Mr. Moore to tell you all about it but I dare say you were too busy with your convention in Philadelphia to listen to "swan songs." So on that subject — Vale!

I was truly sorry to learn from Mrs. Washington that your health has not been of the best of late. I sincerely hope, ere this, you are once more yourself in every respect. Always your friend

Pinchback

ALS Con. 930 BTW Papers DLC.

Emmett Jay Scott to Charles William Anderson

[Tuskegee, Ala.] September Fourth, 1913

Dear Anderson: Principal Washington asks me to send you the names of colored people who have been removed from office by Wilson's administration. I am sending you the list of those of whom I have any information. Namely:

William H. Lewis, Assistant Attorney-General of the United States at Washington

Ralph W. Tyler, Auditor for the Navy Department, Washington

James C. Napier, Registrar of the Treasury, Washington

Harry [Henry] W. Furniss, Minister to the Republic of Haiti

J. E. Bush, Receiver of Public Moneys, Little Rock, Arkansas

Nathan H. Alexander, Receiver of Public Moneys (or registrar of the Land Office, I do not know which) at Montgomery, Alabama

General Robert Smalls, Collector of Customs at Beaufort, South Carolina

Joseph E. Lee, Collector of Internal Revenue, Jacksonville, Florida

There probably have been some others, but if so, I do not recall them. Very truly yours,

Emmett J Scott

You know of Gov. Pinchback and Col. Young @ Raleigh, N.C.

TLpS Con. 64 BTW Papers DLC.

To Emmett Jay Scott

[Tuskegee, Ala.] Sept. 5, 1913

Mr. Scott: Sometime within the next few days I want to decide upon a plan whereby we can have a clerk to take charge of the whole matter of the minutes of the Council and Business Committee. As matters have been handled heretofore, too much of the valuable time of the Business Committee has been taken in matters that could just as well be omitted.

I want, for example, a man who is strong enough to relieve Miss Porter from the duty of taking the minutes in the Council, and to go through all matters that are to come before the Council, thoroughly systematize them, and also to anticipate the action of the Council by writing a definite decision. If we can get the proper man I am sure we can save from one-half to two-thirds of the time now spent in the Council.

Aside from the matter referred to, I want a person who can follow up every order given from my office to a head of department or head of division, also every decision made by the Council, and every unfinished matter left over by the Council. I want both the orders and the unfinished matters followed up until they are finally disposed of. Very often the council reaches important decisions, but the matter is postponed or not followed up and the effect is lost because no one is in a position now to follow up decisions and to follow up orders.

The work that I have in mind will take a good part of the time of some strong person, but I am sure it is worth while.

I have neglected to say that I want the same person to keep in touch with the orders given by the General Superintendent of Industries and follow them up in the same way that he does orders given by the Principal or Acting Principal or decisions reached by the Council.

Our whole organization has been weakened by reason of the fact that heads of departments and divisions have become slack in not following out orders. We must have a system which will make sure of our finding out who obeys orders and who does not obey orders.

I should like very much to have any suggestions from you on the foregoing.

Booker T. Washington

TLS   Emmett J. Scott Papers   MdBMC.

From N. Clark Smith

Wichita Kas   9–5 [1913]

Condition of my eyes and nerves will not permit regular work for some time   we asked Major for three months absence   Mrs Smith & Mother advise giving up the work this year   cannot take doctors treatment and operation till cold weather   band tour has disabled me   beg you release   no salary arrive for band tour yet

N. Clark Smith

TWSr   Con. 931   BTW Papers   DLC.

To Edmund Hext Dryer

[Tuskegee, Ala.] September 9, 1913

Dear Mr. Dryer: You do not know how very much I appreciate your thoughtful and kind letter of September 1st which I found here on my return home a few days ago.

Very few men manifest much gratitude for any unsuccessful effort in their behalf, and therefore it is a matter of great satisfaction for me to think of you as one of the rare exceptions and to know I shall always have you as my friend.

It may be, however, that an opening will yet come by which your ambition will be satisfied. My policy of life is for one to go on doing his full duty every day in the year to the fullest extent of his ability and then not worry about results. Rewards and appreciation will come in due time. Yours very truly,

Booker T. Washington

TLpS Con. 925 BTW Papers DLC.

To Pinckney Benton Stewart Pinchback

[Tuskegee, Ala.] September Ninth, 1913

My dear Governor Pinchback: I have your letter of September 4. You do not know the pressure I have been under during the summer. That alone explains why I did not see you when in New York last, that is, when you were there.

Mr. Anderson and Mr. Moore have explained to me why you decided to retire rather than be retired, and I think you were altogether right in your decision in that matter.

I very much wish I could see you and have a good long talk, and the privilege and opportunity will probably offer itself at an early date.

I am very glad that Mrs. Washington had the opportunity to see and talk with you. Very truly yours,

Booker T. Washington

TLpS Con. 930 BTW Papers DLC.

From John Henry Washington

Tuskegee Institute, Alabama   Sept. 9—1913

Dear Brother: I thank you most heart[i]ly for the amount sent me yesterday to help me in paying for medical treatment.

I do not only suffer with rheumatism but during the last six week[s] have suffered a great deal with my stomach. your brother

J. H. Washington

ALS Con 634 BTW Papers DLC.

Emmett Jay Scott to Wilford H. Smith

[Tuskegee, Ala.] September 10, 1913

Dear Mr. Smith: For some reason which I cannot understand, Mr. Moore refuses to answer or acknowledge any of my letters. I have been trying very hard to have him take over $3500 worth of stock which I hold in the esteemed New York Age Publication Co. I was very much chagrined, however, a day or two ago to see in a published sworn statement that Mrs. Ida Moore[1] was put down as the owner of the paper.

Would it be asking too much of you to ask where in a circumstance like this I and the other stockholders stand? To my mind the matter is a more serious one than Mr. Moore seems to regard it.

I wish very much that you would be good enough at your convenience to let me know where the whole situation leaves me and the other men who are stockholders in the paper. I wish to sell my interest to Mr. Moore! Yours very truly,

Emmett J Scott

Will you take the above up with Mr. Moore — He does not, or will not, write me — & said nothing to me @ Phila: I thought he w'd, but he didn't say a word! Explain all this to him!

TLpS Con. 486 BTW Papers DLC. The last sentence of the letter and the postscript are in Scott's hand.

[1] Ida Lawrence Moore (1861–1939) was the wife of Fred R. Moore.

From Charles William Anderson

New York, N.Y. September 11, 1913

PERSONAL Confidential

My dear Doctor: You may recall our conversation at Saratoga in which we both expressed surprise that Mr. Moore should continue to boost Bishop Walters. I have discovered a reason for this support. Moore came to my office yesterday, and in course of conversation told me that he and Bishop Walters had entered into an agreement by which the Age was to support the Bishop and the Bishop in turn was to push Ralph Langston[1] for a place in the Internal Revenue service. He further stated that Secretary McAdoo[2] and Commissioner of Internal Revenue Osborn[3] had been seen, and Osborn had promised that Langston would be appointed to a place over here as soon as the Tariff Bill, which carries the appropriation for this purpose, is passed. This arrangement, he informed me, was concurred in by Collector Mitchel.[4] Great is Diana of the Ephesians. Fred ought to see that the pushing of a democrat for a place in the Internal Revenue service in this city would give the administration a chance to drop the *big colored officer* and name a little one. We had the same thing to contend with in this state for years with respect to the legislature. Every time we attempted to get behind a man for a clerkship in the legislature some other colored man appeared as candidate for janitor of the same body. The result in every case was, that the clerk failed and the janitor was placed.

Just what influence Langston has over Moore, I am unable to state. He must have seen Moore kill a man. During the time Moore and I were at odds, Langston told me that you did not have influence enough with Moore to compose the differences between us, but a word from him would induce Fred to extend the olive branch. I was not in an olive branch mood at that time, but later on, when Langston first came to realize that Lee was losing out, he induced Moore to stop the fight and get in line with me. Thus you see, he was speaking as one having authority, when he said that he had the power to make Moore "smooth his wrinkled front," and you did not. I am passing this on for your advisement. You are now able to account for the Napier-Walters editorials that appear so regularly in the columns of the journal presided over by that bright luminary from Douglas Street, Brooklyn.

With warm regards to the family and friends, and with warmest thanks for your work at Saratoga, I am   Yours very truly,

C.W.A.

P.S. There is a rumor in the air that Mayor Gaynor died on board ship. I hope — sincerely hope — it is false.

C.A.

TLI   Con. 64   BTW Papers   DLC.   Postcript in Anderson's hand.

¹ Ralph Langston was the son of the black congressman John Mercer Langston, and the brother-in-law of James C. Napier. He received a minor appointment in the Internal Revenue Service as a "special employee." (Charles W. Anderson to BTW, Oct. 10, 1913, Con. 64, BTW Papers, DLC.)

² William Gibbs McAdoo (1863–1941) was U.S. Secretary of the Treasury from 1913 to 1918.

³ William H. Osborn was U.S. Commissioner of Internal Revenue from 1913 to 1917.

⁴ John Purroy Mitchel (1879–1918), collector of the port of New York from June to Dec. 1913, was mayor of New York City from 1914 to 1917. In 1918 he became an officer in the army aviation corps, and was killed in a fall from an airplane while training.

From John Andrew Kenney, Frank L. West,¹ and Ernest Ten Eyck Attwell

Tuskegee Normal and Industrial Institute   September 11, 1913

Mr. B. T. Washington: The Shoe Committee examined the shoes shipped by Sears, Roebuck and Company for Mr. Rosenwald.

Two of the cases of shoes seem to be of such character that they should not be opened for sale here. They might be disposed of through Mr. C. J. Calloway in the rural communities.

One box of mens shoes in our opinion might be sold for from Five to fifteen cents per pair.

In one box of shoes there were both ladies and mens shoes and on the outside of the box the price of the shoes was marked fifty cents per pair. This indicates the value placed on the shoes by Sears, Roebuck and Company, and which the Committee understands Mr. Rosenwald has been charged for each pair of these shoes in this particular box so marked. The price mentioned seems to be much more than we could ever get for such shoes in this section, and for that reason the Committee is sending you two pairs of shoes picked at random without any special direction.

One box of women's and children's shoes can be sold to families at nominal prices.

None of the shoes in the entire shipment seem to be of particularly fine quality or condition. We will make further report as to the outcome of the disposition of these shoes after they have been disposed of. Very respectfully,

	John A. Kenney
Committee:	Frank L. West
	E. T. Attwell

All shoes that will warrant it are to be repaired and polished — Referred to Messrs. E.T.A. & R.R.T.

TLS Con. 636 BTW Papers DLC.

¹ Frank L. West taught shoemaking at Tuskegee Institute, beginning about 1902.

To Joseph Patrick Tumulty

[Tuskegee, Ala.] September 12, 1913

We understand that President Wilson is to be in Mobile October twenty seventh. In that case is likely to pass practically by Tuskegee. We are very anxious to have him make short visit to school. We would extend him hearty welcome if there is possibility his doing so. We could get this invitation reinforced by one from Governor O'Neal, Mayor of Tuskegee and other prominent white citizens of state. I could also see you if necessary regarding further details.

Booker T. Washington

TWpSr Con. 934 BTW Papers DLC.

From Joseph Patrick Tumulty

The White House   Washington   September 13, 1913

My dear Dr. Washington: I have your telegram of September 12th, and beg to thank you warmly in the President's behalf for your cordial invitation to visit Tuskegee in October. If the President finds it possible to undertake a southern trip at that time I shall be glad to call particular attention to your invitation and to advise you promptly in case he is able to include Tuskegee in the itinerary.

Meanwhile, with an assurance that your courtesy is appreciated, I am Sincerely yours,

J. P. Tumulty
Secretary to the President

TLS Con. 934 BTW Papers DLC.

To the Editor of the Chicago *Tribune*

[Tuskegee, Ala.] Sept. 15, 1913

To Editor The Tribune, Did not receive your former communication.

I think the law which bars white teachers from teaching and helping in colored schools in Florida is a very unjust and unreasonable law, and I do not believe it will b[e] sustained either by the courts or by the best sentiment of the people of that state and the South. Our race has been greatly helped at a time when we had few teachers of our own by devoted white teachers, and we have not gotten to the point yet as a race where we can dispense with the help of these devoted white teachers. One of the very best institutions in the South is Paine College, Augusta, Georgia, which is taught wholly by Southern white men and Southern white women. There are other cases of this kind.

As showing the increasing disposition of Southern white people to work in Negro institutions, I also mention the Interchurch College in Nashville, wholly officered and taught by Southern white men and women. The Southern white Baptist Convention has recently inaugurated a movement to establish a theological seminary for Negroes in Louisville, Kentucky, that shall be largely if not wholly taught by Southern white people. Such a law as you have referred to if allowed to stand would check the growing disposition of Southern white people to work in Negro institutions for training Negroes as well as prevent our receiving helpful instruction from Northern white people.

Such a law would prevent Southern white people who are more and more inclined to do so, from doing their part in the elevation of our race. I do not believe that any acts of wrong doing on the part of these white teachers can be pointed to as a justification for the passing of any such law, and I repeat I cannot believe that enlightened Southern public sentiment or the law on appeal will sustain it.

Booker T. Washington

TWdSr Con. 933 BTW Papers DLC. Corrections and signature of this draft in E. J. Scott's hand.

From Nettie J. Asburry[1]

Tacoma, Wash. Sep 15—'13

My Dear Mr Washington: You are of course aware of the Race discrimination now practiced in the Federal buildings at Washington. You must be noting with satisfaction that the colored people all over the United States are holding Mass Meetings protesting against this infernal predjudice. You have noted (and replied to) how the Americans discriminated against the Japanese in the California alien Land Law. Dont you think it is about time you lifted your voice in defense of the American Negro? We acknowledge you as our leader yet we take issue with you in your great fault of *Omission.* You have accomplished a great work, your deeds will live after you have passed away. We all love and revere you for what you have achieved but we could love and honor you so much more if you would speak out for your people. We are human beings with well developed senses and keen aspirations therefore it goes without saying that we are more than mere *money making machines. Of course* we should acquire land holdings and learn trades but there is a birthright which every human being is heir to. Without this natural bequest life is a Comedy. (or a tradegy).

I listened to your lecture when you were here last February and I was greatly entertained. Now be the great man that you would be, and *"strike* while the *iron* is *hot."* Yours for the Race

Nettie J Asburry

ALS Con. 934 BTW Papers DLC.

[1] Nettie J. Asburry was corresponding secretary of the Tacoma, Wash., branch of the NAACP. She was married to Henry J. Asburry, a Tacoma barber.

From N. Clark Smith

Wichita, Kans. Sept., 15/13

"THE LORD HATH HEARD MY PETITION:
THE LORD HEARETH MY PRAYER."
Monday morning   8:30.

My Dear Dr. Washington: Just a line (or) so to keep in touch with Tuskegee and its people; and to let you know of my condition.

I am feeling much improved these last few days of cool weather; yet some times my nerves give completely down, and reading music seems to strain the eye. So I shall not try any work of this sort for some time; but we hope Major[1] will remember that I am ready at any time to come to Tuskegee Band's rescue if necessary.

Your next Bandmaster will have everything ready at hand, all systematized, with the very latest instruments and music, the pride of my ripest and best life; in fact, Tuskegee Band is my child, raised from 14-to-45 pieces and shall always remain very dear to me.

We have decided to remain here all winter with mother, who is now very feeble and begs us to help look after the property.

The people are asking me on every hand to help the colored Y.M.C.A. Boys to their feet, they are completely down, and my white friends have offered me financial aid if I will take hold while in the city. I shall serve "God" the rest of my days, for he has prospered me in every undertaking. The colored boy's in this section are in need of our help and council, though I cannot do much actual work now; but can direct and suggest ways and means to better their condition.

When my eyes will permit, I shall continue at work with my melodies and compositions on Negro Music, especially my "Uncle Tom's Cabin" set to music, with themes of old plantation melodies, with solo voices, chorus and orchestra. We have been asked to arrange the "Negro Folk-Melody Suite" for our local white orchestra's use this fall, at the Wichita College of Music. I shall keep you inform[ed] with regard to this matter. These melodies made a profound impression when the Band play[ed] here last June.

We have quite a number of Tuskegee Song book's on hand if Mrs. Lee[2] or your friends should ask for them. Price 25¢. People out this way are growing very fond of my arrangements. The pastor's and their choir's all use them at regular services.

Love and best wishes to the intire "Student body" at regular pray-e[r]'s especially, and say to the Band and Orchestra Boy's, that I expect them to "hold up the standard" for I may visit Tuskegee in ear[l]y spring.

Remember me to Mrs. Washington and Booker, who I have learned to love so well, say to them I shall expect an early letter from them soon.

Mrs. Smith has intirely recovered from the fever and seems rather cheerful since I came. My daugh[t]er still teaches in the city school with other Tuskegee Graduates and I shall help them stand up for Tuskegee too.

Hope Mr. Scott has recovered from his recent attact.

My Best Wishe's and Thank's to you. I am   Yours

N. Clark Smith

ALS   Con. 931   BTW Papers   DLC.

[1] Julius B. Ramsey.
[2] Jennie C. Lee.

A Circular Announcing a Speech
in Barbour County, Alabama

[ca. Sept. 15, 1913]

Did You Know

===THAT===

Dr. Booker T. Washington

the wizard of the south, and pioneer educator of the negro race is going to speak in Eufaula ?

WELL IT IS TRUE

On Sunday October 5th

1:00 O'CLOCK P. M.

in front of the Barbour County Court House. **DR. WASHINGTON** will deliver an address to the friends and citizens of Eufaula and Barbour County at large.

All of the friends and citizens of Clayton, Clio, Louisville, Ozark, Cuthbert, Comer, Midway, Glennville and all points within the radius of eighty miles are urgently requested to take advantage of this opportunity of hearing this great man

A very excelent program will be rendered, upon which the Mayor of the city will take an active part.

W. D. FLOYD, Pres. of Movement.

E. A. CROCKETT, Secretary.

PD   Con. 636   BTW Papers   DLC.

To Robert Elijah Jones

[Tuskegee, Ala.] September 18, 1913

Dear Dr. Jones: Mr. Scott has just let me see the copies of correspondence you have had with the railroad people. It is perfectly fine. You have done one of the finest things in the interest of the race that has been done since Freedom. Of course these letters mean more than they appear to mean. The mere fact that they took the trouble to answer you at all means that they have begun to think and mean to act.

I am going to speak out plainly in my address before the National Baptist Convention in Nashville on Friday. I am also planning to send copies of my Century article[1] with the portion specially marked bearing upon the railroads to all the railroad people. If we keep firing into these people from different angles we will reach them.

The worst sinner in the whole lot and the one who, in my opinion draws more patronage from our people than any other railroad is the L. & N. It seems absolutely unreasonable, but we must keep at the job. Yours very truly,

Booker T. Washington

TLpS Con. 927 BTW Papers DLC.

[1] See An Article in *The Century,* Nov. 1912, above.

Wilford H. Smith to Emmett Jay Scott

New York, Sept. 18th, 1913

Dear Mr. Scott: In regard to your letter of July 28th, I was assured by Mr. Moore that he would see you at the Business League and take up the matter with you.

Since receiving yours of the 10th instant, I had a conference with Mr. Moore over the matter and he told me that he would write you making a proposition to buy your stock in the Age. He informs me today that he has done so.

With reference to the claim of ownership of the Age by Mrs. Ida Moore would say, Mr. Moore consulted me before taking this step, and it was to protect the Company's properties against judgments and executions that this was done. Under the circumstances Mrs. Moore would simply be a trustee for the benefit of the true owners, and I don't think either she or Mr. Moore would desire to take any advantage of the stockholders by this course.

I hope that you have already received his letter and found it to contain a proposition satisfactory to you.

I was surprised to learn from Dr. Washington that you had been in the hospital suffering with rheumatism. It is a troublesome complaint and I wish to assure you of my cordial sympathy. Very truly yours,

Wilford H. Smith

TLS   Con. 486   BTW Papers   DLC.

To Julius Rosenwald

[Tuskegee, Ala.] September 19, 1913

Dear Mr. Rosenwald: Replying to yours of September 11th signed by Mr. Graves,[1] I would state that we thank you for the suggestion of sending a portion of the hats to some of the other schools, and we would suggest that they be divided as follows:

Tuskegee Normal & Industrial Institute	
Tuskegee Institute, Alabama,	300
Snow Hill Normal & Industrial Institute,	
Snow Hill, Alabama,	
Wm. J. Edwards, Principal,	200
China Agricultural Institute,	
China, Conecuh County, Alabama,	
N. E. Henry, Principal,	50
Utica Normal & Industrial Institute,	
Utica Institute, Alabama,	
W. H. Holtzclaw, Principal,	100
Voorhees Industrial School,	
Denmark, South Carolina,	
M. A. Menafee, Principal,	100

Robert C. Hungerford Industrial School,
Eatonville, Florida,
Mrs. M. C. Calhoun, Principal,   100

Christiansburg Normal & Industrial Institute,
Cambria, Virginia,
E. A. Long, Principal,   100

Topeka Industrial & Educational Institute,
Topeka, Kansas
W. R. Carter, Principal,   100

North Louisiana Agricultural & Industrial Institute,
Grambling, Louisiana,
Charles P. Adams, Principal,   50

Yours very truly,

Booker T. Washington

TLpSr Con. 66 BTW Papers DLC. Signed in E. J. Scott's hand.

¹ William Colfax Graves (1863–1942) was night city editor of the Chicago *Tribune* from 1892 to 1902. Afterward he was private secretary to Julius Rosenwald and several Chicago public officials.

Extracts from an Address before
the National Negro Baptist Convention

Nashville [Tenn.] September 19, 1913

This is the twelfth time you have invited me to deliver an address before the National Baptist Convention which, in my opinion is the largest delegated organization of our race in this country and I believe anywhere in the world.

There is a tremendous responsibility involved in bringing together so large a body of our race once a year. There is responsibility for the expenses of travel and entertainment, responsibility for the loss of valuable time away from one's occupations. How can you make this great gathering so valuable to our race and to our country that everyone will feel that the time and money spent in coming here is worth while?

More and more in an increasing measure the Christian Church has got to face the social problems of the day. The church in an increasing degree must realize that the problem today is to save the soul of the man by saving the body.

I am glad that I have an opportunity in addressing this important organization here in the proud capital of the State of Tennessee in connection with the celebration of the Fiftieth Anniversary of the freedom of our race. There is in the city of Nashville by reason of the liberal spirit shown by the white people and the unusual opportunities for education of our race perhaps the most advanced group of our people, all things considered, to be found any where in the South. This, then, I repeat, is a fitting place and a fitting occasion in which to consider some of the achievements of the past and some of the problems of the future.

What we have accomplished during the past fifty years has been largely through the influence and guidance of the church. What we are to attain to in the near future is going to be largely the result of the influence and teachings of the church.

. . . .

One thing stands out definite, clear and distinct in the way of achievement during the last fifty years. We have proven to the world that we can survive from a physical point of view in a state of freedom. There were not a few who predicted more than fifty years ago when the Negro was made free he would disappear as a race. At the beginning of our freedom we numbered four millions. After fifty years of freedom we now number over ten millions, a population larger than that of the whole of Canada and twice as large as that of Australia. We have in the United States as many of our people as there are persons all told in Norway, Sweden, Switzerland and Denmark.

. . . .

We have not only proven that we could survive in a state of freedom, but that we could live in the presence of the white man and imbibe something from his civilization at every point of contact that has made us stronger, better and more useful citizens. When the white man touched the native Australian years ago the Australian began to disappear. The same was true of the Hawaiian, the same of the American Indian, but the Negro unlike any of these, flourishes and prospers in the presence of the white man's civilization.

. . . .

We have not only survived, but we have proven to the world from an economic point of view that we could support ourselves. There were not a few who predicted before our freedom began that we would prove as a race a perpetual burden on the pocketbook of the nation, that we would not clothe, feed or shelter ourselves.

During all the fifty years of the freedom of our race since the days of Reconstruction we have never called as a race upon Congress to provide for a single dollar to be used in providing either food, clothing or shelter for our people. We have not only done this, but we have accumulated something over $700,000,000 worth of property upon which we pay taxes in this country.

No other emancipated people have made so great progress in so short a time. The Russian serfs were emancipated in 1861. Fifty years after it was found that 14,000,000 of them had accumulated about $500,000,000 worth of property or about $36 per capita, an average of $200 per family. Fifty years after their emancipation only about 30 per cent of the Russian peasants were able to read and write. After fifty years of freedom the ten million Negroes in the United States have accumulated over $700,000,000 worth of property, or about $70 per capita, which is an average of $350 per family. After fifty years of freedom 70 per cent of them have some education in books.

. . . . .

We have met another severe test, and that is the test of being able to work together in harness in organized capacities. This is proven by the fact that we have over 36,000 churches with over 3,000,000 members. We have over 18,000 Baptist churches with as many Sunday schools.

The numerous fraternal and secret organizations which are maintained by our race is another indication of our ability to work in harness, to pull together in organized capacity. There are at least 3,000,000 of our people who belong to some of these secret and fraternal organizations.

We have organized and now sustain 63 banks in various parts of the country, another indication of our ability to work in harness.

So much for the past. What about the problems of the future? Many of the strongest and most powerful leaders who are before me tonight in this audience, must realize as I said a minute ago that the church in an increasing degree has got to concern itself with the social problems that exist in the community where the church is located. Our leaders have got to concern themselves with the problem of teaching our people how to live side by side with the American white man in peace, harmony and friendship. There is no portion of the civilized or uncivilized world today where we can go and not meet a white man, where we can go without living by his side or very near him.

I have studied white people in many parts of the world, and I have no hesitation in saying that if I have got to solve the problem of living by the side of any white man, I prefer to take my chances every day in the year by the side of the Southern white man. There is an inexplainable intangible something in the atmosphere of the South which makes the black man and the white man understand each other, and despite all academic and theoretical discussion there is something in the atmosphere of the South which makes the white man and black man like each other. In some parts of the country there is a good deal of discussion concerning the segregation of the races, but I am not afraid that segregation in the South will ever play any serious part. The average white man, especially in the country districts, does not care to have his black neighbor very far out of calling distance.

The white man of the North and the white man of the South are making friends with each other, are getting closer together. The Negro has got to imitate their example. When the white man who wore the blue and the white man who wore the gray met upon the field of Gettysburg a few days ago and clasped hands, it meant to say to the Negro that no more would the white man of the North and the white man of the South become enemies and do battle with each other because of the Negro.

In my experience with the Southern white man I find that he respects the colored man who talks to him, who tells him in a respectful, kindly and polite way what he wants, tells him about his needs, about his grievances, about the wrongs perpetrated upon him; but the Southern white man does not like to be talked about. This is human nature, and is not peculiar to the Southern white man.

In an increasing degree we, representing the leaders of our race, must talk to the Southern white man in our community. Let him know about our condition, about our needs. We must get hold of the officers of the county and of the city in which we live. We must get the county judge, the sheriff, the mayor, the members of the city council, the members of our board of education to visit our churches and Sunday schools, to visit our day schools. We must let these representatives of the white race see our condition and our needs.

Everywhere I want to see our people get back to the old habit of inviting the best white ministers into our pulpits. There are dozens of the best white ministers scattered throughout the South who would be glad to occupy our pulpits three or four times a year, and in this way we would keep in touch with the white race in a way that we could scarcely do in a better manner.

· · · ·

I have said on many occasions that all things considered, the South is the best place for the masses of our people. I believe this idea should be emphasized by the religious leaders. I believe, further, that it is a part of the duty of our religious leaders to influence our people to live in the country districts and in the smaller towns. We should get hold of the young men who are now burning out their lives, who are ruining in many cases soul and body around the gambling table, the pool table and in the whiskey shops of our large cities, and get them in the country on the soil.

Through the church we must teach our young people they must not mistake the signs of civilization for civilization itself, must teach the young men that cheap, flashy clothing does not make the man; that it is better to be clad in rags or homespun and have real character, real worth, and have some land and a bank account and some education back of it, than to wear the most gaudy and flashy clothing with nothing back of these clothes. In the cities in many cases, the temptation is to get an automobile before we get a home; the temptation in too many cases is to get a dress suit before we get a bank account.

There is the problem of the loafer which is becoming extremely difficult in all of our large cities, which the church must concern itself with. There is the problem of the woman making herself too common in public places, on the streets, in the court house. The church must tackle this problem.

There is the problem of teaching our people how to keep and use property in a way not to injure the value of that property, but to increase the value of the property. In too many cases when a Negro family enters a dwelling it seems that very soon the palings from the fence begin to disappear, that very soon the gate is off the hinge, window glasses disappear and old pillows take the place of window glasses. All this injures the reputation of our entire race and makes life harder for us.

· · · ·

We must not only tackle the problems that concern our race as a whole, but we must be equally frank in a polite, kindly way, letting the Southern white man know what our conditions and needs are. He will listen to us.

For example, in a polite, kindly way we should constantly remind the officers in the cities where we live that our people, except in a few cases, are not treated with justice in the matter of lighting the streets or in the conveniences of sewerage and drainage. We should remind the white man everywhere that if he expects us to live a clean, orderly life that we should have better facilities for the education of our children.

In one county of the South each white child had spent upon him for his education last year about $21, while each Negro child in that same county had spent upon him for his education about 98 cents. There is no white man in the South who will not acknowledge that such a difference is unjust.

We should, too, with equal frankness and equal politeness, remind those in charge of the railroads of the South that in few cases do our people receive justice or are they treated with common humanity when they travel upon the railroads. We should let the officials know that in many cases our men and women are crowded into filthy cars, poorly ventilated, not large enough, and in many cases one toilet room made to serve both men and women, that we seldom have proper facilities for getting food when traveling on the railroads. We should remind those in charge of the railroads that if they take the same money from our people for railroad tickets that they take from the white people that they should have equal treatment on the railroad. If a black man and a white man subscribe for a newspaper or buy a yard of cloth from a white man, the newspaper and the yard of cloth which the Negro receives costs just as much as the newspaper or the yard of cloth sold to the white man, there is no difference in these respects. There should be no difference so far as accommodations are concerned on the railroad.

We should make our appeal to the railroad authorities on the ground of common humanity, on the ground of common justice, and then we should try to convince the people who own and operate the railroads that from a commercial point of view it will pay to treat the Negro with more justice; that there are 9,000,000 black people in the South, a population larger than that of Canada, as I have said, and if these black people are treated in a way to make them feel kindly toward the railroads instead of hating the railroads it would pay from a commercial point of view because of the increased traffic which these millions of Negroes would furnish to the railroads.

At some time in the not far off future, in my opinion a great big, broad, levelheaded, far-seeing railroad man is going to appear in the South who will see the commercial value of treating 9,000,000 millions of people with absolute and unerring justice in reference to railroad travel, and he will be more than repaid for his liberality through the increased patronage that his railroad will enjoy.

After the railroads have done their part, let us as a race see to it that we do our part in helping keep the railroad coaches and depots clean and comfortable.

Say these things directly but in a polite and kindly way to the railroad officials, and everywhere they will listen to our appeals and bring about a changed and improved condition.

We must not content ourselves, however, with occupying a mere negative, complaining attitude. No race of mere faultfinders and whiners ever makes much progress. Fundamentally we must depend upon large constructive work for the progress our race is to make. The leaders of our race must see to it that whenever there is the slightest opportunity for our people, they put themselves in harmony with every great constructive movement that has to do with the progress of the South. Whenever there is a clean up movement or health movement, whenever there is a county fair, state fair or local fair our people should do their part to promote its success. We should become willing and ready taxpayers. We should become a part of every law and order movement in the community. The black leaders in our churches should join hands with the white leaders in all that concerns the prosperity and the happiness of all our people here in this great country, and if we sustain this attitude one toward the other we will set the world an example in showing how it is possible for two races different in color, separate in social affairs, to live together on the same soil in peace and friendship.

TM Con. 835 BTW Papers DLC. Delivered in the Ryman Auditorium.

Nathan Hunt to Emmett Jay Scott

Nashville, Tenn. Sept. 19, 1913

Dear Mr. Scott: Mr. Washington wishes left out of that railroad matter from his speech which I left with you the last sentence on page six, as follows: "Sometime in the near future some great captain of industry in the railroad world will see that it will pay from every point of view to treat 9,000,000 of people who patronize the railroads with absolute justice. In proportion as this is done, I repeat, the railroads will receive an increasing degree of patronage." Yours very truly,

Nathan Hunt

TLS Con. 633 BTW Papers DLC. Docketed: "Advised 12 Negro papers to which report was sent."

To Ralph Waldo Tyler

[Coden, Ala.] September 24, 1913

Dear Mr. Tyler: I have just sent you a telegram reading as follows: "Letter of September 19th received. No criticism intended. For years have found September impossible as business month. Hope you will not be impatient. Better go easy until October. Matters will come out all right. Think you are doing all that can be done under circumstances. Telegraphing Anderson to honor drafts more promptly in future. Am writing."

I am sure that you misunderstood both the spirit and object of my letter. No criticism whatever was intended or implied. The plans which you have been following were those outlined by the Executive Committee, and if they are not the wisest ones all of us are just as much to blame as you are. I do not see how under the circumstances, you can do better than you are doing.

In your great anxiety to succeed I fear you will have to exercise a little patience, especially during the month of September. Long experience has convinced me that it is practically impossible to do business in this country, either North or South, in September. I myself just now am on the Mobile Bay fishing. I find that to attempt to do business is simply throwing away my time and strength in September. I tried sometime ago to get the people in our section of Alabama to come to hear President Roosevelt speak at Tuskegee in the fall of the year when they were picking cotton. They refused to do so. It is practically impossible to do much in the South in the way of definite, constructive work until December or after Christmas. When I say the South, I mean the cotton growing states. I have just returned from the National Baptist Convention in Nashville, where practically every leading minister and layman was present. This illustrates the unsettled conditions in September. People are either away from home or are returning from their vacations and are unsettled.

So far as finances are concerned, I think we shall have to work a little further in advance. Suppose you make up an expense account a little further ahead than you have been doing, and I will see that Mr. Anderson pays over the money. If necessary we could pay your salary a month in advance instead of after the month has expired. We have the money in our treasury or in sight, to meet all the obligations that we have to incur for the year.

I am sure that you will find during October and November that your correspondence will receive more prompt attention from the people whom you write. I happen to know that in several cases the people to whom you wrote had not returned from their summer vacations, and after they do return it will require some days or perhaps weeks for them to take up the work of the year in a serious manner.

As soon as you have reconstructed your itinerary, will you be kind enough to send me a rough outline of it. I am quite sure that by both of us working together we can get definite results.

In the latter portion of your letter you speak of "a lot of discouraging obligations in connection with my association with the work." Really I do not know what these discouraging things are. If all the problems that I had to deal with were as easy as the one that I have had in connection with you and the League, my life would be a bed of roses.

In all of your work you will have to bear in mind that many of our men are not in the habit of answering letters promptly. The writing of a letter is an irksome and tremendous task to them. This is one of the things that the League wants to teach them, the importance of answering business communications promptly.

I think I have already written you to the effect that I had a conference with Mr. Trumbull, who has charge of the railroad system in Oklahoma, and he says that under the laws it is impossible for him to do anything for you, but he does say that when the League goes to Oklahoma in August he will be able to make considerable concessions.

I have been fishing for a week and am having a great time. Yesterday I caught about 100 fish. As I have stated, I have found that fishing is much more profitable and interesting than trying to do business with people in September.

When you get ready to come into Mobile, I want to introduce you to some of the best people you have ever seen, wide-awake business men who are securing results.

I hope that you and family are well. Yours very truly,

[Booker T. Washington]

TLc   Con. 851   BTW Papers   DLC.

From Frank Fox[1]

Sioux Falls, S.D., September 24th 1913

Dear Sir and Brother: I have been grieved and moved to indignation over the recent move of the administration in segregating the colored clerks in the Government offices in Washington.

Some years ago while in Washington I met a number of these colored people at a reception given a former teacher of one of our American Missionary schools. Later I saw them at their work and was deeply impressed with their character, courtesy and efficiency.

It seems so uncalled for to insult these people who are doing such good work that I feel that something should be done. For this reason I write you to know what you think about a carefully planned protest through Representatives and Senators. This should not be a party measure but should be a general protest from all right thinking people. I have the honor of knowing personally several Senators and Representatives and President Wilson. I shall be glad to take this matter up with these men if in your judgment it seems best to have others do the same.

Kindly let me know what in your judgment is the wisest thing to do. Sincerely

Frank Fox

TLS Con. 935 BTW Papers DLC.

¹ Frank Fox was pastor of the First Congregational Church in Sioux Falls, S.D.

From Charles William Anderson

New York, N.Y. Sept. 25th, 1913

My dear Doctor: Enclosed find clipping from the "Amsterdam News" of last week. It is from the pen of Tyler. What do you think of his perfidy? He is afflicted with a strange malady which expresses itself in covert attacks on his friends in the columns of newspapers. Keep your eye on him. A man who will deal dishonorably with one friend is apt to do so with another — particularly if he believes the friend can no longer do favors for him. Perhaps I ought to congratulate myself, for his conduct has relieved me of that severe mental strain under which I have lived for a few years, lest that in an absent-minded moment, while dining with friends, he should seize the vinegar bottle and proceed to shampoo the heads of the other guests at the table. It is possible to get an auditor out of a barber shop, but I fear it is absolutely impossible to get the barber shop out of an auditor. When I think of the earnestness with which I begged Gilchrist Stewart to refrain from denouncing his son as a thief when that young man suddenly left New York with within the neighborhood of $100.00 in his pocket which Stewart had given him to pay bills, I feel like calling myself by the name of one of the ancient kings of Sparta. You may recall that the name of this particular king was Eudamidas. So much for this heading.

Yesterday I sent forward, by parcel post, a bottle of digestive medicine for you. It is being put on the market by a very rich corporation here and is prepared after the formula of New York's greatest stomach specialist. I am sure it will do you a great deal of good, and if so, I wish you would send me a good strong line in commendation of it. The head¹ of this corporation is a warm particular friend of mine and one who has done me many great and lasting favors.

295

Hoping to see you in the near future, I beg to remain, Yours faithfully,

Charles W. Anderson

TLS Con. 64 BTW Papers DLC.

[1] M. M. Looram, of Westchester County, N.Y., with offices on Broad Street in New York City, marketed a patent medicine called Digestine, which BTW apparently endorsed. (See Charles W. Anderson to BTW, Oct. 16 and 27, 1913, Con. 64, BTW Papers, DLC.)

From Gilbert Thomas Stephenson

Winston-Salem, N.C. September 25, 1913

Dear Sir: Mr. Clarence Poe of Raleigh, N.C., editor of The Progressive Farmer and author of considerable note, is advocating the passage by the Legislatures of the Southern States of "a simple law which will say that wherever the greater part of the land acreage in any given district that may be laid off is owned by one race, a majority of the voters in such a district may say (if they wish) that in future no land shall be sold to a person of a different race. Provided such action is approved or allowed (as being justified by consideration of the peace, protection, and social life of the community), by a reviewing judge or board of county commissioners." Through the columns of his paper Mr. Poe is waging an active campaign in favor of such a law. So far I have been able to get only the white people's side of this question, whereas I am desirous of getting at the colored people's side as well, because I do not believe that such a law should be passed, waiving its constitutionality, unless it will [be] for the best interests of both races. Have you expressed any ideas on such a law? Have you any literature bearing on the subject that you could let me have? I am preparing an article on the subject for The Social Service Quarterly of this State as Chairman of the Negro Problem Committee of the Social Service Conference of North Carolina; and I want to put this matter before our people in the proper light.

Thanking you for a prompt reply to this letter, I am   Yours truly,

Gilbert T. Stephenson

TLS Con. 935 BTW Papers DLC.

From Charles William Anderson

New York, N.Y. September 26, 1913

Personal

My dear Doctor: Enclosed please find a copy of Tyler's second attack. I would especially invite your attention to his references to Lincoln Johnson. A short time ago he contributed a signed article to the "Evening Post" in which he gave entire credit for the removal of the objectionable segregation signs in the Treasury Department to Mr. Villard, Du Bois and their committee. Now he takes occasion to praise Johnson for it. He also denies that he is the author of the article, notwithstanding the fact that the proprietor of the News, Mr. Edward Warren,[1] told me without hesitation that the article was prepared by Tyler. This week's article was not inserted but was sent to my office by the Amsterdam News people, and is now in my possession. Cobb writes me that this ex-barber has a mental obsession on the question of getting every colored man out of office because he was turned out. He prates about our coming out against segregation when neither he nor Napier, nor any of the rest of them, said anything about it until after their resignations were demanded. They then suddenly found out that segregation in Washington was a bad thing and deserved to be denounced.

Is it not strange that every time a man holds the position of organizer for the Business League he feels that he is in some way paid to attack me? Moore felt that way when he had the job. Some one ought to talk ["]brass tacks," to that ex-barber. Ever since he came to Washington he has been busy assailing his associates, and other men in public life, in anonymous articles in the Bee. His contributions to the "Sage of the Potomac" column have struck at about everybody in the service, of color. His contributions to the Age, from Washington (unsigned, of course) have done the same thing. Now he is the Washington correspondent of the Amsterdam News, and as the News is under the influence of Robt. Wood, James D. Carr and Prof. Du Bois, he finds a splendid opportunity to strike at me. The editor of the Amsterdam News, last week, promised after reading the article, not to print it. I learned afterwards that the Wood–Carr–Du Bois faction, who are throwing their printing to the News, ordered it in. This week's contribution would have also been inserted had it not been that a dozen or so advertisers in the paper, among them one whose ads are worth from $250 to $500 a year, threatened to withdraw their patronage if I were again assailed in the columns of that journal; this, together with the severe criticism that the editors have received for allowing a coward who fears to sign his own name, and who does not live in this city, to covertly assail a man whom some people here regard as being, at least, a useful citizen caused Warren, who really owns the paper, to immediately send his man to me with the article, of which the enclosed is a copy. So I have Mr. Tyler's original contribution in my possession at this writing. You know how urgent I was that you should name him for Auditor instead of sending President Roosevelt five or six names, as he requested. You also know that during the campaign, Mr. Hilles thought it necessary to send Assistant Secretary of the Treasury Bailey[2] to New York to ascertain why you had taken a trip to Mississippi and induced Banks and his colleagues to change from Taft to Roosevelt. After denying the report unreservedly in your behalf, I wired you for confirmation of the denial. I subsequently wrote you and asked you whether it did not seem strange that Tyler, who was at Hilles' elbow, and on the ground, and familiar enough with the President's Secretary to call him "Dewey," should not be able to tell him that you were taking no part, one way or the other, in the hunt for delegates. It was he that inspired the Associated Press article stating that the two colored men of the country, about whom the administration was then worrying, were yourself and myself, and that an emissary had been sent to Tuskegee to find out where you stood. I mention these things to let you see what kind of a man you are dealing with. Of course, one cannot fight him, one can only drop him and spurn him. You can fight with a lion if he stands in your path, but you cannot fight the cur at your heels. Cobb writes that Tyler is in communication with Col. Roosevelt and is claiming to the Colonel that he was always for him at heart for President. You know as I do, that he was Mr. Roosevelt's bitterest opponent and went from state to state peddling the money to turn colored newspapers from Roosevelt to Taft. But enough of this. It makes my gorge rise. I shall never see that garfish-mouthed ex-barber again without smelling a serpent. But I want to promise you that I will get him before the devil does. I may not be good at hunting bears, but I am very efficient at killing snakes. Happily, Mr. Loeb knows all about his handling the Taft money with the colored newspapers, so when I get ready to strike I will have a very strong witness, and I mean to strike some hard blows, but I mean that they shall be fair ones. This miserable creature who goes "wiring in and wiring out, And leaving the beholder all in doubt, Whether the thing that made the track, was coming out or going back," shall have the sweat brought to his brow before that article which he has spent so many years in dressing and trimming, hair, is much whiter. I certainly would be obliged to you if you would send him a copy of this letter. It might do him good, if, indeed, he has not abandoned himself [to] a career of iniquity.

Hoping you are very well, I remain, Yours very truly,

Charles W. Anderson

TLS   Con. 64   BTW Papers   DLC.   No enclosure found with letter.

[1] Edward A. Warren (1889–1921) founded the New York *Amsterdam News*, a black weekly, in 1909. After his death his widow, Sadie Warren, continued as manager and treasurer of the paper.

[2] Robert O. Bailey.

To Ralph Waldo Tyler

[Tuskegee, Ala.] September 29, 1913

Confidential

Dear Mr. Tyler: This is wholly confidential. I wonder if you realize that certain parties in New York[1] claim that you are the author of certain letters sent out from Washington to a New York paper, and that the paper to whom these letters were sent give out your name regularly to certain other parties in New York as the author of these letters.

I understand that some of your letters are not only not printed, but are turned over in manuscript form to the parties most concerned. Yours very truly,

Booker T. Washington

TLpS   Con. 933   BTW Papers   DLC.

¹ Tyler replied to BTW with a defense of his articles in the *Amsterdam News* and added: "I know all about Charlie. I know how he has 'knocked' every body, with a single exception, the Divine Ruler." (Oct. 1, 1913, Con. 933, BTW Papers, DLC.)

From James Carroll Napier

Washington September 29, 1913

Dear Mr. Washington: I am writing to offer you my sincere congratulations on the bold stand you took at the recent convention of the Baptists at Nashville in regard to the matter of poor accommodations which we receive on the railroads and railroad stations of our southland. I have no doubt but that your words will go far towards remedying these complaints.

I am handing you herewith a letter which I am sending to some twenty of the most substantial men of Washington, looking towards the organization of a bank among our people in this city. It is my purpose before leaving for home to do the same thing at Baltimore, where the people have expressed themselves as being very solicitous that I should come and launch such project. Very truly yours,

J. C. Napier

TLS Con. 929 BTW Papers DLC.

To Sarah Cooper

[Tuskegee, Ala.] September 30, 1913

Mrs. Sarah Cooper: Information comes to me from a party whom I have had looking into the matter for several days to the effect that the shoe shop near your residence and belonging to you is often used as headquarters for people who drink whiskey, and is sometimes used as a place for delivering whiskey after it has been brought from Montgomery to Tuskegee.

I very much hope that if there is the slightest foundation for these charges that you will see that a change is brought about in the future so there will be no opportunity for such criticism to be made in connection with property controlled by you. You have always cooperated with the school in the most hearty manner and we have always appreciated it, and I hope you will do so in this.

Booker T. Washington

TLpS Con. 638 BTW Papers DLC.

From Sarah Cooper

[Tuskegee, Ala., Sept. 30, 1913]

Dear Sir, In regards to the matter of which you wrote me today, I must say, that, about a year ago I had occassion to speak to the party about drinking in there and he faithfully promised me he would do so no more.

Since then if such is true it has been on the quiet to me, however, I shall keep on the watch hereafter. Thanks to you for this information, as I am always grateful to learn of impending danger to myself or the Institute, if by word or act I can prevent it. Respty.,

Sarah Cooper

ALS Con. 638 BTW Papers DLC.

From John H. Palmer

[Tuskegee, Ala.] September 30, 1913

Mr. Washington: As you know, the Liberian students supported here by Miss Stokes, with one exception, have not been making a satisfactory record.

James Duncan[1] was excused in August, at his request, to go to Birmingham, Alabama, to spend a few days with Mr. C. A. Camphor,[2] Principal of the Central Alabama College, and who at one time taught

James in Liberia. Mr. Camphor informed me a few days ago that James has not been to see him as yet. One of our students, who has recently returned from Birmingham informed me that he saw James while there.

Benjamin Neal[3] recently left school without permission, and, I learn, that he is in Birmingham also. He did not apply at the office for an excuse.

Charles W. Williams[4] has not as yet registered and entered upon his school duties. He refuses to register. He recently left school without permission and says that he went to Montgomery to spend a few days. When he returned to school I had both Mr. Scott and Mr. Logan to speak to him, but he continues to refuse to register and enter upon his school duties.

Since these young men are so unsatisfactory it seems to me that it would be a good idea for some arrangements to be made so that they could be sent back to their homes in Liberia. I thought you might care to write Miss Stokes regarding them. I have frequently spoken to these young men and tried to impress upon them the importance of taking advantage of what the school offered them here and endeavor to make a good record in every respect.

Mr. Scott, Mr. Logan and Major Ramsey have done what they could to encourage the young men to remain here and do well, but they have not taken heed of the advice given them. Bishop I. B. Scott has also been written to regarding their unsatisfactory record here.

I am glad to say, however, that Charles Wardah is and has been making a satisfactory record and seems to appreciate what the school is doing for him. Yours very truly,

J. H. Palmer

TLS Con. 633 BTW Papers DLC.

[1] James Wesley Duncan of Monrovia, Liberia, attended Tuskegee Institute from 1910 to 1913.

[2] Alexander Priestly Camphor (1865–1919), a minister of the Methodist Episcopal Church, was president of the Central Alabama Institute in Birmingham from 1908 to 1916. He had been president of the College of West Africa, Monrovia, from 1897 to 1907. In 1916 he was elected bishop for Africa of the M. E. Church.

[3] Benjamin Alexander Neal, of Cape Palmas, Liberia, attended Tuskegee Institute from 1909 to 1913.

[4] Charles Wilmot Williams, of Monrovia, Liberia, attended Tuskegee Institute from 1909 to 1913.

From Susan Helen Porter

[Tuskegee, Ala.] October 1, 1913

Mr. B. T. Washington: I think it would be well to speak to the teachers about the unwisdom of the following:

1st. Making themselves too familiar with students. Each year I have found that there are two or three teachers who encourage the association between student girls and young men teachers.

2nd. The association of lady teachers with that of male students from a sentimental stand point.

3rd. Gentlemen teachers lingering about the Women's buildings. It would be very much better for the gentlemen to call at White Memorial Building for ladies and have a duty girl to go at once to the ladies' building and call for the ladies whom they wish to see. Some of them may not know that there is a pleasant sitting room in White Memorial Building for teachers.

Furthermore, I think it will be well to say to the lady teachers that they will be asked to chaperone the girls and to serve with them generally and to impress upon them the importance of serving with the girls cheerfully and conscientiously.

Some teachers discuss rather freely, the school's business before the students. This I think their attention should be called to; and too, some of them keep money for the students instead of encouraging them to put it in the Savings Department.

Some of the young men teachers have a habit of visiting young women in the Dining Hall and delivering favors (candy, flowers, etc) to them otherwise than through the Dean's Office. This I think should be discontinued. Three Tuskegee graduates are in charge of the Dining Hall now and they are uniform in their desires to have nothing go on in the Dining Hall that will lower the high standard which they hope to maintain there. Sincerely,

S. H. Porter

TLS Con. 484 BTW Papers DLC.

To James Hardy Dillard

[Tuskegee, Ala.] October 4, 1913

Dear Dr. Dillard: There is more fascination and interest in this work of Negro education than there is in hunting for gold mines.

Last Saturday and Sunday I have been making an educational campaign through Russell and Barbour Counties. I spent last Saturday in Russell County. In all my experience in this kind of work I have never met with a more genuine surprise than I did in Russell County. I do not believe you will find in all the South a county that is better prepared for some real advance work in the matter of Negro education than is true of Russell County. In the first place, it is almost purely an agricultural county. The white people there of all classes are in favor of Negro education. They have one of the finest county superintendents that I have ever met. He is not only interested, but is backed up by public sentiment. White people in that county, and I mean the ruling classes, boasted to me of the fact that they have more colored people registered as voters in that county than any other county in the state but one, and they were complaining of the fact that the colored people did not take more interest in registering and voting. I believe that Russell County is an ideal place for you to try the experiment of an agricultural high school.

I wish that you could meet Mr. DeGraffenried,[1] the county superintendent. He is a young man from one of the oldest families in Alabama. He is a large property holder and a first class gentleman. He is enthusiastic over doing something to help the Negro schools. He is just now arranging to set aside two or three weeks in which to visit every colored school in his county. One of his greatest difficulties is to get good teachers, notwithstanding he is ready to pay a good wage. In this regard we are going to try to help him from Tuskegee. I very much wish you would consider seriously the matter of putting an agricultural high school in that county.

I so much wish that we could spare the money to give him a Jeanes Fund supervisor. Even if we could only pay part of the salary he says that the county will pay another part. In fact he is anxious to have two supervisors, a man and a woman. Yours very truly,

Booker T. Washington

TLpS   Con. 64   BTW Papers   DLC.

[1] Frank M. DeGraffenried was Russell County superintendent of schools from 1913 to 1917.

From Clarence W. Allen

Mobile, Ala., Oct. 4th, 1913

My dear Doctor: Your very nice letter received, and wish to say that we are happy indeed to know that you liked Coden and enjoyed your stay there. Glad to know that you feel rested, and stronger for having come. I really felt myself that your rest made you look better and stronger. Our wish is that you shall visit us again soon, we shall be very glad to have you come at any time you would like to fish and rest.

We shipped Ducks and Pelican this week, I hope you received them in good shape.

Mrs. Allen and I thank you very much for your kind invitation to visit Tuskegee, and trust that it will be possible some time soon to accept the same.

Wishing you continued good health. Humbly Yours,

C. W. Allen

TLS Con. 923 BTW Papers DLC. Written on stationery of the Johnson-Allen Undertaking Co., Inc.

To Charles William Anderson

[Tuskegee, Ala.] October 6, 1913

Dear Mr. Anderson: I do not know what to suggest or do regarding our editorial friend.[1] The great display and noise made in the last paper over Langston's appointment is disgusting. One would have thought that Langston had been appointed to a cabinet position or some high Presidential office instead of having been given some insignificant position that was not important enough to go before the Senate for confirmation.

The worst of it is that through such prominence the paper seems to take back all that it has said against the Wilson administration for turning scores of Negroes out of office. It seems willing to compromise the rights of the whole race because of this little insignificant appointment. McAdoo, who has been the leader in the segregation, is forgiven for all of his "high crimes and misdemeaners" because of this little appointment.

I shall talk to him plainly again when I see him, but I do not know what effect it will have.

I do not see how anyone can blame you, as I have said before, for holding on to your office. You are simply doing what hundreds of white men are doing or trying to do. Yours very truly,

Booker T. Washington

TLpS Con. 64 BTW Papers DLC.

¹ Frederick Randolph Moore, editor of the New York *Age.*

To Frank Fox

[Tuskegee, Ala.] October 6, 1913

My dear Mr. Fox: I have your kind letter of September 24th, replying thereto. I beg to say that I think the suggestion you make is a very good one indeed. I feel reasonably sure that a carefully planned protest along the lines of your suggestion will prove effective.

I will be very glad to hear from you. Yours very truly,

Booker T. Washington

TLpSr Con. 935 BTW Papers DLC.

To John Hobbis Harris

[Tuskegee, Ala.] October 7, 1913

My dear Mr. Harris: I thank you very much for your letter of September 22d which I have read with great care.

While neither of us have thought about the matter very carefully, Dr. Park and I have talked over the matter in the rough. My general idea is to visit Europe sometime in the near future with a view of getting a kind of hearing in the various countries of Europe that would react on public sentiment so far as it concerns our race in this country and in Africa. I have found in the past that such visits have been rather helpful in making better conditions for our race in this country.

If I could make the trip, my general plan would be to visit the important cities and seats of learning, colleges, universities, and speak before a few important organizations. I should like, of course, to cover as many countries as possible, not confining the visit by any means to Great Britain. My point would be, in a word, to speak before representative organizations rather than merely local organizations whose influence would be limited.

I would not care to have it savor of a commercial tour, but I would like to get out of it enough to cover my expenses in connection with the trip. I do not know how that feature could be arranged for. In this country I can easily get from $200 to $250 every night in the year if I were to go on the lecture platform, but I do not care to do so in this country or in any other, but in some dignified way I would like to get enough out of it to cover my expenses, including pay for those who might assist in planning for the trip.

After I have made such a trip through Europe, I would then, I think, be in a better position to decide definitely about the African trip in which I am most interested.

I would like to get your opinion of the wisdom of this plan. Yours very truly,

Booker T. Washington

P.S. I have an idea that since practically all of the European countries are interested in the black race in Africa or somewhere else, any discussion of the question would excite some interest most anywhere in Europe.

I had most pressing invitations by cable from the London Missionary Society to come there last March to speak at the Livingstone centennial, but I was compelled to decline as I had made previous engagements.

TLpS   Con. 842   BTW Papers   DLC.

To Gilbert Thomas Stephenson

[Tuskegee, Ala.] October 7, 1913

Dear Sir: Your letter of September 25th received. I have read it with a great deal of care and interest. I have been carefully considering the proposition to segregate the Negro farmers of the South and find, as a matter of fact, that there is no sentiment among the substantial white landowners in this section of the South in favor of such a proposition. The average Southern white man, as perhaps you know, likes to have just as many black people in "calling distance" as possible.

The only embarrassment that the Negro is experiencing in this part of the South is not being able to buy all the land that the white man is offering for sale. The scheme is so utterly impracticable that I cannot feel that thoughtful people will long give it any large degree of serious attention.

It would seem to me so much better and so much wiser for all of us to spend our time and strength in doing something that we are sure will help and strengthen both races than to try to do something that might result in stirring up strife with nothing good accomplished.

If there is an attempt to carry the proposition into effect, racial hatred, in my opinion, will be stirred up in a way that it has not been stirred up in the South since reconstruction days. The one great thing that is needed throughout the Southland is for the white and black people to live together in peace and harmony. I think we should learn a lesson along this line from what is taking place in Baltimore and in other cities where segregation has been attempted. So far as I have been able to ascertain, in every instance there has been a stirring up of racial hatred and, in some instances, rioting. You will also readily see what a handicap would be placed on the Negro in the matter of securing land if the proposed legislation is carried into effect in the various Southern states. As I have said again and again, whatever tends to place a handicap on the Negro and keep him down will retard the progress of the South.

With reference to the white and colored people not being able to live side by side and cooperate in those things that make for the general uplift of a community, or a county, or a state, I think that some things have been done in my own state of Alabama and particularly in the county, Macon, where I live which indicate in a small way what it is possible to do in that direction.

What I believe ought to be done is to carry further the cooperative efforts that have been started, such as where the white people and colored people have worked together in a county or community for better live stock, for better schoolhouses for both white and colored, for better churches and for moral improvement.

I believe that a great educational campaign throughout the South, whereby better school facilities would be secured for both white and black people in which would be taught those things which are of vital interest to the community, would be more valuable to the ultimate interest of the South than attempting by law to segregate the black farmer. My own observation of rural districts in the North and in Europe are that conditions that tend to make social life unsatisfactory are dependent more upon other things than they are upon the presence of two different races. If, for example, the similar things that make for unsatisfactory social life in the rural districts of the South and in the rural districts of the North and of Europe could be tabulated and compared, then we would be able to ascertain to what extent racial conditions enter.

I myself have devoted considerable time to promoting educational campaigns in the South. I am enclosing herewith a copy of a reprint of some comments on my tour through the State of Tennessee some years ago and am enclosing at the same time a report of a visit made only Saturday and Sunday last. The white people who were present at all of these meetings were just as enthusiastic as the black people and, apparently, determined to give the Negroes full opportunity to develop the best that is in them.

Instead of immediately placing, as is suggested, this important question relating to the welfare of the South in the hands of legislators where, in all probability, it would not be calmly and judiciously handled, why not first have a Country Life Commission for the whole South, made up of carefully selected and fair-minded white people who would carefully study the question of the improvement of rural conditions in all of its phases. For example, this commission might make or have made "social surveys" of black and white counties and find out what are the exact conditions in these respective counties.

In the Progressive Farmer for July 12th, on page 779, a Mississippi Negro farmer and a North Carolina Negro farmer give their views on Mr. Poe's proposal. You have, no doubt, already read what the Negro from North Carolina said. In the Progressive Farmer for September 20th, Professor T. S. Inborden,[1] Principal of the Joseph K. Bricks Industrial School, Enfield, North Carolina, gives the view of a principal of a Negro industrial school. I mention these that you may get a line on Negro opinion as published in Mr. Poe's own publication. Very sincerely yours,

Booker T. Washington

TLpS Con. 935 BTW Papers DLC.

[1] Thomas Sewall Inborden, born in Upperville, Va., in 1865, educated at Fisk and Oberlin, was principal of Joseph K. Bricks Junior College, near Enfield, N.C., from 1895 to 1926.

From Charles Banks

Mound Bayou Miss, Oct. 9th. 191[3]

Mound Bayou oil mill began manufacturing today.

Charles Banks

TWSr Con. 64 BTW Papers DLC.

To Sinclair Lewis[1]

[Tuskegee, Ala.] October 11th, 1913

My dear Sir: Unfortunately for me my life is such a busy one that I do not have time for very much reflective reading, but during the past year I have been helped, diverted, and instructed from time to time by each of the following books,

"The Biography of Mark Twain"	Albert Bigelow Paine.
"Psychology and Industrial Efficiency"	Hugo Münsterberg.
"The Inside of the Cup"	Winston Churchill.
"The Woman Thou Gavest Me"	Hall Caine.
"The New Freedom"	Woodrow Wilson
Virginia	Ellen Glasgow

It seems to me that the biography of Mark Twain should be read by everyone. The sidelights on the character of the genial, cheerful philosopher have lightened many an hour for me. Yours very truly,

Booker T. Washington

TLpS   Con. 935   BTW Papers   DLC.

¹ Sinclair Lewis (1885–1951), the novelist and playwright, was in 1913 the editor of the Publishers' Newspaper Syndicate.

Notes for a Sunday Evening Talk

[Tuskegee, Ala.] Sunday evening, Oct. 12, 1913

Self Mastery.

Parents
Keeping under body
Gentleman
Bully.

Snake
Bull
Bear

Temper,
Making body do it
Early in morning
When sick.   Bad.
Mood

Putting off
Hot climate
Slighting work
Stealing
Vanity in dress

Drinking
~~Temper~~
~~Passion~~
No *control* over
   temper.
Fighting
Razor
Pistol
"Kill some one"

Controling talk

Thinking it over
Not sorry for what
   was not said

Calm
Dignified
Self mastery

TD   Con. 634   BTW Papers   DLC.

From Joseph Booth[1]

On S.S. Benalla, en route London to Capetown   Oct 14. 1913

Dear Friend, Twelve years ago you were kind enough to introduce me to Mr Peabody of Vine St, New York & he advised me to see Mr Carnegie. I did not then try to do so as I went on to Central Africa almost immediately.

I am now prohibited from entering Nyassaland, but all other sections are still open.

The enclosed printed papers will show the present way which seems most hopeful to me for the largest *final* gain to the Natives of, so called, British Africa. I have just completed, & am returning from, a 5 months tour through England & Scotland & have 300 Members pledged against "forceful" methods.

I went to Mr Carnegie's place, in the extreme north of Scotland, Skibo Castle, but only saw Mr Bertram, his secretary, who gave me the letter of which I enclose you a copy. This shows he can best be approached in USA & so far as the Washington £2,000,000 fund is concerned *only* on peace lines.

Possibly, in this age of murderous armaments of race against race, when whites of various European States, as well as those colonially born, are steadily preparing to convert Africa into a human-slaughter-house, the most hopeful method of nullifying the power of sanguinary-handed-foes is that of purely "peaceful penetration."

To this end special effort should be made to get for the African Family of two hundred Millions, their one-eighth proportion of the "International" Carnegie peace fund, comparitively speaking, at your doors. The fund I am informed brings in £100,000 yearly in interest. Africas & African's share, to preserve the race from exterminating operations (now stealthily & resolutely at work in many ways not known in USA) would be £25,000 yearly, if that, by judicious effort on your side of the water, can be moved *into line,* before it is absorbed in directions where responsibility "to do justly" is not marked so emphatically as in the case of those of the African race & those of kin.

I am trying to start the ball rolling in this direction by a lengthy letter to Dr James Brown Scott[2] of Washington D.C. the Secretary of the International Peace Fund, as suggested by Mr Carnegie's letter.

Now I have many enemies in Britain, to whom if Dr Scott refers (particularly in Scotland, as in Central Africa I am teaching Native Preachers to cast off Church bonds & establish *Native* "Free" Churches) many such would try to veto *my* appeal, as they do not consider me sufficiently loyal to British ideals; which is true, since I try to be loyal to the Fatherhood of God & the Brotherhood of men, particularly those most needing & appreciating true Brotherhood on *equal* terms.

To counteract this in advance, & to more effectually get in the thin end of the wedge for Africa's preservation, advancement, & unification, & in the hope of gaining your influential aid to *that* end, the following sentence occurs in the letter to Dr Scott, leaving by this mail, viz: (after showing that at an early date £3000 yearly is needed to educate students & subsidise Native Agents on peace principles throughout all parts of "British" Africa & regions beyond)

"As regards Africa the B.C. Union program is designed to save the unarmed Native African from exterminating conflict with Troops prepared by colonial conscription; as also British & often Indian troops, armed with modern weapons & machines for the purpose of dealing out slaughter & death rapidly, ruthlessly & thoughtlessly on small provocation, or assumed cause. It is an attempt to preserve Africa as the natural home of the African-born Negro, & of the Negro of the Dispersion so far as he elects, as the race matures in unity of interests & ideals.

"To this end it is suggested that Mr Booker Washington be invited to select & send, with your approval, one or two Negro co-workers, as Tutors for Native African peace students."

I may say *to you* that I am hoping this may lead to the establishment of a Carnegie Fund, as half suggested by Mr Peabodys statement, that his friend Carnegie had a lump sum I understood (20 Million pounds) put aside for something of the kind.

Be that as it may the Cotton supply of £50 Millions yearly needed by Britain *ought* to be, before 50 years pass, produced on Negro *owned* & Native worked plantations in "British" tropical, or subtropical Africa.

The 300 BC Union Members have it before them to secure the reserve of 10 or 20 Millions of suitable land, as *Free* grants, for this purpose, for 40 or 50 years to come.

See also copy of letter (which please return) from brother[?] Lyman Abbott showing how the settlement plan struck *him*.

Hoping you may plan some sort of African, or USA, auxiliary to tap the Peace Fund, I am, Sincerely yours for the right

J Booth

ALS Con. 935 BTW Papers DLC.

[1] Joseph Booth (1851–1932), born in Derby, England, migrated to New Zealand at the age of twenty-nine. Becoming a Baptist minister, he heeded a call to become a missionary in Nyasaland in 1892. There he met John Chilembwe, whom he brought to the United States to be educated for the ministry. A passionate advocate of justice for the African blacks, Booth imbued Chilembwe with his spirit. In 1915 Chilembwe headed an uprising against British rule that led to his death and the ouster of Booth, who later returned to missionary work in South Africa. (Shepperson and Price, *Independent African.*)

[2] James Brown Scott (1866–1943) was trustee and secretary of the Carnegie Endowment for International Peace beginning in 1910. He was editor-in-chief of the *American Journal of International Law* from 1907 to 1924.

From Charles William Anderson

New York, N.Y. October 16, 1913

Personal

My dear Doctor Washington: I am working day and night to elect Mr. Mitchel and the entire Fusion ticket. I am making an especial and strenuous effort to defeat that unspeakable Judge Zeller[1] who is running for re-election on the Tammany ticket. Judge Wadhams,[2] who is running for the same position on the Fusion ticket is a fine lawyer and a first-class man in every respect. I am helping get up some independent organizations for Wadhams and against Zeller, among colored democrats. In this work, I have been unable to get much assistance from the Age as its proprietor is too busily engaged in supporting John Royal,[3] an independent candidate, for alderman in my own district. Langston and he are helping Royal all they can. I would do likewise if Royal had a chance to win. He has no more chance than I have to be made president of the Argentine Republic. The very best he can possibly do is to poll enough colored votes in the black belt to elect the democratic candidate. The district is nominally about a thousand republicans and there are about eighteen hundred colored republicans. My private opinion is that Tammany Hall is financing the whole thing. Moore is also supporting the Tammany candidate for Comptroller[4] against Mr. Prendergast, who is Colonel Roosevelt's friend here and who has appointed a colored man in his office. It is true he appointed but one, but that is better than his democratic predecessor did. So much for that heading.

I wish you would write me a good strong letter of endorsement of Digestine. I am writing one. The proprietor of this remedy is a particular personal friend of mine and one who has done me many valuable services. I know of no man in this city who, in an emergency, would go further to serve me than this man. This is the first time he has ever asked me a favor and I am very anxious to do it for him. He wants a few letters from prominent men to be printed in his circulars.

Thanking you in advance, I remain, Yours very truly,

Charles W. Anderson

TLS Con. 64 BTW Papers DLC.

[1] Lorenz Zeller was a judge of the three-member Court of Special Sessions who had voted to dismiss the charge of assault against Henry Albert Ulrich in Nov. 1911. A lawyer in New York City since 1880 and formerly counsel for the local Brewers' Association, he was appointed a city magistrate in 1899, and in 1904 was appointed a judge of the Court of Special Sessions. He held this post until 1913, when he ran for election as a Democrat to the Court of General Sessions. Partly through the efforts of Charles W. Anderson, as shown in the correspondence below, Zeller was defeated by the Fusion candidate Charles C. Nott, Jr., who had the endorsement of the city bar association and the New York *Times*, by a vote of 123,911 to 105,226.

[2] William Henderson Wadhams (1873–1952), a Republican and Fusionist, was a judge of the Court of General Sessions of New York from 1914 to 1928. He was a noted international lawyer and a supporter of the League of Nations.

[3] John Mabery Royall, born in Virginia in 1874, was a prominent black real estate broker in Harlem, president of the Negro Business League of New York City, a Progressive party leader in 1912, and an unsuccessful candidate for alderman in 1913.

[4] Herman A. Metz (1867–1934), president of a dye and chemical company, was city comptroller (1906–10) and congressman (1913–15). He ran for comptroller in 1913 while retaining his seat in Congress.

From Reed Paige Clark

Monrovia. Republic of Liberia. October 16, 1913

PERSONAL AND CONFIDENTIAL:

Dear Doctor Washington: A long, long time ago (on June 16th) I received your letter of May 23d and to-day I have your letter of September 17th. I have been busy indeed since I last wrote you, often none too well, and at times more than discouraged at the outlook from all but the financial point of view.

Naturally, your letter in regard to the new Minister is disquieting. I had hoped that he would be a man of culture. I knew of course that he would be inexperienced as regards the Diplomatic Service and Liberian affairs (that was my only objection to Mr. Moore), but I had hoped that he would be at least cultured and possessed of a certain amount of savoir faire. To learn that there is perhaps but little to expect in this regard is a hard blow to say the least. I shrink from the contrast that will inevitably be drawn by non-Americans between the American Minister and the British, German and French representatives at Monrovia, all of whom are men of intellect, culture and experience and all of whom will be outranked by our Envoy.

The new Minister,[1] however earnest and hard-working he may be, under the circumstances will necessarily lack influence with the Liberian Government and our own Department; the foreign Governments, none of whom are to be counted upon to help Liberia to get on her feet, will be quick to gauge his worth; in the face of the apparent indifference of our State Department to matters Liberian (an indifference from which the foreign Governments are not slow to profit), and the natural apathy of the Bankers, how can those of us who have a real interest in the upbuilding of Liberia expect to accomplish anything of permanent value? It is with great difficulty that the Liberians themselves can be made to realize their own best interests. I am increasingly of the opinion that the officials in power are but little disposed to embark upon the program of reforms that we consider necessary for the Republic's welfare and that they are prone to evolve wild schemes of their own calculated to make matters worse even than they are. With no power at hand to help us force the Liberians to carry out in good faith the tacit pledges of the Loan Agreement I am convinced there is but slight prospect of success here. In what has been accomplished the American Legation has been my chief dependence, and I shall continue, under all circumstances, to do my utmost to co-operate with the American Minister. Please rest assured of this.

If Mr. Bundy should remain and the new Minister would be guided by his counsel we might continue to make a creditable showing, but it must be borne in mind that the Minister is under no obligation to accept the advice of the Secretary of Legation or even to consult him. Moreover, I fear Mr. Bundy will be able to remain here longer only at a great personal sacrifice. I believe he is sincerely desirous of retaining his post but the salary paid him is totally inadequate in a country where the prices of necessities are well-nigh prohibitive, and he has a wife to care for. He has told me privately that he has expended practically his entire earnings during the nearly four years he has been in Monrovia and that the expenses of a vacation, of which he is sorely in need, would leave him nothing to show for his years of faithful and efficient service. I know something of living conditions here and I can tell you truthfully that my expenses at the end of the year, single man though I am, will exceed in amount the sum paid Mr. Bundy for his services, and no one can accuse me of living extravagantly. Mr. Bundy's salary as Chargé is $2500.00 per annum, but he will receive only $2000.00 when the Minister comes. Can not something be done to bring about an increase in his salary?

Pardon me for writing you such a long, plain and doleful letter. There may be a way out of the situation in which I now find myself but I do not see it, and I am feeling deeply the humiliation of the position in which I am placed. Believe me, I shall continue in office only so long as I see some prospect of success. The Refunding Loan is held wholly in Europe; there is no occasion for the services of an American on the Board of Receivers unless he be permitted — and helped — to work out or attempt to work out the country's salvation.

I thank you more than I can say for your helpful and kindly letters; your active interest in Liberian affairs is more than ever needed.

With best wishes to yourself and Mr. Scott, I am   Cordially yours,

Reed Paige Clark

TLS   Con. 473   BTW Papers   DLC.

¹ George Washington Buckner, a black man born in Green County, Ky., in 1855, was U.S. minister to Liberia from Sept. 1913 to Aug. 1915. Educated at Indiana State Normal School in Terre Haute and with an M.D. degree from the Indiana Eclectic Medical College, he practiced medicine in Evansville, Ind., from 1890 to 1913.

Emmett Jay Scott to Isaiah Benjamin Scott

[Tuskegee, Ala.] October Twenty-second, 1913

My dear Bishop Scott: Your letter came to me during the summer, but I was not able just then to send a proper reply to it for the reason that, unfortunately for me, I suffered a slight break down which put me under the weather for about a month. I am now all right again.

I was very glad indeed to hear from you and to learn that your work proceeds so satisfactorily. I still find myself looking forward eagerly for news of Liberia, and especially for anything that is in the nature of good news.

The new Minister to Liberia has been here for a little conference with the Doctor and me. I took particular pains to emphasize two things: First, that he talk with you as soon as he reaches there, assuring him that you will be glad, unofficially, to advise him in those things where an official would be diffident about it. In the second place, I have urged upon him that he keep Mr. Bundy as his guide, philosopher, and friend because of his familiarity with Liberia and its situation in all of its many phases. He seemed to appreciate these suggestions, and I think will act upon them. He is a singularly abrupt and apparently uncultured man, but nevertheless, seems to have a stratum of good common sense; and I believe he is sincerely anxious to do anything that he can to help our brothers across the Sea.

So far as we here at Tuskegee are concerned there has not been very much of anything happening. I have been trying to keep my ears to the ground in church matters, but have not learned anything of particular interest aside from the fact that there is some growing difference between Jones¹ and Lucas.² Lucas seems to be the aggressor. The particulars, however, have not come to my attention. I got this little word from Roscoe Simmons and afterward talked it over with Dogan,[3] who tells me that he is doing everything he can to bring them into line. I trust that there may be no further fights between our men in the church. The past "scraps" they have had at their meetings of the general conference sessions have not helped us very much.

Now, with reference to your boys, Duncan, Neal, and Williams, all are in Birmingham. They slipped off from here one by one, going there to work. Duncan is a tailor, and the other two have work of which I have not yet been informed. We are somewhat in a quandary as to our responsibility because of their lack of appreciation for what was done for them while they were here.

Bishop Ferguson[4] has just written that he is willing to take Neal back with him, but we have not had time to write Miss Stokes for the money to cover his passage; and as above stated, we are somewhat in a quandary as to how far we are responsible, in view of their having left the school grounds.

Wardah was in to see me yesterday. He is, of course, the native of the crowd, and the only one really worth his salt. They have not turned out well here from our point of view; and yet I am sure they got something from their Academic and Trade work, which will be helpful to them when they return to Liberia.

My folks get on about as well as usual. The children, of course, are growing quite fast. The three older ones are now on the Institute grounds, but the twins are still at the Children's House.

Please let me hear from you whenever you can spare the time to write me of your good self and of your work.

With all good wishes, I am   Yours sincerely,

Emmett J Scott

TLpS   Con. 465   BTW Papers   DLC.

[1] Robert Elijah Jones.

[2] William Walter Lucas (b. 1870) of Meridian, Miss., was assistant general secretary for Colored Conferences, Epworth League of the Methodist Episcopal Church.

[3] Matthew Winfred Dogan.

[4] Samuel David Ferguson (1842–1916) emigrated with his parents to Liberia in 1848. He became bishop of Cape Palmas and adjacent areas in 1884, and in 1885 he was the first African consecrated as a bishop of the Protestant Episcopal Church in America.

To Bowser & Company[1]

[Tuskegee, Ala.] Oct. 23d, 1913

My dear Sirs: When in Chicago a few days ago I meant to have written you or talked to you through the telephone.

I do not want my son to engage in any business directions while in Chicago. He is there for the purpose of studying,[2] and anything in the way of business, however profitable, takes his attention from his books. Later on he may be in a position to do business, but just now I have asked him not to engage in such matters. This will explain why I have suggested that he go no further in the matter of buying a house from you. Yours very truly,

Booker T. Washington

TLpSr Con. 471 BTW Papers DLC. Signed by E. J. Scott.

[1] A real estate firm in Chicago.
[2] BTW, Jr., was studying at the Northwestern University School of Pharmacy.

To Emmett Jay Scott

[Tuskegee, Ala.] Oct. 23, 1913

Mr. Scott: We can get a strong and striking news item for the colored papers out of the fact that Dr Park is being employed as an associate professor in the University of Chicago, his subject being the Negro in America. Incidentally I would weave in the fact that he is associated with the work of this institution and is inspecting schools in the South half the year and devotes the other part of the time to work as a professor at the University. Our friends will soon see the significance of our having a man who thinks as we do in such an important position as a professor at the University of Chicago. Dr. Thomas tells me Dr. Park is making a great hit with his work. Of course the letter ought to be dated from Chicago.

B. T. W.

TLI Con. 58 BTW Papers DLC.

To Frank Trumbull

[Tuskegee, Ala.] Oct. 23—1913

Dear Mr. Trumbull: I am sure you will be interested in the enclosed letter[s] from railroad people whose roads operate in the South.

At your suggestion, I sent a marked copy of my Century article, "Is the Negro Having a Fair Chance." to practically all the railroad officials whose roads touch the South, I also send a personal letter[1] with each article. You will note that some of the replies are very encouraging and indicate that the heads of these roads take a broad view.

I believe that the time will soon come when these railroad officials are going to recognize the fact that they are dealing with a population of over ten millions of people which constitutes a population larger than the whole population of Canada and twice as large as that of Australia, and that it is worth while to encourage ten millions of people to do more business with railroads.

As a matter of fact, there are thousands of colored people both in the North and the South, who never travel except as they are compelled to do so because of the poor accommodations. There are thousands of colored people in the North who would come South to visit their friends, but never travel into the Southern States, and as I have said, there are thousands in the South who never leave home to travel on a railroad except under compulsion.

I believe that the time will soon come when the railroads will begin to see that it is a matter of business to treat the Negroes better, that in many cases their receipts would be increased by a large per cent through having the friendship, cooperation and good will of millions of colored people who live along the trackage of these railroads instead of their enmity and bitterness. Yours very truly,

Booker T. Washington

TLpS Con. 933 BTW Papers DLC.

[1] In his cover letter to the railroad officials BTW said: "I often feel that those who hold the higher positions in connection with the operation of the railroads do not at all times know the actual conditions that exist so far as our race is concerned. I believe that improvement in the accommodations extended our race would help the railroads immensely as well as add to the comfort and happiness of our race and mutual friendship between white and black people." ("Copy of Letter Sent to Railroad Officials," ca. Oct. 13, 1913, Con. 933, BTW Papers, DLC.)

From Susan Helen Porter

[Tuskegee, Ala.] Oct. 24, 1913

Mr. B. T. Washington; The attached matter is self-explanatory. I appreciate the increase in salary which has been allowed me, but as it is not the amount for which I have asked I am not altogether satisfied.

I regret that I have not been able, so far, to give the impression that my services are worth the amount for which I have asked, namely: $100.00 a month.

There are certain teachers in the institution who are receiving $100.00 a month for services rendered, whose work is of no more importance than this which I am doing and who are giving no better service than I would be able to render in the particular positions which they are now filling. I am referring especially to certain teachers in the Academic department.

I am wondering, if it is contrary to the general policy here, as is true in other places; to pay a woman as much for her work as a man receives; although she may be doing as much work or even more than the man is doing?

I will render as thorough service for $10.00 under certain conditions; as I would render for $100.00; but I cannot say that I would be unmindful of any lack of certain considerations, which I may justly claim.

I am not making here any request for any further consideration for this year, but I will appreciate it, if I am allowed the amount for which I have asked, during the next school year, if it is my good fortune to be connected with the institution.

Permit me to state that I am delighted to be engaged in the work here again and I am enjoying it very much indeed. Sincerely,

S. H. Porter

ALS   Con. 634   BTW Papers   DLC.

Charles William Anderson to Emmett Jay Scott

New York, N.Y. Oct. 24th, 1913

Personal.

My dear Emmett: You probably know that I am making a special fight against that infamous Judge Zeller. I collected all ascertainable facts about the Civil Rights cases which came before him and were decided against us. It made a very formidable array. I placed these facts in the hands of Mr. Guthrie,[1] President of the Bar Association, and then verbally called his attention to the doctor's "frame-up." The Bar Association met the other day and endorsed several candidates for judicial positions on both tickets, but unanimously declared that Zeller was unfitted by training and by his actions on the bench to serve as a judge of General Sessions, for which position he is now a candidate on the Tammany ticket.

Fred is supporting Judge Foster,[2] who is one of the candidates on the Tammany ticket for General Sessions. This is a very foolish thing to do. There are but two candidates on each ticket for Judges of General Sessions, and it would be very difficult for a man to vote for one of them without voting for the other. Besides, the judges do not run one against the other, as other candidates do; that is to say, one particular Fusion judge is not running against one particular Tammany judge, as in the case of Mayor, Comptroller, County Clerk and other offices. The two judges receiving the highest number of votes will be elected. They may be both Fusionists, or they may be both Tammany men, or it may turn out to be one Fusionist and one Tammany man. Thus you see every colored vote given to Judge Foster on the Tammany ticket takes away one from one of the Republican candidates. In this way, Judge Foster would receive the solid Tammany vote plus the colored Republican vote; Judge Zeller would receive the solid Tammany vote plus the German vote, for he is himself a German. This would leave Judges Wadhams and Nott[3] with the Fusion vote minus a part of the colored Republican and a part of the German vote, and would probably elect Zeller with a vote less than his colleague, Judge Foster, but considerably above either of the Republicans. I am giving you this exposition to show you that Fred's action in supporting one of the Tammany candidates for Judge of General Sessions is directly helping the infamous Zeller, against whom I have been fighting with might and main since the opening of the campaign. However, it is a foregone conclusion that we will elect the entire Fusion ticket and bury old Zeller.[4] Put this down as a prophecy from me.

Many thanks for your last installment. Please let the good work go on, and when you need funds notify me. Yours faithfully,

Charles

P.S. Zeller was formerly cou[n]sel for the Brewers As's'n and since he has been on the bench, has never held a bartender or a proprietor of a hotel or restaurant or saloon for refusing to serve colored people. These were the cases I brought to the attention of the Bar Association.

TLS Con. 64 BTW Papers DLC. Postscript in Anderson's hand.

¹ William Dameron Guthrie (1859–1935) was a Wall Street lawyer and Ruggles professor of constitutional law at Columbia University from 1909 to 1922.

² Warren William Foster (1859–1943) was judge of the Court of General Sessions of New York County from 1899 to 1914.

³ Charles Cooper Nott, Jr. (1869–1957), a graduate of Williams College and Harvard Law School, was judge of the Court of General Sessions of New York County from 1914 to 1939.

⁴ Near the end of the campaign to defeat Judge Zeller, Anderson wrote to Scott: "From the time I rise in the morning, which is quite early, until I retire at night, which is quite late, I am busy on Zeller." Anderson told Scott that when the election results were in "be sure and take a drink on the result, and be assured when you do it that there will be an answering hiccough from New York." (Oct. 29, 1913, Con. 470, BTW Papers, DLC.)

To Sartell Prentice¹

[Tuskegee, Ala.] October 25th, 1913

Dear Mr. Prentice: I SHALL BE VERY MUCH DISAPPOINTED IN THE COLORED PEOPLE OF NYACK IF THEY DO NOT PLACE THEMSELVES UNRESERVEDLY ON THE SIDE OF LAW AND ORDER AND TEMPERANCE. WE HAVE NOTHING TO GAIN BY LENDING OUR INFLUENCE TO THOSE WHO WILL DEGRADE AND IMPOVERISH OUR RACE BY TAKING FROM THEM THEIR HARD EARNED MONEY FOR DRINK. I VERY MUCH HOPE THAT OUR MINISTERS AND OTHER LEADERS WILL COOPERATE WITH THE LEADING WHITE PEOPLE AND CAST THEIR VOTES IN FAVOR OF THE CLOSING OF THE SALOONS.

BOOKER T. WASHINGTON

TWSr Con. 542 BTW Papers DLC.

¹ Sartell Prentice (1867–1937) was minister of the First Reformed Church of Nyack, N.Y., from 1905 to 1923.

From Charles William Anderson

New York, N.Y. Oct. 27th, 1913

Personal.

My dear Doctor: Many thanks for your commendation of "Digestine." It is just what I wanted.

I will see Mr. Macy's manager to-day and will cheerfully do what I can to advance his interests.[1]

We will elect Mitchel and defeat that old scoundrel Zeller, as surely as night follows day. The stars in their courses are battling with us. I have been going steadily night and day, and intend to keep it up until the end. Fred and Wibecan are together for once in their lives. They are both against most everybody on the Fusion ticket, and yet both claim to be supporting some parts of it. Fred is supporting Judge Foster, which is most unfortunate. There are four candidates running for Judge of General Sessions, and as only two can be elected, the two highest will succeed. Hence, the criminal folly of turning any votes from either Mr. Nott or Mr. Wadhams to Judge Foster, as it might elect old Zeller, who, in addition to the regular Tammany vote, will probably receive a great German Republican vote. You know how the Germans stick to each other. I am, however, confident of the result. Yours very truly,

Charles W. Anderson

TLS Con. 64 BTW Papers DLC.

[1] BTW endorsed V. Everit Macy for the office of County Superintendent of the Poor for Westchester County, N.Y. (BTW to Rev. King, Oct. 23, 1913, Con. 924, BTW Papers, DLC.) Macy was elected to the office. (Anderson to E. J. Scott, Nov. 7, 1913, Con. 470, BTW Papers, DLC.)

To Henry Power Bull[1]

[Tuskegee, Ala.] October 28, 1913

My dear Sir: The boy, John Swift, about whom you telegraphed sometime ago, has reached Tuskegee.[2] We have been waiting to hear from you with regard to this boy but so far nothing has come to hand aside from your telegraphic communication.

This boy warmly and cordially insists that he is colored, that he does not wish to "pass" for white, and that it will be doing him a serious injustice not to permit him to enter school as a colored student. In the meantime we have no word whatever from his parents either in favor of his admission or disapproving of his admission.

Before finally disposing of the case, we have asked the boy to go to Montgomery, forty miles away, and to await some word from you or his parents regarding him.

It is very desirable that the money be sent for his return to Boston in case he is not to be permitted to enter here. He states that he worked his way from Boston on boats, etc. Yours very truly,

Booker T. Washington

TLpSr Con. 932 BTW Papers DLC.

[1] Henry Power Bull was an Episcopal clergyman in Boston.

[2] John L. Swift of Roslindale, Mass., claimed he was black, the son of a black physician and a Norwegian mother. He sought entrance into Tuskegee Institute, but Rev. H. P. Bull informed BTW of the case and Swift was sent away from the school. Bull wrote BTW, "We are very much disturbed at John Swift's attitude. It is a most undesirable thing that anyone should disown their own race." (Nov. 11, 1913, Con. 932, BTW Papers, DLC. See also E. J. Scott to S. E. Courtney, Nov. 7, 1913 and BTW to H. P. Bull, Nov. 26, 1913, Con. 932, BTW Papers, DLC.)

From Lucius E. Johnson[1]

Roanoke, Virginia. October 28th, 1913

SUBJECT: Complaint as to Separation of Races.

Dear Sir: Your letter of the 13th instant with marked copy of an article written by you which was recently printed in the Century Magazine. I have read your article and I apprehend that there is some cause for criticism as outlined by you. Whether or not this applies to the Norfolk & Western Railway I am at this moment unable to advise definitely. Permit me to suggest that in presenting matters of this character to the public that it might be well to be more specific and not include all of the railroads that perhaps have reasonably well provided the same conditions for the colored people as they have for the white people. I know that in some instances the railroads have endeavored to do this and I further know that generally speaking it is the purpose of the executive officers of the railroads which operate in the states in which the separation of the races is made necessary in traveling, to do this, and great pains have been taken and a very considerable amount of money expended to bring about a condition that complies with the law, and all should not be condemned for the failure of some. I may write you further regarding this matter at a later date. Yours truly,

L. E. Johnson

TLS Con. 519 BTW Papers DLC. Written on stationery of the Norfolk and Western Railway Co.

¹ Lucius E. Johnson (1846–1921) of Roanoke, Va., was president of the Norfolk and Western Railway from 1904 until his death, except for Jan.-June 1918, when he was chairman of the board.

To Robert Elijah Jones

Boston, Mass., November 3, 1913

Dear Dr. Jones: I think I am finding a way to have street railway conditions improved for our race.

Will you be good enough to let me have in the form of a letter the actual facts bearing upon the method of separating our race in the street cars of New Orleans? Also facts as to the humiliations to which they are subjected. Write me a letter that I can show to certain bankers who furnish the money. Also state if it is true, to what extent colored people refrain from riding on the cars because of the discrimination. Bring out especially the point that they do not have room enough. Yours very truly,

[Booker T. Washington]

P.S. Please send me copy of the law bearing upon the separation of the races in the street cars. Write to Tuskegee.

TLc Con. 927 BTW Papers DLC. Marked "Copy to Mr. Scott."

Charles William Anderson to Emmett Jay Scott

New York, N.Y. Nov. 5th, 1913

Personal.

My dear Emmett: Did you hear anything drop yesterday? Something fell up here with such a dull sickening thud that I am sure you must have heard it even in Tuskegee. I think I told you that it was going to happen. Among the thronging reasons for rejoicing, there is one predominant, supreme and unfading one — and that is, the defeat of old Zeller. That old scoundrel got the worst drubbing that I have ever seen administered to a human being, not excluding the one that Mr. Jack Johnson handed out to Mr. Jeffries on that memorable day out West. The Tammany ticket was buried. Not a man was left alive to tell the tale.

I thought I would send you this news. It might improve your appetite a little.

Hoping you are very well, I remain, Yours faithfully,

Charles

P.S. The prominent colored leaders were all on the other side in this fight. Fred did not support the ticket. He wanted the "long green" before coming out, and as he was supporting Metz the Tammany candidate for Comptroller, and Judge Foster on the Tammany ticket, and Royall the darktown candidate for Alderman, the Fusion people wouldn't give him any coin, so he sulked. Harris went over to Tammany. The Amsterdam News was controlled by Wood. McDougald declined to help. So you see I was left in full possession of the field.

CA

TLS   Con. 470   BTW Papers   DLC.   Postscript in Anderson's hand.

To J. Harada[1]

[Tuskegee, Ala.] November 10, 1913

Dear Sir: I have given careful consideration to your letter of October 4th in regard to the causes for prejudice against the Japanese in this country, as well as to the solution of the problem which your letter suggests.

There are reasons — I shall not venture to say how valid they are — why some restriction should be put upon all forms of immigration to this country. There are, perhaps, other reasons in the case of the Japanese and other oriental people, why immigration should be even more restricted. One of these is the very fact that there is prejudice, in some parts of this country, against people who are not white.

I believe, as you can well understand, that this prejudice is unfair, unjust, unchristian and un-American. But as long as it exists it is a fact to be reckoned with. The United States has not reached a point where it can fully protect its own citizens, when they do not possess a white skin. It is reasonable that this country should not desire to increase its difficulties in this direction.

There are, I fear, a good many people, white people and colored people, who believe this question of race prejudice should be pushed to a final issue at once, no matter what the cost. I have never been able to bring myself to see the matter in that light. I believe there is wisdom, humanity and Christianity enough in this country to solve this question without partisan, sectional or racial strife and without war. It will require patience and forbearance to accomplish this.

I should favor any proposal that is inspired by good will and based on a mutual understanding on the part of both races and all sections of this country.

The plan suggested by The Outlook[2] seems to me one which answers that description and, I believe, if acceptable to the people of Japan, would be endorsed by the majority of people in this country.

In any case I can assure you of the hearty sympathy of Negro people in the effort you are making for a solution of this problem, which, after all, is quite as much the problem of the Negro in this country as it is of the Japanese.

I am, Sincerely,

Booker T. Washington

TLpSr Con. 935 BTW Papers DLC.

[1] J. Harada was editor of the *Middle-Western Japanese Year Book* for 1914, published by the Japanese Christian Association in Chicago, Ill. He was also editor of the *Hokuto Sei* (North Star), a bi-weekly review of literature and current events published in Japanese. Harada asked BTW for his opinion of the relations between Japan and America. (Oct. 4, 1913, Con. 935, BTW Papers, DLC.)

² An editorial in *Outlook,* 104 (Aug. 2, 1913), 739–41, concluded that Japan and the United States should agree to limit immigration to the United States to avoid a massive influx of Japanese citizens. On the other hand, well-educated and qualified Japanese immigrants should be allowed to enter the country, and those already in the United States should have the right to be naturalized.

To Joseph Booth

Tuskegee Institute, Alabama   November Thirteenth, 1913

My dear Sir: I have your very interesting letter of October 14, outlining your plans for racial peace in South Africa. I shall be glad to do anything that I possibly can to further the plans and purposes you have in mind. I do not believe it possible, however, to induce any considerable number of American Negroes to emigrate to Africa as long as conditions are as you describe them. In my opinion the introduction of another alien element into South Africa would only increase the present irritation and make conditions worse.

I am certain that all Negroes in America have a sentimental interest in Africa and many of them would gladly go out to Africa as missionaries. But the Negroes of America regard this country as their home and are convinced that they are better off here than they would be in any other part of the world. For that reason, they have no desire to emigrate. For my part, I cannot help feeling that any funds that were raised to assist Negro emigration to Africa might better be used in sending back home the class of white people in South Africa who are making most of the trouble. In fact, I wish that when the South African Constitution was framed a clause might have been inserted that no one, who did not show a disposition to live on terms of peace and good will toward the natives, should be allowed to enter or live in South Africa.

I wish that rule might be enforced in every part of the continent just as we do not admit to this country people whom we have reason to believe will disturb the peace. Of course, I do not imagine such a suggestion would ever arouse much enthusiasm in South Africa. That is the sad thing about the situation.

In conclusion, let me assure you that I wish you every success in the work you are doing to secure justice for the African people. My task is here but my heart is with you in your work in Africa. Yours sincerely,

Booker T. Washington

TLS   Woodrow Wilson Papers   DLC.   Enclosed in Booth to Woodrow Wilson, Jan. 8, 1919. A press copy is in Con. 935, BTW Papers, DLC.

To Robert Sterling Yard[1]

Tuskegee Institute, Alabama   November 14, 1913

My dear Sir: I am very anxious to have published in the near future an article, showing the changing opinion for the better of Southern white people regarding the Negro.

I have gotten together in the rough, and it is very rough, what I have in mind; and I am sending it to you, not with the idea of your publishing it but to get your advice concerning how it might be put in such shape that it will be useful for publication, and how it might be best used if it is put in such shape.

Please return the matter. Yours very truly,

Booker T. Washington

TLS   Century Collection   NN.

[1] Robert Sterling Yard (1861–1945) was editor-in-chief of *The Century* (1913–14.)

To Willard N. Baylis

[Tuskegee, Ala.] November 14, 1913

Dear Mr. Baylis: I want to make some investments near Tuskegee, since interest rates are cheaper here, and am thinking of trying to secure an additional loan on my Northport property. Would it be possible for me to secure any more on it and how much? I should like to get as much as possible. Would like $2000.

I have given orders to have the property repainted, repaired and put in better shape. I think the repairs are now going on; when they are completed I am sure the whole house and outhouses will present a more attractive appearance. Yours very truly,

Booker T. Washington

TLpS   Con. 471   BTW Papers   DLC.

Lester A. Walton to Emmett Jay Scott

New York, Nov. 14–13

Dear Friend: Just returned from office of New York Evening Post. Oswald Garrison Villard wrote me a letter the other day asking me if I would call to see him. Anxious to ascertain what it was all about I made an appointment and called at noon to-day. Was cordially received and he thanked The Age for running account of his speech made in Baltimore some weeks ago. Said he thought probably it meant that there was an inclination on the part of The Age to get together with him. I told him that we ran article because we deemed it worthy of consideration and that our actions possessed no significance.

I was then asked how paper was doing, and the answer was very good, better than ever. The next question put to me was what financial position did Mr. Moore occupy on The Age and I replied — owner. Then he wanted to know what was Dr. Washington's influence with The Age. I said that the doctor was Mr. Moore's personal friend; that Mr. Moore was a warm admirer of the doctor, and as Mr. Moore was known for either being with or against you he could readily understand Mr. Moore's position.

Mr. Villard then proceeded to tell me that he admired Dr. Washington but that he disagreed with him on some points; that in the chair I was then sitting he had made known to the doctor where he had disagreed with him; such as writing optimistic letters about the Negroes being thankful, etc. I informed him that I was a warm admirer of Dr. Washington because he was doing great constructive work. On this he agreed with me, declaring that even his Tuskegee work, in his opinion, was not as great as his work in the South telling the white people of their faults on the race question — something no other person could do. Then we disagreed somewhat on the terms "cowardice" and "diplomacy."

Mr. Villard complained that when his association sent out its letter none of the strong papers favorable to the doctor published a line. This seemed to hurt him very much. The fact that The Age did not use matter particularly seemed to affect him. I told him that we were making our fight in our own way, and he admitted that we were doing much good. The fact that Dr. Washington is so influential with the colored press seems to worry him.

Then, after I kept leading up to Du Bois for sometime without any results, I told him that while I thought the doctor had the greatest admiration for him (Villard) I did not think he was so kindly disposed to the impractical methods of some of his friends. We finally brought up Du Bois. He said he admired both Dr. Washington and Du Bois; that he had criticised both and did not think there should be any ill feeling for taking issues. I told him I thought the doctor a very broad minded man and declared I did not think he could have accomplished so much had he not been broad. I then dropped the opinion that I did not think Du Bois broad. He disagreed with me, but declared that Du Bois lacked tact and he was ill-tempered. My reply was that tact and a good temper were two requisites one who aspired to be a leader should possess. Mr. Villard assured me that he thought Du Bois was a leader and acclaimed him the scholar of the race. He pointed out the Crisis as a great piece of literary work and said it had a circulation of over 33,000. I congratulated them on their effort.

I was also told that the National Association was gaining friends daily, and that even the Hampton people were being won over. I again stated that I was glad to learn of such a victory, as co-operation was necessary in our fight. I also recall that Mr. Villard said he was opposed to the doctor dealing in politics, but from what he said to me later he seems to be desirous of controlling the colored vote himself — if he could. Talked about Wilson being frightened about colored vote in Illinois, Indiana, Ohio, New York and other debatable states. He seems to have talked with Wilson.

We discussed other matter for a short time and he asked me to think out a plan whereby we could get together. I promised to do so, but before leaving suggested that he also talk with Mr. Moore, as I did not control policies of The Age.

I have told Mr. Moore of the conversation I had with Mr. Villard. It only goes to show that The Age is feared and could be more of a power if conducted rightly. There is no better proposition in this country. But, alas! If the doctor could only show our friend a few pointers and the latter would act accordingly what great work we could do, as well as make some money?

Your letter of recent date received. Expect to hear from you soon. Regards to Mrs. Scott and family. The two doctors were over from Philadelphia Sunday. We had a fine time. Sincerely yours,

Lester A Walton

P.S. I also told Mr. Villard about a conference held some years ago at which both factions agreed to work together and that a few days later Du Bois broke his word. Villard said he could not believe it.

TLS   Con. 489   BTW Papers   DLC.

To Jeannette Tod Ewing Bertram[1]

[Tuskegee, Ala.] November 15th, 1913

Dear Mrs. Bertram: Mrs. Washington and I are sending you by express prepaid today, what we consider a very fine Southern opossum; we are also sending with it some sweet potatoes grown on our farm. Of course, the sweet potatoes naturally go with the opossum. In the South, the people combine the opossum, sweet potatoes and sometimes, beer, but I am not sending the beer for the reason that I fear it would require a good while for you to learn to drink it. We sincerely hope that you and Mr. Bertram will enjoy the opossum and the sweet potatoes.

A Southern colored woman knows how to cook the opossum better than anybody else. However, I hope you may get someone to prepare it for you.[2] Yours very truly,

Booker T. Washington

TLpS   Con. 64   BTW Papers   DLC.

[1] Janet (Jeannette) Tod Ewing Bertram (d. 1949) was the wife of Andrew Carnegie's secretary, James Bertram.

[2] Mrs. Bertram replied that the opossum and sweet potatoes "were so heartily enjoyed & appreciated that I hardly know how to thank you enough." (Nov. 20, 1913, Con. 64, BTW Papers, DLC.)

To Frank Trumbull

[Tuskegee, Ala.] November 17, 1913

Dear Mr. Trumbull: Enclosed I send you copies of correspondence which explains itself. I am not inclined to let this matter pass by easily. I do not know what is back of this move. If these people get into the habit of declining risks on colored people they will keep it up, and no colored person or organization will be able to get accommodation.

I rather think that this move has been brought about by reason of the fact that there have been one or two cases in Alabama lately where colored men connected with banks have gone wrong. It would be manifestly unfair to discriminate against us as a race. Each individual should be judged by his own performances, it seems to me.

I am wondering if you would think it wise to have a conference with these people? Perhaps Mr. Willcox can help in the matter.[1] Yours very truly,

Booker T. Washington

TLpS Con. 933 BTW Papers DLC.

[1] The National Surety Company had adopted a general rule against bonding Negroes. After Tuskegee trustees Frank Trumbull, William G. Willcox, Seth Low, and Charles E. Mason met with the president of the company, he agreed to reinstate Warren Logan and another Tuskegee employee. (National Surety Co. to BTW, Nov. 12, 1913, and Frank Trumbull to William G. Willcox, Dec. 17, 1913, Con. 933, BTW Papers, DLC.)

From Charles William Anderson

New York, N.Y. Nov. 17th, 1913

Personal.

My dear Doctor: Your favor of the 15th is at hand, and I thank you most cordially for the marsupial, which I am sure will arrive in the near future. When it does, I shall invite two or three choice spirits here to dine with Lucullus.

Did you know that the Emancipation Commission is at loggerheads? James D. Carr and Du Bois have had a falling out. Du Bois is said to have sworn some brave Spanish oaths at Carr, and Carr is reported to have retorted in kind. Wood and Carr have also had a serious difference, but this was about campaign funds alleged to have been supplied by Tammany Hall, and appropriated by Wood to his own personal uses. It is further reported that the Governor has sent auditors to go over the accounts of the Commission. On the appearance of these auditors, I am advised, that Wood, Carr and Anderson[1] took to the high brush and attempted to unload the responsibility for $1800 which is missing, on the eminent sociologist. The said eminent sociologist seems to be in danger of being made the scapegoat for the rest of the Commission. Wood maintains that the editor of "The Souls of Black Folks" was in debt to him to the extent of $800, before the celebration opened, for printing "The Crisis." He seems to have put him on the Commission in order that he might be able to settle up. This gave the distinguished editor a taste of warm blood and he appears to have developed the appetite of Gargantua. Carr accuses Du Bois of having stated that he, Carr, was leading an improper private life, and has expressed his opinion of "The Educator" in terms which I dare not consign to paper. "The Educator," in turn, referred to Carr as a one-eyed something or other. The Deputy Assistant Corporation Counsel did not seem to relish the inferred similitude between himself and the cyclops, and threatened to impair the personal beauty of the professor's cephalic configuration, and so on "ad infinitum."

This is the unenviable state of affairs existing in the camp of our friends, the enemy. In the meantime, I am possessing my soul in patience and quoting Goldsmith's elegy on the death of a mad dog.

You may be interested to know that during the last campaign "The Age" did not support Mitchel, and while it did not support McCall[2] openly, its editor talked rather strongly in private conversation against Mitchel. "The Amsterdam News" and "The New York News" were both for McCall. Wibecan of Brooklyn was for the same man; Macdougald did not open his mouth during the contest, except in private, and then in favor of McCall; Ransome was for Tammany, as were nearly all of the other so-called leaders. So you see the atmosphere has been pretty well cleared.

With warm regards to the family and friends, and with renewed thanks for your thoughtful gift, I remain, Yours faithfully,

Charles W. Anderson

TLS Con. 64 BTW Papers DLC.

¹ James Henry Anderson.

² Edward Everett McCall (1863–1924) was a justice of the Supreme Court of New York (1902–13). He was the Democratic candidate for mayor of New York City in 1913.

To Frederick Randolph Moore

[Tuskegee, Ala.] November 18, 1913

Dear Mr. Moore: Last week's issue of your paper presents a very creditable appearance.

In writing you a few days ago, I meant to have made one other suggestion: It is this, "The Age" only contains an impartial report of all the important occur[r]ences in New York and the country among our people.

Whether "The Age" agrees with the heads of movements or not, people naturally look to your paper for the news, and if they cannot get it in your paper, they will buy another paper.

If "The Age" continues to be silent on news items because it dislikes the individual concerned, the temptation will be for somebody to start a paper that will print all the news. You will notice that the New York dailies, while they have personal animus against individuals, always publish an impartial account of anything bearing upon the activities of these individuals. A newspaper should never be used by an individual as a means of punishing one's personal enemies. Yours very truly,

Booker T. Washington

TLpS Con. 65 BTW Papers DLC.

To Lester A. Walton

[Tuskegee, Ala.] November 18, 1913

Dear Mr. Walton: I send you herewith two copies of letters I have recently written to New York.[1]

Mr. Scott and I are trying to think of a plan by which improvement will be made that will be more satisfactory to you. We hope to write something definite soon.

I am very glad you wrote Mr. Scott as you did, concerning your visit to Mr. Villard. Your letter makes very interesting reading. I am sure you handled the situation finely. Yours very truly,

Booker T. Washington

TLpS Con. 489 BTW Papers DLC.

[1] One of these enclosures was probably BTW to Fred R. Moore, Nov. 18, 1913, above. It is not clear what the other letter was.

From John Andrew Kenney

[Tuskegee, Ala.] November 18, 1913

Mr. Washington: I am enclosing to you a note from Mr. W. W. Thompson which he says is a permit for you to hunt on his place and to take any of your friends with you that you wish to take.[1] He says that he thinks it will do you good to take this outing. He also advises that while you are there you will drink some of the water from the well that is just beyond Mr. Leslie's house, as he claims that it has special medicinal virtues. Very truly,

J. A. Kenney

TLS Con. 933 BTW Papers DLC.

[1] An enclosed note signed by William Watson Thompson gave permission to BTW, Logan, and any invited guest to hunt on his company's lands for the 1913–14 hunting season.

Fragments of Washington's Financial Account

[Tuskegee, Ala.] Nov. 18, 1913

B.T.W. personal

OBLIGATIONS

At Macon County Bank, notes	$7808.83
" " " " overdraft	1314.81
Bank of Tuskegee, notes past due	1062.35
Travelers Insurance Co.	2396.00
Northport Mortgage	5000.00
Mutual Insurance Co.	6634.00
School Account, about	1500.00
Report "	854.45
Total	20,570.44
Amount obligations last report	19,455.63
Increase	1,014.81

SECURITIES

Southern R.R. Pref. 20 sh. (Macon Co. Bank)	$2000.
Douglas Shoe Co., Pref.9 sh. " " "	900.
Central Leather Co.,1 sh. " " "	100.
First Lien 20 yr.Gold Bond " " "	100.
United States Steel Corporation " "	100.
Ala.Agri.Fair Association 1 sh.	100.
Tuskegee Building & Loan Assn. 1 sh.	25.
Probable value of publications about	10,000.
Annual interest on pub.	$600.
Total	13,525.
Value of securities at Macon County Bank	3400.

ROYALTIES

J. L. Nichols & Co., "Story of My Life & Work"	6¢ per copy
Doubleday, Page & Co., "Working with the Hands"	18 " "
" " " " "Up From Slavery"	22½ " "
" " " " "Character Building"	18¾ " "
" " " " "My Larger Education"	15 " "

339

"	" " "	"Story of the Negro"	18¾ " "
"	" " "	"Man Farthest Down"	15 " "
Small, Maynard & Co.,		"Future of the American Negro"	15 " "
Hertel Jenkins & Co.,		"Negro in Business"	6 " "

RESOURCES

Value of Real Estate	$ 50,900.
" " Life Insurance	28,025.
Held by Trustees	150,000.
Value of Securities	13,525.
On deposit with Union Trust Co., Montgomery	30.44
" " " Farmers Loan & Trust Co., N.Y.	32.69
Grand total	242,513.13
less amount of liabilities	20,570.44
	221,942.69
Less	150,000.00
Net total	71,942.69

TMf   Con. 255   BTW Papers   DLC.

To the Editor of the Boston *Transcript*

Tuskegee Institute, Alabama   November 19, 1913

Editor: The Transcript, Boston, Massachusetts. At the end of six months of the present year there had been 24 cases of lynchings. At the end of ten months (November 1st) there had been 45 lynchings; a reduction of 4 as compared with the same period for 1912. Within the past four months, July, August, September and October, since I last called attention to the subject, there have been 21 lynchings, making a total, as I have said, of 45 lynchings for ten months. Of this number only 7 individuals or 1.5 [15] per cent were charged with rape.

It is worth while I think to note a few typical cases for which human life was taken by a mob:

July 10th, a Negro near Blountsville, Florida, charged with being lawless and assisting a criminal to escape.

July 27th, a Negro at Dunbar, Georgia, supposed to be a burglar, charged with shooting a proprietor of store.

Also in July, two colored farmers were lynched near Germantown, Kentucky. No motive was assigned for the lynching. The Commercial Appeal, the leading white newspaper of Tennessee, in commenting upon the lynchings, said: "Two apparently inoffensive Negroes, good farm hands, real wealth producers, were assassinated." No motive was assigned for the lynching. The Commercial Appeal further stated, "As far as anyone knows, they were quiet orderly country people."

August 18th, the sheriff at Spartanburg, S.C., in spite of the fact that dynamite was used, prevented a mob from lynching a Negro accused of assaulting a white woman; he [was] tried later before a white jury and found not guilty.

August 23rd, a half-witted Negro near Birmingham, Alabama, for frightening women and children.

August 25th, a Negro accused of murder, at Greenville, Georgia. A few days later, another Negro was arrested and confessed. An innocent man had been lynched.

August 27th, a Negro at Jennings, Louisiana, for striking an Italian merchant who had swept dirt on the Negro's shoes as he was passing the store.

September 20th, a Negro at Louisville, Mississippi, because he frightened a white woman in her home by his strange actions.

September 21st, at Franklin, Texas, a Negro for killing two white men and wounding a third.

September 25th, at Marks, Mississippi, a Negro accused of attempted rape. The opinion of the mob was divided on his guilt or innocence; a mass meeting held condemned the lynching.

September 26th, a Negro at Litchfield, Kentucky, accused of rape.

October 22nd, at Monroe, Louisiana, a Negro for making insulting remarks to a white woman.

In ten months, as above stated, 45 persons have been put to death by mob-law. A reduction of the number of lynchings by four, though small, means something in the way of a higher civilization.

Booker T. Washington

TLSr James Thomas Williams Papers NcD. Signed in E. J. Scott's hand.

To Reed Paige Clark

[Tuskegee, Ala.] November 19, 1913

My dear Mr. Clark: Thank you so very much for your good and full, frank letter under date of October 16th.

Though at a distance, I think I can appreciate some of the difficulties that you are experiencing, but assure you I sympathize with you most deeply. I had no idea, however, that the loan was now only held by foreign people. This, of course, adds to your difficulties.

Another element, I presume, which is making itself felt is the new policy enacted by the present administration to the effect that it would not take up such matters with foreign countries in the way that past administrations have been doing.

In regard to the new minister, I think you will find that while he has a rather crude exterior, deep down at the bottom, he has a lot of common sense and will finally win his way. The more I saw of him and the more I talked with him, the more I was pleased with him, notwithstanding the impressions formed at first sight.

I very much hope the Liberian people will ultimately be led to see the importance of getting right down to business, throwing aside all superficiality and devote themselves to the improvement of their country along fundamental lines of civilization. This, in my opinion, is the last chance for Liberia.

Now, regarding Mr. Bundy, I am very glad you have written me so frankly about him. He seems to have made an unusually good impression upon everybody: he must be a man of an unusually strong character. I should like to keep in touch with him even if he leaves Liberia. I wish I knew what to say or to do about having his salary increased. As you perhaps know, I am not in such close touch with this administration as I have been with other administrations. I am a Republican and the present administration is Democratic. If you or Mr. Bundy will point out some practical way in which you think I can be of service, I shall be glad to consider the matter.

Judging by what Mr. Scott tells me, I can easily appreciate what you say regarding the high cost of living in that country.

Please do not fail to call on me when you think I can prove of the slighted [slightest] service.

By this mail, I am sending you a marked copy of the "World's Work" which contains an article from my pen.[1] I think it has some suggestions that might prove helpful to the people of Liberia. Yours very truly,

Booker T. Washington

TLpS Con. 70 BTW Papers DLC.

[1] This presumably was BTW, "What I Am Trying to Do," *World's Work*, 27 (Nov. 1913), 101–7, below, though the article contained no explicit reference to Liberia.

Emmett Jay Scott to Bertha Ruffner[1]

[Tuskegee, Ala.] November 20th, 1913

Dear Madam: I notice that you are in charge of the special Hotel Bureau, conducted in the interest of the readers of THE INDEPENDENT. I am writing to ask if you know of a single hotel of the better order in New York City which accepts colored people of character and responsibility as guests. I frequently go to New York, but since the old Astor House retired from business, I know of no hotel of substantial quality to which a black man can go with the assurance that he will not meet with specious excuses for refusing him.

I enclose stamped envelope for reply, and will thank you if you will let me hear from you at your convenience. Yours very truly,

Emmett J. Scott

TLpS Con. 485 BTW Papers DLC.

[1] Owner of the Bertha Ruffner Hotel Bureau with offices in the Hotel McAlpin in New York City and the St. Charles Hotel in New Orleans, La.

To Grover Cleveland Thompson

[Tuskegee, Ala.] November Twenty-first, 1913

Dear Mr. Thompson: I am sure that you will not misunderstand me in regard to the matter about which I am writing. I am sure you will consider it an act of friendship.

I think you ought to know that a good many colored people feel that the hearse which is used in burying colored people could be greatly improved in appearance. I have heard many express this feeling in the matter.

I feel, too, that if you could induce the driver to be more careful in his dress and general appearance, it would help your business a great deal among the colored people. The driver does not dress himself in accordance with funeral customs. Very truly yours,

Booker T. Washington

TLpS Con. 933 BTW Papers DLC.

Charles William Anderson to Emmett Jay Scott

New York, N.Y. Nov. 21st, 1913

Personal.

My dear Emmett: Some time ago I mentioned, in obiter dictum, that you were a sufferer from rheumatism, to Mr. Looram. To-day, he called at my office and gave me a pamphlet and two small packages of rheumatism medicine, which he said several of his friends had taken with most excellent results. I am sending them forward to you by parcels post, to-day. Read the pamphlet carefully. I hope you will reap real benefit from it.

Please tell the Doctor that his marsupials reached me last night, but owing to the fact that the box was addressed to me at 156 West *152nd* Street, instead of *132nd* Street, it was delayed, until the marsupials had spoiled. You can imagine my disappointment when I found that they were not edible. However, I thank him just the same. Yours very truly,

Charles

TLS Con. 470 BTW Papers DLC.

To Valentine Everit Macy

[Tuskegee, Ala.] November 23rd, 1913

Dear Mr. Macy: I am very glad that you feel that my efforts were of some value in bringing about your election. I realize that you were in the district of one of the severest "bosses," I mean Mr. Ward.[1] I have had a little experience with him in the past, and know something of his methods and attitude. Nevertheless your election will prove of great value in many directions.

With all good wishes, I am Yours very truly,

Booker T. Washington

TLpS Con. 928 BTW Papers DLC.

[1] William Lukens Ward.

From Lester A. Walton

New York, Nov. 23–13

Dear Dr. Washington: Your letter of the 18th inst. with enclosures received. The information that you and Mr. Scott are trying to think out a plan by which improvement will be made that will be more satisfactory to me, and that you hope to write something definite soon came at an opportune time and was very inspiring. I certainly need some good news to excavate me out of my none too cheerful mental state.

I am glad you think I conducted myself finely on my visit to Mr. Villard. During my twenty-minutes talk with him I think I was given an excellent chance to study him at close range. While he impresses me as being sincere in his efforts to help the Negro, I also formed the conclusion that he aspires to be a Moses of our race. I don't think we need white men as leaders. What we need is their earnest co-operation, moral and financial support. Although Mr. Villard seems to be averse to you delving in politics, he talked to me about what the colored voters in the doubtful states could do if they used judgment, and it seems that he and Wilson have been talking on that subject. He said

345

President Wilson had made known to him that he was worried over the situation. My impression of Mr. Villard is that he would use the colored vote, if he could.[1]

I am going to be frank and tell you that you are going to need a strong publication to help teach the gospel of common sense in the future. While you and Mr. Scott are in a position to learn what is going on, yet one who has ostensibly taken an impartial stand on racial matters as myself can learn much valuable information. There is no need of me disguising the fact that the Crisis is getting stronger daily, and that its backers are planning a more active campaign than ever before. While the Crisis does not deal with racial matters as it should, yet it is the only publication which is put out on a high class, dignified scale. Therefore, it creates a good impression and makes friends. The Age has an opportunity to wield more influence than the Crisis and all the colored papers put together. And it is because advantage is not taken of the opportunity that causes me much worry.

Trusting that I shall receive some good news from you soon, I am, Sincerely yours,

Lester A Walton

TLS Con. 489 BTW Papers DLC.

[1] Walton wrote even more frankly to E. J. Scott on the same date: "The sending of Mr. Villard for me evidently had some significance. I am at first inclined to think he heard that I was dissatisfied with The Age and either wanted to talk some business with me or wanted me to tell him some Age secrets. However, I do know he wants The Age influence. His first question was how was business, and when I told him it was better than ever before, he wanted to know if we were making money, to which I answered in the affirmative. Then he switched and abruptly asked me about what was the Washington influence on The Age, and when I told him that Mr. Moore owned The Age and that he was a warm friend and admirer of Dr. Washington he (Villard) looked at me in a queer sort of way. I think he anticipated that he was going to confuse me with his 'august' presence, but he did not know that for six years I mingled with judges, etc., on white papers in St. Louis and had become well acquainted with the white brother. Mr. Villard seemed to be very disappointed in my answers and soon changed his cross-examination to holding a conversation." (Con. 489, BTW Papers, DLC.)

Bertha Ruffner to Emmett Jay Scott

New York   November 25th 1913

Dear Sir: Replying to your favor of recent date beg to say that we have made inquiry at several of our hotels of the better class, regarding the accommodation of colored people and regret to say that thus far we have not been able to locate any to which we can refer you. We are, however pushing the inquiry further and shall communicate with you again as soon as we have satisfactory data.

Regretting the delay in the matter, I am, Yours sincerely,

Bertha Ruffner

TLS   Con. 485   BTW Papers   DLC.

To Andrew Carnegie

[Tuskegee, Ala.] November 26, 1913

Dear Mr. Carnegie: Owing to the growth of the school, it has become absolutely necessary to enlarge our Library Building. I am putting the matter rather frankly before you because of your kindness in giving it to us; and because it bears your name we do not like, of course, to ask anybody else for the funds with which to enlarge it.

You can see the necessity for enlargement when I say that you gave us $20,000 for the building in 1899. At that time we had 1200 students and 115 teachers. Now the students and teaching body and the community which has grown up around the school have nearly doubled.

The building is constantly full of students, teachers, and people living in the community; and ever since we have had this library building we can note a rapid and constant growth of students, and teachers, and all who use the library in the direction of higher and better ideals of living. The library building and the books have served a genuine purpose in the way of a better and higher civilization.

At the time you gave us the building we had only 6,000 books and 500 magazines. Now the number has increased to 23,000 books and 12,000 magazines. For some time we have been compelled to store away a lot of our most valuable books and magazines in basements and sheds for lack of space.

Since the building was erected, as I am sure you will realize, the price of all kinds of building material has increased twenty per cent, hence in order to provide a sufficient addition to the building to answer our purposes, we ought to have $18,000. Of course the students would make the bricks and do the greater part of the work of putting up the addition, as they did on the original building.

I am sure you will not misunderstand my frankness in putting the whole matter before you just in the way I have thought you would like me to do. Yours very truly,

Booker T. Washington

TLpS Con. 64 BTW Papers DLC.

Emmett Jay Scott to the City Editor
of the Montgomery *Advertiser*

[Tuskegee, Ala.] Nov. 27, 1913

A Twenty pound Macon County bred turkey with Macon county products including sweet potatoes, parsley and lettuce, in a wicker basket garnished with cranberries, apples and autumn leaves, was sent as a gift by the Tuskegee Institute for Governor and Mrs. O'Neal's Thanksgiving dinner. It was delivered by special messenger at the Executive Mansion.

Emmett J. Scott

TWSr Con. 928 BTW Papers DLC.

To James Longstreet Sibley[1]

[Tuskegee, Ala.] November 28, 1913

My dear Sir: Thank you for yours of November 24th:

My idea for the Colored State Teachers Association is as follows:

1st — To have the meeting at the same time and place as the white association.

2nd — To have the meeting center itself around the following points:

(1) Securing good schoolhouses.

(2) Extension of the school term.

(3) Securing better pay for teachers.

(4) Getting strong, representative white men to speak to the colored teachers.

(5) An industrial exhibit representing especially what is being done in the small, rural schools.

(6) Show through means of the stereopticon as far as possible what is being done in the rural districts in improving school conditions.

(7) Confine the speakers as far as possible to those who have actually done something in bringing about better results in either of the three directions mentioned under Numbers,[2]

(8) In the case of white speakers to get men who favor Negro education, with the view of influencing public sentiment throughout the state in this direction.

The foregoing represents my wish. Whether I can get the Executive Committee to adopt it or not, I am not sure. Please, however, let me have your frank criticism on this suggestion. I should be very glad to have any suggestions from you. Yours very truly,

Booker T. Washington

TLpS Con. 931 BTW Papers DLC.

[1] James Longstreet Sibley (1883–1929), a white teacher in the state normal school at Jacksonville, Ala., became Alabama state supervisor of rural black schools in 1913, through a cooperative arrangement between the state and the General Education Board. From 1925 until his death he was educational adviser for a group of mission boards in Liberia. He prepared a system of textbooks for Liberian schools, and introduced to Liberia the Jeanes system of supervising teachers. He founded the Booker T. Washington Institute in Liberia. (Dabney, *Universal Education in the South,* 2:521–26.)

[2] BTW presumably intended to add numerals from the foregoing list.

From George Ruffin Bridgeforth

[Tuskegee, Ala.] November 29, 1913

Mr. B. T. Washington: I have studied very carefully the use of the automobile, and from what information I have been able to collect, I am sure it has not served the institution as was originally planned. The main thing for which we bought the machine was to transfer students to and from the farm, and to hasten farm deliveries, thus making the distant parts of the farm nearer to the school, so to speak. While I have been waiting for the newness of the thing to wear off and let the people on the campus get acquainted with it, yet it has consumed considerable gasoline running up and down the roads, carrying three and four persons simply riding to be riding.

It is my plan, beginning the 1st of December, to put the truck practically out on the farm for use in transferring students, hauling potatoes, hay, and whatever other things we need to haul, and make it serve the purpose we had in mind; and when it is needed for special purposes on the campus it could be brought in. But at the present time it is almost a dead expense, doing work that was not intended to be done in a great many cases. This is for your information. Yours very truly,

G R Bridgeforth

TLS Con. 634 BTW Papers DLC.

From Andrew Carnegie

New York November 29 1913

My dear Friend: Don't you think Tuskegee has had its share from your humble servant, and that Hampton has prior claim on anything I have to give for Negro education? Just think this over my friend Always very truly yours,

Andrew Carnegie

Take part of the revenue from the six hundred thousand dollars given Tuskegee & extend Library & it will still be all Carnegie Library.

A C

TLS Con. 64 BTW Papers DLC. Last sentence and postscript in Carnegie's hand.

Emmett Jay Scott to Bertha Ruffner

[Tuskegee, Ala.] November 29th, 1913

My dear Madam: I am in receipt of your letter of November 25th written from Hotel McAlpin, Greeley Square, New York City.

It would be interesting to learn of the attitude of the managers of the Hotel McAlpin with reference to respectable colored people who have regard for the "eternal fitness of things"!

It would not be my purpose to ostentatiously parade myself — nor would it be the attitude of any thoughtful black man — about the corridors of a hotel. In fact, as a rule I have my meals always outside of rather than in the hotels where I have stopped.

I am greatly obliged to you for your assurances that you are still pushing the inquiry and that you will advise me again when you have satisfactory data.

Thanking you for your kindly good offices in this matter, I am Yours very truly,

Emmett J Scott

TLpS Con. 485 BTW Papers DLC.

An Article in *World's Work*

November 1913

What I Am Trying to Do

Soon after I settled down for my life's work near the little town of Tuskegee, Ala., I made up my mind to do as an individual that which I am striving to get my race to do throughout the United States. I resolved to make myself, so far as I was able, so useful to the community, the county, and the state that every man, woman, and child, white and black, would respect me and want me to live among them.

I foresaw, before I reached Tuskegee, that I should be classed as an "educated Negro," and I knew that this meant that people would expect me to be a kind of artificial being, living in the community but not a part of it in either my dress, talk, work, or in my general interests. My first duty, therefore, was to convince the people that I did not have "education," but only a head and heart to serve.

This personal illustration will, perhaps, suggest one thing that I am striving to do, that is, to get the Negro race as a whole to make itself so valuable and so necessary to the community in which it lives that it will not merely be tolerated, like a poor relation, but rather welcomed and sought after. To do this I learned years ago from my great teacher of Hampton Institute, Gen. S. C. Armstrong, that it would first be necessary to get out of the Negro's mind the idea that education un- fitted a man for any kind of labor, whether with the hand or head. So from the first I have striven to get the educated Negro to feel that it was just as honorable and dignified for him to use his education in the field, the shop, the kitchen, or the laundry as to use it in teaching school or preaching the gospel.

The most difficult and delicate task that Tuskegee, in common with institutions like Hampton and others, had to perform has been to convince members of my race that in preparing them to use their knowledge of chemistry, mathematics, or any other form of knowledge, to improve the soil, develop the mineral resources, to construct a house or prepare and serve a meal, it was not necessary to limit or circumscribe their mental growth or to assign them to any special or narrow sphere of life. I have constantly urged upon them that we must begin at the bottom instead of at the top; that there will be little permanent gain by "short cut" methods; that we must stick to that which is fundamental and enduring — and we must overcome evil with good.

But in all this I have not sought to confine the ambitions, nor to set limits to the progress of the race. I have never felt that the Negro was bound to behave in any manner different from that of any other race in the same stage of development. I have merely insisted that we should do the first things first; that we should lay the foundation before we sought to erect the superstructure.

At one time, when I was a young boy working in the coal mines of West Virginia, I came out of the mine after a hard day's work feel- ing tired, sick, and discouraged. A neighbor, wishing to cheer me up and make me feel better, offered me a large red stick of candy. That candy looked good to me and I took it eagerly. My mother, who knew my condition and needs, told me that it was not candy that I needed, but a good big dose of vermifuge, which is about the worst tasting and smelling medicine, I firmly believe, that was ever concocted. However, it was in general use in those days for almost every real and imaginary ailment. In fact, vermifuge was about the only medicine on sale at that time in the coal mining districts of West Virginia.

Contrary to my mother's advice I took the candy and put the vermifuge aside. The next day I came out of the coal mine feeling no better, and the next day I was still worse. Finally I decided to follow the advice of mother and take my medicine. So I threw back my head and held my nose while my mother forced the nasty stuff down with a large spoon. The next day, however, I felt fine.

Now, in my experience in working with my race I have found that the Negro meets with two classes of advisers, each of which is equally well-meaning and kindly disposed. One class of advisers hands him the red candy and the other offers the vermifuge. Very often it has been a hard task for me to make certain kinds of colored people see that it is the vermifuge the race needs rather than the red candy. Still, the Negro is learning this lesson, and nothing gives me more genuine satisfaction at the present time than to note that the great masses of my race, in every part of this country, are willing to take the vermifuge in place of the red candy.

I recall another experience that I had while working in the coal mine that has helped me in trying to lead my race in the direction of things that are permanent and lasting rather than the things that are merely showy and temporary. As a boy I long cherished a desire to own a suit of "store" clothes. I worked hard in the mine and finally saved enough to gratify this desire. It was a flashy, showy suit with many colors, called, in those days, I think, a Dolly Varden suit. It cost at wholesale, I suppose, about five dollars. At any rate, I purchased it for ten or twelve. The following Sunday I wore it with great pride to church. On my way home, however, a heavy rain came that drenched both me and the suit. Monday morning I put the suit out in the sun to dry. Presently I noticed that the colors had begun to flow. In fact, they had gotten all mixed up with one another and the whole suit seemed to be in a process of disintegration. My mother had advised me that it would be wiser to spend my money in buying some "homespun" cloth which she promised would make into a good, sensible, and serviceable suit. Eventually she did make me a "homespun" suit which was far from being showy. However, I wore it for several years.

The lesson which I learned in this simple fashion at home was of great value to me when, later on, I went away to school, for though I learned many new and interesting things at Hampton Institute, it did not take me long to discover that, back of all else, the lesson which General Armstrong was trying to teach us was the same that my mother had taught me. He stated it in other words, and gave it a deeper and broader significance, but what I learned at Hampton, through the medium of books and tools and through contact with my teachers, was at bottom what I had learned at home, namely, to distinguish between the real and the sham, to choose the substance rather than the shadow, to seek the permanent good rather than the passing pleasant. And so it is a source of great satisfaction to me to observe throughout the whole country that my race is beginning to prefer "homespun" to "Dolly Varden."

It is not easy to teach a new people, just out of slavery, the kind of lessons I have described. For a number of years the purposes of General Armstrong and of Hampton were misunderstood by a number of the Negro people. The same has been true at Tuskegee. I have had some mighty interesting experiences, both in school and out, in trying to teach the members of my race some of those simple but fundamental lessons, the meaning and significance of which I learned at Hampton Institute.

At one time, while stopping for a day in one of the border states, I visited a colored family whose son had recently graduated and returned home from college. The mother of the young man was naturally very proud of her son and told me with great satisfaction how he had learned to speak Latin, but lamented the fact that there was no one in the neighborhood who was able to talk Latin with him. She had heard that I had some education and felt rather confident that I would be able to converse in the Latin language with him. When I was obliged to confess that I could not, her feathers fell, and I do not believe she ever afterward had the same respect for me. However, I got acquainted with the son, and, as I knew more of the young man, learned to like him. He was an ambitious, high strung young fellow, who had studied books, but he had not studied men. He had learned a great deal about the ancient world, but he knew very little of the world right about him. He had studied about things, through the medium of books, but had not studied things themselves. In a word, he had been infected with the college bacillus and displayed the usual symptoms. However, I had seen cases of this kind before and felt sure that he would in time recover.

This young man was exceedingly sensitive concerning the "rights" of his race, and propounded to me the very popular theory that the only reason the Negro did not have all the rights coming to him was that he did not protest whenever these rights were infringed upon. He determined to put this theory into practice and so wrote a very learned lecture which he delivered on every possible occasion. The subject of his lecture was "Manhood Rights." As he was really a rather brilliant speaker he was able to work up an audience with this lecture to a high pitch of enthusiasm and indignation in regard to the wrongs committed against the Negro race.

For a season this lecture was quite popular and the author was in some demand as a lecturer. During this time he was invariably present at every indignation meeting that was called to pass resolutions condemning some wrong meted out to members of the race. Here, again, his eloquence and burning words could excite an audience to the highest degree of indignation. This was especially true when he quoted some striking passage from Demosthenes or Cicero.

Like most young colored orators he was strong on quotations from people who have been a long time dead. At the same time he forgot the fact that most of the men he quoted never so much as dreamed that the average man had any rights at all, and he totally overlooked the really thrilling fact that never in the history of the world before were there ten million black men who possessed so many rights and enjoyed so many opportunities as the ten millions of Negroes in the United States to-day. I mention this, let me add, not because I want to minimize or make light of the injustices which my race has suffered and still suffers, but because I believe that it is important that we view our present situation in its true light and see things in their proper perspective. In no other way can we gain the courage, the wisdom, and the patience that will help us to go forward, not only steadily and persistently, but cheerfully.

In the course of time it gradually began to dawn upon my young friend and his mother that neither indignation meetings, the passing of resolutions, nor his lecture on "Manhood Rights" were providing him or the family with shelter, food, or clothes. For a while the old mother was quite puzzled to know why it was that neither eloquence nor Latin quotations would provide the family with the common necessities of every-day life. The young man himself grew morose, peevish, and miserable. He could neither eat nor sleep properly, because he was constantly thinking of the wrongs of his race. He was not only unhappy himself but he made everyone he came in contact with unhappy. Nevertheless, for a number of years, he went on in the way that he had started. Finally he seemed to have struck bottom. He found himself face to face with, not a book world, but an actual world. Home, food, clothes, rent were now pressing so hard that something had to be done.

At this point I had an opportunity to renew my acquaintance with him. In fact, he called to see me. He had now become quite softened, mellowed, and even sweet, but I could discern that he was still troubled about the "rights" of his race, and he ventured to suggest a little vaguely once or twice that he would be willing to "die for his race." I noticed, however that he was not quite so emphatic in his desire to "die for his race" as he had been a year or two before, when I heard him pouring out his soul before a small but enthusiastic audience. In one of the first conversations I had with him after the mellowing process had set in, I ventured to suggest to him rather mildly that there were other methods by which he could help the Negro race to secure those rights and opportunities which both he and I were so anxious they should possess and enjoy.

At first he was rather taken aback at the thought that I was just as much interested in the rights of the race as he was, and he was still further surprised when I told him that I felt just as indignant and outraged when my race was insulted and persecuted as he did. This opened the way for a heart to heart talk, which was followed by others, all which resulted in a changed life for my young friend, a change not in the end that he was seeking, but rather in the method of seeking that end.

The story of the young college man that I have just tried to sketch is not different, except in particular circumstances, from that of many other young men that I have known. Several of these young men I have come to know intimately and, as we came to understand one another, they have become faithful friends and supporters of the work I am trying to do. Let me now relate as briefly as possible the sequel of the young college man's story.

After several backsets, my friend persuaded his mother to sell her little property and invest the proceeds in a farm some miles from the city. Here my friend began a new career. He began to study the soil, to observe and study animals, birds, and trees. Soon he became so absorbed in his new life and work that he forgot that he had ever been to college. After a time, however, it began to dawn upon him that his college education could be serviceable in the highest degree by applying all that he had learned to the development of the soil, and so he proceeded to do this. The result was that for the first time in his life he experienced real joy and satisfaction in living. In finding that he could apply his education he had found out what education really is.

He has continued to prosper as a farmer and is looked up to as the leader among his people in his community. He has the respect and confidence of his white neighbors as well as of those of his own race. Although he lives in a county where it is not common for colored people to vote, my friend votes regularly and his white neighbors seem glad to have him do so. He has not only made himself a useful citizen but has become a large taxpayer and keeps a considerable balance in the local bank. He has a wholesome and happy family. Through his influence the local school has become, instead of a mere form, a real power for good in the community. My friend has become so influential in his own community that his word or wish controls the colored church. He virtually decides who shall teach the public school, what wage shall be paid, and how many months the school shall continue in session. He is not only the leader in church and school, but he is president of the farmers' institute, and has control of the county fair. If difficulties arise between white and black people, his advice and counsel are invariably sought. His children, with better preparation than he had, will perhaps attend the college from which he graduated.

I do not pretend that my friend has secured all the rights and privileges that he thinks belong to him. What man of any race or color ever does? Some of the most miserable and ineffective people that I ever met are those who, when viewed from a distance, seem to have all the privileges that the world can confer. No man ever enjoys privileges in the highest sense until he has had the experience of having privileges withheld from him. The people who get the most enjoyment out of wealth are those who have experienced poverty. Sometimes people ask me how I can get so much happiness out of my work and my surroundings when I must be conscious of the suffering and wrongs endured by my race. I usually reply that I am happy because I can compare the present with the past, that I know the depths from which we have come as well as the heights to which we have attained.

During a recent trip through Europe for the purpose of studying the condition of the poorer classes in that part of the world, it was a source of encouragement to me that, wherever I found misery, almost without exception the people told me that things were better than they used to be, that people were looking up, not down. It is not so much what we have as it is the upward look, the knowledge that we are making progress, which makes life worth living.

And so it is with my friend as I observe him to-day. Instead of being miserable he is happy. He is happy because he is engaged in a definite, vital, and constructive work, and through this work, and because of it, he exerts a larger social and political influence than would ever come to him by pursuing the mistaken course on which he first set out. In fact, with all his handicaps, I believe I am safe in saying that he exerts more real influence than nine out of every ten persons of the white or colored people either in the North or in the South.

As the solution of the problems of the individual colored man consists very largely in turning his attention from abstract questions to the concrete problems of daily life — consists, in other words, in interesting and connecting himself with the local, practical, commonplace work and interests of the people among whom he lives — so, too, the solution of the Negro schools consists in connecting the studies in the classroom with the absorbing and inspiring problems of actual life.

Another thing that I am trying to do, therefore, is to get people to see that education in books and in the schoolroom can be articulated into the life and activities of the community surrounding the schoolroom in a way to make the local activities the basis for much of the mental training that is supposed to be furnished by the old traditional and abstract education. In using the local and practical activities as a means of education nothing is sacrificed in culture and discipline, and much is gained in interest and understanding and in earnestness. Children who hate the schoolroom and love the fishing pond, the berry patch, or the peach orchard frequently do so because one is artificial and the other real life. There is often a better opportunity to do this kind of work, I am convinced, with a new race as mine is, whose ancestors for generations have not been educated in the old formal methods, than with a race that has much to unlearn.

I have had some experiences in helping teachers to connect schoolroom work with real life. Often so simple a thing as a button can be used to make this connection. I have often referred to the "button" connection. Early in my experience as a teacher in Alabama I was called into a community to help compromise between parents and teacher. The parents wanted their children educated. The teacher was earnest and a hard worker, but somehow she was at "outs" with the parents and the parents were at "outs" with the teacher. One of the complaints was the far-reaching one that the school did not seem to accomplish any good.

On my first visit to this community I spent some time in the schoolroom listening to the recitations, which were of the usual sort. But, as I have said, the teacher was in earnest, and, in the effort to be of service, she had got hold of a text book on embroidery which she had seen advertised somewhere. The children were first required to read some lessons from this text book on embroidery a number of times; then they were instructed in the art of embroidery in the most up-to-date and approved fashion. There was about as much difference between the garments which the people actually wore in their homes and the embroidery the children were making as there is between the pictures that you sometimes see in a fashion magazine and an actual human being.

In the first place, about half of the children in the school were more than half naked, and so, as I told the teacher, embroidery was not what they needed most. The teacher complained that although she had gone to considerable expense to prepare to teach embroidery the people showed no interest in what she was trying to do for them. Looking the school over, I noted that there were few buttons on the clothes of any of the children, even of those who were fully dressed. That suggested to me a point of attack upon the situation. As gently and tactfully as I could, I suggested to the teacher that she had missed a step in the evolution of the people in this community and that from almost no garments to embroidery was too sudden a transition. I suggested that she defer her lessons in embroidery for eight or ten years until she could work the people up by gradual processes to the point when they needed embroidered garments and the other things that go with them. She readily consented. Then we began on the "button" connection. The teacher asked the children to count the missing buttons on their garments. The number was amazing. Here was an interesting problem in mathematics.

After that the teacher asked every pupil to get permission from his parents to bring to the school the next day all the garments from home that needed buttons sewed on, and what was her surprise to find that we had about all the spare clothing in that community in the school. When the hour for the sewing lesson came it was a mighty interesting hour, one that pupils and teacher looked forward to, because every child felt that the lesson in sewing on buttons was of vital interest to him and to his family. When the clothes were taken home by the pupils at the close of the day, with all the buttons in their places, the parents for the first time in their lives began to understand what education meant; for the first time in the history of the community a vital connection had been made between the schoolroom and the home. As a result new interest was awakened in the subject of education. The parents now felt that the school was a part of themselves. The teacher found that her work in the school room was no longer a burden, that it was no longer a treadmill of dull routine, but a living reality. The reason was that she was touching and teaching life. Instead of dreading the hour for the reopening of school, pupils and teacher were impatient for the hour to come. It was the "button" connection that did it all. The school continued to grow and expand in the directions which the teaching had taken. Garments that needed darning and patching were regularly brought to the school to be mended. Later, vegetables were raised by the pupils in the school garden and the pupils were permitted to carry home specimens of vegetables that they themselves had raised. Some of them were better vegetables than their parents had ever raised. Still later, the pupils were encouraged to have their own plots at home for the growing of vegetables, and after a while one of the teachers was appointed to make weekly visits to the homes of the pupils to inspect the vegetable plots.

On these activities as the basis, real problems in arithmetic were constructed — problems as to the cost of cloth, of buttons, the time required to sew on the buttons or to do the darning and patching; compositions were written describing how parents, teachers, and pupils had worked together in bringing about these results. The children no longer dreaded the sound of the word "composition," because in a natural, simple way they were describing something that they were all genuinely interested in.

Another thing that I have tried to do has been to bring the white people in the Southern States and throughout the country into what seems to me a proper and practical attitude toward the Negro in his efforts to go forward and make progress. I am seeking to do this not only in the interest of my race, but also in the interest of the white race.

There are in the Southern States nine million Negroes. There are three million Negro children of school age. Fifty-three per cent., or more than half, never go to school. Many of these Negro children, particularly in the country districts, are in school only from three to four months in the year. I am trying to get the white people to see that, both from an economic point of view and as a matter of justice and fair play, these conditions must be changed. I am trying to get the white people to see that sending ignorant Negroes to jails and penitentiaries, putting them in the chain gang, hanging and lynching them does not civilize, but on the contrary, though it brutalizes the Negro, it at the same time blunts and dulls the conscience of the white man.

I want the white people to see that it is unfair to expect a black man who goes to school only three months in the year to produce as much on the farm as a white man who has been in school eight or nine months in the year; that it is unjust to let the Negro remain ignorant, with nothing between him and the temptation to fill his body with whiskey and cocaine, and then expect him, in his ignorance, to be able to know the law and be able to exercise that degree of self-control which shall enable him to keep it.

Still another thing that I am trying to get the people of the whole country to realize is that the education of the Negro should be considered not so much as a matter of charity, but as a matter of business, that, like any other business, should be thoroughly studied, organized, and systematized. The money that has already been spent by states, institutions, and individuals would have done vastly more good if there had been, years ago, more thorough organization and coöperation between the different isolated and detached members of the Negro school system in the Southern States.

I am trying to get the white people to realize that since no color line is drawn in the punishment for crime, no color line should be drawn in the preparation for life, in the kind of education, in other words, that makes for useful, clean living. I am trying to get the white people to see that in hundreds of counties in the South it is costing more to punish colored people for crime than it would cost to educate them. I am trying to get all to see that ignorance, poverty, and weakness invite and encourage the stronger race to act unjustly toward the weak, and that so long as this condition remains the young white men of the South will have a fearful handicap in the battle of life.

World's Work, 27 (Nov. 1913), 101–7.

A Circular Announcing *The Negro Farmer*

[Tuskegee, Ala., ca. November 1913]

THE NEGRO FARMER

Something New: Something Needed

A PAPER THAT HELPS PEOPLE TO BECOME
BETTER FARMERS IS AN AID TO THE CHURCH,
THE SCHOOL AND TO THE SECULAR AND RELIG-
IOUS PAPERS

It has been decided to publish at Tuskegee Institute Post Office, Every-Other-Week for the present, a national farm paper to be known as THE NEGRO FARMER. It will be published in the interest of Negro landowners, tenant farmers and of those who employ Negro labor. There is no other strictly farm newspaper in the world devoted to the interest of Negro farmers.

Many of the white farm newspapers enjoy huge circulations and there is no reason why a farm paper in the interest of Negroes should not prove equally successful. In fact, occupying an exclusive field it should enjoy a success far beyond that of the usual farm publication.

It is proposed to circulate this paper among the 2,000,000 black farmers of the United States. The paper will be eight pages, of about the size of "The Country Gentleman."

Dr. Booker T. Washington States:

The Tuskegee Institute has no financial interest or control over this new publication, but some of the active officers of the institution are interested in its success and believe that it will not only accomplish great good but will be a paying investment. The paper is backed by a strong organization and funds have been provided in advance to assure its publication. Those in active control of The Negro Farmer have my entire confidence and good will.

— Booker T. Washington

The success of this project is assured because of the solid and sensible lines upon which it is being laid out.

All the capital stock has been subscribed for.

The subscription price is $1.00 a year and Subscriptions and Advertisements are invited. Clubbing rates with important Negro newspapers will be arranged for on a satisfactory basis. We are now ready to receive Subscriptions and Advertisements.

The first issue of the paper will appear February first, 1914.

Address all communications to:

THE NEGRO FARMER
Tuskegee Institute, Ala.

PD Con. 483 BTW Papers DLC. Enclosed in Thomas J. Edwards to BTW, Nov. 25, 1913.

From John Davison Rockefeller, Jr.

New York December 1, 1913

My dear Mr. Washington: Your letter of November 13th was duly received. I am gratified to know that steps are being taken to put the physical equipment of Tuskegee on a better and more economical basis. It would be contrary to our custom, however, for either my father or me to take up a matter of this kind personally, for since the organization of the General Education Board we have referred all applications to the Board. May I suggest, therefore, that you take the matter up direct with Dr. Buttrick? Very cordially,

John D. Rockefeller Jr.

TLS   Con. 931   BTW Papers   DLC.

Bertha Ruffner to Emmett Jay Scott

New York   December 1st 1913

Dear Sir: Referring to your favor of recent date beg to say that we regret that we have been unable to secure the name of any hotel in this city, to which we can refer you. We have written and telephoned several, but their restrictions are such that they are unable to accommodate you. It is impossible for us to be of service to you in this connection. Yours sincerely,

Bertha Ruffner

TLSr   Con. 485   BTW Papers   DLC.

Viola Spencer[1] to Susan Helen Porter

Tuskegee Inst Ala. Dec 1, –13

Miss S. H. Porter. I recd a letter from my mother saturday stating that I may be Excused from Tuskegee, and go to Bishop College.

I dont like Tuskegee Inst well enough to stay here. The first reason is, the food dosnt agree with me, it gives me the heart burn.

Second, walking so much dosent agree with my feet, they are sore with corn's.

Third, it works you so hard to leave breakfast at six thirty, and clean up your room and get to work at seven o'clock.

When you get to work you are so tired you can hardly breath.[2]

I would like to leave rite away if possiable for Bishop College, which is in Marshall Texas.

My mother has written Mr. Palmer, a letter about the matter. Oblige you

Viola Spencer

ALS Con. 640 BTW Papers DLC.

[1] Viola Spencer of Temple, Tex., attended "part of the term" 1913–14 in the A preparatory class, according to the Tuskegee Institute catalog.

[2] S. Helen Porter forwarded the letter to BTW, explaining that Viola Spencer had entered the school the previous month. "The expressions in the letter," Porter wrote, "are very similar to statements made by other girls who leave the Institution and will not be persuaded to remain here." (Dec. 1, 1913, Con. 640, **BTW Papers,** DLC.) A few days later BTW ordered that Viola Spencer receive special food "in the dining room or at the hospital" until she was better. (BTW to John A. Kenney, Dec. 5, 1913, Con. 640, BTW Papers, DLC.)

To Henry C. Watson[1]

[Tuskegee, Ala.] December 2, 1913

Mr. Henry Watson: Several of the gentlemen teachers are going against the policy of the school and embarrassing it by reason of smoking on the public roads and other public places as well as in their rooms. This is to be stopped in the future on the part of persons connected with the school.

A club room has been provided on the grounds for the use of gentlemen who wish to smoke.

Booker T. Washington

TLpS Con. 638 BTW Papers DLC. The same letter was sent to eight other teachers and staff members on the same date.

[1] Henry C. Watson was in charge of student accounts in the chief accountant's office at Tuskegee Institute in 1913. He began working for the school in 1909.

To George Ruffin Bridgeforth

[Tuskegee, Ala.] December 3, 1913

Mr. Bridgeforth: I have received yours of November 29th regarding the truck, and think your policy of using the truck is a wise one. I wish you would let me know to what extent it would be a paying proposition for us to get a smaller truck or a similar one for use on the school grounds.

Booker T. Washington

TLpS Con. 634 BTW Papers DLC.

To D. Peter French[1]

[Tuskegee, Ala.] December 4, 1913

My dear Sir: I have received your letter of the 30th of November and thank you very much for writing me. I am very glad to hear that my son is doing well. As you suggest, the greatest difficulty will be not yielding to the temptation to spend too much time in social matters.

I sent him a check yesterday to be handed to Mrs. French to cover the matter of his room. He seems very happy in your home and we are very glad he is there. Yours very truly,

Booker T. Washington

TLpS Con. 934 BTW Papers DLC.

[1] D. Peter French of 3366 Calumet Avenue, Chicago, was listed in the Chicago city directories as a porter. BTW, Jr., boarded with the Frenches while attending the Northwestern University School of Pharmacy.

From Paul Moritz Warburg

New York, December 4th, 1913

My dear Dr. Washington: You know that I have taken a warm interest in the development of Liberia. My friends in Hamburg ask me whether it would not be possible to encourage immigration of colored men from the United States to Liberia. They believe that if about five-hundred men a year would come to that country, it would be a great help. I know, of course, that Mr. Scott has given this matter very careful consideration, and as I understood, the results of his investigations in this respect were rather of a negative nature. I wonder, however, whether you have given up entirely the idea of encouraging some groups of efficient people to go down there. Very truly yours,

Paul M Warburg

TLS Con. 70 BTW Papers DLC.

From Seth Low

New York December 4th, 1913

Dear Doctor Washington: I am writing to suggest that you send out, as early as practicable, the preliminary announcement of the February visit of the Trustees. Washington's Birthday next year falls on Sunday; so that Monday, the 23rd. will be the day upon which it is observed. Under these circumstances I think the party had better leave New York on Saturday morning, February 21st. For the purposes of the preliminary notice to our friends it will suffice, I think, if you say that the car will leave on or about February 21st. and reach New York, on return, on or about February 27th, and that the details will be furnished later to all who think they might like to make the trip.

In this connection I want to say that Mr. Trumbull took luncheon with us the other day, and Mrs. Low and he both agreed that this annual visit has become so strenuous as to threaten its destruction. In particular, Mr. Trumbull, speaking for himself and I think for many other Trustees, regrets to visit the Institute year after year and to see so little of it. In other words, we hope that next year there may be fewer gatherings of the students, and much less speaking. A year ago both Mrs. Low and myself were so exhausted by the demands made upon us at Tuskegee, and from the necessity of talking during our waking hours all the way from New York to Tuskegee and back, that it is quite plain to me that it will be impossible for us to continue to make this trip much longer, unless the fatigue of it can be in some way lessened. I do not see how the fatigue incident to the journey can be abated, if a party of visitors is to be formed every year; and this is so valuable for the Institute that it would be a pity to abandon it. On the other hand, while we are at the Institute I am sure you can do very much to lessen the demands upon the time and strength of the visitors.

One thing more — the numbers included in the two parties last year were so large that I think it imposed a very great strain upon the Institute itself, both upon the teachers and upon the students. The size of the party also added greatly to the fatigue of every member. I am wondering whether it is not possible, in some way, to limit the number of those to be included in any one visit. I speak of this somewhat doubtfully; but I would like to have your ideas on every aspect of the question. Very truly, yours,

Seth Low

TLS   Con. 65   BTW Papers   DLC.

To Travers Buxton

[Tuskegee, Ala.] December 5th, 1913

My dear Mr. Buxton: I am very glad to see in a cable published in the New York Times this week that your association is proposing to organize a movement in this country to deal with the matter of slavery in South America and elsewhere. I very much hope that you will do this. I trust that the cable is correct.

There is much of slavery, and that which is equally as bad, peonage, existing in South America, and I am sorry to say, in some of our Southern States. I will state, however, that we are gradually getting rid of peonage in this country.

If I can be of the slightest service at any time in aiding your efforts in this country, please do not hesitate to call upon me.[1] Yours very truly,

Booker T. Washington

TLpS   Con. 924   BTW Papers   DLC.

[1] Buxton replied that the Anti-Slavery and Aborigines Protection Society would count on his help when it organized in the New World. (Dec. 19, 1913, Con. 924, BTW Papers, DLC.)

To William Alden Smith[1]

[Tuskegee, Ala.] December 12, 1913

Dear Senator Smith: I know that several bills, bearing upon agricultural education are soon to come before Congress, and I want to venture the suggestion: that in all of these bills, unless some definite provision is made for the colored people, sharing in the money in states where there is a separate public school system, the colored people are likely to get very little.

Enclosed I send you copy of a resolution on that subject which was passed recently at a meeting of Southern white educators held in Nashville. You can easily see if these Southern white people, and they are the more advanced type, have such a feeling, they must have great justification for it. Your very truly,

Booker T. Washington

TLpS Con. 931 BTW Papers DLC.

[1] William Alden Smith (1859–1932) was a Republican representative from Michigan from 1895 to 1907, and U.S. Senator from 1907 to 1919.

To Paul Moritz Warburg

[Tuskegee, Ala.] December 13, 1913

Dear Mr. Warburg: I am glad you wrote me in reference to Liberia.

We too, are deeply interested in anything that concerns Liberia, but it is a very trying and difficult problem to decide what to do in reference to that country. Mr. Scott, I think, knows more about it than anybody I have seen and he will send you a memorandum next week, bearing upon the matter of emigration of colored men from the United States to Liberia.[1]

I often wish that we knew just what to do and how to do it. A good friend sometime ago placed a sum of money at my disposal for the starting of a small industrial school in Liberia, but I confess I have not been brave enough to begin the expenditure of it for the reason that I am not sure as to the right course to pursue. Yours very truly,

Booker T. Washington

TLpS Con. 70 BTW Papers DLC.

¹ Scott's memorandum stated that it was the unanimous opinion of the American commission to Liberia "that the time is not ripe for Negro-Americans to emigrate to Liberia in larger numbers except under conditions more favorable than were in sight when we visited that country in 1909." Scott promoted the idea of sending a group of farm demonstration agents to Liberia to teach the Natives how to cultivate the soil. "The native," Scott wrote, "in my opinion is the hope of Liberia, and I hope that such selected leaders as I have indicated may be secured to help train these native Liberians." (Memorandum for Mr. Warburg, Dec. 17, 1913, Con. 65, BTW Papers, DLC.)

To the Editor of the Montgomery *Advertiser*

Tuskegee Institute, Alabama, December 15, 1913

Editor The Advertiser: In many parts of the country where our race lives in large numbers, a cloud of gloom is spread over the Christmas holiday season because of the large number of people who are murdered or wounded. Many of our people seem to feel that Christmas is for the purpose of drinking whiskey, carrying pistols or shooting or murdering somebody. This kind of thing is not confined to the negro race, but just now I am trying especially to advise my race.

A careful study and observation convinces me that these shootings and murders are brought about by two causes. The first cause is drinking. Many of our people who, during the other months of the year seldom touch whiskey, feel at liberty, in fact feel the necessity of drinking and making fools of themselves during the Christmas holidays.

These murders are brought about in the second place by the senseless and useless habit of carrying pistols on one's body for the mistaken purpose of self-defense or protection. I have not carried a pistol in all my life, and do not keep one in the house, for I found that the carrying of a pistol or other weapon gets one into trouble in nine cases where it keeps one out of trouble in one case.

It used to be that the Fourth of July was a noisy, senseless occasion, where hundreds of people were murdered through the shooting off of fire crackers and firearms; a reform has been brought about so that the Fourth of July is now a safe, sane season. Why cannot we as a race, do our part in bringing about some kind of a reform with reference to the Christmas season? Why cannot we change the policy of whiskey drinking and carrying firearms so that Christmas will not bring sorrow, but only joy and gladness?

Think of it, instead of Christmas being a day of thanksgiving, joy and gladness, it is too often turned into a day of misery and woe, even for a lifetime. Christmas leaves behind it penniless widows with children to support. It leaves disappointed, broken hearted parents, whose children, heated with liquor, have committed some shameful or criminal act. Hundreds of young men who would otherwise lead decent, upright lives, have begun their careers as jail birds on Christmas day, and almost equally as many a young woman, due to the license of the season has started on a course of shame and disgrace.

My special purpose in writing this letter is to make a definite, strong and personal appeal to every minister, to every Sunday School teacher, to every public school teacher and every parent to use his influence to have drinking of whiskey and the carrying of firearms stopped during the Christmas season. If something could be said by the ministers and teachers, and other leaders in every church in the South on this subject, on Sunday, December 21st, I am sure it would accomplish great good. Perhaps we might designate the day as "Anti-Whiskey and Anti-Pistol Day." I very much wish that all the ministers and teachers in the day and public schools might set aside this special Sunday, or a special day where attention through the medium of sermons or lectures might be called to this important matter. Our young people need to be spoken to plainly about the senseless and useless habit of drinking whiskey and carrying pistols. I realize fully that the type who are most guilty of these acts do not attend church, Sunday or day school, and know of the difficulties in this direction, but nevertheless, if each one who reads this communication will begin now in some way to do his part to bring about a reform, I am sure that the coming Christmas season will show an absence of whiskey drinking and pistol carrying that will be most gratifying and encouraging.

Booker T. Washington

Montgomery *Advertiser,* Dec. 17, 1913, 4.

From P. C. Jackson

Lometa, Texas [ca. Dec. 15, 1913][1]

Personal

Respt Sir, I was raised in Tuskegee Ala and served in C. S. Army with all who went to the War from old Macon Co. I have lots of kin folks in Tuskegee now — also in the Co around Mrs. Campbell is my sister. Judge Cobb (deceased[)] was my uncle. The Torrances and others are kin to me. I have been in Texas over 40 years married here and have grand children near grown. I am a great admirer of you Prof look upon you as one of the greatest men on Earth. I am told by my people in Ala and other States that my Father, W. S. ("Scott") Jackson, Wilbur Foster and other old pioneers of Ala and comrades of mine in army, that the friendship between you and them was like that of Damon & Pythius — all of which God knows — makes me love you. Did you know if I were to go back to dear old Ala I would be as glad to see any of the old negroes of our family as I would any of my kin folks — they are dear to my heart yet. I have 2 negro neighbors. They are well fixed farmers and ranchmen — we are good friends. As a token of my friendship for them I want to present them this Xmas with a book that will inspire and impell them to keep on in the road of Justice right and usefulness like yourself; hence I want two (2) histories of life of Booker Washington.

Will you be so kind as to send them to me C. O. D. I read your life years ago and it done me good. I believe you should rewrite the book — tell more — tell about you W. S. Jackson Wilbur Foster & others how you worked and pulled together &c.

With best wishes for you, your people and work I am   Very Respty

P. C. Jackson

ALS Con. 935 BTW Papers DLC. Written on stationery of the Jackson House, P. C. Jackson, proprietor. The letterhead described the fifteen-bedroom house as "Brand New and First-Class," and boasted: "Lometa ships more live stock, wool, cotton and pecans than any place in Texas to its size. It is in the very center of the State, and is the best trading point in Texas."

1 While no date appeared on the original letter, it was obviously written before Christmas. See BTW to P. C. Jackson, Dec. 29, 1913, below.

To Mary A. Davidson Elliott

[Tuskegee, Ala.] December 16, 1913

My dear Mrs. Elliott: Mrs. Washington has let me read your letter of December 5th, and you do not know how very glad we are to hear from you again. It seems a long time since we have had a line from you. I am glad to hear that you have gotten on your feet after the flood but I am sorry to learn that Mr. Elliott is not well and Hiram has lost his wife. I shall hope to see you, however, sometime in the near future. Tell Hiram I hope he will write me a line.

By this mail I am sending you some pictures taken sometime ago of Booker and Davidson. Mrs. Washington I think had already told you that Booker is studying pharmacy at a college in Chicago and Davidson is taking a course in a business college in New York; they are both fine young men. Booker says he is going to have the largest drug store of any colored man in the South. Portia, as you know, is married and is living in Dallas, Texas. She has three bright children.

I am going to see that "The Student," the paper published here at the school is sent you twice a month hereafter.

By this mail, I am sending you one of my latest books, "My Larger Education" which I hope you can find time to read. I am also sending one of my books for Hiram which I wish you would see that he gets.

Please remember us to all. Yours very truly,

Booker T. Washington

P.S. I think you already know that Booker graduated.

TLpS   Con. 476   BTW Papers   DLC.

To John Andrew Kenney

[Tuskegee, Ala.] December 17, 1913

Dr. Kenney: Without making any noise about it, I wish you would reduce the pay of the nurses and other employees in the hospital, beginning January 1st by 15 per cent on an average. You will, of course, use your own judgment as to just how to treat individuals, but I wish the general reduction to average 15 per cent, covering the total number employed, aside from instruction.

Now, this does not mean that you will have to reduce the pay of every individual. There may be individuals who, for certain reasons, ought not to be considered under this order.

Use your own judgment in these matters, but let the average be 15 per cent.

Booker T. Washington

TLpS   Con. 637   BTW Papers   DLC.

To John Robert E. Lee

[Tuskegee, Ala.] December 17, 1913

Mr. Lee: I am of the opinion that the force of our workers in the Library is too large. I wish you would let me have a recommendation on that matter. I feel sure we can have the work done in the Library with a smaller force, and thus reduce expenses. I think there are too many students working at the Library, and I feel that three instructors are as many as we ought to employ there.

Booker T. Washington

TLpS   Con. 632   BTW Papers   DLC.

To John Henry Washington

[Tuskegee, Ala.] December 17, 1913

Mr. J. H. Washington, General Superintendent of Industries: Without making any noise about it, I wish you would have the pay of the students in the Day School reduced by 10 per cent, beginning January 1st. This only applies to boys.

Booker T. Washington

TLpS   Con. 634   BTW Papers   DLC.

To William Colfax Graves

[Tuskegee, Ala.] December 18, 1913

Dear Mr. Graves: I have gone through Mr. Ferris' two volumes,[1] and while Mr. Ferris does not agree with my views that would not prevent in any way my commending the two volumes if I felt that they had anything of real helpful value in them to the South or to our race. I cannot see that they have any value to warrant the expense of publication.

Mr. Ferris knows little or nothing about real conditions in the South, and what he does say is such a jumble of ancient and modern history that it is hard to understand just what he is driving at. Besides, I think it a pretty safe rule in passing on a case of this kind to find out what reputable publishers think of the manuscript. As you know the large publishing concerns are constantly on the lookout for valuable manuscripts; they not only seek them but are willing to pay for them. Mr. Ferris has tried practically all the publishers and they have refused his manuscript. The book is now being printed by a private printing firm. I think this is an indication of what publishers who have had wide experience in such matters think of the value of his work.

By this mail I return the books. Yours very truly,

Booker T. Washington

TLpS   Con. 66   BTW Papers   DLC.

[1] William Henry Ferris, *The African Abroad, or, His Evolution in Western Civilization, Tracing His Development Under Caucasian Milieu*, 2 vols. New Haven, Conn.: The Tuttle, Morehouse and Taylor Press, 1913.

To Robert Robinson Taylor

[Tuskegee, Ala.] December 18, 1913

Mr. Taylor: I do not like the idea of the school being put to so much expense to put steam into my house alone, and I wish you would consider again the matter of putting steam into the houses of Mr. Logan and Mr. Scott, and your house. In view of the saving which we are likely to make on the original estimate, I am wondering if it would not be possible and practical to put steam into these houses now. Please let me hear from you.

Booker T. Washington

TLpS Con. 637 BTW Papers DLC.

From John Robert E. Lee

[Tuskegee, Ala.] December 18, 1913

Mr. Washington: I have gone over the matter of the Library very carefully alone, and then with Mr. Wood. I am convinced that it will be impossible for us to successfully carry on the work there in an efficient manner, such as is being done now with three teachers. Every teacher there has an absolutely definite amount of work and plenty of it.

We have worked out a schedule, however, whereby we are able to drop one of the day school girls, Mattie Robinson[1] who works every other day, and a boy Shadrack Stevens[2] who has been doing some special help. With these two persons taken out there will be a reduction of somewhere nearly $10 a month.

With reference to reducing the teaching force I know you can easily see that Mr. Wood is away from the Library a good deal of his time by your direction. We had caustic criticism at the close of school a little more than a year ago because of the poor work that is being done. This was due to the fact that Mr. Wood was away and one teacher was out for a time.

I should be very glad to reduce the teaching force there if the work could be done as I know you want it done, with such a reduction. Yours very truly,

J. R. E. Lee

TLS Con. 632 BTW Papers DLC.

[1] Possibly Mamie Robinson, of Guerryton, Ala., a student in the C preparatory class in 1913–14.

[2] Shadrack Smith Stephens, of Girard, Ala., listed as a senior in the 1913–14 Tuskegee Institute catalog.

To Robert Sengstacke Abbott[1]

[Tuskegee, Ala.] December 19, 1913

Personal and Confidential

Dear Mr. Abbott: In addition to what I said to you yesterday, I want to make the following suggestion:

We are pursuing the policy for the first time so far as we know in the history of any colored institution to have our strongest successful business men come before our students as lecturers. This is the policy being pursued by the great universities of the country like the University of Wisconsin, Harvard and others. Carrying out this policy, we have here now at our special invitation Mr. W. A. Wallace,[2] who, as you know, is the successful baker of Chicago. Mr. Wallace is delivering a series of talks to the high class students on his experiences as a baker.

As soon as Mr. Wallace returns to Chicago, I want to ask that you have one of your representatives see him and get a good live interview, describing his impressions and experiences at Tuskegee, and if you can put this interview in good shape and send us 200 copies. We shall be glad to pay for them and distribute them in a way that will be of service to your paper; thus you will be helped and we will be helped. We have wasted too much time as a race in spending our time and energy on the non-essentials rather than the essentials of life.

I am glad to see that your paper is taking this sensible view. Another thing we must learn sooner or later, and that is, that no matter how much a certain type of white people may promise to do for us in the way of securing "rights" in the last analysis, we have got to help ourselves.

Mr. Wallace will leave here on Sunday evening, stop in Louisville and reach Chicago Wednesday evening. Yours very truly,

Booker T. Washington

TLpS   Con. 932   BTW Papers   DLC.

[1] Robert Sengstacke Abbott (1870–1940), a Hampton graduate, was the founder and editor of the Chicago *Defender,* the most militant black newspaper in Chicago. He avoided identification with either the Washington or the Du Bois faction.

[2] William A. Wallace in the 1920s gave up a thriving business as a baker to devote full time to organizing for Marcus Garvey's Universal Negro Improvement Association.

An Extract from a Report by
John Andrew Kenney, John Henry Washington,
and Julius B. Ramsey

[Tuskegee, Ala.] December 19, 1913

Mr. Washington: Memoranda of proposed changes at the hospital as reported by the Committee:

(d)

That from now until the first of June the present prices of the hospital treatments be reduced by ⅓ to outsiders and teachers.

(e)

That for the remainder of the term the teachers who are run-down and tired at the end of the week be encouraged to go to the hospital to rest from Saturday evening to the time to go to their duties on Monday morning, and that the charges for same be reduced to 50¢ per day which includes everything except special treatments. The teachers not being charged for board in the Boarding Department during such time as they are in the hospital. This same rate to hold good for the families connected with the school, under similar conditions.

(k)

We suggest that at any time nurses can be spared from the hospital that they be sent out into the community among outsiders and families to do social work as we believe that this will not only aid in the matter of their health, but will also bring the people in closer touch with the usefulness of the hospital, and that people of means will probably be more willing to give more for this sort of work.

And we further recommend that in order to get the people of our community to take greater advantage of our electric and water system of treatments of which so many of them stand in need, we reduce the present charges for same by ½, which will be 50 cents for one and 25 cents for the other.

John A. Kenney, Medical Director

J. H. Washington

J. B. Ramsey

TLSr Copy   Con. 636   BTW Papers   DLC.

From William Henry Tayloe[1]

Uniontown, Ala. Decr 20, 1913

Dear Doctor. The above institution does business with a great number of the best negroes in this section and is therefore financially interested in their welfare. They constitute the only labor in this part of the County. Now the boll weevil is coming and the country is not prepared for their advent. This bank wishes to do what it can to aid the coming situation. On thing that occurs to the directors is that you might aid in the matter and I write to enquire what it would cost per month to get one of your best men to work with the negroes here in the spring and inspire them with the desire to make food stuffs and do what may be necessary in the premises. Mr. Taylor[2] the president of this bank proposes to work with the white people; he wants some one to assist him with the negroes and we think a negro is the best one to do the work.

I shall be glad to hear from you on the matter. Very truly,

W H Tayloe

TLS Con. 933 BTW Papers DLC. Written on stationery of the Canebreak Loan & Trust Co., W. H. Tayloe, vice-president.

[1] William Henry Tayloe (1852–ca. 1920), an Alabama lawyer and banker, was formerly a member of the Alabama Senate (1886–90), and was a delegate to the Alabama constitutional convention in 1901.

[2] The letterhead of the Canebrake Loan and Trust Co. listed "Val Taylor" as president.

To John Andrew Kenney

[Tuskegee, Ala.] Dec. 23, 1913

Dr. Kenney: It seems to me that there should be a rule existing in the hospital to the effect that no gentleman teacher is to go into the room of a lady teacher to visit her when she is sick except under very exceptional circumstances and of course the reverse of this ought to be true in reference to men teachers.

B. T. W.

TLpI Con. 637 BTW Papers DLC.

From William Colfax Graves

Chicago   December 23, 1913

Dear Dr. Washington: Thank you very much for the confidential letter, re: Ferris books. Mr. Rosenwald will not undertake to help in the publication of volume 3. The volumes which you sent back were duly received.

With compliments of the holiday season, I am always, Very sincerely yours,

William C. Graves

TLS   Con. 66   BTW Papers   DLC.

From Walter Hines Page

American Embassy, London   23d, Dec. 1913

Dear Mr. Washington: Judge McCants Stewart (you know him, of course) of the Supreme Court of Liberia was here a little while ago. He has a plan to try to induce Mr. Carnegie to give a library to Monrovia — after he secures the consent of the city or of the Government to maintain it. He wish[e]d me to ask if you'd take enough interest in this to speak to Mr. Carnegie when some favorable chance presents itself.

One of the old Peace Societies of London — an anti-slavery & anti-war Quaker group of old standing and most reputable record — have approached me with the question wh they would do you a good turn to invite you to come here next year. I said "Yes, if you'll open a way definitely to Mr. Washington to enable him to carry home enough money for his work to make it worth his while."! They have rich friends. I didn't see why I shdn't remind them of the real use they can be in the world. The Secretary spoke hopefully about it & said that he wd confer with his fellows. It occurred to me that possibly it might be a good plan — if you think well of it & shd come — to bring a quartette.[†] It's been a long time, I hear, since the old melodies were heard here; &, if you shd come in the fashionable "season," perhaps the duchesses & other rich ladies wd open their drawing-rooms and their check-books. I do not know; but this is worth thinking about.

I hope that all goes well with you & your work. With my very heartiest good wishes for the New Year, Sincerely Yours,

Walter H. Page

† Too many t's?

ALS Con. 69 BTW Papers DLC.

From George Walter Stevens

On line — December 23, 1913[1]

Dear Sir, I have read with interest your pamphlet entitled "Is the Negro Having a Fair Chance." One hundred copies of this article have been received and distributed among the officials and in the employes' reading rooms.

As you are well aware, both in Virginia and Kentucky, the railway lines furnish the same accommodations for colored passengers as are furnished white passengers and it is a requirement that these accommodations shall be equal in every way to those furnished the white race. If it comes to your knowledge that equal service is not being given, I shall be glad to hear from you personally. In the other three states through which this Company operates, West Virginia, Ohio and Indiana, segregation laws do not exist and the negro is accommodated in the same cars as the white race.

As to employment by the railway companies, the negro is accorded the same treatment as the white man, and in some particular classes of employment is preferred to the white man.

I am deeply interested in the work that you are doing and am quite convinced that it is along the right lines. If, in any way, I can aid you, do not hesitate to call upon me. Yours truly,

Geo. W. Stevens

TLS Con. 519 BTW Papers DLC.

[1] Written on stationery of the Chesapeake and Ohio Railway Co., of which Stevens was president. His office was in Richmond, Va., but he was on a train when this letter was drafted.

To Ernest Ten Eyck Attwell

[Tuskegee, Ala.] Dec. 26, 1913

Mr. Attwell: I gave an order yesterday to the effect that I wished a small chicken from the Commissary, sent over to Mr. George Cunningham's[1] house. I take for granted that this was done. As you know, he was in the employ of the school for a long while. He is now completely disabled. Two or three times a week during the month of January, I want you to see that he gets either a small chicken or some beef or some other kind of meat out of which soup can be made as he is unable to take any nourishment except soup. Mr. Logan will know just how this can be charged.

B.T.W.

TLpI Con. 635 BTW Papers DLC.

[1] The name does not appear in the Tuskegee Institute catalogs.

From David Page Morehouse[1]

Oswego, N.Y., Dec. 26, 1913

Dear Sir: I write to inform you that Col. Wardwell G. Robinson, who died in this city Dec. 8, 1913, by his will left to Tuskegee Normal & Industrial Institute the sum of five thousand dollars ($5000). Mr. John T. Mott, President of the First National Bank of this City and myself are the executors. I send you under separate cover a copy of the will. As there are many heirs to cite it will be some weeks before the will can be admitted to probate, and probably some months more will elapse before the payment of the legacies can be made. The estate is in high class securities, and much larger than required to pay the bequeaths of specific amounts.

I think you will be interested in the history of this legacy. Some years ago you published your autobiography in the Outlook. The Hon. Alanson S. Page[2] of this City read it there and was so impressed by it that when the history came out in book form, he purchased twenty-five copies for distribution among his friends, giving one to me. I loaned mine to Col. Robinson who in turn read the autobiography with much interest. It happened that he was then engaged in preparing his will, and a little later he told me he had given your institute five thousand dollars. It is just possible however that you will have to share to some little extent the credit for the inspiration of this good deed with some colored Cavalry men who were under command of Col. Robinson at Harrisons Landing, Va., where his regiment, the 184th N.Y. Infantry was stationed in 1864–65. He always spoke very highly of the soldierly qualities of those Cavalrymen.

When the time for distribution shall arrive, Mr. Mott and I will take great pleasure in forwarding this legacy to Tuskegee. Yours very truly,

D. P. Morehouse

TLSr Copy   Con. 473   BTW Papers   DLC.

¹ David Page Morehouse (d. 1958) was special surrogate judge of Oswego County, N.Y. (1911–28). He later served on the New York Supreme Court, beginning in 1935.

² Alanson S. Page (d. 1905), former mayor of Oswego, N.Y., for four terms beginning in 1869, was an Oswego window-shade manufacturer and lumber dealer.

Emmett Jay Scott to Frederick Randolph Moore

[Tuskegee, Ala.] December 26th, 1913

Dear Frederick: You wrote me about four months ago that you meant to make me an offer on my New York Age stock; Mr. Wilford H. Smith wrote me to the same effect. The thing I am trying to get settled in my mind is how I stand with reference to this stock. *I hold certificates calling for 3,500 shares of this stock,* but according *to the affidavit, published in your paper,* the *ownership seems to be vested in someone else.* Now, what I would like to get settled is, how were the bona fide, *legal stockholders* disposed of in this transaction. I set too much value upon this stock to let it lapse without some kind of an understanding about the matter, and I certainly would like to settle it in an open, frank, square manner without misunderstanding or difficulty of any character.

I am sure that you appreciate the spirit in which I write; it is one of entire frankness and at the same time an earnest desire to find out just where I stand. Yours very truly,

Emmett J. Scott

TLpS Con. 459 BTW Papers DLC.

To Isaac Fisher

[Tuskegee, Ala.] December 27th, 1913

All arrangements for starting paper[1] completed. You were elected editor last night. Salary to begin January first; should get here as soon as possible.

Booker T. Washington

TWSr Con. 483 BTW Papers DLC.

¹ *The Negro Farmer.*

To P. C. Jackson

[Tuskegee, Ala.] December Twenty-ninth 1913

My dear Sir: In some way, your kind letter of recent date was delayed in reaching me. I think the delay came about by reason of the fact that the mail has been three to four days late during the last few weeks.

You do not know how very much I appreciate your letter, especially because you were raised in Tuskegee and Tuskegee I love better than any spot on earth. I know all the people to whom your letter refers and those of them now living are among my best friends. I do hope that at some time you will return to Tuskegee and see the work we are now doing. We are trying many changes for the better, in Tuskegee and Macon County.

As you request, I am sending you for your colored neighbors, two of my books by express and the young man who has charge of selling them, will send you a bill. Will you be kind enough to tell your two colored farmers that I think they are very fortunate in having so good a man as yourself for their friend. The fact that you were raised in Tuskegee in Macon County, shows within itself that you have a broad and liberal spirit and that you are generally interested in colored people. I have met white people in all parts of the world, but I have never met any who are more broad, more liberally disposed than those in Macon County and I am sure you have carried to Texas this same spirit and disposition. I hope that the two books which I am sending will inspire your colored friends to a higher and more useful life.

With sincere holiday greetings, I am, Very truly yours,

Booker T. Washington

TLpS   Con. 935   BTW Papers   DLC.

From Robert Elijah Jones

New Orleans   December 29th, 1913

My Dear Doctor: Your interest in the Race in all parts of the country, and your constant exertion in our behalf leads me to call your attention to the separate street car situation here in the city of New Orleans, with the hope that you may be able to do something to bring us relief.

The separate street car as operated in New Orleans is the most abominable arrangement in the whole country. In many of the cities where the separate car law is in force, the White people fill the car from the front to the back, and the Colored people from the back to the front, but here we are separated by a screen. In some of the cars the screens are large and cumbersome, and fits on the top of the back of the seat, and invariably is inclined toward the face of the Colored patrons, so that when a Colored woman gets on the car she must hold her neck backwards or her hat is constantly bumping against the screen. In some cars these screens rise from the top of the back of the seat to a height of 12 or 14 inches. The newer screens, however, are not more than six inches, and of course reduces in a measure the objection alleged.

But the screens are unlike anything else, even in the State of Louisiana. Just across the river from New Orleans, in Algiers, which as a matter of fact is a part of the city, a very small moulding indicates the line of separation, and is not so noticeable. In some other towns the marking is over-head.

I should say that the screens are perhaps the least objectionable of the operation of the separate car here. The passengers are not permitted to move the screens. This is made to apply almost absolutely to the Colored Passengers, when the White passenger moves the screen backward at will, and there are only a few conductors that will call a halt to the White passengers.

The accommodation for Colored passengers is inadequate on all the lines, with the exception perhaps of the Peters Avenue and Louisiana Avenue lines, where the Colored people constitute the largest percent of the patronage of those lines. In this case they are therefore given a little better accommodation, but even in these cars, if there is any disadvantage to be offered the passengers, the Negro passenger must suffer it. Take for instance the Tulane Belt, St. Charles Belt, Jackson Avenue, Carondelet, etc., the usual accommodation is one seat that runs lengthwise of the car, while all the other seats in the car run crosswise. There are two seats of this kind allotted to Colored passengers, one on each side, but please note that even this seat is shorter by several inches than the regular seat in the car which runs crosswise. This makes it very crowded for two passengers. As a matter of fact two stout passengers cannot occupy such a seat. But the most objectionable feature of this lengthwise seat is that it faces the aisle, which permits the passengers in crowded hours who persist in standing in the rear part of the car, to tread upon and mash the feet and toes of the Colored passengers who are seated in those seats. If it happens that the car is full, with the exception of these two seats allotted Colored people, before Colored people board the car, this space is usually taken up by White passengers, who stand and at times there are men who rest their feet upon these seats. I know of one specific case where my wife was involved, when a White passenger did not want to remove his foot from the seat, even when she wanted to sit. It is this crowding upon the Colored passengers and reducing even the small space allowed them that makes the separate car situation so objectionable.

Now I could give you specific instances almost without number where the space allotted to Colored passengers was taken in full, and where there were a number of seats ahead in the part of the car allotted the White passengers, and still there would be Colored passengers standing. There would be room enough for the Colored passengers to sit if the screens were moved forward.

Here is one case just given me by the Rev. B. M. Hubbard,[1] Pastor of our First Street Church. He was on the car where there were three seats, one allotted to Colored passengers. All of these seats were taken with yet six Colored passengers standing. Above the screens in the part of the car allotted to White passengers there was not a person. The car was absolutely vacant, except for the Colored passengers that were on the car, and still the conductor would not move the screen forward.

Another case when my family and some friends were making the trip from the Y.M.C.A. home a few nights ago on the Jackson Avenue line, we were forced to sit two deep in one of these lengthwise seats, while nearly every seat in the part of the car allotted to White people had only one passenger each, and this situation existed in spite of my earnest request for accommodation.

I had a most humiliating experience when Mr. Napier was here, and when I made a request for a seat for him, the request was only to be denied.

Now I think that I ought to say that now and then you will find a conductor who makes an effort to give the Colored people accommodation, but such men are scarce. The whole trouble in the situation is that the street cars in New Orleans are operated as if the Colored patronage was not wanted, or that the Colored people must take the accommodation offered without regard to convenience and comfort.

I am sorry I have taken so much of your time, but I wanted you to know something of the situation here as it pertains to the separate car law. A copy of the law under which these cars are operated is enclosed.

With every good wish, I am, Yours truly,

Robert E. Jones

TLS Con. 519 BTW Papers DLC.

[1] Berry M. Hubbard, pastor of the First Street Methodist Episcopal Church.

To Robert Lloyd Smith

[Tuskegee, Ala.] December 30, 1913

Dear Mr. Smith: I am pleased to acknowledge receipt of your check for Sixty ($60.00) Dollars, covering your subscription in full to the "Negro Farmer."

I am pleased to tell you that we have formally organized, by electing a Board of five Directors and Officers as follows:

> Booker T. Washington, President
> Emmett J. Scott, Vice President
> Charles H. Gibson, Secretary
> Warren Logan, Treasurer
> Robert R. Taylor

That is to say; these five gentlemen constitute the Directorate and officers of the Corporation.

Application for the charter will be made at once. The Directors have decided to employ Mr. Isaac Fisher as Editor and Mr. C. B. Hosmer as Business Manager.

We hope to launch the paper early in February. Further details as to the affairs of the Concern will be sent you from time to time. Yours very truly,

Booker T. Washington

TLpS   Con. 483   BTW Papers   DLC.

To Andrew Carnegie

[Tuskegee, Ala.] January second, 1914

Dear Mr. Carnegie: I am writing to say that your card on "Peace" has just been received. It is strong, beautiful, direct and unanswerable; I am sure it will accomplish great good. It shall have a place among my most precious and cherished documents.

In an humble way, I have been trying to bring about a reform in the manner of celebrating Christmas in the South — trying to get rid of the pistol, the shotgun and the fire-cracker. I have had a letter similar to the one which I am enclosing published in practically every white daily paper of importance in the South[1] and most of them have backed up what I have said editorially. I am sending herewith a clipping from the CHARLESTON NEWS AND COURIER and the ATLANTA GEORGIAN. I am sure that we have had a much more peaceful and civilized Christmas than we have had in a good many years.

With best wishes for the coming year, I am   Yours very truly,

Booker T. Washington

TLpS   Con. 68   BTW Papers   DLC.

[1] See To the Editor of the Montgomery *Advertiser,* Dec. 15, 1913, above.

To Officers and Teachers of Tuskegee Institute

[Tuskegee Institute, Ala.] January 2nd, 1914

To ALL OFFICERS AND TEACHERS:

Hereafter it will mean instant dismissal from the services of this institution for any teacher or teachers to get married secretly.

Booker T. Washington

TLSr   Con. 638   BTW Papers   DLC.

John Brown Bell to Emmett Jay Scott

Houston, Texas, January 3 1914

My dear Mr. Scott: I received a telegram from Mr. Washington Sr. saying his son Booker T. would arrive in Houston Tuesday night Dec. 30 '13. on his way to Prairie View and would spend Tuesday night with us. I met him at the depot and found Mrs Hancock[1] and daughter[2] there, after Mr. Washington's arrival he held a short conference with them, then said to me that he would like to remain in the city for one or two days, which was very agreeable with me. His marriage in our city was a total surprise to me and my wife, for not an inkling did we know of it until we read the marriage license in the paper the next morning.

I approached him and asked if it was true, and he acknowledge[d] it. They married at the Court House some time during the day of Dec. 31th. He remained at my house and she stopped at Dr. Jackson's[3] residence. His last night in Houston which was Thursday night Jan 1th he spent with his wife at Dr. Jackson's home. I wrote Mr. Washington today concerning the same. Had I or my [wife] even known it before it happened, I would have used my influence to have it stopped until after hearing from Mr. Washington Sr. however we knew nothing until the next day. Trust Dr. Washington will not feel badly towards me as I am indeed sorry it happened as it did, however the young lady is a very deserving young woman. My wife met her for the first time after the marriage. I hope you spent a very pleasant holiday. I wanted to write you for I knew nothing of the marriage before it occurred. We send best regards to your self and family. Yours truly,

J B Bell

TLS Con. 471 BTW Papers DLC.

[1] Mrs. S. E. Hancock was a faculty member at Prairie View State Normal School (Tex.).

[2] Nettie Hancock, born in 1887 in Austin, Tex., married BTW, Jr., on Dec. 31, 1914. She was at that time a teacher in the Texas State School for the Deaf in Houston. She was a graduate of Fisk University, where BTW, Jr., was a classmate. She later did graduate work at the University of Southern California and New York University in social work, and taught for many years until retirement at the California State School for the Deaf. She died in Bethesda, Md., in 1972.

[3] Charles A. Jackson, a black Houston surgeon, was a friend of BTW, Jr.

Margaret James Murray Washington
to Mrs. S. E. Hancock

[Tuskegee, Ala.] January 3, 1914

If it meets with your approval we will prepare the following Announcement.

> "Mrs Hancock wishes to announce the marriage of
> her daughter Nettie to Booker T. Washington, Jr.
> in Houston, Texas, December 31st, 1913."

Can send portion there for you and Nettie to send out and we can send portion from here. Can send names we are to use so as to avoid duplication. Telegraph answer as Mr. Washington is to be in Chicago this week, and wishes to have engraving or printing done there.[1]

Mrs. Washington

TWSr Con. 17 BTW Papers DLC.

[1] Mrs. Hancock replied: "Your proposition meets my entire approval." (Jan. 5, 1914, Con. 504, BTW Papers, DLC.)

An Article in *The Country Gentleman*

January 3, 1914

TWO MILLION FARM HANDS

The Right and Wrong Way to Handle Negro Labor

"I just can't learn to work free Negroes." Thirty years ago, when I was establishing Tuskegee Institute, this was the plaint made to me by a wealthy planter in Alabama who had formerly owned and worked slaves, and in this sentence is the crux of the problem of Negro labor. In slavery the Negro could be worked. In freedom he must be induced to work. There is a vast difference between being worked and working. But the problem in nearly every county in the South is how to use Negro labor successfully on the farm.

Of the nearly 9,000,000 colored people living in the Southern states it is safe to say that more than 2,200,000 work on farms as hired hands, as independent farmers or croppers, as renters or as independent owners. Included in this number are a great many girls and women, for it must be kept in mind that especially in the cotton-growing states it is a common thing for girls and women to work in the fields.

Despite all theory and academic discussion as to the value of the Negro in the economic life of the South, it is true in the cotton-growing states that a large part of the banking business has for its basis the Negro and the mule. If a planter wants to borrow money the decision of the bank will hinge largely on the question of the number of reliable Negro tenants he can control.

Here, then, is a tremendous amount of labor, and in it there are tremendous possibilities. These more than 2,200,000 people are not likely to leave the Southern states. Where they remain in large numbers no other class of laborers is likely to come in large numbers, and I also find that the majority of Southern white landowners do not want any other.

To put the matter in another form, forty per cent of the tillable land in the Southern states is in the hands of colored people in one form or another. The large number of colored laborers and the vast territory that they occupy make up a serious but interesting question for the South and for the whole country. In my opinion, in this mass of Negro labor is an undiscovered gold mine.

TOO MUCH PROSPERITY

Before I attempt to suggest how to use Negro labor successfully let me tell how not to succeed with it. I can best do this by using some illustrations that have come under my own observation.

Some years ago, when I was in Mississippi, a planter asked me to visit his farm. I found he had a large number of colored tenants, but I was surprised at the small acreage assigned to each family. In one case I happen to remember a family that had three or four strong persons at work every day that was allowed to rent only about ten acres of land. When I asked the owner of the plantation why he did not let this family have more land he replied that the soil was so productive that if he allowed them to rent more they would soon be making such a profit that they would be able to buy land of their own and he would lose them as renters. This is one way to make the Negro inefficient as a laborer — attempting to discourage him instead of encouraging him.

Another illustration: In one of the cotton-raising counties of Alabama a colored tenant brought six bales of cotton and delivered them to the merchant from whom he had been renting and who had been furnishing him "advances." The colored farmer had kept pretty good account of his purchases and of the rent due. When he entered the store he told the merchant he thought he had made enough cotton to settle all he owed. After looking over his books the merchant agreed with him that the six bales would "bring him out clear." But before the colored man left the store the merchant learned that he had not brought in all the cotton he had grown, having two more bales at home. Immediately the storekeeper called the farmer aside and told him that he was sorry he had made a mistake in the accounts, and in going over the books again he found enough omitted charges exactly to cover the two bales the Negro tenant had left at home.

Here is another method of how not to succeed with Negro labor. Of course this Negro tenant was not long in putting an account of how he had been treated on the "grapevine telegraph," and soon every Negro in the neighborhood knew about it.

Through such practices, in not a few sections of the South, Negro tenants have been thoroughly convinced that no matter how much they economize or how hard they may work they are going to come out in debt at the end of the year, and they have become so discouraged and hopeless that they try to do only enough work to "make a showing" in order to get their "advances."

If they work little they get nothing at the end of the year, they say, and if they work hard they get the same nothing.

Let me give another example of how not to succeed with Negro labor: Some years ago a rather prosperous and intelligent farmer asked me to send him a man from Tuskegee Institute to work round the house and take charge of the garden. We sent a modest, hard-working, sensible young man who was not afraid of any kind of work. He was to be paid so much a month, with board and lodging. The young man reached the place in the morning and worked hard all day. At night, after he had milked the cows and done the chores about the house, the employer called him to the house, handed him two pieces of bread and some fat meat from the kitchen door, and told him he thought he could find a good place to sleep in the loft of the barn. The boy left the next day.

A LOYAL LABORER

I know I am speaking plainly, but I am doing it in the interest of the white employers of labor and Negro employees.

One more example as to how not to succeed: I know a white man who owns thousands of acres of the best land in his state. He is a high-toned gentleman and would not cheat his Negro tenants out of a cent for any consideration. He means to be just to his hundreds of Negro tenants, but the trouble is here: To my certain knowledge this large landholder has not seen the greater part of his land for twenty years.

He knows nothing of the personal needs of his tenants, nothing of the condition of the tenant houses, of the fences, ditches, and what not. He knows nothing of the morals of the people or to what extent they have opportunity to improve themselves through the church and the day school. All this landlord knows is that he is expected to make "advances" and receive so many bales of cotton for rent. His ignorant Negro tenants are left absolutely to themselves. His lands and houses depreciate in value each year. Under these conditions there cannot be much success, and when failure comes the Negro is likely to be blamed.

In brief, I am simply trying to say that if one would succeed with Negro labor there must be the constant human touch maintained between tenant and landlord. With all his weakness there is no laborer in the world who is more responsive to this personal and human touch than the Negro. When rightly treated he does not maintain that cold-blooded "dollars-and-cents" relation to his employer that the foreign laborer does; he manifests deep interest and even pride in the success and happiness of his employer.

Another way not to succeed with Negro labor is constantly to curse and abuse the Negroes who work for you both in public and in private. I know men whose every meal is cooked by black persons, whose children are nursed by black persons, whose garments are laundered by black persons, who are nursed when sick by black persons, whose land is cultivated by black persons, whose houses are built by black persons, whose graves will be dug by black persons, who have been able to accumulate immense fortunes through the labor of black hands, yet who in spite of all this never seem to think they are doing any injustice to the colored man or discouraging him when in private conversation and public print they delight in damning the Negro. I know, however, that fully half of what is said in condemnation of the colored laborer is not meant. Some employers simply have the habit of speaking disparagingly of Negro labor, and because they think it popular they don't stop.

Not long ago I read an editorial in a prominent Southern daily paper that contained this sentence: "It is a well-known fact that Negro labor cannot be depended upon, and that Negroes are shiftless, lazy and dishonest." Now a sweeping general statement like this simply results in discouraging some of the best colored labor in the South. What the writer meant was that *some* colored people cannot be depended upon to labor faithfully, and that *some* colored people are worthless and dishonest.

I wish I might impress upon employers of Negro labor the fact I have learned by personal experience and observation: That one can get more out of members of my race, whether they work on the farm, in the shop or in the kitchen, by mixing in a bit of praise when it can be honestly given than by constant condemnation, which tends to make laborers discouraged.

Having called attention to the negative side, let me now tell how a number of Southern white men who are large planters are succeeding with Negro labor. I am confining these examples almost wholly to Alabama, for these in most cases are personally known to me.

First I mention J. W. McLeod, who owns a large tract of land in Macon County, Alabama. He is a good example of the white planter who treats his tenants well. Mr. McLeod believes in having a good school in the community, so he gave an acre of ground upon which the schoolhouse was built, and $100 in addition to help put up the $700 schoolhouse. He deeded the land to a set of colored trustees. Mr. McLeod also offers annual prizes for the best-kept stock, best-kept farm, best-kept house, best-cared-for children, best attendance at Sunday school and church. The man or woman guilty of taking intoxicating liquors or engaging in family quarrels is not eligible to prizes and must go at the end of the year.

J. C. Pinkston, of Macon County, Alabama, owns several thousand acres of land. He sees to it that the colored people are encouraged in building good schoolhouses and that their children are sent to school. He has given $200 toward the building of two $600 schoolhouses, but on condition that the tenants themselves raise a large amount of money for the building. He discourages whisky drinking. He encourages churchgoing.

Judge William Henderson, of Wilcox County, Alabama, with a plantation of about ten thousand acres of good land on the Alabama River and several hundred tenants, is a staunch supporter of Negro farm demonstration work. He not only calls his tenants together in gatherings of from two hundred and fifty to three hundred and fifty, but in the midst of pressing business comes to the meetings himself. Judge Henderson always makes it a point to comment on the instruction given in such a way as to impress every farmer.

On one occasion, to show how his tenants stood financially, he stood up in a gathering of about three hundred tenants and made this statement: "If there is a tenant here from my plantation who owes me or anybody please stand." Out of the large number of tenants from his place there was only one man who stood, and his account was so small that he was more than able to take care of it. He gave the land for the erection of the Millers Ferry Industrial School in order that his tenants might send their children there and at the same time keep them in the community.

Probate Judge J. C. Woods, of Lowndes County, Alabama, urges his tenants to have a hog and a cow apiece, and to raise their own foodstuffs at home and stay out of the store. He gave $50 in 1913 for the improvement of the Negro schoolhouse, and promised at the close of school in May that if the pupils would continue to improve he would give them $50 more.

Another method of accomplishing the same thing is used by W. W. Campbell, of Macon County. Mr. Campbell is a banker and a large planter. Since his banking business prevents his being on his farms and giving personal attention to the tenants, Mr. Campbell has a graduate of the agricultural department of the Tuskegee Institute who lives right among the tenants and directs and helps them, not alone in their farming but in their schools and churches as well.

In 1909 W. W. Thompson, of Macon County, purchased a farm of about three thousand five hundred acres. Before he came into possession of this place it was operated on the old "absentee-landlord" system and passed from owner to owner; it was usually looked upon as a hopeless business proposition.

There were many colored tenants on the farm; but since the owners seemed to manifest little interest in the permanent success of the place it was natural that the tenants should manifest little interest. As soon as Mr. Thompson bought the farm he moved his family on it and began to let the tenants know that he was interested in them as well as in the farm. Instead of abusing them he began praising them and impressing upon them the fact that in proportion as they prospered he would prosper. Among the first things he did was to tear down the little one-room cabins and build comfortable cottages with two and three rooms.

On this point Mr. Thompson says: "As a result of improving the houses a better class of tenants has been secured, and this means a permanent tenant instead of a shifting and roaming one." Near his farm is a church and a day school that is in session seven or eight months of the year.

See how the colored tenants respond to this new kind of treatment: A Birmingham newspaper, in speaking of one of the tenants on Mr. Thompson's farm, says: "On one patch of an acre and a half this year Kelly Sparks has grown three crops — Irish potatoes, cotton and pea-nuts — and has produced crops to the aggregate value of about $100 per acre." The paper further says: "The story of Kelly Sparks should be a lesson to the farmers, white and colored, of Alabama."

The net result on this place within four years, according to Mr. Thompson's report, is as follows: In 1909 the farm grew 129 bales of cotton, 500 bushels of corn and 500 bushels of oats. In 1913, four years later, the same farm has grown 850 bales of cotton, 16,000 bush-els of corn, 6000 bushels of oats, 300 head of hogs, 100 head of cattle. Converted into money these lands made more than $7.50 in 1913 for every dollar that they made in 1909.

Some time ago the Hon. Walter Clark, one of the most prominent and wealthy Southern planters, living at Clarksville, Mississippi, said: "I am sick and tired of this eternal abuse of the Negro. The Negro is what the Southern people have made of him. We are absolutely responsible for nine-tenths of his shortcomings, and we should, like men, shoulder our share of his faults. There is no question but that he has some of the worst traits of any human beings, but he also has some of the noblest."

All persons who deal with Negro labor must bear in mind that the colored man is extremely social. He likes to have a let-up now and then; he likes to have a good time; he is fond of attending church, funerals, camp meetings, lodge meetings, revivals, frolics, and going to town on Saturday. I have noticed that colored landowners very often control colored labor more successfully than white owners for the reason that they understand this element in colored labor better than the white man. And here let me remark that the average man, especially the one living outside of the South, does not realize to what an extent colored people themselves are becoming employers of colored labor. There are not a few colored men scattered through the South who em-ploy on their farms and in one way or another as many as two hundred or three hundred colored laborers each.

Nearly every one of the white planters I have held up as examples of employers who know how to use Negro labor successfully has once or twice a year a barbeque for his tenants. It is made a great holiday, when the people are not only amused and entertained but are instructed by persons who are experts in various lines of farming.

I know that a great many people will say that this large social element in the case of the Negro constitutes his weakness. This may or may not be true. Any one who has visited Southern Europe and has noted the tremendous amount of time thrown away in holidays will say that the Negro is far above the average of the European workman in the matter of time wasted in holidays and the like. Where the Negro wastes one day I am safe in saying the average workman in the Latin countries of Europe or in Mexico wastes three or four days.

How can the colored laborer be kept on the farm where, in my opinion, he is best off, and out of the city where in most cases he is worst off? This is not an easy question to answer, for the tendency all over the world in recent years has been toward the cities. It can hardly be expected that the Negro will not be influenced by this tendency, even though he likes the rather free life in the country. Why do so many leave the land then?

WHY THEY LEAVE THE FARMS

From direct investigation I find that many valuable colored laborers leave the farm for the reason that they seldom see or handle cash. The Negro laborer likes to put his hands on real money as often as possible. In the city, while he is not so well off in the long run, as I have said, he is usually paid off in cash every Saturday night. In the country he seldom gets cash oftener than once a month or once a year.

Not a few of the best colored laborers leave the farms because of the poor houses furnished by the owners. The miserable condition of some of the one-room cabins is almost beyond description. In the towns and cities, while he may have a harder time in other respects, he can find a reasonably comfortable house with two or three rooms.

No matter how ignorant or worthless a colored man may be, he wants his children to have education. A very large and valuable element of colored labor leaves the farm because education cannot be secured in many cases. In a large section of the farming district of the South the Negro finds public schools provided for him which run only from two to five months in the year. In many cases children have to walk miles to reach these schools. The schoolhouses are poor, in most cases beyond description. The teacher receives perhaps not more than $18 or $25 a month, and of course poor pay means a poor teacher.

In the larger towns and cities the Negro laborer finds schools provided by the public missionary or denominational agencies. These schools are in session eight and nine months in the year, the schoolhouses are good and the teachers are competent.

More and more each year the South is being forced into competition with other farming sections. This means that the South has to use in an increasing degree more labor-saving machinery of a complicated character. Ignorant persons cannot understand or successfully use complicated labor-saving devices. There is only one way out of this — to make the laborer of the South just as intelligent and skilled as the laborer of other sections.

Again, a large number of the most industrious, conservative and law-abiding valuable colored laborers leave the country districts and go to the towns and cities to get police protection. In the country these colored laborers fear that if they are charged with crime they will be dealt with by the mob or without trial by jury.

EDUCATION IN FARM METHODS

This same element of colored people, too, often leaves the country to avoid the constant harassing to which they are subjected in many sections by petty officers of the law. Few white men realize to what an extent minor officers get into the habit of following up colored people in the country districts and arresting them on all kinds of petty charges. These arrests are often made for the sake of the fee, which goes either to the man making the arrest or to some local magistrate who in many cases is anxious to put as many persons as possible into the chain gang in order to increase the revenue that will come from prison labor.

But, as I have just stated, if in every country district the Negro could be sure that when he or members of his family were accused of crime the charge would be impartially investigated and a legal trial of the case would be held it would keep many colored people on the farms.

It would help tremendously to make the Negro more efficient and contented as a farm laborer if more were done in the way of educating him as to the importance of farming and better methods of farming. I know that the usual objections will be urged — that educated Negroes do not often go back to the farm. Be this as it may, it means much to the masses of my race for the teachers, the ministers and other leaders to know about farming and to be interested in country life, even though they do not earn their living by farming, for these leaders, both directly and indirectly, exert a great influence on the average working man and woman.

In every state in the Union thousands of dollars are being spent to instruct people in farming. Farmers' institutes are being held. County, district and state agricultural schools are being maintained at public cost. The average white employer of Negro labor does not realize how little is being done to make the Negro more efficient as a farmer and keep him interested in the soil. Let me give one example:

The state of Georgia has the largest Negro population of any state — 1,176,000. About 700,000 of these are engaged in farming for themselves or for some one else. To make these people more efficient as farmers the state of Georgia, through its Negro Industrial College, annually spends $23,000. A good proportion of this amount comes from the Federal Government, and much of it is spent for other kinds of training than farming. Taking, however, the $23,000 as a basis, there is spent for the better training of Negroes engaged in farming in that state about three cents per capita. In contrast, the state of Kansas, which has a total population of a little over a third more than the Negro population of Georgia, is spending annually more than $500,000 for the improvement of those engaged in farming, or more than fifty cents per capita.

But conditions are changing for the better in all parts of the South. White people are manifesting more interest each year in the training of colored people, and, what is equally important, colored people are beginning to learn to use their education in sensible ways; they are learning that it is no disgrace for an educated person to work on the farm. As white people see this they are going to be willing to spend more on the Negro for farm training.

Country Gentleman, 79 (Jan. 3, 1914), 5–6. BTW prefaced the article with the statement: "In this article I know I have spoken plainly, but I have done so from an honest motive — that is, to be of service to the white people of the South as well as to my own race. My experience has taught me that in proportion as the business men of the South find that a man is frank and straightforward he is respected and believed in by them. By each race being frank with the other and each trying to help the other, the South can be made one of the greatest agricultural countries in the world."

Ralph Waldo Tyler to Emmett Jay Scott

Washington, D.C. January 4th., 1914

My dear Emmett: I do not know whether or not the Doctor is at Tuskegee at present, and for that reason I will write you about what I desire to say to him, and you can communicate same to him if you consider it worth the while. Writing you is the same as communicating with him direct anyhow.

The N.A.A.C.P. is growing fast, and it has all but blanketed this community here. I found in my travels its influence was rapidly spreading, and wherever it was increasing in numbers I found a very noticeable decrease in proper respect and appreciation for the Doctor's work. In Washington its leaders are either avowed opponents of the Doctor or indifferent friends. On my return I found The Bee, all along our "constantly" watched ally was slowly, but surely getting into the enemy's camp. While I was absent it seemed it was none of our friends' concern to keep an eye on it. Some of "our friends" here whose past success was due almost entirely to the Doctor's influence in their desire for retention under the present administration have changed from strong Washington partizans to middle of the road men.

Villard's appearance here, a couple of months ago, and his billed second appearance here this month, has invigorated our opponents, and made luke warm some of our friends.

The Bee, unquestionably, has the call here, no matter how much of a Hessian its editor may be, and, The Age is a practical nonentity here.

When in office I looked after helping The Bee financially, and "our friends in" cooperated to some extent, although I was forced to make up deficiencies, and now am carrying some of their unkept promises to liquidate in full. If The Age's course was such as to support, and at the same time placate the opposition our organization, once strong organization, might have been held in tack [intact], and concern about the local organ here reduced to a minimum, but its course, and its (The Age) dwindling prestige and dwindling circulation neither helps us or the bear. If anything, it helps the bear.

I now find myself a practically unassisted champion here, and when I start on my next trip, if I start, there will be the devil to play.

I am not sounding a false alarm, and neither am I exaggerating the situation and conditions.

In the past two months the local branch here of the N.A.A.C.P. has collected and forwarded to Villard almost $2000. This alone tells, in a few words, of its activity and growing strength. They had practically (when the administration changed) captured Thompson who was disseminating their news while he tightened up on news in the Doctor's interest, to whom he is greatly indebted. There was only one alternative — close him up and out. And I have done this effectually. Have placed him in a jam — he can neither hurt us or help the bear.

Growing strong, the enemy now sees the need of good organs, and a good publicity man. With funds at their disposal they will secure both.

I have studied the situation closely, and in my travels made careful observations, and have arrived at this conclusion:

A sturdy, but fair organ in New York, national in influence, and local in a field extending over New England, New York, Delaware, New Jersey, Pennsylvania, Maryland and the District here is imperative; a fair supporting organ at Chicago, a fairly helpful organ at St. Louis, and a strong advocate at Memphis. Memphis really offers a splendid field for a newspaper to cover Tennessee and the South.

There is no reason, in my opinion, why a newspaper at Memphis should not only be powerful in influence, but a financial success, with close application. St. Louis, with its many advanced school teachers, I found ripe for N.A.A.C.P. propagation.

The fact is we have, and are losing ground, and the enemy is gaining. We cannot afford to openly oppose the N.A.A.C.P. for the reason that its fundamental principles are precisely what we all desire to see in force. With its present leaders, we cannot afford to go over to it in a body. As I see it, we must not withhold approval — we surely must not antagonize, while emphasizing, in no offensive manner the things which the Doctor is trying to do.

Now here is the situation, and here is the confronting condition. We have friends who were with us strong when we were serving their meals and washing their clothes. Now that they believe we can no longer feed or clothe they are preparing to hurdle the fence. We held them by favor then. We must hold them now by fear. Sincerely,

Ralph

TLS Con. 851 BTW Papers DLC.

To John Hobbis Harris

[Tuskegee, Ala.] January 5th, 1914

Dear Mr. Harris: I thought you and your committee might like to see the enclosed record of lynchings in the United States. It is not a document of which one feels proud to send out of his country, but there is consolation in the fact that the number of lynchings is constantly decreasing, though slowly, and public sentiment throughout the South is growing in favor of blotting out this evil altogether. Yours very truly,

Booker T. Washington

TLpS Con. 842 BTW Papers DLC.

To John Brown Bell

[Tuskegee, Ala.] January 6th, 1914

Dear Mr. Bell: Mr Scott tells me that you are somewhat agitated because of the marriage of my son in Houston, and that you fear that we blame you and Mrs. Bell. The fact of the matter is that we are not sorry at all that the marriage took place. He had informed his mother as to what he planned to do, but that he was not certain when or where. We also, of course, knew that he had intended marrying Miss Hancock. We have known her for a number of years and feel perfectly sure that he has found a fine, worthy young woman. There is no blame whatsoever attaching to anybody in the matter. I sent you a telegram last night reading as follows:

"WE THANK YOU AND MRS. BELL FOR YOUR KINDNESS. HIS MOTHER KNEW ABOUT HIS INTENTIONS AND BOTH

OF US ARE VERY MUCH PLEASED AND SATISFIED.
WE KNEW MISS HANCOCK TO BE AN EXCELLENT AND
WORTHY YOUNG WOMAN."

Our son, Booker, we are proud to say, has developed into a fine, thoughtful self-controlled young man and in most cases we have found it wise to follow his judgment as to what he is to do. He has high ideals in life and we never fear of his doing an immoral or unwise thing. He is now taking a course in Pharmacy in the Northwestern University at Chicago, with a view of establishing a drug store somewhere in the South; he has an ambition to have one of the largest and most successful drug stores operated in the South by colored people, and I very much hope that he will achieve this result.

Mrs Washington will be writing you shortly, if she has not already done so regarding the beautiful Christmas present which you sent us.

Both Mrs. Washington and I appreciated it most heartily. Yours very truly,

Booker T. Washington

TLpS Con. 493 BTW Papers DLC.

From Ralph Waldo Tyler

Washington, D.C., Jan. 6., 1914

Dear Doctor: Villard meeting, last evening, was a big success, in p[o]int of attendance, enthusiasm and funds raised. In addition to Mr. Villard, Senator Clapp, Justice Stafford, Archie Grimke and Rev. I. N. Ross[1] spoke, the latter spilling the cup, and giving the white press an opportunity to feature a sensational statement.

Mr. Villard quoted you in his address, saying that "Dr. Booker Washington never said a better thing when he said that 'you cant keep a man down in the ditch without staying down there with him.' "

To date, the local branch here has raised about $2500 in cash, sending same to New York. Rosco[e] Bruce is a grand high priest now in the N.A.A.C.P. movement, hurdling from his past friends who saved him to hoped for new friends. Rosco[e] is for any port in time of storm.

After the meeting they gave Mr. Villard a dollar banquet at the Y.M.C.A., and kept him over today to show him around through the schools. I did not attend the banquet, and know nothing of what took place there, not having, as yet, met any one who was in attendance. Hastily

R. W. Tyler

TLS Con. 14 BTW Papers DLC.

1 Isaac N. Ross, an A.M.E. clergyman residing in Washington, D.C. In the 1890s he was minister of the Wiley Avenue A.M.E. Church in Pittsburgh. Later he served the Ebenezer A.M.E. Church in Baltimore.

To Nettie Blair Hancock Washington

[Chicago, Ill.] Jan. 8, 1914

Booker is sending money to repay loan and to pay your traveling expenses here whenever you desire to come. His mother and I are very anxious for him to go on with his studies. Mrs. Washington and I think it well for you to come here and stay as long as you desire then if you wish to go to Tuskegee. Both of us send you our most hearty good wishes and congratulations.

Booker T. Washington

TWcSr Con. 526 BTW Papers DLC. Addressed to Austin, Tex.

Emmett Jay Scott to Hamilton Holt

[Tuskegee, Ala.] January Eighth 1914

Dear Mr. Holt: I think you probably may recall the writer as Dr. Washington's Secretary. I called upon you in your office in New York and have also talked with you here at Tuskegee when you came here several years ago.

It occurred to me that you might be interested in the enclosed correspondence[1] with "The Bertha Ruffner Hotel Bureau" of the Independent. The correspondence so clearly explains itself that I am sure I need add no further word. It reveals a condition of affairs, however, in New York City, which is most depressing so far as self-respecting, decent Negro Americans are concerned.

I am not writing this letter however, as I am sure you know, for the purpose of attracting any attention to myself. It is written only to call your attention to a condition of affairs of which you may not be advised. Yours very truly,

Emmett J Scott

TLpS Con. 11 BTW Papers DLC.

[1] See Emmett J. Scott to Bertha Ruffner, Nov. 20 and 29, 1913, and Bertha Ruffner to Emmett J. Scott, Nov. 25 and Dec. 1, 1913, above.

An Address on the Negro Race at the First National Conference on Race Betterment[1]

Battle Creek, Michigan, January 8, 1914

Mr. Chairman, Ladies and Gentlemen: I am very glad that those in charge of this conference have seen fit to consider the race to which I belong, in connection with the subject under discussion. Before I begin what I have to say, I wish to express my personal obligation to Dr. Kellogg and to the teaching for which he stands, because of the benefit which I have received as an individual.

Some three years ago I found myself almost out of commission physically. Without my knowledge or consent, my wife in some way got hold of a colored man trained here under Dr. Kellogg, by the name of Mr. Crayton. He came to Tuskegee, was installed in my home by my wife, and for six months he had charge of me. At the end of that six months I was a new man, and not only a new man, but I knew more about living and enjoying life than I had ever known before. And so I want to express to you, Dr. Kellogg, my deep personal gratitude.

Some years ago I was traveling through a certain section of the South with a friend. We chanced to stop overnight in one of the cabins which are common to that section of the country. The next morning,

when we went to the breakfast table, the good hostess asked us whether
we wanted long or short sweetening in our coffee. (I am aware that I
am getting on tender ground when I attempt to discuss the question of
food here, and especially coffee.) But this good lady asked whether we
wanted long or short sweetening in our coffee. Neither of us had ever
heard the question put in that form before, and each was puzzled. She
looked at me and then at the other for an answer. I punched my friend
rather gently and slyly in the side and suggested that he answer first.
With a good deal of courage he finally said he would take long
sweetening. With that the good woman put one of her fingers into a
cup of molasses — that is allowable — and then she put that same
finger into his coffee. Now that was long sweetening. Then she turned
to me and asked what I wanted, long or short. I said I would take
short. Then she put her hand into another cup, took out something
that resembled a lump of maple sugar, put it between her teeth, bit it
into two parts, put one part into her coffee and the other part into my
coffee. That was short sweetening. Now, Mr. Chairman, I do not know
what you want or expect of me in the way of an address, but I wish to
assure you in the beginning that both my long and short addresses are
rather disagreeable. Under the circumstances I shall have to choose
short sweetening, if any at all.

Few races in history have been subjected to so many sudden, violent,
and trying changes as is true of the American Negro within a short
period of years. First, there was a tremendous transition from Africa
to America, from free life to slave life, then from slave life to free life,
and then there has been a change which a large portion of my race has
experienced of moving from the South into the North. But in spite
of all these changes, the Negro has lived and is still living and intends
to live, in my opinion. Now I know sometimes people get a little impatient with us because we do change so suddenly and frequently. I
remember that some years ago I was in Jacksonville, Florida, visiting
a friend who had become a prosperous lawyer. He had recently built
a new house, and he took me into his rooms and showed me over the
fine mansion which it really was — into his bedrooms, bathrooms,
kitchen, and dining room. When we went into the beautiful dining
room, there was a bell under the table, and he put his foot on it and
pressed it, and a servant appeared at the door. He pressed it again and
the servant appeared the second time. Then a third and a fourth time
he pressed on the bell and the servant appeared. And I said to him,

"My friend, why in the world are you calling that servant through the medium of that bell so often when you do not seem to have any need for the servant?" "Why," he said, "Mr. Washington, the fact is, only a few years ago I used to be a Pullman porter and I always came when the bell rang, and I am trying to readjust myself to the changed conditions in life."

So you have to be a little patient with the Negro while he is trying to readjust himself, through all these changed conditions — changed conditions physically, industrially, socially, morally, from almost every point of view.

We have in this country about ten millions of my race. The number, in spite of predictions to the contrary, is not decreasing. We are growing at a reasonably healthy rate, not only from within, but from without. Some years ago the United States began to manifest an interest in the people of Cuba, Porto Rico, Hawaii, and the Philippine Islands, and those people began coming over here in pretty good numbers. I noticed that when they landed, either on the Pacific or Atlantic coast, the white man looked at them very closely, critically. He examined their skin through a microscope, felt of their hair, looked at their noses. He did not know exactly how to classify those people, and he finally said, "We had better be on the safe side and give them to the Negro." Now we are getting almost all of them, so that we are increasing at a reasonably rapid rate. Nine millions of the families of black people reside in our Southern states, one million reside in the Northern and Western states. Eighty-five per cent of those residing in the Southern states are at present to be found either in small towns or rural districts of the South.

Now, in my opinion, these people are worth saving, are worth making a strong, helpful part of the American body politic. They have already indicated, within their fifty years of freedom, some signs of being worth saving. In the first place, from a physical point of view they have lived — that is, they have survived. That is not an easy thing for any dark-skinned race to do when it is near you. Now, my friends, study history and you will discover that the American Negro is practically the only race with a dark skin that has ever undergone the test of living by the side of the Anglo-Saxon, looking him in the face and really surviving. All others that have tried that experiment have departed or they are departing. Now we have lived. Not only that, but we have supported ourselves from a physical point of view.

When Mr. Lincoln said fifty years ago, or a little more, that he was going to free us, some people said, "Don't free those Negroes. They will prove a perpetual burden upon the pocketbook of the nation." Somebody said that from a physical and economic point of view they would not support themselves, they would not clothe themselves, they would not shift for themselves, they would not feed themselves. If you will study the records of the American Indians — and I have nothing but the highest respect and love for the American Indian — you will find that Congress is called upon to appropriate every year between ten and twelve millions of dollars to be used in providing food, clothing, and shelter for about three hundred thousand American Indians. My own race in this country has been free fifty years, and never, since the days of Reconstruction, has the American Negro asked Congress to appropriate a single dollar to be used in providing food and clothing for his people.

Absolutely, from a physical point of view, we have cared for ourselves — and once in a while we have had a little something to do in caring for somebody else. Some time ago in Dallas County, near where I live, the white people were having a convention. There was an old colored man who was janitor of the court house who usually managed to find out what was the object of every meeting the white people held in that court house. But this was a new kind of convention, and the old colored man could not seem to analyze it. After it was over, he found the president of the convention, Colonel Jones (who used to own him), and he said, "Colonel Jones, you white people is up to something. You is havin' a meetin' in this court house, and I can't understand what you drivin' at. What is the object of this here meetin', Colonel Jones?" He replied, "Uncle Jim, it is simply an immigration convention. We are trying to devise ways and means by which we can induce more white people from Europe and the West and North to come and settle in Dallas County." The old colored man scratched his head and said, "Oh de Lord, Colonel Jones, we niggers in Dallas County have got just as many white people now as we can support." We have had to support ourselves and we have had a little to do once and again in supporting somebody else, and while we have not paid a great deal of taxes directly to the support of the government, we have made it mighty convenient for somebody else to pay the taxes through our labor.

If you will study the economic life of the South, you will find that a very large part of the expense of the government in the South, as I said — and I say it, my friends, with regret — a very large part of the expense of carrying on the government comes from the labor of convicts, a very large proportion of whom are black people. That is, we have not yet gotten out of the condition where we yield to the temptation of using the convicts for profit. Of course, the more convicts, the more profit. That is something that the civilization of the South is working away from gradually, but, in my opinion, slowly.

Some years ago we discovered that the people of Great Britain were spending annually not far from fifty millions of dollars in an attempt to rescue the drunkard, the gambler, the loafer, and the misfits of life; in a word they were spending not far from fifty millions of dollars in an attempt to get people up out of the ditch. Now, my friends, with all our weaknesses and shortcomings — and I fully recognize what these weaknesses and shortcomings are surrounding my race — we are not yet in the ditch. How much wiser it is, how much more economical it is, how much more interesting it is, for us not to wait till these millions of black people get into the ditch and then have to spend millions in getting them out, but to spend millions, if necessary, in saving them before they get into the ditch. That, in a word, is a problem that is before the people of this country.

Then, in a word, I represent a kind of new race. You know some races are so old. They have been where they are going. They have their history behind them. Mine is before it. Some time ago I met an old colored woman on the public road at Tuskegee one Sunday morning, and I turned to her and said, "Aunt Caroline, where are you going this morning?" Quick as a flash she turned and said, "Why, Mr. Washington, I's done been where I's goin'." These black people in the South are tremendously interesting from this point of view, in that they have not been where they are going. They are just on the way, and if we deal with them wisely, intelligently, frankly, sympathetically, I repeat that we will make them a strong, helpful part of our citizenship.

Now how? In the first place, we should use our influence, if we would better the condition of my race, to keep the masses of our people in the country districts and out of contact with the large, complex problems of city life, either North or South. The Negro, as I have observed and studied him, is best off near the soil, near nature, in the rural districts, as a rule. He is worse off in contact with large, complex city life. And I go further. The Negro on the whole (I know there are many fine exceptions) is better off in our Southern states than he is anywhere else in this country. He finds opportunities for progress in the South that he does not find in like degree outside of the South.

Those of you who would keep the body of my race strong, vigorous, and useful should use your influence to keep whiskey away from the Negro race. I am no professional advocate of temperance, but I have observed the effects of the use of liquor on my people in the South, and I have no hesitation in saying that in the counties and in the states where we have no open barrooms, the black man, from every point of view, is 50 per cent better off than he is in the counties and states where they have the open barrooms. I know it is often said that shutting up the barrooms does no good, because people get whiskey by other means. I am speaking of conditions in the South where I know them. The difficulty in judging correctly grows out of the fact that you hear of a man who gets whiskey in a closed barroom, but you do not hear of the ten men or nine men who fail to get whiskey in these prohibition counties. In my own county in Alabama — and it is typical of a large section of the South — we have had no open barrooms for twenty years. A barroom in our county would be a curiosity to a large proportion of children, white and black. That means that the people have become weaned from the love of whiskey, even from the taste of whiskey. And so if you would help my race better itself physically, use your influence everywhere to keep the barroom closed, and to keep whiskey away from them.

And then, with equal emphasis, I want to ask you to use your influence to keep the patent medicines away from my race. Now I suspect I am getting a little personal here in the North, because most of these things are manufactured up here and the South seems to be a kind of dumping ground for them. When a patent medicine is so vile that you cannot find a market for it in the North, it is dumped down in the South on my race. Now keep the whiskey and patent medicines from my race and you will help make them a strong and better race of people.

Now I have said, in connection with that, keep them in the country districts, but, my friends, the Negro has a great deal of human nature, and he wants education for his children, and he is not going to stay in the country districts unless he finds as good school opportunities, as good church facilities, as he finds in the smaller towns and larger cities of this country.

Again, from an industrial point of view — and this applies to all sections of the country, North and South — those who would better my race I hope will learn to reward the race more as individuals and not so much as a race. There are certain opportunities in industrial directions that are closed against the Negro simply because he belongs to a certain race. You know what I mean. Now that is unfair, my friends; that discourages and holds back some of the strongest and best men of my race.

Now, my friends, more and more the American white man should come to the point where he deals with my race as individuals, and not so much with the race as a whole. That is the way other races are dealt with. You will find that in proportion as my race is studied and helped and encouraged, it will add to the strength of the economic life of this country.

In that section of our country where the Negro is dependent upon others largely for work — I do not mean the discussion of the theory of work or these economic theories, but actual work; I do not mean the discussion of home economics and domestic art and domestic science, but I mean only one thing — the Negro woman is depended upon for cooking. You know sometimes you get cooking mixed up with domestic art and domestic science and have a lot of trouble. Now down there where the Negro woman is depended upon for cooking, where the black man is depended upon for work in the field and in the shop, there is a tremendous waste of economic life to the white man because of the weak and sickly bodies of thousands of my race. I speak with care when I say that at the present time there are, at least in the Southern states, two hundred thousand black people who are sick, who ought to be well. And somebody is paying the cost of that sickness. There are two hundred thousand colored people in the South today who are sick from preventable causes, and your duty as American citizens will not be accomplished until you reach this class of our people.

You cannot help the Negro very much and you do not help the white man very much by yielding to the temptation of trying to shut the race off in certain segregated parts of American cities. The Negro is just as proud of associating with his race as the white man is of associating with his race. I would not change races or colors with the whitest man in America. No man can be more proud of his race than

I am of mine. No man can be better satisfied in association with his race than I am when associating with members of my race. But, my friends, according to our complex form of republican government, when you shut the Negro off in any certain section of a city or community, the Negro objects because he knows that he is going to receive an unfair deal. Where? How? In the first place he knows that when you shut him off from the rest of the population, he is not going to have a fair chance from a health point of view, from a moral point of view, from a physical point of view. He knows that the lights in that section of the community are not going to be so good as they are in the other section. He knows that the streets are not going to be so well kept as is true in other sections of the community. He knows, above all things, that the sewerage is going to be neglected in his portion of the city. He knows that he is not going to receive the same police protection that other people receive in the same city. He knows that he is going to be kept out of churches, out of the influences of the Y.M.C.A., out of the library, out of the hospital. And he knows, further, that he is going to be compelled to pay a tax that is equivalent to the tax paid by the rest of the community who receive the benefit of all the comforts and conveniences of civilization.

Now, my friends, our two races are going to remain in this country together. We are going to touch each other at some points. You cannot shut the Negro away from the white man. If you would build a wall around the Negro, he would get over that wall, and then you would have to build five walls around the Negro to keep the white man away from the Negro. We are going to live in this country together. In fact we are more like you than any other race, aside from the color of our skin, that comes into America. We speak the same language that you do, we eat the same food that you eat, we profess the same religion that you profess, we have all the ambitions and aspirations that you have, we understand the genesis of your local institutions, we have the same local and national pride that you have, we love the same American flag with as great fervor as you do. We are American citizens and we are going to stay here with you. That means we are going to help you, or we are going to hurt you, and we want you to help us to get to the point where we can help you. We want to help you, and we want to help ourselves.

I am interested in the Negro race. I am equally interested in the white race in this country. I used to be a hater of the white race, but

I soon learned that hating the white man did not do him any harm, and it certainly was narrowing up my soul and making me a good bit less of a human being, and so I said, "I will quit hating the white man." I want to get the Negro on his feet for his sake and equally for your sake. I protest against the lynching and against the burning of human beings in the South, not only because of the interest that I have in my race, but equally because I do not want to see any of God's sons and daughters having their souls narrowed, lowered, and embittered by inflicting unjust punishment upon any section of the human family. As I said, I am interested in my race and interested in your race. We touch each other everywhere. In the South, especially when food is to be prepared, the Negro touches the life of the white man. When clothes are being laundered, the Negro touches the life of the white man. Often the clothes in the South go from the rich mansion to the dirty and filthy hovel of the ignorant colored woman who has had no opportunity to learn the lessons of health. We are bound together by ties we cannot tear asunder if we would. In their most tender years, thousands and hundreds of thousands of little children in the South spend their years in the presence and in the hands of colored women, or rather colored girls. It is immensely important, for the sake of the colored women, and equally important for the sake of the health, happiness, and upbuilding of your race, that that colored woman or girl who plays such an important part in the rearing of a large portion of the white people — it is mighty important that she should be intelligent, that she should be clean, that she should, above all things, be virtuous. We want you to help us.

You can help the Negro in two ways — by being frank with him, telling him about his faults, and by praising him just a little more. The Negro likes praise. I know him pretty well, and there are few races that will improve so much under the influence of praise as will my race. I remember when I was a young fellow, just about the close of the war, I had a few dollars. I had said that when I got enough money the first thing I was going to buy was a store suit of clothes. So I went straight to the store when I thought I had cash enough. The man in charge of this store, when he found I had the money and wanted to buy a suit of clothes, said he had exactly the suit of clothes I needed, bought for my special benefit. He began to describe the suit of clothes, and I looked it over. He was looking at my pocket at the same time. The first thing I knew he had the coat on me. I began to feel around, and the sleeves were about six inches too short. But the storekeeper caught hold of the sleeves and began to pull them down and press them and praise the coat. Then he went around and pulled down the back part of the coat and began to praise that — said it was an imported coat, bought for my special benefit. Before I knew it, I thought it was a pretty good coat. He got the pants on me and they were about six inches from my shoes, but he praised the pants, pulled the legs down, patted them, and pulled them down until I thought it was a pretty good pair of pants and a pretty good suit of clothes. He got my money and I got the suit of clothes. I went home. The next day was Sunday and I went to church. While at church a rainstorm came on and the suit of clothes got wet. When it dried out it was about the size of a fig leaf. Now it was a pretty good suit of clothes, friends, so long as it had somebody to praise it. I have found that you can make, very often, a good man of an indifferent man by praising him a little bit more. Whenever you have an opportunity, praise my race. As you come in contact with them as individuals, or in large numbers, whenever you can honestly do so, praise them.

And, lastly, when you go back to your own homes, seek an opportunity to actually get acquainted with my race. There are a lot of people in this country who know about the Negro, who hear about him, who have examined him at a distance, but, my friends, very few people actually know my race. If you will take the time and the trouble to go into their homes, to get into the life of my people, to go into their churches, into their Sunday schools, in every one of your communities, you will find the Negro has virtues you never dreamed of. I was in Sicily some years ago. I had always trained myself to hate the Sicilians and thought they were the most lawless and hateful and dreaded people in the world. I went away out into the country. I went among the peasant classes in Sicily and I ate their food, lived in their houses, lived their life for a number of days, and I came back loving the Sicilians and honoring them more than I had ever loved and honored any others outside of my own country before. I found I had not known the Sicilians. So when you go back home and find a Negro, just one, say to yourself, "I am going to know this individual, I am going to put my life to touch with his life." I was in a college town a few months ago, where there was great interest in the education of the colored people. After I had spoken to the students, as I usually do, I said to the college president, "Now I want to go to the colored church. I want to speak there." And he turned up his ears and eyes and said, "Well, where is the colored church?" Now there were seventy-five colored people right there in the shadow of that college, and yet the college president did not know where the Negro church was. So, my friends, every one of you, in your own way, at your own turn, get into the life of the members of my race.

And finally let me thank all of you, notwithstanding the fault that I have seemed to find with you — let me thank all of you for what you have done in bringing about race betterment among my people. Despite all the faults of America, and despite all the shortcomings of white men and black men, when we look at this matter in the large, not in the little, you cannot find ten millions of Negroes anywhere in the civilized or uncivilized world who have made such tremendous progress industrially, educationally, morally, and religiously as is true of the ten millions of Negroes in the United States, and a very large proportion of that progress is owing to the fact that you have been more generous in helping forward my race than was ever true in all the history of the world when one race of a different history, of a different color, was dealing with the members of another race.

And so, Dr. Kellogg, we thank you for this opportunity of coming here and getting this inspiration, coming here and getting opportunity to resolve again and again that each will go back home and do our part in making our races better, more useful, more righteous. In doing that we shall have to overlook the little things that will be perplexing, the short-lived things of life. I was once traveling with an old man in South Carolina. When we got to Columbia, he went up to the city and stayed longer than he should. In order to catch the last train by which we were traveling, and in his haste to get to the railroad station, he went to the first hack driver he saw and said, "Take me to the railroad station right away." The hack driver was a white man. He had never driven a black man in his hack. He said, "I have never driven a black man in my hack." The Negro said, "Boss, I have just got to get to the railroad station, that is all. I ain't got no time to discuss details." Then he said, "Mr. White Man, I will show you how to fix it. Just keep quiet. You take the back seat and do the riding and I will take the front seat and do the driving." Overlooking perplexities, overlooking all these details, in a few minutes the white man and the black man, together, were at the railroad station. The white man got his quarter and the black man got his train. Overlooking all these little perplexing, tantalizing, short-lived details, through the leadership of this great movement let us go forward with the surety that every day in the North and in the South and throughout the country, white people and black people together are moving in the direction of the railroad station.

Ernest Davidson Washington, ed., *Selected Speeches of Booker T. Washington* (Garden City, N.Y.: Doubleday, Doran and Co., 1932), 218–34.

[1] The conference was held Jan. 8–12, 1914. BTW spoke on Jan. 8. He left Battle Creek on Jan. 9 for speaking engagements in Massachusetts.

To Emmett Jay Scott

Parker House, Boston. Jan. 16, 1914

Dear Mr. Scott: I have been getting somewhat into the heart of things since I have been North. First, I have had an interesting conference with Bishop Walters about which I will tell you when I see you.

Second, I find that all the old, strong forces have either been put out of Villard's organization, or have withdrawn. This is true with few exceptions. There seems to be a general spirit of unrest and dissatisfaction among them. Dr. Mossell has withdrawn or been put out. The same is true of Ida Wells Barnett, and Trotter of course. The most interesting of all, I have learned from a reliable source that Villard and Du Bois do not speak to each other. They have been at daggers points for a good many weeks.

There are a good many colored people who resent the idea of a white man assuming to lead and control the colored people. One point that Bishop Walters and [I] agreed upon was that we use our influence in all the colored publications to emphasize in every way possible the matter of Negro leadership for Negroes, that we welcome the assistance and advice of such disinterested men such as Dr. Frissell, Mr. Ogden and others, but we are not ready to be taken charge of bag and baggage by any white man. The Bishop is heartily in agreement with this program. Yours very truly

[Booker T. Washington]

TL Con. 71 BTW Papers DLC.

From William Gaston Caperton[1]

Slab Fork, W.Va., Jan 19–14

Dear Sir: Some months ago you published through the Century Magazine[2] an article treating on the best home for the colored man, finally concluding that the South is his most logical home.

In the Spring and Summer there is an exodust of our miners from our coal fields to the Northern fields, and almost invariably the men that go return with no good report from their experience; however this move more or less disorganizes our mines, and unnecessarially cuts into the miners earnings.

And by distributing some good literature amongst the men, it might be possible for us to lessen the evil.

So I write to know if you can furnish us with 1000 pamphlets of your address, and at what cost?

And can you give us the names of a few lecturers, as there is a move to try and establish a lecture course taking in a dozen or more mines. Thanking you in advance. Yours truly,

Slab Fork Coal Co.
W Gaston Caperton

TLS   Con. 498   BTW Papers   DLC.

[1] William Gaston Caperton (1869–1945) was general manager of the Slab Fork Coal Co.

[2] See An Article in *The Century,* Nov. 1912, above.

To Walter Hines Page

Tuskegee Institute, Alabama   January 26, 1914

My dear Ambassador Page: I thank you so much for your good letter of recent date. I think our letters must have crossed:

I note what you say regarding the library from Mr. Carnegie for Liberia. I have tried several times to get Mr. Carnegie interested in Africa. He seems to have absolutely no interest in that country, and in fact has told me so rather bluntly several times. I fear there is little hope of succeeding with him.

Thank you very much for your suggestion regarding my coming to England. I am thinking over the matter seriously and I hope carefully, and shall reach a decision soon, and when I do reach a decision on the broad question of making the trip, shall write you regarding the plan. When [What] I have in mind, if I go to England, is not to confine my visit to Great Britain but to go to several influential centers of thought on the continent as well, and in that way try to create public sentiment that will react upon conditions in this country.

I am glad to say we are making progress in the South. I feel quite sure there has never been a time when racial conditions were so friendly, everything considered, as they are at present. As an indication of this, the New Orleans Times-Democrat, you know what that paper has stood for in the past, gave a Christmas tree to all the poor colored children in New Orleans. Yours very truly,

Booker T. Washington

TLS Walter Hines Page Papers MH. A press copy is in Con. 69, BTW Papers, DLC.

To Emmett Jay Scott

Tuskegee Institute, Alabama   Jan. 26, 1914

Mr. Scott: In the reorganization or changes that will take place in my office in the near future, I want you to keep in mind the getting of somebody who has a fine literary taste and will have time to thoroughly go through everything I write; I mean for everything to be thoroughly studied, criticised from a logical, rhetorical and literary point of view. I find that much I am now preparing in the way of speeches and even newspaper articles is very weak and defective. This was especially true regarding the article on public schools which went to The Outlook sometime ago.[1] The right man can be very serviceable in this direction.

Booker T. Washington

TLS Con. 644 BTW Papers DLC.

[1] See An Article in *Outlook,* Mar. 14, 1914, below.

To Timothy Thomas Fortune

Hartford, Conn. January 28, 1914

My dear Mr. Fortune: I have yours of January 23d. I am very glad to hear from you. I will not write much in detail at the present time as I hope to have Mr. Scott see you while he is in the North. He will be in the vicinity of New York for several days and can be reached, I think, in care of Mr. Moore.

I note very carefully what you say in your letter,[1] and shall ask Mr. Scott to let you know more fully what I think of your idea.

Certainly, from one point of view, we are having the old game played over again of white people trying to lead colored people. I am not, however, alarmed, as I have passed through many sand storms in the past.

I am very sorry that there was not an opening on the Negro Farmer for you. Later on as the paper develops strength and secures an income there may be some opening. Yours very truly,

[Booker T. Washington]

TLc   Con. 502   BTW Papers   DLC.

[1] Fortune wrote that O. G. Villard and J. E. Milholland "are attempting to run and control the destinies of the colored race through Du Bois." He thought that Villard and Milholland would have a difficult time because blacks were going to do their own thinking "and not be second fiddle to a few white men, who feel that the Negro race belongs to them." (Fortune to BTW, Jan. 23, 1914, Con. 502, BTW Papers, DLC.)

An Account of an Address
in Hartford, Connecticut

[Hartford, Conn. Jan. 28, 1914]

BOOKER WASHINGTON
PLEADS FOR NEGRO

Delivers Address before Inter-
Churchmen

SAYS RACE IS NOT
FULLY DEVELOPED

Colored People Profit by
White Man's Example

Declaring that the negro race was a new race and in that silly period peculiar to boys between the ages of 12 and 15, but that there had been a great development in the last twenty-five years, Dr. Booker T. Washington spoke before the inter-churchmen at the Allyn House yesterday noon in an address remarkable for its native humor and forceful sincerity. Although it taught a lesson of need and plead[ed] for aid, similar to many demands made today by speakers who have some cherished hope that they desire fulfilled, still the convincing arguments and cleverness of the man in his stories of little incidents of the Southern states and his powerful and earnest personality made the address one of intense interest.

The first impression that one received when he arose to speak was that he had a solemn and important matter on his hands and a matter that must be dealt with in a careful and sober manner — but one was partly deceived. Next in interest to his description of negro life at Tuskegee Institute and in the smaller Southern schools, came his relation of personal experiences which he told in a clever and humorous manner. All through his address [he] showed that his view of life was broad and that he firmly believed in the ultimate redemption of his race.

Mayor Cheney Speaks

Following the introduction of Mayor Louis R. Cheney by Harvey B. Brainerd, chairman of the arrangements committee, who said that it was unnecessary to dwell at length on the introduction since the mayor was such a well known man; Mayor Cheney introduced the speaker. He said:

"It is a great honor and pleasure to have you visit the city in any capacity and you will be, as you always have been, welcomed and listened to by the people of Hartford with the deepest admiration and respect for what you are doing. Mr. Washington has told me that he was born in the year 1859, as was I, so we have both decided to call the day of his birth April 27, the day of mine, which I consider a great honor. He told me a story that I want to repeat. A certain colored man made an appointment with another colored man who kept him waiting nearly an hour before he finally came running along, all 'het up' and excited. The darky who had been awaiting his arrival asked the cause of his delay and he responded, 'Laws, man, when I'se getting up dis morning I saw dat de chicken coop door was open and when I went out there I found dat the chickens had all gone home.' We all realize the great work that Booker T. Washington is doing and the unselfish way in which he is doing it so I repeat that it is with great pleasure that I introduce to this audience Booker T. Washington."

DR. WASHINGTON SPEAKS

"Some years ago while traveling with a friend through a certain section of Alabama," Mr. Washington said, "we stopped for the night at a cabin presided over by an old mammy. At supper that night we were asked whether we wished long or short sweetening in our coffee and, as I did not know the meaning of her words, I nudged my companion as an intimation that he should take the first chance. He said that he would take long sweetening, whereupon the mammy dipped her forefinger in a jug of molasses and put it in the coffee. I quickly decided upon short sweetening and she took a lump of maple sugar from the cupboard, placed it in her teeth, bit it in two pieces and put one piece in my coffee. Now, my speeches are somewhat similar to that mammy's method of sweetening. Both the long and the short are liable to be disagreeable.

"Youth is prone to narrowness of conception. When I was 9 or 10 years old, I believed that a Methodist could not go to Heaven, but now I sometimes think that he's got a better chance than I. This country is now reaching the time when there is a broadening out of all things and the activities of the churches and the religious denominations are becoming stronger. My race is one of the great national problems but there is no race in the history of man that has been so helped by the church and religion as my race has been and is being helped. Some of you probably have little idea of our number. We have in this country, a nation within a nation. There are, in the South, about 9,000,000 negroes and in the northern and western parts of the country about 1,000,000. We are a new race, but I would rather take a new race with its whole optimistic future before it than one with an obscured past. It's something like this story: One time I met an old negress. 'Where you goin',' I asked. 'Laws, sir,' she answered, 'Aunt Caroline done been there and she's comin' back.' As a race we have the virtue that we are still 'gwine' on."

WORK OF NEGRO SCHOOLS

The speaker then passed on to a description of the conditions in the negro schools of the South. He told of the great opportunity before the negroes there who were working on the farms and thereby gaining commonsense ideas. He said that as it was better to study the horse in person rather from a book, so was it good for men to get right down to the bedrock of nature.

"We believe in women's rights there," he said, "and let the women come out into the cool, fresh, fragrant morning air with us and work in the cotton fields and enjoy the same privileges as we can do. They enjoy the same privileges in the schools. One thing that I have done at Tuskegee Institute that I am very proud of is the abolishing of the regular form of the commencement address. Usually, it was something about 'After the Alps Lies Italy.' Now that didn't seem to take after several repetitions, so I suggested that something else be tried. I was asked what might be substituted and replied, 'eating.' At the next commencement, a girl gave a demonstration of an inexpensive farm dinner, preparing and distributing it from the platform in full sight of all.

"She cooked as choice a lot of turnips as it was ever my good fortune to see. She didn't dissertate on the philosophy, psychology or history of turnips either. She told how she grew them. There were two advantages to that arrangement. The student knew what she was talking about and the audience knew too.

"I remember when I was rather young and in the hills of Virginia that I thought I ought to deliver a lecture on 'Family Government' and did so in many nearby places. Now that I have married and have three children I have quit delivering it. I know more but say less. Boys, when they are at that silly period, try to run the home. My race is in the silly period. In the last twenty-five years we've been keeping down to earth and getting some good, commonsense ideas. The first thing that we must do is to convert the Southern man to giving to the school fund for our children.

"We have now, thanks to your many and generous contributions, reached the point where we can accomplish much and we have accomplished much, too, in these last few years. You ask what are the results I speak of? My race owns about $700,000,000 and has now about 16,000 more farms in its possession than in previous years. We are going into every kind of business in the South. We own grocery stores, plantations and other valuable pieces of property. The average negro in the South now has as good [a] chance as the white man in business. He can borrow at a bank or from an individual as readily as can the white man under similar circumstances. He is following the white man's example and profiting by it. Only the other day I read in a paper where a negro down in Texas had even robbed a bank.

VALUE OF WHITE ADVISORS

"Of course, on the other hand, there is much to be condemned as bad and disagreeable in the South. Take, for instance, the numbers of lynchings which, thank God, are decreasing every day. That is a horrible example for humanity to set. It is never right to take and burn and lynch a human being without a fair trial. Whenever that happens in the South, I always go to the spot immediately, take a white man's hand there in mine, look him in the face and try to make a friend of him. Nearly every negro has a white man who is a friend. Think of the 10,000,000 acres of land that my race owns. How did they get it? Nine times out of ten, a Southern white man has showed the way to the negro by lending him money or advising him. The attitude is daily becoming better and more honest. When I last left Tuskegee, there was a convention of negro teachers there getting ideas for their own schools. Fifteen years ago that would have been impossible."

"A wonderful change is taking place," he said in continuing. "The power and the education of Christian religion is being felt. We are just finding the way to solve our problems and, thank God, we are succeeding in doing it. I am selfish enough to say that I also thank God that they are not all solved yet for I like problems and I like this work. O, the glory of the imperfect! I love the work. As long as there is work to do in the South, and there will be as long as this ignorance, narrowness and foolish prejudice exists, so long will I be working.

"Let me tell you another story of a colored man who had spent much of his time in close communion with nature and who visited a town with me one day. I waited at the station for him to take the return trip with me but he did not show up until the train pulled in. The town, with its numerous delights, had fascinated him, so that he did not realize how long a stay he was making. When he saw that it only lacked ten minutes to train time and he was in the center of the city, he called a cab with a white cabby to take him to the station. The man refused, saying that he had never yet driven a colored man. 'Why,' said the darky, 'dat's easy. You get in the back seat and I'll drive.' That shows how the black man is working out the little tantalizing details in his life and also that he will continue to do so and God, in His own good time, will take care of the rest."

Hartford *Courant,* Jan. 29, 1914, 3.

To William Gaston Caperton

Hartford, Conn. Jan. 29, 1914

My dear Sir: I received your kind letter of January 19th just as I was on the eve of leaving Tuskegee for a trip in New England. I did not have time to answer your letter or to send you the things which you suggest. If you will be a little patient with me, I shall attend to the matter just as soon as I return to Tuskegee.

I appreciate something of the condition of things among the colored miners in that section. I used to mine coal myself and lived, as perhaps you know, for a number of years in Kanawha County. I am anxious to be of service to the miners. I will send you the documents that you refer to, and will try to suggest to you the names of some people who may prove helpful to the miners in lecturing to them. It is not easy,

I fear, to find people who can talk to the miners in a way to have them profit by what is said, for the reason that comparatively few lecturers know the real condition concerning the miners.

I think your plan to establish lecture courses covering a dozen or more mines is an excellent one, and I want you to call upon me for any service at any time you think I can render it in this direction. I agree with you thoroughly that the colored man has a better opportunity in the South than he has in the North.

If the miners could be induced to cultivate a little patch of land during their spare time I think it would go a long ways in keeping them contented and satisfied, especially in the spring and summer months. When I used to work in the mines in West Virginia, I observed that the miners who cultivated a plot of land usually stayed at home, did not become demoralized when the mines were not running or when there was a strike on hand.

I will write you more fully as soon as I return to Tuskegee.

By this mail I am sending you a copy of one of my books, "Up From Slavery," which I thought perhaps you might like to see. Yours very truly,

[Booker T. Washington]

TLc Con. 498 BTW Papers DLC.

To Charles H. Fearing

Hartford, Conn. January 29, 1914

Dear Mr. Fearing: During my absence I wish you would be careful to give Davidson some short dictation every day so that he can get practice in writing from dictation. Also give him some of the more simple letters to be answered in a way that he can use his own judgment and initiative in answering them. I wish you would give him as much work in both these directions as you think he can do well. Yours very truly,

B. T. W.

TLI Con. 653 BTW Papers DLC.

From Adelia Hirshfield[1]

Mobile Ala   Jan. 29, 1914

Sirs, Please be so kind as to give me two pieces of information. First, — For what purpose is the organization "Association for the Advancement of the Negro?" Is this for advancement along educational lines, or is it for vocational and industrial training? Second question — Is it true that your reply to those requesting cooks and housemaids is that your girls are trained for wives & mothers, and not for service. We need trained maids in Mobile worse than any city in the South, and would like to know if there is a possibility of getting them later from your Institute. Kindly send this information at once as I have a most urgent need for it. Yours truly

Mrs. A. Hirshfield

ALS   Con. 504   BTW Papers   DLC.

[1] Adelia Hirshfield was the wife of the Mobile County coroner and physician Henry P. Hirschfield.

From Garfield McCaster

Tuskegee Institute, Alabama   January 30, 1914

My dear Principal: No doubt you will be surprised to receive this letter, and too, you may not exactly solicit one of this kind. But it is one that I feel and have long felt should be written. It is not the purpose of this letter to place myself before you to be popular or to seek notoriety in any way whatever. It is not with any ill feeling or will toward any particular person. It is simply for the best good of all concerned and to give you some such information as I feel that you should have.

I came to this institution and entered as a student November 2, 1905, and was graduated in May, 1911. Since my graduation I have been employed as a hired man in the Printing Division. During the time here, and some time before coming, I have never failed to hear your instructions whenever possible. And as I noticed in a recent issue of the New York Age a letter published that had been written to you by a white man, the mayor of a certain city, who was about to appoint a Negro man on the Board of Education of that city. He asked you to advise this man as to what features of education to advocate for the Negro children there. He said that he never failed to read whatever he could get that you had to say about any thing. This has been no less true of myself. When you travel in the North and other sections of this country I am anxious to get the papers for your speech; when I hear [you] in our own chapel I am each time filled with new inspiration. I read your articles in the various magazines that come to our library. I do this because I know in them I will get nothing but the sanest, the soundest, and most truthful and trusted advice for the most practical and useful living, and too, because I know they are from, in my opinion, the broadest and most generous and sympathetic heart existing in any man living today. I am a firm believer in the spirit of my Alma Mater — "The Tuskegee Spirit." All I am and all I hope to be Tuskegee is the foundation of it.

Now, my dear principal, as for the criticism I wish to make is upon the members of our faculty, in whom the students and graduates should at all times be able to take much pride and confide. I think it is through them that our teaching may be more or less effective upon the lives of the students and graduates. But I am exceedingly sorry that during the last three or four years the larger majority of our faculty has not represented just what I believe to be your ideals of real dignified representative men and women of the highest standards of culture, refinement, and moral character. It is sad but nevertheless true that a large majority of them are walking statures of impoliteness and discourtesy and are not worthy in any way of being emulated by the students and no one else. It is common to hear slang expressions frequently made use of among the teachers that suggest low ideals — just the opposite to you[r] teaching. I have in mind a certain teacher who is very careless about the use of curse words in the presence of his students. They [are] loud and boistrous on the streets. And too, I think on a whole our teachers dress rather loud and seemingly beyond their income for a place like Tuskegee. The practice of economy as emphasized and taught here is not maintained. It is notic[e]able here that when some of the members of the faculty meet the students and others on the streets they do not even give them respectful recognition but turn their head in another direction. I do not consider this a lack of education but a lack of putting education to the proper use.

It is often that the student boys are punished for smoking cigarett[e]s or cigars and for the use of intoxicants — whiskey. I do not see how it is possible to keep the students from practicing these habits when the teachers themselves are guilty. I often see teachers passing down the streets in Greenwood smoking cigarett[e]s and I can most any day go into the divisions and smell the wiskey on their breath ten feet away. I have in mind a certain teacher whom I have heard tell students during the flag rush to go ahead they had not done any thing until they had disobeyed the Principal — How absurd. This particular teacher is a cigarett[e] fiend. And he said that it is college life to disobey the President. I hope the time will soon come when teachers may be chosen for merit not merely because of being the son or daughter of a friend or some prominent person as I have been told is the case.

As I come in contact with the students and hear them talk and see just how they live now as compared with when I came to Tuskegee I am inclined to believe that the religious life of the institution is on the decline. And I firmly believe that the carelessness and indifference on the part of teachers in this direction and ragtime music and dancing are largely responsible. I am not particularly oppose[d] to either but I know that they are fast taking precedence to the sacred life and higher classed amusements. I believe that it is a mistake to allow so much dancing and ragtime music in the school, as they will get enough of this after they have gone out of school. When I came to Tuskegee dancing was not allowed and it seemed to me that we got along as well or better. As the case is now I often know two dances to be going on at the same time. It is almost impossible to have any kind of amusement now without dancing and ragtime music. Nothing but ragtime music is played in the dining hall during the meal time. I remember when, here in Tuskegee, the boy or girl that did practice singing ragtime songs or dancing because of the respect they had for his or her mother's religious and home teaching and the laws of the home church was highly respected by all others, but now it is just the op[p]osite. They are called slow and dull and non-society. The majority of our girls and boys are able to tell the origin and author of many of the ragtime songs but are not able to do the same of "The Tuskegee Song," "The Star Spangled Banner," or "Jesus Lover of My Soul."

It appears that persons employed here and placed at the head of Departments and Divisions should serve more as teachers to teach, persuade, influence and build up this mass of young Negro life to the highest standards of ideal living. Rather than that some of them seem to serve more as foremen, or "bosses," owners of a large lumber plant, ordering, commanding and driving the students and putting them out [of] the Divisions for most any trivial cause or offense at their will without ever being questioned as for the cause for sending the student out, and merely using the school for their own convenience and as a money making proposition. It is a common occur[r]ence for as many [as] five or six teachers to meet in a certain Division and stand and converse aloud from one to two hours at a time about a game at the club or something else not pertaining to the business of their Divisions or the institution in any way. This is frequently done in the presence of students and I have often heard them talk about it. It does not seem that any instructor should draw a large salary and be able to remain away from his work so long for such minor causes. I said that they use the institution for a money making proposition. As an example, I know very recently in a certain Division where the students were put away from a certain phase of their trade work for some minor offense and a hired man placed in their stead. This was said to be only temporary but later another man was hired and the first man was allowed to hold the place where the students were supposed to receive instructions thus making a way to employ the second hired man. The majority of students are members of the Senior Class.

Great care should [be] exercised in the use of hired help. It has been my observation, that they are merely parasites. They are not at all interested in the welfare of the students nor the institution. It is in most cases a matter of making money. I have known them to slight their work during the day and tell the person in charge that work at night was a necessity, thus depriving the student of the practice that they should have during the day. I do not believe that it is possible for a man to work nine or ten hours each day and three or four hours nearly every night in the week and give good efficient service. I have known many times students who were Seniors in both their academic and industrial work and were not able to master some of the simplest work. This is because of too much of hired help. Any student of average ability in the third year at his trade should be able to do most any thing a Division may have to do, that is if the instructor has done his duty.

Experience has taught me that the hired men are usually of such a class that are detrimental to the student body. I have known student boys less than 17 years of age to be told such fa[s]cinating stories and jokes by these hired men that they become restless, left school "to try the world" as they call it for some of those wild experiences that had been told to them by these vicious persons. I have in mind one Division where there are several hired men employed and it is frequently [that] these persons report to work five and ten minutes after the bell rings and they quit some times five and ten minutes before time. I know these persons are paid from two to two dollars and fifty cents per day for their services. I have also known articles to be made for exhibition by the hired help and labeled as "made by students." This of course teaches untruthfulness, unreliability, dishonesty and deception.

In connection [with] all this there is so much "eye service" practiced among the teachers during your absence that the students practice the same when the teacher is absence. For example, When you are absent things grow very slack throughout the institution. The student's dining hall is a striking example. The services rendered are not carried out as I have heard you say that they should be. The students are poorly fed. The food is not properly prepared. And on the other hand when it [is] known that you are here or coming an extra effort is put forth to get things in order. The meals are better prepared and served more promp[t]ly. And every thing is made to appear as if it is kept in this manner during your absence. This teaches absolute "eye service," unreliability and dishonesty. It is dishonest because the person in charge is drawing a salary to do something that he claims that he has done that he has not done. It is stealing the character from 1200 to 1500 young people. It [is] depriving them of their health and strength by giving them improperly prepared food. I have seen as many [as] five boys fall out on the drill ground while standing in ranks waiting for inspection and was carried to the hospital. When I saw these boys again I asked them what seemed to be to their trouble and they said that they had weakness at the stomach and swimming at the head. They attributed [this] to the improperly prepared food given to them to eat in our dining hall. There is constant complaint among the students of being hungry and large sums of money are being spent annually without satisfactory results. I don't believe the students should ever have to go off the Tuskegee campus for the want of something to eat and to go into such places as they do to get what they call something fit to eat. I consider it a reflection upon our own "Tuskegee the pride of the Swift Growing South." It is a reflection upon our own Principal, "the Moses of his race," and the pride of every Tuskegee boy's and girl's heart. It is not the "quantity" but the "quality" of the food.

The last but not the least thing I wish to mention is that the habit of extravagance is taught in the case of charging for every phase of athletic sport. I believe that when a visiting team comes from a distance the student body should and would give ample support. But in case of games between classes and the foot race and potato race where there are no expenses incur[r]ed it is unreasonable to charge. I have known boys to spend their last penny to get into these games and borrow more.

Now, Mr. Washington, I sincerely hope that you will not feel that I am in any way trying to dictate the policy of the institution but simply have tried to remind you of some things which I doubted seriously that you knew. I am not particularly finding fault nor seeing the dark side of things. Hoping you will see it in the light as I have tried to place it, I am sincer[e]ly And truly yours,

Garfield McCaster

TLS Con. 509 BTW Papers DLC.

From Charles H. Fearing

Tuskegee Institute, Alabama February 2, 1914

Dear Mr. Washington: I have your note with reference to Davidson's work in the office:

I have given him a number of letters to answer and also have dictated to him from time to time. I shall continue to do so and do whatever I can to help him. May I venture the following suggestions with reference to his work; I make them for the reason that I believe they will help him:

Davidson is weak as to his spelling. I believe if you could get him to concentrate more upon this feature it would help him build the foundation which he needs.

I note that he does not write shorthand. This is not surprising for the reason that it is a very difficult matter for any person to acquire the ability to write shorthand within the space of three or four months. If he could confine himself to more regular study of this subject, it would perhaps enable him within the next two or three months to take slow dictation.

He is very careless. For example, in copying simple matter he makes errors that are inexcusable for the reason that he does not give close enough attention to what he is doing.

I hope you will take these suggestions in the spirit that I make them. I am intereste[d] in his development and make them only for that reason. Yours truly,

Chas. H. Fearing
Acting Secretary

TLS Con. 653 BTW Papers DLC.

To Adelia Hirshfield

[Tuskegee, Ala.] February 3, 1914

Dear Madam: The Association for the Advancement of the Negro is a society with headquarters at 70 Fifth Avenue, New York. Its main business so far as I understand it, is to agitate in favor of equal rights for colored people.

All the girls in our school are taught to cook. A portion of our graduates become teachers of cooking. Very few, I fear, take positions as cooks in private families. One reason is the competition of other employments in which the pay is better. Another is that parents do not, as a rule, like to have their daughters work as servants. They complain that the associations which young girls make in positions of that kind are not good. It is true that most of the girls who graduate here do, as a matter of fact, become housewives.

Practically the only way which a Normal School can help to solve the servant question in the South is to prepare teachers of cooking and try to get that subject taught in all the public schools. Yours truly,

Booker T. Washington

TLpSr Con. 504 BTW Papers DLC. Signed in Charles H. Fearing's hand.

Extracts from an Address at Harvard University

Harvard University, February 4, 1914

Every man going out from this great University has a duty to perform not only in relation to his personal success, but in helping to solve the various problems relating to state and nation. Because of the superior advantages which you are enjoying, in a peculiar manner the solution of these problems will rest upon you. Just in the same degree in which you have received broad liberal culture, you should be willing and anxious to give your service in lightening the burdens of others; in seeing that every man, no matter what his race or color is, has a fair chance, is permitted to have all the opportunities for growth and usefulness that is accorded to every other human being.

I hope that when you go away from here and enter upon your life career, whether it is in private business or in some public service, that you will seek an opportunity to let the members of my race know that you are interested in it; not only interested in the race as a whole, but interested in the individual members of the race. It is not always an easy task for one to manifest interest in persons who are members of what is commonly considered an unpopular race, but just in the degree that you manifest the courage and the deep interest to break through prejudice and custom and show that you are interested in the members of all the human family and desire to benefit humanity regardless of race or color, just in the same degree will you yourselves be strengthened and broadened and your life sweetened.

*   *   *   *

My race owes much to Harvard University; much for its spirit of fairness and justice. Here above all places a man is measured by his

434

ability, and I hope that this spirit and this disposition will always be manifest at Harvard.

* * * *

My race is often classed as an unfortunate race. I do not sympathize with such classification. On the other hand, I am proud that I am identified with the colored race in America. I would rather be classed as a black man in this country than as a white man. I belong to a race that has problems to solve, difficulties to overcome every day in the year, and one of the means by which the young colored men and women throughout this country are developing themselves in mind and in spirit is through the service which they are rendering to their less fortunate brothers and sisters, and in proportion as educated colored men and women render this service they receive a breadth of mind and sympathy and have brought into their lives a sweetness and satisfaction which rarely comes to the educated men and women of any race.

I would not care to live in any age or in any country where there were not problems to be solved and difficulties to over come, and the educated men and women of my race are striving to do their share in solving America's problems, and just in proportion as they strive to do this they should have the sympathy, the encouragement and the cooperation of every American citizen and especially of those who are placed as you are with the opportunities of receiving the highest and best university training.

TDc   Con. 957   BTW Papers   DLC.

To Booker Taliaferro Washington, Jr.

[Tuskegee, Ala.] Feb. 7, 1914

Think good plan for Nettie to take lessons in domestic science at some of institutions there. Mrs. Hall[1] I think might suggest good institution.

B.T.W.

TWcIr   Con. 526   BTW Papers   DLC.   Addressed to Chicago.

[1] Mrs. George Cleveland Hall.

From G. B. Zahniser

New Castle, Pa. Feb. 7, 1914

Sir, The proposition has been made in this city of 40000, with 6500 school children, 104 of whom are colored, to segregate these colored children, and give them a colored teacher. This for the purpose of holding out an inducement to these 104 children to fit themselves for teaching, &c &c.

As a real friend of the colored people I doubt the wisdom of such a course here, however I do not know enough about the matter to judge so take the liberty of writing to you for advice. There is no race feeling against these children either in the community or in the schools, and they are scattered all over the city in our 16 schools. Respectfully

G B Zahniser
Member New Castle School Board

ALS   Con. 521   BTW Papers   DLC.

To Daniel Edward Howard

[Tuskegee, Ala.] February [8?], 1914

My dear President Howard: Thank you many times for sending me a copy of your Inaugural Address. I have read every line of it. It is fine. I am especially interested to note that you promise to emphasize the amalgamation in some form of the Liberian and native population. It seems to me that the whole future of Liberia hinges upon its ability to get hold of the native population. The grasping hungry European governments, I feel, will not long permit only a few thousand Liberians to occupy so large and valuable a territory, unless they can show that the natives are a live, vital part of the national life.

We have not forgotten the school project and you will hear from me regarding this later on.

I wish for you the greatest success in your administration. Yours very truly,

Booker T. Washington

TLpS   Con. 918   BTW Papers   DLC.

From Robert Heberton Terrell

[Washington, D.C.] February 8, 1914

My dear Dr. Washington, Bishop Walters has worked indefatigably in carrying out the plans upon which you and he agreed with reference to my appointment. He saw the President Thursday and was informed that I would be surely reappointed. The President said that I had the best endorsements, written and oral, that had been brought to his notice. On Friday the Bishop and I called on a number of Democratic Senators who assured us that my nomination would be confirmed if sent in.

Yesterday we had a most satisfactory talk with the Attorney General.[1] I beg to thank you for your deep interest in my case. Sincerely yours,

R. H. Terrell

ALS Con. 525 BTW Papers DLC.

[1] James Clark McReynolds.

From George Wesley Harris

New York February 12, 1914

My Dear Doctor: Owing to the trouble I met with in finding the emigrant's boat I could not get back to the station until nearly eleven. You said, I think, that you would be there at eleven and possibly at ten. However I found about fifty very ignorant, with one or two exceptions, plain, negro farming people on board the old vessel which is in Crane's dry dock for repairs. The general overhauling of the vessel has not yet begun and will await Chief Sam's[1] return who left, they told me on Monday evening for New York and New England points. Their faith in him while almost childlike is however seemingly beginning to waver just a little. I told them, however that if I could do anything for them I was at their service and it being such a blizzardy night on the seashore none of those directly in charge, a Prof. W. H. Lewis,[2] Revs. A. Davis[3] and G. W. Lane[4] could be induced under any circumstances to go anywhere till the following morning and then of

437

course I knew it would be impossible for them to see you. I am keeping in close touch with the situation and if Chief Sam does not return Monday as they expect something will turn up, I believe. They also expect to sail for Galveston, early in the week but you can see how it will be impossible for them to get away under any circumstances within two weeks if the Curityba is to undergo overhauling. They paid $69,000, they say, for the ship and altogether $20,000 additional has been raised. Of this fund the white agent Smith,[5] of high rolling reputation in Harlem, is sole custodian. The ship is 27 years old and would not, seamen told us, stand an ocean voyage. A great dry dock repair bill will result and a shipbuilder's lien would tie it up there indefinitely. To this end I think Chief Sam is scouting for funds and Smith may be manuvering for his 'shakedown'. Smith is not bonded. I shall let you know everything on Monday and will await your orders. You will find Times story, correct, enclosed.[6] Yours Very Respectfully

George W. Harris

ALS Con. 504 BTW Papers DLC.

[1] Alfred Charles Sam was born about 1880 in the Gold Coast (present-day Ghana) but was probably not the chief he claimed to be. In 1911 he founded the Akim Trading Co. in New York for trade between the United States and his homeland, but when this company encountered legal problems he withdrew and started another company in South Dakota.

In 1913 Sam began to recruit emigrants from small farms in Oklahoma, where disfranchisement and cotton depression made his promise of a better life in Africa especially appealing. Mass meetings raised the money needed to purchase a ship, and Sam and his followers ignored warnings from the British government and many prominent blacks that they would not find a welcome or livelihood in the Gold Coast.

Since there were more would-be emigrants than Sam could transport at once, he and delegates of the emigrants gathered in New York in Oct. 1913 to take over a German-built, Cuban-owned steel ship, the *Curityba,* which they rechristened the *Liberia.* They brought the *Liberia* around to Galveston, where additional emigrants boarded, and the ship sailed for Africa in Aug. 1914. Sixty chosen passengers with Sam at their head reached Saltpond, Gold Coast, on Jan. 13, 1915, traveled overland to Sam's birthplace, but found they could only borrow the tribal land, which was of poor quality. After an eight-month stay and some deaths, the party tried to leave. But the *Liberia* was seized by the courts, Sam abandoned the group and became a cocoa buyer, and the crew of the ship, after being hospitalized with fever, were returned to the United States. A majority of the emigrants returned to America on a British ship in late 1915; few if any settled permanently in West Africa. (Redkey, *Black Exodus,* 291–93.)

[2] W. H. Lewis, a graduate of Fisk and a teacher in Wewoka, Okla., was one of A. C. Sam's principal lieutenants in Oklahoma. He addressed the local black

citizens in behalf of the emigration proposal and was one of the most zealous of the emigrants. He died soon after the arrival of the party in the Gold Coast. (Bittle and Geis, *The Longest Way Home,* 82, 106–7, 197.)

[3] Reverend A. Davis, one of the passengers, spoke and sang at the christening of the *Liberia* at Galveston, Tex., July 5, 1914.

[4] Reverend G. W. Lane of Wewoka, Okla., with another black supporter of Chief Sam, secured an interview with the governor of Oklahoma, who gave him a letter of introduction to the British ambassador in Washington. (Bittle and Geis, *The Longest Way Home,* 93.)

[5] A. E. Smith, New York agent of the Akim Trading Co., was the only white man at a high level in Sam's movement. He received all of the funds which Sam collected in Oklahoma and sent in money orders, gave ambiguous but friendly information to the New York press, and arranged the purchase of the *Curityba.* After it set sail he disappeared. He and Sam were cleared of allegations of fraudulent use of the mails by a federal postal inspector. (Bittle and Geis, *The Longest Way Home,* 97–100, 113–16, 125, 134.)

[6] The enclosed clipping from the New York *Times,* Feb. 11, 1914, described in detail the emigration scheme of Alfred Charles Sam, his arrangements with Oklahoma emigrants, his Akim Trading Co., and his relations with the white promoter A. E. Smith. His ship *Curityba,* built in Hamburg in 1887, was purchased from the Munson Line, which had used it in trade between New York and Havana.

From Cornelius Bailey Hosmer

Tuskegee Institute, Ala. Feb. 13, 1914

Dear Dr. Washington: For the week ending today, I am pleased to make the following report:

The Negro Farmer is gradually increasing its circulation. We have received entirely by mail this week twenty-three (23) subscriptions — which makes a total of one hundred forty-six paid up subscriptions. We have two hundred four subscriptions now. It is noticeable, however, that so far, stockholders of the publication are not subscribing for it. We trust, eventually, each stockholder will become a subscriber to the Negro Farmer.

We have had printed and mailed the second issue. 2,100 copies were made; and we have shipped and mailed 1,800 copies of this second issue, which is dated Feb. 14th. The front page picture is a striking feature.

After consulting Mr. Scott, Mr. Logan and Dr. Park, we decided it would be a good thing — a good advertising stroke, to let Mr. Fisher, editor, take the trip to Demopolis, Uniontown and Snow Hill, Ala., with several hundred copies of the paper — visiting with Mr. T. M. Campbell farmers' conferences and meetings at those places. The purpose of the trip by Mr. Fisher is to create interest in our new publication, to secure subscriptions for it and advertise it. This kind of advertising ought to prove especially helpful.

We are making progress. Very sincerely yours,

C. B. Hosmer

TLS Con. 512 BTW Papers DLC.

To G. B. Zahniser

[Tuskegee, Ala.] February 14, 1914[1]

Personal

Dear Sir: There are some advantages, no doubt, in what is called the segregation of the races in their schools and this is especially true where there is active race prejudice. But there are also many disadvantages, some of which we know and some of which we have no knowledge.

I should regard it as a misfortune to have this question of the separation of the races raised in a community where there was no demand for it on the part of either race. The best thing to do for both races is not to disturb them if they are getting on together. This is my candid opinion about the matter. Yours very truly,

Booker T. Washington

TLpSr Con. 521 BTW Papers DLC. Signed in E. J. Scott's hand. Addressed to "G. B. Lahmiser."

[1] The year was typed as 1915, but the letter is in response to G. B. Zahniser to BTW, Feb. 7, 1914, above. Zahniser's letter and the reply are filed in Container 521, which is a 1914 file.

To the Editor of the Macon *News*

[Tuskegee, Ala.] February 16, 1914

Dear Sir: I note what you say in your editorial under date of January 22d regarding my letter on lynching.

I think if you will re-read what I have said on lynching you will find I have not in any case referred to the South. I have preferred to treat the subject in a national way rather than in a sectional way. No one has a higher regard for the South or more love for it than I have. Yours truly,

Booker T. Washington

TLpS   Con. 509   BTW Papers   DLC.

From Leola Chambers

Moodus Conn. 2–16–1914

Dear Sir; This clipping from the 'Hartford Courant' is something that I have wanted to know your opinion about, but didn't dare to write until I read this.[1] It may be foolish of me to think of such things, and to want you to tell me what you think about it, but do you suppose if we should stop telling so many jokes about our chicken stealing, the white people would soon think we had quit stealing and begun to raise our own? (a good many of us are doing so). I heard your lecture in Hartford Jan 22,[2] and I did enjoy it so much. I hope I will hear you again soon. I wanted to shake your hand, but didn't have the opportunity.

Com. Moton said something I didn't like, but I guess he meant well. He was speaking of you and your home, and said, 'He was up and out among his *own* chickens at 5 o'clock." Do you think it was necessary for him to emphasize the word 'own' as he did? I have been staying with white people since I was 17, (21 now) I've never told them one story about colored people stealing chickens & I think it is awful. please let me know as soon as possible what you think about it. Yours truly

(Miss) Leola Chambers

ALS   Con. 522   BTW Papers   DLC.

[1] See An Account of an Address in Hartford, Connecticut, Jan. 28, 1914, above.
[2] Actually Jan. 28.

To William Colfax Graves

[Tuskegee, Ala.] February 17, 1914

Dear Mr. Graves: I have received your kind letter regarding Mr. Banks's cotton seed oil mill situation.[1] I have no direct information on the matter, but shall proceed to get as reliable information on the points your letter raises as soon as possible and let you hear from me. I am very glad you wrote so promptly.

We hope Mr. and Mrs. Rosenwald are having a restful time. Our Trustees come this week and we are all going to miss the visit of Mr. Rosenwald and the Chicago party more than I can explain. Yours very truly,

Booker T. Washington

TLpS Con. 255 BTW Papers DLC.

[1] Graves wrote BTW on Feb. 14, 1914, asking him to find out discreetly the current financial status of the Mound Bayou Oil Mill Co. Julius Rosenwald had subscribed $25,000 of a total bond issue of $40,000, the remainder being purchased by B. B. Harvey of Memphis. Hearing during Rosenwald's vacation in Europe that I. T. Montgomery was recently in Chicago and St. Louis trying to sell additional stock, Graves sought information in anticipation that Rosenwald would be asked for further assistance. (Con. 255, BTW Papers, DLC.)

To George Wesley Harris

[Tuskegee, Ala.] February 17th, 1914

How is African party coming on? If you think they are inclined to give up trip and locate in this county we could offer encouragement. Am attending to other matter which I spoke to you about today. Answer my expense.

Booker T. Washington

TWSr Con. 504 BTW Papers DLC.

To George Wesley Harris

[Tuskegee, Ala.] February 17, 1914

Dear Mr. Harris: I have your two letters. I am very much obliged to you for the information you sent with reference to the "Chief Sam" expedition. I have carefully noted all that you wrote, as well as all that the clipping from "The Times" states. You have received my telegram by now. I shall be glad to hear further from you.

I am enclosing herewith a small amount, $15.00, covering special advertising in The News, your newspaper. I wish I could do more but our advertising resources have been drawn upon so considerably, lately, that at this time this is all that I am able to send you. Yours very truly,

Booker T. Washington

TLpSr Con. 504 BTW Papers Signed in E. J. Scott's hand.

Charles William Anderson to Emmett Jay Scott

New York, N.Y. February 17, 1914

My dear Emmett: Only a line to say that I have concluded to resign from the League[1] because of that scoundrel Tyler. I cannot support any man or body of men, giving support to such a viper as this. He is now attacking Terrell. The dirty coward has assailed every one who has ever served him. He has made our politics bad and he is now trying to make our business bad. He is arraying friend against friend and brother against brother, causing discord where there should be harmony, promoting hatred where there should be concord and mutual respect. He is teaching men whose friendship for the Doctor has been sincere and loyal, to fight for their own sword. I, for one, am willing to take up the gauge. I have had quite enough of following people whose friends are flying at my throat, and I have concluded to put an end to it. Hereafter those who dislike me will find that there are blows to give as well as blows to take. Yours very truly,

Charles W. Anderson

TLSr Copy Con. 849 BTW Papers DLC.

[1] National Negro Business League.

To Quincy Ewing

[Tuskegee, Ala.] February 18th, 1914

My dear Mr. Ewing: My wife read to me last evening your fine letter published in THE EVENING POST, of February 13th on Senator Vardaman, and I want to thank you again and again for your fine, brave expressions.[1] I am sure that there will be great good accomplished.

It is all the more deplorable that men of the type of Vardaman should be misrepresenting the South, when in my opinion there is a very friendly feeling existing between the white and colored people of the South. I have never known a period when there was such a disposition on the part of the white people to help the colored people.

I am sure that the career and influence of a man like Vardaman can only be short-lived at best.

It might interest you to know that I received through a committee of colored citizens, an invitation from the Governor of your state[2] to make a tour of the state sometime in the near future.

Please come to see us whenever you can, we shall always extend to you a hearty welcome. Yours very truly,

Booker T. Washington

TLpS Con. 501 BTW Papers DLC.

[1] Ewing attacked Senator James K. Vardaman's allegation that white women in the South were living in a "state of siege" because of the large black population. He stated that the real reason Vardaman was such a negrophobe was his desire to keep his Senate seat, since it was his abuse of blacks that got him elected in the first place. He said: "But let it be here added that there are thousands of good people in Mississippi whom Mr. Vardaman is not fooling today, and *never has fooled.*" (New York *Evening Post,* Feb. 13, 1914, 6.) Ewing replied to BTW's letter that he knew Vardaman was "deliberately employing abuse of the Negro" and that BTW's work at Tuskegee "makes the Vardamans of to-day ridiculous." (Feb. 23, 1914, Con. 501, BTW Papers, DLC.)

[2] Luther Egbert Hall, governor of Louisiana 1912–16.

From George Wesley Harris

New York City, February 18th, 1914

African party tells me tonight tied up here indefinitely, but not willing to admit failure. Will report at first break. Need matter for today's issue, will you wire me at once?

George W. Harris

TWSr Con. 504 BTW Papers DLC.

From Robert Heberton Terrell

Washington, Feb 18, 1914

My dear Doctor Washington, The President sent my name to the Senate today. I am the only one of the four retiring judges reappointed. This appears to me to be rather a compliment.

I thank you for your support. Sincerely yours,

R H Terrell

ALS Con. 525 BTW Papers DLC.

To Robert Heberton Terrell

[Tuskegee, Ala.] Feb. 19, 1914

My warmest and most cordial congratulations upon your reappointment by President Wilson. It is an honor well deserved.

Booker T. Washington

TWSr Con. 525 BTW Papers DLC.

To Ralph Waldo Tyler

[Tuskegee, Ala.] February 20th, 1914

Dear Mr. Tyler: Replying further to yours of February 14th, I will say that I see no way out of the dilemma except to let the present hysteria run its course, which it will do within a few days. Then, perhaps, we can decide upon some definite, constructive plan.

Regarding your suggestion that radical newspapers pay better than the others, I wonder if you know about the experiences of our friend Trotter at Boston, whose paper is in the front rank of the radical papers. He has to go about on Saturdays with his hat in his hand to collect money in order to get his paper out of the printing office. In the meantime, he has lost every cent of property he owned, and is in a miserable condition financially.

I have spoken recently, at Boston, Springfield, Hartford, and Pittsburgh and had a tremendous reception at every point. I did not hear the Advancement Movement mentioned in any case. Yours very truly,

Booker T. Washington

TLpS   Con. 525   BTW Papers   DLC.

To Garfield McCaster

[Tuskegee, Ala.] February 20, 1914

Mr. Garfield McCaster: I have received your communication of January 30th, and I want to thank you for your thoughtfulness in writing me.

I assure you I appreciate what you say and shall take measures to look into the whole matter and do whatever is necessary to bring things into better condition wherever I feel that a remedy ought to be put into effect.[1]

I shall be glad to hear from you at any time whenever you have anything to say that you think will improve the condition of the institution.

Booker T. Washington

TLpS   Con. 509   BTW Papers   DLC.

¹ BTW appointed a committee to investigate the charges in McCaster's letter of Jan. 30, 1914. See From Charles G. Kelley *et al.*, Feb. 28, 1914, below.

To Charles William Anderson

[Tuskegee, Ala.] February 20, 1914

My dear Mr. Anderson: I have just seen the letter written by you to Mr. Scott:

I have directed Mr. Scott not to accept your resignation but to leave the matter in my hands for a few weeks, and I think you will find conditions will change. We cannot afford to accept your resignation. Yours very truly,

Booker T. Washington

TLpS Con. 849 BTW Papers DLC.

From George Wesley Harris

New York Feb 20 1914

My Dear Dr Washington: I want to thank you for your letter just recieved with its enclosure, receipt for which you will find enclosed. It comes at a time when it is badly needed as it enabled me to finish a bill for this week. But I am, too, sorry, Doctor, that you could not help me substantially at this time. The Amsterdam News has not been able as yet to get its paper out for this week and as their printer is the same as ours I am sure of what I am telling you that if I can get the News out for the next two weeks I am saved and will have the field practically to myself. I was hoping that you would lend me about two hundred dollars personally for about 6 months on my note. I am sure that you would never regret it for it would be the means of saving what I am determined must be someday a genuinely great and strong race institution. Unless I can get this amount by Wednesday or at least one half of it by that time I fear I can not get the paper out next week.

If I can get the News out for the next weeks I am saved for all time, Doctor. If you can do this for me will you wire me Monday, please.

I am still keeping close watch on the Chief Sam party and something will develop in a very few days. Am going down to the boat again tomorrow. Dr. Sinclair was in to see me Monday and told me that Mr. Milholland sails from England on February 28 and that things will hum when he arrives. Relations between the "scholar" and editor[1] are becoming more strained he said despite the fact that the former is siding on every vital question with the latter. Hoping that you will strain a point Doctor, and help me in a way that will be a lifesaver to The News I am As Ever   Yours Very Respectfully,

George W. Harris

ALS Con. 504 BTW Papers DLC.

[1] W. E. B. Du Bois and O. G. Villard.

A Memorandum on Washington's Itinerary

[Tuskegee, Ala.] Feb 20/14

Memorandum covering Mr. Washington's time at the school and engagements away from the school following his California trip through April and May.

Return to Tuskegee from California March 27th
At Tuskegee March 27th to April 6th, inc. This includes Palm
   Sunday, April 5th, ... 9 days
April 5th to 8th, Southern Sociological Congress, probably
   Louisville, Kentucky
" 10th. Birmingham, Ala. State Teachers' Assn.
Leave Birmingham for New York.
In New York April 12th to 21st .... 10 days
Wisconsin tour April 23rd to 30th inc. eight days
New Jersey tour May 3rd to 9th inc. seven days. The major
   portion of these seven days may be spent in N. Y. .... 7 days
May 10th, Concord, N.H. St. Paul's School
Following this meeting you could return to Tuskegee, or, you
   could remain in New York until the 18th, an additional ... 7 days

You could then arrive at Tuskegee four days before Commencement, which will begin May 24th.

Total days in New York April and May .... 24 days

Number of days in Tuskegee:
9 days in April.

10 days in May if you do not return to Tuskegee immediately after the engagement at Concord, N.H., May 10th. If you return immediately after the Concord engagement, you will have 20 days at Tuskegee.

Engagements — Decided

February	21 —	Tuskegee Institute Trustee Meeting
March	7–22 —	California Trip. Dr. John Willis Baer,[1] Occidental College, Los Angeles
April	5 —	Palm Sunday. You wish to be at Tuskegee this date.
"	5–8 —	Southern Sociological Congress. Place, probably Louisville.
"	10 —	Birmingham, Ala. State Teachers' Assn.
"	12 —	Easter. You wish to be at Tuskegee this date.
" Last week		Wisconsin trip
May first week	—	New Jersey trip
"	10 —	Concord, N.H. St. Paul's School. Mr. G. M. Brinley[2]
"	24–28 —	Tuskegee Institute Commencement
June bet.	10–15 —	Auburn, N.Y. Unveiling of Harriet Tubman Memorial. Rev. Paul Moore Strayer,[3] Rochester, N.Y. Mr. C. G. Adams,[4] Bank Building, Auburn, N.Y. While on this trip, visit Prison. Mr. Thomas Mott Osborne,[5] Auburn, N.Y.
July	21 —	Tuskegee Institute for meeting of Mosaic Templars. Mr. J. E. Bush, Box 36, Little Rock, Ark.
August	7–9–10–11 —	Under auspices of Co-Operative Chautauqua Assn. Mr. James L. Loar,[6] Bloomington, Ill. One address Friday, Aug. 7; two Sunday, Aug. 9; one Monday, Aug. 10 and one

> Tuesday, Aug. 11. Total fee for five engage-
> ments $775.

" 19–20–21 — Muskogee, Oklahoma. Business League Meet-
> ing

" 23 — Camargo, Ill. Patterson Springs Chautauqua.
> Mr. W. D. Higdon,[7] 4031 Wyoming Street,
> St. Louis, Mo.

October 11–17 — 150th Anniversary of Founding of Brown Uni-
> versity

" 19–24 — Macon County Fair

TD Con. 842 BTW Papers DLC.

[1] John Willis Baer (b. 1861), whom BTW had known in Boston as an official of the United Society of Christian Endeavor, was president of Occidental College in Los Angeles from 1906 to 1916.

[2] Godfrey Malbone Brinley, headmaster of St. Paul's School.

[3] Paul Moore Strayer (1871–1929), minister of the Third Presbyterian Church of Rochester, N.Y., from 1903 to 1920.

[4] Charles G. Adams was secretary of the Auburn, N.Y., businessmen's association.

[5] Thomas Mott Osborne (1859–1926) was a prison reformer. After a successful business career and a term (1903–6) as mayor of Auburn, N.Y., he was appointed chairman of the New York Commission on Prison Reform in 1913. He spent a week in prison to learn conditions at first hand. He was warden of Sing Sing (1914–16), commanding officer of Portsmouth Naval Prison (1917–20), and author of three books on prison problems.

[6] James L. Loar was a lawyer.

[7] William D. Higdon, a teacher in McKinley High School in St. Louis.

To George Wesley Harris

[Tuskegee, Ala.] February 24, 1914

Dear Mr. Harris: I very much wish I could without hesitation comply with your request for a loan of $200 to help tide your newspaper over its present difficulties, but unfortunately I have no source from which to secure the money at this time. I need not tell you how much of a pleasure it would be for me to serve you if it were at all possible for me to do it. Yours very truly,

Booker T. Washington

TLpS Con. 504 BTW Papers DLC.

To Leola Chambers

[Tuskegee, Ala.] February 25, 1914

Dear Miss Chambers: In reply to your letter of February 16th, permit me to say that I do not think it is very good taste to tell chicken stealing jokes. My experience teaches me, however, that white people have a good deal more respect for us when we tell them on ourselves than they do when we try to make ourselves believe there are no such jokes going around.

On the other hand, if we take these anecdotes too seriously, people are likely to think that they are something more than jests. If we treat a joke merely as a joke, people will at least recognize that we have a sense of humor, and every man — I won't say anything about every woman — has respect for every other man who will laugh at the same jokes he does, particularly if the joke is on the man who tells it.

Thanking you for writing me, I am   Yours very truly,

Booker T. Washington

TLpSr Con. 522 BTW Papers DLC. Signed in E. J. Scott's hand.

To Woodrow Wilson

[Tuskegee, Ala.] February 25, 1914

Dear President Wilson: I want to thank you for re-appointing Judge Robert H. Terrell. It was my pleasure to recommend him a number of years ago for the same position to President Roosevelt, and it has been a great satisfaction to know that he has lived up to the recommendation that was given him. The whole race feels grateful to you. Yours very truly,

Booker T. Washington

TLpS Con. 526 BTW Papers DLC.

451

Timothy Thomas Fortune to Emmett Jay Scott

Harrisburg, Pa., Feb 25, 1914

My Dear Mr. Scott: I have been too unwell since I came here on the 12th instant to acknowledge receipt of your kind letter of the 11th instant. I am doing a little work for The Verdict and the usual for The Age.

I appreciate your faithful and affictionate sentiments for me and know you would serve me if you could. *But the seven years* have been lived in death, and have just reason to be believe[d] that I shall make my way in the future as I did before stricken in 1907. There are a few of the old friends remaining, you of them, but all the others are personally dead to me, including the Wizard.

With great affection, Yours as ever,

Thomas Fortune

ALS Con. 11 BTW Papers DLC. On stationery of the Harrisburg *Advocate-Verdict*.

Emmett Jay Scott to Lelia Brown Walters[1]

[Tuskegee, Ala.] February 26th, 1914

Dear Mrs. Walters: Doctor Washington asks me to write you immediately and say that he will be glad to have his name entered as one of the honorary members in connection with the celebration of the tenth anniversary of the African Redemption Society.

Doctor Washington received his knighthood because of his interest in the Liberian people prior to the trip of the American Commission to Liberia. Others also who have received such knighthood, are, Fred R. Moore, of the New York Age, Doctor Ernest Lyon, former American Minister to Liberia, Bishop Walters, of course, and myself. My award came after the American Commission had made its trip to Liberia and returned.

With kindest regards to Bishop Walters, I am   Yours very truly,

Emmett J. Scott

TLpS Con. 526 BTW Papers DLC.

[1] Lelia Brown Walters was the second wife of Bishop Alexander Walters.

From Tom Johnson

Margaret, Ala   Feb 27. 1914

Dear Sir. I was instructed by the Paper that yo an Mr chief-Sam —
was caring the colord Peoples to Aferica, to their own homes an if it
is true I wants to go my Self an four other familys. we or wating for
an ancer from yo an then we or ready to go as soon as we get a ancer
from yo. Yours Truly

Tom Johnson

Please ancer at once. we will meet yo at any Place that yo say for
us to meet yo.

ALS   Con. 507   BTW Papers   DLC.

From Charles G. Kelley, Edward W. Cummings, Marian R. Brown,[1] Henry C. Watson, John D. Stevenson, Emily Chun Moore,[2] and T. Jarvis Taylor[3]

[Tuskegee, Ala.] February 28th, 1914

Dr. B. T. Washington: Principal. The Committee appointed to look
into the statements made in a letter from a Graduate of the Institution,
feel that you have used rare judgement in selecting *them* to make this
investigation as, in a degree each member is able to answer directly
as to the truthfulness of one or more of the statements.

As a body they do not feel that a *true* bill should be returned by
them, as all of the charges as stated are not borne out by the facts in
the case. Concerning the different counts in the Indictment we wish
to reply to them, as they are set forth by the author in his letter.

Count #1.

That the larger majority of the faculty does not represent what (the
writer) thinks, are your ideals of real dignified representative men and
women of the highest standards of culture, refinement and moral
character.

453

We feel that this charge is without foundation and there is no truth in it. In fact the conditions in this respect are just the opposite to what he claims. The larger majority of the faculty are what would be, regarded by any sane individual to represent the best type of our race to be found anywhere, this is borne out by statements of the many visitors that come to our Institution from time to time. In regard to the use of curse words by a teacher before a student, this might and does happen once in a while at a moment of anger or unguarded thought, but we are positive that there are no habitual users of profanity that are members of our faculty.

Count #2.

While there is considerable slang expression used by some teachers and students, we do not regard this a serious habit, and in any degree detrimental to the development of good manners to the student body, for where ever you find a large body of teachers as it is true of condition here, it would be almost impossible to eliminate slang expressions altogether.

Count #3.

Concerning faculty members dressing beyond their means, we are unable to find out positively what the means are, and we doubted if the writer of the letter could positively state what their income is.

Count #4.

If the author has definite knowledge as to persons on the faculty or otherwise employed who smoke cigarett[e]s and use intoxicants we would suggest that you ask him for these names and you as Principal take the matter up with them as individuals. As in the absence of any definite information we are unable to verify this charge.

Count #5.

In the matter of selecting members of the faculty this is entirely in your and the council hands, and if the charge as stated about the method of choosing teachers is true we suggest that you as Principal will investigate this matter.

Count #6.

We feel that at the present time the religious life of the Institution (while it could be better) is far above what it has been, in the past, and we are sure is much better than when, as he says, he entered the Institution.

Count #7.

In regard to dancing, we concur in this statement, but feel that you have amply taken care of this condition. In reference to rag time music it is something that appeals to the average person of this generation, and it would be impossible to eliminate it entirely from among us, but would suggest that it not be indulged in too often in the Dining Hall during meal hours.

Count #8.

We feel that a person is no less an individual because he or she is unable to tell the author of "Jesus Lover of my soul," but might happen to know the author of some rag time song.

Count #9.

In regard to statement of the author, that the heads of department and divisions, send students out of their division without cause, and the handling of students in a way which the writer of the letter feels it not right, and using the school as a convenience and money making proposition, we are unable to verify, and we think that if this condition is true, that the heads of departments who are members of the council should have knowledge of it.

Count #10.

We find that the statement, that as many as five or six teachers congregate during work hours, and conversing for one or two hours about happenings at the Club or other matters not pertaining to the Institution, is utterly false.

Count #11.

We feel that the matter of employing hired men, if it is done, to perform work that a student could do is a matter that the Executive Council has knowledge of and should be dealt with through that body.

Count #12.

In regard to the hired men not giving value received in work for monies paid them, we are unable to verify this charge, but if such condition exist the heads of departments and divisions employing such men should have knowledge of such a condition and alter them.

Count #13.

In regard to the vicious influence that hired men might have over some students to such an extent that it would cause them to leave school, we are unable to find any instance where this has been true.

Count #14.

In the statement of articles being made by hired men and exhibited as being "made by students" is to some extent true, and should be discontinued.

Count #15.

While to some extent "Eye service" might be indulged in by some teachers, we feel that on the whole there is not a more loyal body of co-workers to be found anywhere than is true of your force here at Tuskegee.

It is a natural characteristic of any individual, or any group of individuals to put forth an extra effort to have conditions at their best, on the return after an absence of one who they look to as their leader.

Count #16.

In regard to the complaint about preparation of food in the dining hall, this is nothing new, and there is considerable ground for such a complaint, and we feel that much improvement could be made in the preparation of the food.

Count #17.

In regard to the criticism about charging an admission fee to Athletic sports. We feel that no other similar school anywhere gives to the students and others, such excellent entertainment along this line at so small a cost to them as we do here. In the matter of income from athletics no individual receives any financial benefit therefrom, but the entire income is used to defray expenses [in]curred in handling this phase of the school's duty to the student. Concerning the charge as set forth in the letter about teachers smoking cigarett[e]s and cigars, we feel that so little of this habit is seen around the campus and the village, that there is little cause for complaint of this account. This custom is being indulged in less in public now than ever before around here.

Chairman Chas. G. Kelley
E. W. Cummings
Marian R. Brown
H. C. Watson
J. D. Stevenson
E. C. Moore
T. Jarvis Taylor

TLS Con. 648 BTW Papers DLC.

[1] Marian R. Brown was instructor of ladies' tailoring in the department of women's industries at Tuskegee Institute from 1912 to 1914.

[2] Emily Chun Moore taught vocal music at Tuskegee for many years beginning in 1904, the year she graduated from Tuskegee.

[3] T. Jarvis Taylor taught history and geography at Tuskegee from 1909 to 1914. In 1914–15 he was in charge of the academic division office.

A Press Release

Tuskegee Institute, Alabama, February 28, 1914

RAILROAD ACCOMMODATIONS
FOR NEGROES

Editor: Some months ago, I sent out marked copies to railway officials in every part of the South of an article written for the Century Magazine in which I referred to the unjust treatment of colored people on railroads. In addition a letter was written, calling attention to the portion of the article marked.

It might interest those of our people who are seeking to improve the bad conditions that exist on many railroads, to read some of the replies from these officials to these communications. In one case, for example, the president of the railroad had a copy of the "Century" article placed in the hands of every officer on his road.

I am asking that you publish the extracts from these letters, because a little later on it is my purpose to urge our people to set aside one day in the year that might be called "Railroad Day" upon which throughout the country wherever conditions demand it, we can go to the officials of the railroads and speak to them about the bad conditions that exist with a view of our co-operating with these railroad officials in order to bring about better conditions.

I think the extracts from these letters indicate that the railroad officials are now in a state of mind where in most cases they are willing to recognize the justice of our claim for better things; in fact, some of them have already acted.

When the proper time comes, we should take up with the officials concerned, the matter of accommodations provided in restaurants, sitting rooms, street cars, steam cars, steamboats, etc. For the present, I am giving you these extracts for publication in order to show that there is an opportunity, if we go about it in the right way, to do away with what has been a long standing source of complaint.

BOUND TO RECEIVE ATTENTION

Mr. C. J. Millis, Assistant to President William Sproule of the Southern Pacific, writes: "Am very much obliged by your letter of October 9th transmitting your printed article 'Is the Negro Having a Fair Chance,' and note with interest your reference to transportation facilities afforded in the South. These matters are bound to receive attention and we hope the objections will be overcome in due course.

ALREADY MAKING IMPROVEMENT

Mr. William J. Black, Passenger Manager of Atchison, Topeka & Santa Fe Railway System, wrote as follows: "I am in receipt of your favor of the 8th inst., enclosing an article by yourself recently published in the 'Century' Magazine, which I have read with interest. You will, no doubt, be pleased to learn that the Santa Fe has already provided equipment for colored travel in conformity with the plan outlined in your article. At the present time 75 per cent of the coaches used in Oklahoma and Texas for colored people have two compartments, one being a smoking compartment and the other for men and women, and they have separate toilet facilities for each sex. As new cars are purchased, or present ones are converted, they will be of that type, and we expect before long to have all of our cars for colored traffic on the same plan."

COMPLAINTS WELL-FOUNDED

Mr. J. M. Parker, Receiver and General Manager, The Arkansas, Louisiana and Gulf Railway Company, says: "I have your favor with enclosure, being marked copy of an article which recently appeared in the Century Magazine. I shall take pleasure in reading this article and from glancing through it, I am inclined to think that the statement that the Negro is not getting a square deal in the way of transportation facilities, is well-founded."

APPRECIATES COLORED PATRONAGE

Mr. W. Coughlin, General Superintendent, Missouri, Oklahoma and Gulf Railway Company, wrote: "I have carefully read the article to which you have called special attention and in connection therewith wish to say that while, no doubt there is ground for complaint at times, am inclined to the opinion that as a whole the situation alluded to is improving. In fact, accommodations for white and colored passengers on our motor car trains are identical. On other trains there is not much difference except in emergency cases where it becomes necessary to use temporary equipment that was not intended for passenger trains, but such cars as are used for the handling of both white and colored passengers, as well as employees on freight trains. I assure you that our company appreciates the patronage of the colored people, and that it is our desire to do what we can consistently for their comfort and convenience while traveling on our road."

RAILWAYS NOT PHILANTHROPISTS

Mr. W. B. Biddle, Receiver and Chief Traffic Officer of the St. Louis and San Francisco Railroad, writes: "I have read yours of October 10th and the pamphlet enclosed with a great deal of interest. I am quite sure that there is a disposition on the part of the carriers to do anything that they properly can to improve the conditions of the colored race. The conditions under which the carriers are operating at this time are, in many respects, so burdensome as to leave very little opportunity for the adoption of any philanthropic movements. I shall be very glad, however, to discuss this subject with the executive officers of other lines as opportunity offers."

DOES NOT APPLY TO MISSOURI PACIFIC

Mr. B. F. Bush, President of The Missouri Pacific Railway Company, states: "The conditions cited in the article are not applicable to the Missouri Pacific. It is a fact that separate cars are maintained on the St. Louis, Iron Mountain & Southern for the Negroes, but my information is that they are cleanly kept and adequate to meet all demands. However, I thank you for bringing the matter to my attention."

ARE MAKING IMPROVEMENTS

Mr. N. M. Leach, Traffic Manager, The Texas & Pacific Railway Company, writes: "In recent times the T. & P. R'y has made some improvement in the service afforded our colored patrons, and we are making an effort to further improve this service. We have received a number of expressions of appreciation from our colored patrons in Louisiana and Texas. I have read all of your article with a great deal of interest."

Given Careful Consideration

Mr. W. G. Van Vleck, writing for the president, Mr. W. B. Scott, of the Sunset-Central Lines, says: "The matters referred to in your letter October 10th have been given very careful consideration by these Lines. A few months ago we installed in our Sunset Express all steel equipment and precisely the same character of car is used for colored as well as white passengers. Later on we did the same thing with Nos. 7 and 8, and still later Nos. 11 and 12. These cars are all-steel and all of the same kind. On the Central Lines North of Houston, trains 15, 16, 17 and 18, and on H. E. & W. T. trains 1 and 2 are similarly equipped. Local trains will be taken care of as fast as more equipment of this kind is available."

Letter Forwarded to Mr. Gould

Mr. George H. Taylor, Vice-president of the International and Great Northern Railway Company, writes as follows: "I have your letter of the 11th instant, addressed to Mr. Frank J. Gould, enclosing copy of your article recently printed in 'The Century Magazine' entitled 'The Greatest Source of Dissatisfaction to the Negro in the South'; namely, Railway Travel conditions. I have forwarded your letter and its enclosures to Mr. Gould in France."

Statement Entirely Right

Mr. J. E. Franklin, President of the San Antonio, Uvalde & Gulf Railroad, replies as follows: "I think you are entirely right in what you say in the pamphlet you enclose me. So far as this Railroad is concerned, we are in a section of Texas where there is not much Negro travel, but we are giving the Negroes just as good accommodations as we are giving to the whites."

Appreciates the Colored Travel

Mr. J. C. Haile, General Passenger Agent of the Central of Georgia Railway Company writes: "Yours of recent date, with marked copy of an article which recently appeared in the Century Magazine, has been duly received. The same will be given consideration and I hope to write you further later. The management of this company appreciates the colored travel and we desire to handle it satisfactorily."

SUBJECT RECEIVING ATTENTION

Mr. A. A. Matthews, Superintendent of the Missouri, Kansas & Texas Railway System, says: "I have read with interest, your article entitled, 'Is the Negro Having a Fair Chance,' which you enclose with your letter of October 9th. The subject of better accommodation for Negro passengers is one that is receiving much thought by the railroads of the South and I think, as our lines are improved and better coaches are used, that the Negro will share in the benefit. As for the Texas Central except for a short distance, we very seldom handle Negro passengers but when we do their compartment in our coaches is upholstered the same and receives the same care as the part provided for white passengers."

RECEIVED THE ARTICLE

Mr. C. B. Rhodes, General Passenger Agent of the Georgia, Southern & Florida Railway Company, replies as follows: "I wish to acknowledge receipt of your letter of the 13th inst., enclosing marked copy of an article of yours which was recently printed in the Century Magazine, for which please accept my thanks."

WILL LOOK CAREFULLY INTO THE MATTER

Mr. Albert T. Perkins, President of the New Iberia and Northern Railroad Company, writes: "Your letter of October 8th with copy of article reprinted from Century Magazine was duly received, and I have read the article through with care and much interest. I have realized to some extent the situation as to rail road accommodations which you described, and hope I have been instrumental in some cases in bettering certain features on various roads in Texas, Louisiana, etc., in which I have been concerned. As to the New Iberia and Northern Railroad, the passenger service is for the most part given by large steel motor cars in which the accommodations for whites and blacks are equipped in identically the same manner. Your letter will have the effect of my examining with some greater care the arrangements on several other railroads with which I am connected; and I thank you for sending me your article."

WILL BE GLAD TO READ IT

Mr. C. H. Hix, President of the Norfolk Southern Railway Company, says: "This is to acknowledge receipt of yours of the 14th, with enclosure, which I will be glad to read."

POLICY IS TO IMPROVE

Mr. W. W. Finley, President of the Southern Railway Company, states: "I have noted what you say as to the treatment of Negro travelers on railways in the South. The matter of accommodations for Negroes is one which has been having the attention of the management of this Company and it is our policy to improve those accommodations so far as it is practicable for us to do so."

I am sure your readers will be interested in the above extracts and in those which are to follow next week.

(Signed) BOOKER T. WASHINGTON

PD Con. 519 BTW Papers DLC. A galley proof "Released March 5, 1914."

Ralph Waldo Tyler to Emmett Jay Scott

Washington, D.C., Mar. 1, 1914

My dear Emmett: Yours apprising me of the possibility of the Doctor writing me, regarding Charley's threatened resignation as member of the League, came to hand, and since then I have received the advised of letter, to which I have replied. Charley's letter and his complaint was a most childish thing to do. I seldom defend myself, I employ my efforts at defending and boosting friends, and bear silently, as a rule, the open or intimated criticism of presumed friends. I am, when made an enemy, however, just as uncompromising a foe as I am a friend.

When I came to Washington I came an acknowledged follower of the Doctor. Knowing this to be true, and I never deserted my colors even when surrounded by odds, I was the target for the anti-crowd. I marshalled our few friends together here — some times driving some by threats, and in due course of time you and the Doctor know how well his friends had control here. Some of "our" friends, as I have frequently confided to you, were opportunists; some were worth while to have even though they were more of a liability rather than a real asset. Few were as strong in their fealty when the Ides of March last rolled around as they had previously been.

I protested against segregation of the race in the departments. I felt I was right in so doing, and would repeat the offense again. A commendable desire to hang on to their jobs caused some of "our" friends — all who were "in," to regard my protest as a bid for notoriety, simply because their tenure might become involved, and as a consequence the erstwhile warmth, "the Three Guardsmen" loyalty underwent a change, and the spirit which once prompted "all for each and each for all" had been, presto change, crystalized into "we and him." I noticed the change — felt it, but this has been the first time I have unsealed my lips to speak of it. What had usually been regarded as "our cause," and "our interests" became an abandoned project in the effort of each to hold on to his job. I could have brought influence to remain — influence was offered me without asking, but I would not accept and use it. I have not blamed others for their mindfulness of self preservation because I was so deaf to it. I do blame, however, any man who spurns the hand which once fed him, or attempts to destroy the bridge which carried him over.

I know of the criticism leveled against me — have known of it, and knew it was prompted by selfish ambition and self-preservation rather than any actual offense I had committed. It is my nature to be always ready to go down with friends just as I am ready to go up with them.

Take Moore for instance. Time and time again his peddled criticism of me has come to me. He has voiced it to those he thought would transmit it to me. Yet, examine the debit and credit side of the ledger and see to whom is due the credit balance or to whom is due the deficit.

Fred holds me alone responsible for an attempt to secure management of The Age. His antipathy for me is built upon this assumption, and yet you yourself know how clearly wrong is his assumption. As I recall, very distinctly, it cost me fully $100 for two trips to "confer" on the matter, upon request. I have never said to Fred, nor to those who brought me his criticism of me, how I became interested in the prospective management of The Age, and shall not. Charley and Fred who before seldom overlooked an opportunity to knock each other, now are together knocking me, and because of The Age incident Charley employs "I told you so," with Fred.

Of course I have been aggressive — times were when it was necessary here to maintain "our" control, and to beat back the anties. The aggressive fellow is bound to make some enemies, and every conservative must have a few aggressives around as "suppers" if nothing more.

The "Federals" — the anties, have approached me with offers, but I have refused. When I join in with friends, I respect the reserve clause as a part of the moral contract.

That bit of oxygen — Thompson, has tried to injure me, on the assumption that I was the "Sage," and yet the man least suspected (Roscoe Bruce) is the "Sage," and I have indisputable evidence of it. Confidentially — Sherlock-like, I chased down his copy. Also chased down some other copy of his which puts him in the despicable ingrate class.

Out of these three pages you may be able to fathom what I am driving at — the reason why I am now considered, by the anxiously anticipating holdovers, inharmonious.

They say turkeys average three full grown from a setting. The average of real, lasting friends made in politics, or as the result of political association, is even less. Sincerely,

Tyler

TLS Con. 14 BTW Papers DLC.

To Members of the Alabama Colored State Teachers Association[1]

[Tuskegee, Ala., ca. Mar. 1, 1914]

With the co-operation and with the consent of Mr. William Pickens, President, Executive Committee, and other officers of the Alabama Colored State Teachers Association, I am addressing you on a very important matter:

Alabama, as you know, is perhaps near the bottom of the list in the matter of educational efficiency. The white educators of the state are making strenuous efforts to improve the educational condition in this state. It is important that those engaged in the education of colored people co-operate in every way possible with the white officers and educators with the view of improving the public schools throughout the State of Alabama.

After considering the matter very carefully, the Executive Committee of the Colored State Teachers Association has decided to make the coming meeting of the State Association in Birmingham, which occurs on April 8th, 9th and 10th, at the same [time] that the White State Teachers Association occurs, an epoch making affair. Plans have been carefully thought out by which, in my opinion, the meeting in Birmingham will be the largest and most important educational gathering that has ever taken place for our race in Alabama.

There are many advantages in having this meeting at the same time and place as the white association; many of the strong speakers who address the white association will be glad to address the colored association; besides, reduced rates can be secured and the colored association can share the benefit of the general enthusiasm which will be in Birmingham at the time in the direction of better education and more education for all the people of Alabama.

In view of the importance of this meeting, may I urge upon you to come yourself and to influence as many educational workers, as you possibly can, also to attend the meeting. Yours very truly,

[Booker T. Washington]

TLc Copy   Con. 522   BTW Papers   DLC.

[1] BTW also wrote a letter to be sent to each county superintendent urging him to encourage black teachers to attend the meeting. (Draft copy, ca. Mar. 1, 1914, Con. 522, BTW Papers, DLC.)

From Woodrow Wilson

The White House   Washington   March 2, 1914

My dear President Washington: Thank you sincerely for your letter of February twenty-fifth. It gave me real pleasure to recognize Mr. Terrell's very successful services as a magistrate.

In haste   Sincerely yours,

Woodrow Wilson

TLS   Con. 525   BTW Papers   DLC.

A Speech at Western University

[Quindaro, Kan. Mar. 4, 1914]

PRES. KEALING, MEMBERS OF THE TEACHING BODY AND STUDENT
BODY.

Mr. Weaver has just whispered in my ear to the effect that I must
speak to you only five minutes. Now, I regret this because it has been
seldom my privilege to look into the faces of as fine a set of boys and
girls as I find here this morning. I should be tempted to talk to you
as long as I could. The longer I talk, the less studying you will have
to do. I have known your President for a number of years, knew him
before he came to Kansas, knew him in Texas and other parts of the
south and north, and I have known him only to admire him, and I
congratulate you, that you have such a man as this at the head of
your institution; and I congratulate the people of Kansas and this part
of the country that they are so fortunate in having Mr. Kealing at the
head of this institution.

Some months ago when Bishop Grant passed away, it was ours to
select some one to take his place on the Jeanes Fund Board of Education. The fund, the sum of One Million Dollars, was left by a good
old woman in Philadelphia some years ago for the education of the
negro in the south. We searched the country over to find someone of
our race to take his place and we settled upon Mr. Kealing, and he
was unanimously elected. So I congratulate you upon having such an
able man as your head and leader.

I am very glad to hear the beautiful songs, not only the classical
song, but to hear with how much earnestness you sang the last song,
and I hope that in no part of this country will our race forget the songs
created by our mothers and fathers, and I hope, more in the future
than in the past, that in every institution of learning [of] all our race
in all the country, not only more time would be given to songs created
by us, but to the history of our people.

It is indeed true that many of our own race go to institutions where
they study the history of all races, history of the Jews, history of the
Greeks, history of the Germans, but they never study the history of our
own race. You can devote a good part of the month to a study of the
history of men of our own race. There are many in this room who
have begun at the bottom in business, in education, in church, who

466

have begun in poverty and in many cases have gradually struggled upward, and who have grown just as popular and just as worthy of trust as some of those fellows who lived thousands of years ago.

Now before I depart from you let me impress upon you this one word. When you return home, do not be ashamed of your mothers and fathers. Many of you come from the country don't you? Huh? Huh? Don't be ashamed, speak up. You speak timid. Many of you come from the country, out in the sticks, don't you? Huh? Huh? Don't be ashamed. I want you girls and boys that come from the country away out from the railroad to be just as proud as those that come from under the glare of the electric lights. Those of you who live in the country are better off than those in the city, because you own your own property in which you live, and those in the city live in property owned by someone else.

When you go back home, your people are going to expect great things. They have heard that you have an education, and expect you to show signs of it as soon as you get back home. They are expecting big things of you. I want you to disappoint them in two directions. They expect you to show it in the way you talk. Using a language which you or no one else know anything about. If you want to show them that you have an education, be the most simple person in the community. When you talk, use the shortest words that you can get hold of in the English language. Use the shortest sentences that you can get hold of in the English language. You must talk in a way that everyone can understand you. When they expect you to show signs of the big head, you show signs of the little head. You show signs that education has taught you to be of service to the humblest and to the poorest in the community in which you live. Many of you are studying chemistry, aren't you? You know chemistry is a peculiar thing which is of no value, unless you are going to use it. When you left home there had not been any paint on the outside of the house for one or perhaps five or ten years. You remember how the house looked when you left. You remember how it looked. It is looking just like that now. This is how you use that chemistry. When you go home, say to your mother and father, I have been studying chemistry and I am going to use my chemistry by mixing paint or whitewash and putting on a coat, as it will beautify the home as it has never been before. Do not commence anything unless you are going to use it when you go back home, where you can put into practise the knowledge you have thus received.

Many of you are studying mechanical art. It is of no value unless you are going to use it. You know when you left home, part of the palings were off the front fence. You remember that from time to time when you tried to go through the gate which hung on one hinge. That gate is waiting for you to come back home. You remember some of the rooms in the house, when you tried to go in the door and caught hold of the knob. What happened? The knob fell off. Didn't it? It is waiting for you to go back home. Use your knowledge of mechanical art in building up and beautifying the community in which you live. My friends that means service, education, practise, and culture for our entire race. I congratulate all of you, teachers and students, boys and girls that you are grasping all of the knowledge in your power; that you have such a glorious opportunity at this present day. Get all the knowledge that you can, and use it in some way in your home or community, put it into practise for the glory of God and to the service of man.

TD Con. 11 BTW Papers DLC. Stenographically reported by the commercial students of Western University.

To Tom Johnson

[Tuskegee, Ala.] March 5, 1914

My dear Sir: Replying to your letter of some days ago, I write to say that I have no connection, whatever, with the scheme of "Chief Sam" to carry a colony of Negroes from the South to Africa.

Personally, I am not in favor of such a movement, for the reason that there are better opportunities offered to Negroes in this country than in any other country in the world; and my advice has always been that they remain in this country, and, as far as possible, in the South. Yours very truly,

Booker T. Washington

TLpSr Con. 507 BTW Papers DLC. Signed in E. J. Scott's hand.

Robert Russa Moton to Oswald Garrison Villard

[Hampton, Va.] March 5, 1914

My dear Mr. Villard: You remarked to me after my little talk at Ethical Culture Hall that you would like to have stated your side of the situation. I have been thinking much since of that remark and have been wondering what you had in mind. I cannot see but one side of the situation.

I was very sorry not to see you in New York when I talked with Mrs. Villard over the telephone week before last. I am very sorry you have been sick and hope you are yourself by this time.

Now, it would be a good thing if you and I, who have been generally frank with each other, might talk out in absolute frankness the whole situation, as man to man and friend to friend. I am in no sense lacking in appreciation of what you are doing for the Negro and the Nation. I do question seriously, sometimes, the methods of the National Association. There is no doubt that there is plenty to do and the Association has a splendid opportunity.

I was a little disturbed by the report that the Chairman of your Executive Committee was rather severe in his criticisms of Dr. Washington in Chicago, but that might not be an accurate report. I feel that Mr. Spingarn is anxious to help and I want to be fair in my judgment of him.

Inasmuch as I could not talk with you in New York, I am going to make this suggestion, that you and Mr. Fred R. Moore of the "New York Age" talk the situation out. You tell him all that is in the back of your head and let him tell you all that is in the back of his. I have no doubt but that each of you will help the other; certainly you should come to a better and more sympathetic understanding. I remember once your remarking to me that the "Age" had been generally hostile to the Association, and I am sorry this is true, but I think if you two could spend an hour talking out the situation it would be a very good thing. It has always seemed to me most unfortunate that men working for the same cause should seem to be antagonistic to the other. I don't mean, of course, that we must think or act alike, but I have sincerely wished there were more harmony among the forces that are working for the good of colored folk.

I am sending Mr. Moore a copy of this letter. I don't, of course, know how it will strike him, but I have always been frank with him, as I have been with you. Yours sincerely,

R. R. Moton

TLSr Copy   Con. 525   BTW Papers   DLC.

To Emmett Jay Scott

Los Angeles, March 9th, 1914

Dear Mr. Scott: I am sending you the following memorandum regarding my visit here, which you can use in any way you want in the colored press:

A large delegation met the train, with Dr. Baer and other white educators, and practically all the leading colored people, who gave a very enthusiastic demonstration.

One thing for your private information which will interest you. I met a group of the most prominent colored men at Mr. Owens' house last night. Most of them for the main part were those who were engaged in bringing Dr. Du Bois here some months ago. Without my referring to the subject, they volunteered the information that Du Bois, notwithstanding they had been friendly to him, had practically killed himself in this vicinity, and without any hesitation they said he would not be invited here again. It seems he made a perfect fool of himself by trying to snub everybody. So far as I can judge from what they said, his address seemed a failure. I find nobody here who has a good word for him.[1]

I spoke at the First Congregational Church yesterday morning, and I was told the people began going to the church an hour and a half before the service opened. The crowd was so large I had to speak twice, once in the main auditorium, and in the parish house. Yesterday afternoon in connection with the meeting in the interest of the colored Y.M.C.A. I had the privilege of speaking to the colored people and many of the white people. The meeting was held in the First M. E. Church, the largest white Methodist church in the city. It was literally packed with a fine audience of colored people with a large sprinkling of white people. There were many hundreds who could not get in. I was told in connection with the meeting in the afternoon, that some of the people went to the church at 12 o'clock and stayed until 3 o'clock, the hour of the meeting.

I hope matters are going well at the school. You can use your judgement as to what matters to send me. Yours very truly,

B.T.W.

TLI Con. 520 BTW Papers DLC.

[1] BTW wrote Scott from Los Angeles a few days later: "I think if we wanted to get rid of Du Bois as an influence, the best way would be to send him through the country and let the people meet him." (Mar. 17, 1914, Con. 645, BTW Papers, DLC.)

From John C. Leftwich

Cleveland, Ohio—Mar—9th 1914

Personal
Dear Sir — I have read with considerable interest in the "Age" and "Freeman" the number of replies to your excellent appeal on behalf of the Negroes for better treatment by the rail roads. You certianly deserve the thanks and gratitude of every Negroe in America. I for one want to record my thanks for your timely efforts. Of all your good works for the race, I firmly beleive this is one; is your crowning act. I have long thought along the same lines, but was unable to accomplish the good you have done. The colored people of America should hold meetings all over the country, praising and thanking you for the Second Abolition, ye [i.e.] — rail-road Slavery. I didnt see a reply or Statement from any of the rail road officials of the Fort-Smith & Western R.R., which runs through our town — Boley. This road pulls the smallest and dirtiest coaches for Negroes than any other road in the south-west. If you have not, I beg of you to write — Mr. A. C. Dustin, pres. Fort Smith & Western, R.R, Western Reserve Building, Cleveland, Ohio.[1] If you succeed in changing conditions on said road, you will have done the greatest help to the largest bunch of Negroes in America.

May the Lord preserve you to live long to do much good for the race. Respectfully

John C. Leftwich

ALS Con. 508 BTW Papers DLC. On stationery of the Creek-Seminole Agricultural College, Boley, Okla., John C. Leftwich, president.

[1] Replying for BTW, who was in California, E. J. Scott urged Leftwich to complain directly to Alton C. Dustin, the president of the railroad. (Mar. 13, 1914, Con. 508, BTW Papers, DLC.)

Oswald Garrison Villard to Robert Russa Moton[1]

[New York City] March 9, 1914

Confidential

Dear Major Moton: I have your letter of March 5th. I should like very much indeed to see you and talk with you, and I have no objection to talking to Mr. Moore, as I talked with his editor, but I doubt very much whether Mr. Moore and I will progress very far. His newspaper is so essentially the organ of Dr. Washington and regards everything from the point of view of one defending him that I do not believe we shall have very much in common.

It is true that Dr. Spingarn, the new Executive Chairman of the Association has a different policy in regard to Dr. Washington than I have, and I understand that his criticisms in Chicago were very severe. As for my own personal attitude towards Dr. Washington, I have never said anything about him to others that I have not said to Dr. Washington himself. My present feeling for him is one of regret and sorrow, and I can best illustrate it by quoting from a letter which I wrote recently to Mr. Roger Baldwin of St. Louis:

"It is, however, very hard for us not to comment on the pitiful position in which Booker Washington finds himself. He is like Nero, fiddling while Rome burns. One right after another is being taken away from the colored people, one injustice after another being perpetrated, and Booker Washington is silent. There has developed in North Carolina the greatest menace yet, a movement under the leadership of Clarence Poe, which will undoubtedly result in legislation, segregating the Negro on the farm lands, thus giving the lie to Washington's advice to his people that if they will only be good and buy land they will be let alone and will flourish. He is silent about the segregation in Washington, in Baltimore and in nine other Southern cities, and then he believes that he is a leader of his people. It is pitiful beyond words, and pains me particularly as I have always been a loyal supporter of Tuskegee and of Washington, standing by him in his trouble here in New York, and raising the Baldwin Fund for him. His name is getting to be anathema among the educated colored people in the country, and he is drifting further and further in the rear as a real leader."

As for yourself, I need not tell you that my esteem and regard for you and the work you are doing is of the highest. As I told Dr. Frissell the other day, my only feeling about that address was that in one or two points you seemed to be weakening and compromising, and rather leaning in Dr. Washington's direction of saying to the audience things that are pleasant to hear, but which are often taken as indicating a recession from the only proper position, that the colored man is entitled to every single right that the white citizen of the United States has. Sincerely yours,

Oswald Garrison Villard

TLSr Copy   Con. 525   BTW Papers   DLC.

[1] Moton enclosed a copy of this letter to Scott, objected to the comparison with Nero, and asked for a few strong quotations of Washington's public references to segregation to use in his reply. Scott noted in the margin: *"keep private."* (Moton to Scott, Mar. 11, 1914, Con. 511, BTW Papers, DLC.)

To James Edward McCulloch[1]

Los Angeles, Cal. March 11, 1914

My dear Dr. McCulloch: Replying to yours of February 28th, I would state that the afternoon of May 7th will suit me as to the time of my address.

As to the subject. I would prefer to speak on some such subject as this — "The Negro and Crime." That would give me an opportunity to treat the subject rather broadly, that is, to speak of the white man's duties and the Negro's duties regarding the matter of lynching as well as other crimes for which both races are responsible.

As to the matter of land segregation, especially in the country districts, I really hope that the Congress will not give much attention to that question. I have watched it pretty carefully, and aside from one or two men I have found there is little interest in that subject and there is no danger of the movement becoming dangerous or widespread. I very much fear the more attention the Congress gives to that subject the more it will be dignified and thus please those who are advocating what, in my opinion is a silly policy. Outside of one state I have never heard the question of segregating the Negro on the farming lands of the South even mentioned, and I fear that there is great danger of our putting up a straw man in this case if too much emphasis is placed on this matter.

Will you be kind enough to write me at Tuskegee, indicating whether my subject is satisfactory so that I may prepare to speak on it. Yours very truly,

[Booker T. Washington]

TLc   Con. 841   BTW Papers   DLC.

¹ James Edward McCulloch (1873–1939) was a sociologist educated at Vanderbilt University. He was the general secretary of the Southern Sociological Congress (1911–19) and director of the American Interchurch College for Religious and Social Workers (1912–15).

To Emmett Jay Scott

Los Angeles, Cal. March 14th, 1914

Dear Mr. Scott: In sending in my last memorandum, I forgot to say that I was invited by all the judges, eighteen in number, covering this city and county, to meet them at noon this week. I did so. They are a fine lot of men. I was asked to sit on the bench with one of them but I have not had time to do so. Yours very truly,

B.T.W.

TLI   Con. 520   BTW Papers   DLC.

An Article in *Outlook*

14 March 1914

BLACK AND WHITE IN THE SOUTH
SCHOOLS FOR NEGROES

For a number of years I have had the feeling that the more liberal and advanced thinkers of the South among the white people do not know the poor school facilities that are provided for members of my race in certain sections of the South. Often when I have been traveling through the South upon educational campaigns I have reminded white people in my audiences of the poor school facilities that existed right in their own town or county for the education of the Negro. Frequently these white people have not only expressed surprise but have thanked me for my frankness in letting them know about these bad conditions, and then they have taken hold of matters and have greatly changed conditions. In many cases the white people are so busy about their own affairs that they do not take time to find out how the Negro is faring in the matter of education.

When speaking to the white people in the South from the platform I always try to speak with perfect frankness, but in a spirit of friendship and sympathy. I intend to pursue that policy in this article. I have seldom encountered any direct or stubborn opposition to Negro education among the white population, but what I have found is indifference growing out of ignorance of conditions. Certainly we must have truth and facts as a basis for any progress that both races are to make.

A few weeks ago three of the most prominent white men in Mississippi were shot and killed by two colored boys. Investigation brought to light that the two boys were rough and crude, that they had never been to school, hence that they were densely ignorant. While no one had taught these boys the use of books, some one had taught them, as mere children, the use of cocaine and whisky. In a mad fit, when their minds and bodies were filled with cheap whisky and cocaine, these two ignorant boys created a "reign of murder," in the course of which three white men, four colored men, and one colored woman met death. As soon as the shooting was over a crazed mob shot the two boys full of bullet-holes and then burned their bodies in the public streets.

Now, this is the kind of thing, more or less varied in form, that takes place too often in our country. Why? The answer is simple. It is dense ignorance on the part of the Negro, and indifference arising out of a lack of knowledge of conditions on the part of the white people.

Let me not mince matters, but state facts as they are, since it is only through knowledge of actual facts that progress for both races can be made. It is true that in a few sections of the South there is little to complain of with reference to Negro education either in city or country districts. In other sections of the South, however, the opportunities for Negro education are deplorable, and so long as there is little or no opportunity for Negro youths in these sections of the South to get the education which will teach them to keep their bodies clean, to know the law, to exercise self-control, to labor for its own sake, so long will there be crime, so long will the lives of the best white people and the best black people in the South be in danger from ignorant colored people and ignorant white people.

Take, for example, the State of Mississippi, the State in which this crime was committed. By the last enumeration in that State the school population was 712,000; of this number 400 were Indians, 302,000 whites, and 410,000 colored. During the year 1912 244,000 colored children were enrolled in the public schools; this is just a little over fifty per cent. The average attendance, however, in the public schools was 143,000, or about thirty-five per cent of the total number of colored children in Mississippi. In other words, sixty-four per cent of the colored children in Mississippi attended no public school during the year 1912. In Hinds County the average salary of colored teachers during that year was about $16 a month for five months.

South Carolina is another Southern State which is backward in Negro education. According to official reports, in district 9, Beaufort County, of this State, there was expended on the white children enrolled in the public school in 1911 $127.30 per capita, and on the colored children enrolled in the same district $2.74 per capita, or forty-six times as much on the white children as on the colored children.

In district 10, Charleston County, there was expended $202 for each white child, $3.12 for the colored; in district 39, Abbeville County, $11.17 for the white, 69 cents for the colored; in district 3, Edgefield County, $7.45 for the white, 48 cents for the colored; in district 5 of this same county, $23.12 for the white, 58 cents for the colored; in district 9, Fairfield County, $13.67 for the white, 48 cents for the colored; in district 12, same county, $11.50 for the white, 29 cents for the colored.

Under these conditions, let us see how long the colored children are in school during the year in certain typical districts of South Carolina, then we may get further light as to the cause of crime and idleness in portions of the South.

In district 28, Edgefield County, the public school for colored children was kept open by public funds about two and one-half months, and the teacher was paid at the rate of $15 per month. In Anderson County, district 40, the colored public school was open two months and closed ten months. In Barnwell County, district 31, the public school was in session one month and closed eleven months. In South Carolina the average length of the school term for the colored people, outside the cities and large towns, is from two to four months.

The seriousness of this can be understood when it is kept in mind that there are almost a million colored people in South Carolina and that eighty per cent of them live in rural districts. Thus in one State of our great free country 200,000 colored children are provided with public education for but three or four months in the year. Under these conditions it would require twenty-eight years for a child to complete the eight grades of the public school.

Of course any one knows that a two months' or a three months' school, with a mere pittance of a salary for a teacher, means almost no school. The buildings in which these schools are conducted, as a former State Superintendent of Education in South Carolina said some time ago, are in many cases not fit for stables. But South Carolina is by no means the only State that has these breeding-spots for ignorance, crime, and filth which the Nation will, sooner or later, have to reckon with. In Alabama, my own State, we have one of the finest and most liberal Governors of any State in the Union. The Superintendent of Education, as is true of many county superintendents of education, is also generous in the matter of Negro education; and yet in Alabama we have counties where conditions are almost as bad as those in South Carolina.

Take, for example, Wilcox County, Alabama. Here there are 6,200 white people and 27,600 black people. There are 1,884 white children of school age and 10,667 black children of school age. For the education of these white children there was spent in 1912 $33,000, or $17 per capita; for the education of the 10,000 black children there was spent $3,750, or 37 cents per capita. According to the report of the State Superintendent of Education of Alabama, there are 328,024 colored children in Alabama. Of this number 190,000 did not enter any school at all during the last year, and 90,000 of those entering were in school only from two to three months. Thus it is seen that in the single State of Alabama there are almost 200,000 colored children who apparently are growing up in ignorance, notwithstanding all that has been done and is being done. In Alabama, as in other States, some are being educated in the elementary departments of the industrial schools and colleges, but their number in proportion to the total is very small.

Some of the more touching and heart-reaching letters that I receive regarding accommodations for colored children come from Southern white people of both sexes. The following is one example of many. A Southern white lady, the wife of a former official in Alabama, in a letter speaking of the rural schools in her county, says:

"Dr. Washington:

"Since being elected President of the School Improvement Association of this county, I find conditions gloomy enough for both races, but it is strictly relative to the colored race that I am writing this.

"There was some irregularity in the application to Dr. Dillard, of New Orleans, for the fund for the supervisor of the colored schools, and this leaves me absolutely without means with which to supply this crying need.

"Now I am asking you to send me one of your best teachers — I mean most conscientious teachers — to visit each colored school in this county in the capacity of supervisor. If once a quarter would be too much to ask, then let them come at least twice during the scholastic year. The county superintendent has promised to appoint me a president of the School Improvement Association, and I shall personally undertake the direction of her work. If only you could see the heart-breaking need as I see it!

"You have been called the 'Moses' of your race; then this call is to you to help lead your people out of the wilderness of ignorance and inefficiency. This is one of the opportunities to prove your sincerity.

"Allow me to recall to your remembrance the liberal and sympathetic attitude held toward the Negro race by my husband, not only during his incumbency as a State officer but in all his dealings with them in private as well as in public life. The matter of improving the schools of this county has become a question of conscience, and *something must be done*. This appeal goes to you in the name of our Christ in behalf of his needy little ones. Yours for betterment, etc.

"P.S. — We have only sixteen colored schools. After I had determined on this step, I consulted my superintendent, and he heartily sanctioned it."

In a letter to the Montgomery "Advertiser," December 29, 1910, explaining why the black counties of Alabama, Macon County excepted, had lost population from 1900 to 1910, I said: "I do not believe that the leading people, and especially landowners, of the 'Black Belt' counties know how little money some Negro schools receive. More money is paid for Negro convicts than for Negro teachers in Alabama. About $46 per month is now being paid for first-class, able-bodied Negro convicts, $36 for the second class, and $26 for the third class for the twelve months in the year, while in some counties Negro teachers get from $15 to $17 a month for a period of three or four months in the year."

While I have dwelt a great deal upon conditions in Mississippi, South Carolina, and Alabama, I do not mean to imply that these are the only States where such conditions exist. I have used them merely as examples of conditions existing in some portions, at least, of practically all of the States of the lower South.

On my visits to the country schools in these and other States I have seen some very pathetic sights. In some of the so-called school buildings the roofs leak, the winds blow up through the cracks of the floors and down through the ceilings. I have seen in many of these schools five little boys and girls trying to study out of the same book. In some cases two children would occupy the front seat with the book between them, with two others peeping over their shoulders, and a fifth trying to peep over the shoulders of the four.

The ignorance and stupidity that control in some of the schools are almost beyond belief. I have seen scores of little children sitting for hours on a rough bench with no back to it and their feet dangling in the air six or seven inches from the floor. In other cases I have seen, during the very cold, windy, winter weather, schools conducted in malarial districts where there was no provision made on the inside of the houses for warming the room. A fire would be built on the outside of the school-house, and teachers and pupils would study on the inside for a few minutes until they got so cold that they were compelled to go outside to warm their fingers and feet, and then, after a few minutes, return to their studies on the inside. When these conditions exist in a school with a term of only three or four months, conducted by a poorly paid teacher, it is wonderful that any progress at all has been made in such places in the matter of public education.

Now, as I often say when speaking in the South — and I never say anything out of the South that I do not say in the South — in those counties and districts in which this color line is drawn in the matter of fitting these people for the duties of life under free conditions, no color line is drawn in the payment of taxes or in the punishment of crime. The colored boy who has $1.50 a year spent on him for his education is punished by the same court under the same rules of evidence as the white boy who resides in the county and has $15 a year spent on him for his education. Aside from other results of this kind of short-sightedness and injustice, this lack of school facilities is fast driving some of the best colored farmers from the farms, where they are of best service to the white people and to themselves, to the large cities, where, in spite of certain disadvantages, they are reasonably sure of finding some kind of school for their children.

Any one living outside of the South cannot realize how heavily the Southern States have taxed themselves within the last quarter of a century for education and what tremendous sacrifices they have made. It is hard to put in words a true or adequate description of the awakening that is now spreading all through the South in educational matters. While all this is true, we must not fail, however, to look facts in the face, even though they be disagreeable and discouraging facts. The best friend of the South is he who will tell the truth.

It would for this reason be manifestly unfair, while calling attention to the deplorable conditions that exist in some sections of the South, to ignore the many counties and cities in which the public authorities have vision enough and such a high sense of justice that good opportunities are furnished, in length of terms, salaries of teachers, and in the kind of school-houses, for the education of Negro children. This is notably true in the State of Texas.

Outside the large cities and towns in the Southern States the opportunities of Negro education are generally poor, but there are rural districts in which good schools are furnished for the Negro people, almost as good in some cases as those for white children. This is true of both Virginia and Texas. In fact, I think Texas is ahead of all the Southern States in its wisdom, generosity, and farsightedness in the distribution of the public school money. And I am sure that the State of Texas has not lost anything, but has gained, in having a high and useful type of Negro citizen.

I was born in the South, have lived in the South, and am just as proud of the South as any white man could be. For this very reason I want to see it get to the point where it will cease to be continually held up to the civilized world as the most criminal section of our country. But we can get rid of this reputation only in proportion as education replaces ignorance, as thrift and industry replace idleness and laziness, as high moral character replaces immorality.

These bad and unhealthy conditions exist in many parts of the South, I repeat, because liberal and thoughtful white people too often do not actually know what is going on with reference to Negro education. These white people are so absorbed with their own personal business, or in matters that concern white people, that they do not have time, or take time, to find out the actual conditions in which colored people live. This leads me to hope that what I have said in this article may impress the leading white people in the South with the importance of looking into and making known the facts in regard to Negro education.

In some parts of the country public attention has already been directed to the importance of this matter. In Russell County, Alabama, for example, where I have recently been, the white people are pleading for more Negro schools, more Negro teachers, and they are not ashamed to let the world know that they are in favor of Negro education. The same is true of many counties and cities in the South; but, when all this is said, we must face the fact, disagreeable as it may be, that when we consider the growth in population among the colored people in the rural districts of the South, where eighty-five per cent of the Negro population lives, the Nation still has a serious problem which we must meet in a spirit of generosity and handle with wisdom, and, above all things, with courage.

Outlook, 106 (Mar. 14, 1914), 590–93. A typed draft dated Dec. 31, 1913, is in Con. 66, BTW Papers, DLC.

From Edward Pearson Moses[1]

Nashville, Tenn., March 16, 1914

Dear Sir: I have two reasons for writing you a second time in twenty-four hours.[2] The first excuse is finding my note of just what was said by U.S. Senator Hoke Smith about your graduates. Here is my entry:

Congressional Record Feb. 6, 1914 page 3193.
Mr. Cummins[3]*:* What does Booker Washington teach in his college?
Mr. Smith of Georgia: I do not know. I never see any of his graduates doing anything anywhere in my State. I do not know one of his graduates who is at work in my State.

My second reason for writing this letter is to say that today I read in The Outlook your criticism of the discrimination practised in some many places in such flagrant form against the colored schools. This abuse of governmental power has long been a source of genuine regret to me who am a native of Tennessee, a Democrat and an opponent of illiterate voting. Your article rings clear. Hit 'em again! Yours truly,

Edward P. Moses

ALS Con. 936 BTW Papers DLC.

[1] Edward Pearson Moses (1857–1948) was born in Knoxville, Tenn., of New Hampshire parents. He organized the graded schools at Knoxville and at Goldsboro and Raleigh, N.C. During the 1880s he became the leader of young teachers and school reformers in North Carolina, notably Charles D. McIver, Edwin A. Alderman, and James Y. Joyner, whose efforts to increase public support and improve the quality of instruction led toward the Ogden Movement at the turn of the century.

[2] Moses had written the preceding day to urge Washington to reply to Senator Hoke Smith with a summary of what Tuskegee graduates had accomplished in Georgia. (Mar. 15, 1914, Con. 936, BTW Papers, DLC.)

[3] Albert Baird Cummins (1850–1926) was governor of Iowa from 1902 to 1908, and served in the U.S. Senate from 1908 to 1926.

To Clara Johnston

Los Angeles, Cal. March 17, 1914

Dear Clara: Enclosed I send you ten dollars which you can use in getting your incubator. I very much hope you will be successful in raising a large quantity of chickens.

I sent your mother a box of oranges from California a few days ago which I hope she received in good shape.

I shall be going back home in a few days. I hope that the whole family is well. Your uncle,

[Booker T. Washington]

TLc   Con. 507   BTW Papers   DLC.

Emmett Jay Scott to Robert Russa Moton

[Tuskegee, Ala.] March 18th, 1914

Dear Major Moton: I cannot for the life of me feel that anything will be gained by continuing a correspondence with Mr. Villard. Temperamentally, his mind is closed as far as Doctor Washington is concerned, that is, nothing will satisfy him except complete abdication on Doctor Washington's part to any claims to leadership of the Negro race. Of course, Doctor Washington does not claim to be a leader, but our friends on the other side are angry even if other people believe in him and trust him, as a leader.

My point of view may not coincide with yours, but somehow, as I stated in the beginning of this letter, I cannot believe that anything is to be gained by attempting to state Doctor Washington's position with reference to matters which are open to every fair-minded man. What do you think?

Believe me now as always. Ever sincerely yours,

Emmett J. Scott

You have done your part in trying to soften him (Mr. V.).

TLpS   Con. 71   BTW Papers   DLC.   Postscript in Scott's hand.

To Warren Logan

Los Angeles, Cal. March 20, 1914

Dear Mr. Logan: Judging by the reports Mr. Palmer sends me, I very much fear that we are making a mistake in sending too many students away from the school, and giving too many warnings for trivial offenses. It is the easiest thing in the world to get into the habit of doing things in a machine-like way when dealing with students.

I cannot believe that it is necessary to send so many students away from the school or to give so many warnings. We do not really help the students in this way. I believe if each teacher would put a little more heart into his work and get a personal influence over the students and show them what is wrong, it would be much more effective than these routine warnings. I think a warning ought to be given as a matter of last resort, and in each case it ought to be investigated very fully before the warning is passed on by the Council.

I shall hope to be starting home soon. Yours very truly,

[Booker T. Washington]

TLc   Con. 654   BTW Papers   DLC.

To Felix Signoret McGinnis[1]

Hotel Alexandria, Los Angeles. March 20th, 1914

Dear Mr. McGinnis: This note will be handed you by my secretary, Mr. Nathan Hunt.

I hope you will not think it presumptuous in me if I seem to take advantage of a very short acquaintance to put before you a matter of business.

I may find it desirable to return East by the Southern Pacific, and of course if I do so, I want to use a compartment or drawing room in a Pullman car. As you know, there is sometimes some question about colored people using the Pullman cars through the state of Texas. When Judge Lovett[2] was in charge of the Southern Pacific, he was kind enough to arrange this for me whenever I have found it necessary to travel in Texas. No trouble has resulted.

In case I desire to use the Southern Pacific returning, I am wondering if you could help me arrange the matter so that everything will be agreeable with the railroad authorities. My experience has been, that with the consent of the railroad authorities there has been no trouble in any direction and everything has been very pleasant.

The attached telegram I thought you might like to see. I have not heard anything as yet from the San Francisco people. Yours very truly,

[Booker T. Washington]

TLc   Con. 838   BTW Papers   DLC.

¹ Felix Signoret McGinnis, born in Los Angeles in 1883, was city passenger agent of the Southern Pacific Railroad in Los Angeles (1912–15), and later was a vice-president of the Union Pacific system.

² Robert Scott Lovett, born in San Jacinto, Tex., in 1860, was general counsel, then president and chairman of the board of the Union Pacific and Southern Pacific railroads.

To Emmett Jay Scott

Los Angeles, Cal. March 20, 1914

Dear Mr. Scott: I have just finished speaking at the Los Angeles Friday Morning Club, which is the largest and most exclusive woman's club in California. It was an extraordinary affair. Every one tells me that it was the largest attendance they have ever had. Women of the highest and best class flocked in such numbers that people had to stand out in the yard. The luncheon which the club tendered me afterwards was equally well attended. I have never seen so many exclusive, rich and fashionable women assembled in one audience. They seemed tremendously enthusiastic. The strange thing is that white women from the South seemed to be just as much interested as others. Yours very truly,

B.T.W.

TLI   Con. 520   BTW Papers   DLC.

Robert Russa Moton to Emmett Jay Scott

Hampton, Virginia   March 23, 1914

My dear Mr. Scott: You are probably right in what you say regarding Mr. Villard and his group. All the same when I get a chance I am going to tell him a few things. You know my writing him grew out of a conference with Mr. Moore which was concurred in and understood by Dr. Washington.

Our friend, Moore is very anxious to tell Mr. Villard some things which we think he ought to know regarding Dr. Du Bois and some others. I think, however, that it is a thankless task for accomplishing anything. The trouble is, Dr. Washington is a Leader and cannot help it, he is a born Leader, and the others are leading but they have nobody following them. Yours sincerely,

R. R. Moton

TLS Con. 511 BTW Papers DLC.

From Gifford Pinchot[1]

Philadelphia, Pa. March 27, 1914

Dear Doctor Washington: You may have heard that I am running for the United States Senate in Pennsylvania against Boies Penrose. Mitchell Palmer[2] will be the Democratic candidate. The colored vote in the State, especially in Pittsburg and Philadelphia, will be very influential in determining the result. You are perhaps familiar with my attitude toward the colored people, and with what I have been trying to do in Conservation. A letter from you which I could give out would, of course, be of the utmost value.

On the other hand, I realize that you may not want to put yourself in the position of taking part in any degree in a political conflict. The issue in this case is, however, so clear cut that it might be possible for you to make an exception. If you can, I shall appreciate it greatly. If you find yourself unable to do so, I shall understand it perfectly. I do not want you to do anything that would hamper you in your great work. Sincerely yours,

Gifford Pinchot

TLS   Con. 516   BTW Papers   DLC.

¹ Gifford Pinchot (1865–1946), a champion of conservation, was the first professional forester in America. In 1903 he began a thirty-year career as professor of forestry at Yale. He also served two terms as governor of Pennsylvania, from 1923 to 1927 and from 1931 to 1935.

² Alexander Mitchell Palmer (1872–1936) was a Democratic congressman from Pennsylvania (1909–15), U.S. alien property custodian (1917–19), and U.S. Attorney General (1919–21). He was responsible for the "Palmer raids," the mass arrest and deportation of alien radicals in 1919. He was a contender for the Democratic presidential nomination in 1920.

To George Washington Albert Johnston

Tuskegee Institute, Alabama   March 28th, 1914

Dear Albert: I wish you would look around in Birmingham and see if it is not possible to find a place for John Washington with some of the colored business men there. I have just been seeing John in Los Angeles. He looks very well, but I fear is not making any headway in Los Angeles. I feel he would do much better if he could get a good position with some of the colored business men in Birmingham. He does good work on the typewriter and takes dictation in shorthand. He does not want to leave the West until he has achieved some success there, but I think Birmingham will be a far better place for him. Please write me as soon as you have had time to investigate.

Perhaps a position might be gotten for John in one of the banks in Birmingham.

I see that the Teachers' Association matter has been settled satisfactorily. It came out just about as I told you it would.

I hope all of you are well. Your uncle,

[Booker T. Washington]

TLc   Con. 507   BTW Papers   DLC.

To William G. Willcox

[Tuskegee, Ala.] March 29, 1914

Dear Mr. Willcox: I find that through some oversight the report of the committee on the land scheme was sent to you before it had been passed on by the Executive Council or myself; for this reason, I wish you would disregard the report and await an amended report or the confirmation from the Council or myself regarding the report which is in your hands. You will hear from me regarding the matter very soon.

I feel sure that there is no danger of any sentiment among the white people being created against the institution on account of this effort to help our graduates to get land. In fact, the whole trend of public sentiment, with slight exceptions, among white people in the South is in the direction of helping the colored man to get land. If it becomes known in any community that a colored man has a few hundred dollars to invest in land, he is constantly beset by white people who want to sell him land.

The incident to which Mr. Low refers[1] is evidently in North Carolina. North Carolina has been very much misunderstood and greatly exaggerated. There is an editor of a farm paper in North Carolina, who, in my opinion, in order to advertise his paper conceived the idea of segregating or separating white and colored farmers into separate farming districts and preventing colored people, of course, from buying anywhere except in their own special district. This matter has never been taken seriously by anybody aside from the editor of this paper. He has tried to get the North Carolina legislature to pass on the matter, but the legislature refused to have anything to do with it.

There is not the slightest disposition, so far as I can discover in the South, to take this movement seriously or to give it any attention outside of a little group of people in North Carolina. For a number of months, the editor of this paper carried an advertisement, offering a generous sum to people who would write letters favoring the segregation of the colored people and white people in the farming districts, but, notwithstanding his flattering offer, he got very few people to endorse his view.

I am sure for these and other reasons that the element of opposition from the white people might wholly be disregarded in connection with our scheme. Yours very truly,

Booker T. Washington

TLpS   Con. 989   BTW Papers   DLC.

[1] Willcox had written to BTW that Seth Low feared that any effort of Tuskegee Institute to secure land would lead to opposition and possibly legislation to prevent it. (Mar. 3, 1914, Con. 989, BTW Papers, DLC.)

BIBLIOGRAPHY

This BIBLIOGRAPHY gives fuller information on works cited in the annotations and endnotes. It is not intended to be comprehensive of works on the subjects dealt with in the volume or of works consulted in the process of annotation.

Bittle, William Elmer, and Gilbert Geis. *The Longest Way Home: Chief Alfred C. Sam's Back-to-Africa Movement.* Detroit: Wayne State University Press, 1964.

Book of the Fourth American Peace Congress, St. Louis, May 1, 2, 3, 1913. St. Louis, 1913.

Dabney, Charles W. *Universal Education in the South.* 2 vols. Chapel Hill: University of North Carolina Press, 1936.

Dittmer, John. *Black Georgia in the Progressive Era, 1900–1920.* Urbana: University of Illinois Press, 1977.

Fletcher, Marvin. *The Black Soldier and Officer in the United States Army, 1891–1917.* Columbia: University of Missouri Press, 1974.

Fredrickson, George M. *The Black Image in the White Mind: The Debate on Afro-American Character and Destiny, 1817–1914.* New York: Harper and Row, 1971.

Kellogg, Charles Flint. *NAACP: A History of the National Association for the Advancement of Colored People, 1909–1920.* Baltimore: Johns Hopkins University Press, 1967.

Meier, August. "Booker T. Washington and the Town of Mound Bayou," *Phylon,* 15 (Fourth quarter, 1954), 396–401.

Pringle, Henry Fowles. *Theodore Roosevelt, A Biography.* New York: Harcourt, Brace and Co., 1931.

Redkey, Edwin S. *Black Exodus: Black Nationalist and Back-to-Africa Movements, 1890–1910*. New Haven, Conn.: Yale University Press, 1969.

Shepperson, George, and Thomas Price. *Independent African: John Chilembwe and the Origins, Setting, and Significance of the Nyasaland Native Rising of 1915*. Edinburgh: University Press, 1958.

Washington, Ernest Davidson, ed. *Selected Speeches of Booker T. Washington*. Garden City, N.Y.: Doubleday, Doran and Co., 1932.

INDEX

Note: The asterisk indicates the location of detailed information. This index, while not cumulative, does include the major identifications of persons annotated in earlier volumes of the series who are mentioned in this volume. References to earlier volumes will appear first and will be preceded by the volume number followed by a colon. Lyman Abbott's annotation, for example, will appear as: *3:43-44. Occasionally a name will have more than one entry with an asterisk when new information or further biographical detail is presented.

Abbott, Lyman, *3:43-44; 313
Abbott, Robert Sengstacke, *377; letter to, 377
Acorn Club, 126
Adams, Charles G., 449, *450
Adams, Charles P., 206, 285
Africa: American Negroes have sentimental interest, 330; BTW opposes migration to, 468; Chief Sam delivers migrants to Gold Coast, 438; plans of Joseph Booth, 312-14. *See also* Liberia; South Africa
African Methodist Episcopal Church, 239; praised by BTW, 139
African Redemption Society, 452
Akim Trading Co., 438
Alabama Agricultural Fair Association, 339
Alabama Board of Inspectors of Convicts, 198
Alabama Colored State Teachers Association, 348; letter to, 464-65
Alabama governors. *See* Emmet O'Neal
Alabama Penny Savings Bank, 180
Alabama State Teachers Association, 465
Alcohol: cause of holiday crime, 370-71; distributed from shoe shop near Tuskegee Institute, 300-301; influence on crime, 475; seen as source of

misery, 411. *See also* Drug use; Prohibition
Alderman, Edwin Anderson, *6:150; 482
Alexander, Nathan H., *8:272; removed from office during Wilson administration, 270
Allen, Clarence W., *101; letter from, 305
All Nations Baseball Club, 108
Amalgamated Association of Iron, Steel and Tin Workers, 213
Amalgamated Meat-Cutters and Butchers' Workmen, 214
American Baptist Home Mission Society, 195
American Bar Association, 223; and black members, 8-9
American Church Institute for Negroes, 205
American Federation of Labor, 215; urges blacks to join ranks, 209, 211
American Indians: compared with blacks, 409; considered in good financial circumstances, 185-86; fail to develop land according to BTW, 16
American Interchurch College for Religious and Social Workers (Tenn.), 278, 474

Bean, J. H., 221
Bebbington, Joseph A., *11:577; 83, 165
Beck, James Montgomery, *134
Bedford, Robert Charles, *2:219; 191
Behr, Mrs. W. F.: letter from, 204-5
Bell, John Brown, *11:330; letter to, 403-4; letter to E. J. Scott, 389-90
Benson, William E., *4:244-45; 128
Bertha Ruffner Hotel Bureau, 343, 405
Bertram, James, *8:217; 312, 334; letters to, 131, 172-73
Bertram, Jeannette Tod Ewing: letter to, *334
Biddle, W. B., 459
Biddle University, 166
Bishop College, 364
Bivins, Robert L., 243, *244
Black, William J., 458
"Black Cabinet," 60
Black life: attitudes toward labor, 206-7; BTW's advice to Black Belt farmers, 15-20; comparison of opportunities in North and South, 64-67; career of W. H. Lewis, 223-26; chicken-stealing jokes criticized, 441, 451; compared with American Indians, 185-86; crime rate related to alcohol consumption, 21-30; discrimination in professional baseball, 102-3; emancipation celebration planned, 112-13; emigration to Africa planned, 437-38, 445, 453, 468; graduate of Tuskegee criticizes conduct of faculty, 427-32; in Northwest, 135-40, 141-44; juvenile delinquency, 91-92, 100-101, 102; letter from southern migrant to Detroit, 61-64; literacy increases, 35-39; more money paid for black convicts than for black teachers, 479; Mormons, 152-53; rural blacks described, 191-92; segregated streetcars in New Orleans, 385-87; slavery in Franklin County, Va., 265-67; treatment in New York hospitals, 118-19; treatment of tenant farmers, 392-94; whiskey drinking near Tuskegee Institute criticized, 300-301
Black officeholders: BTW shocked by hasty dismissal of W. H. Lewis, 146-47; F. R. Moore as U.S. minister to Liberia, 131-32; J. C. Napier loses position, 147; lose positions during Wilson administration, 259, 270-71; P. B. S. Pinchback resigns rather than face removal, 270, 273; R. H. Terrell retains judgeship during Wilson administration, 169-70, 437, 445; R. W. Tyler loses position, 147; Republicans dismissed by Wilson administration, 133, 134; Robert Smalls loses office, 168
Blaine, Mrs. Emmons, 97
Blumenthal, George, 97
Boll weevil, 379
Bonaparte, Napoleon, 33, 175
Bonner, M. Lee, 51, *52
Booker T. Washington Institute (Liberia), 349
Booth, Joseph, *314; letter from, 312-14; letter to, 330-31
Boothe, Charles Octavius, *3:271-72; 180
Boston Guardian: in financial trouble, 446
Boston Riot, 32
Boston Transcript: publishes letter by BTW on lynching, 232-33, 340-41
Bowser and Co.: letter to, 320
Boxing: Jack Johnson criticized for behavior, 43-44
Boyd, Billy: letter from, 111-12
Brainerd, Harvey B., 421
Brais, E. J. 215
Brandt, Ralph V., 211
Breckenridge, Sophonisba Preston, 159, *160
Bridgeforth, George Ruffin, *9:134; 94; letter from, 350; letter to, 365-66
Brinley, Godfrey Malbone, *450
Brotherhood of Locomotive Engineers, 210
Brotherhood of Locomotive Firemen and Enginemen, 210
Brotherhood of Railroad Freight Handlers, 215
Brotherhood of Railroad Trainmen, 210
Brown, Arthur A., 109, *110
Brown, Joseph M., 243

leadership, 417; gaining support at
Hampton Institute, 333; growth
threatens BTW's power, 401-3; member criticizes BTW, 279; methods
questioned by R. R. Moton, 469;
O. G. Villard criticizes BTW for de-
clining to attend meeting, 159-60;
protests segregation of federal employees, 234, 247; purpose mentioned,
433; strategy of dealing with movement proposed by BTW lieutenant,
402-3
National Baptist Convention, 283, 293
National Conference on Race Betterment: BTW speaks before, 406-17
National Educational Association, 123
National League for the Protection of
Colored Women, 119
National Medical Association, 115
National Negro Baptist Convention:
BTW speaks before, 285-91
National Negro Business League: BTW
addresses, 259-65; C. W. Anderson
threatens resignation, 443; involved in
cotton oil mill at Mound Bayou, 56;
many local chapters inactive, 239-40;
R. W. Tyler criticized, 297-99; R. W.
Tyler encouraged to continue work as
organizer, 292-94; report of R. W.
Tyler on attempts to organize locals,
237-40
National Press Association, 32
National Religious Training School
(N.C.), 205
National Surety Co., 335
National Urban League: investigates
discrimination in New York hospitals,
115, 118-19
Neal, Benjamin Alexander, *302, 319
"Negro": BTW urges capitalization of
word, 10-11
The Negro Farmer, 388, 420; circula-
tion increases, 439; publication an-
nounced, 362-63; publication plans,
384
The Negro in Business, 6
Negro Year Book, 6, 228-29
Newberg, Moses, 97
New Iberia and Northern Railroad Co.,
461

New Jersey Emancipation Commission,
10
New York *Age,* 471; considered hostile
to NAACP, 469; considered organ for
BTW, 472; critical of W. Calvin
Chase, 99; E. J. Scott plans sale of
stock, 274; editor criticized, 337;
editorials criticized, 230; little influence in Washington, D.C., 401;
O. G. Villard investigates BTW's control, 332-34, 346; publishes accounts
of BTW's tour of Northwest, 135-40,
141-44, 149-53, 154-58; stock sale dis-
cussed, 283-84; stock transaction
sought between E. J. Scott and F. R.
Moore, 383-84
New York *Amsterdam News,* 295, 297,
299, 328, 336; in financial trouble,
447; influenced by Du Bois, 297
New York City Board of Health, 115
New York Colored Medical Society, 97
New York Commission on Prison Re-
form, 450
New York *News,* 336; editor seeks loan
from BTW, 447-48
New York University, 390
New York University Law School, 50
NNBL. *See* National Negro Business
League
Norfolk Southern Railway Co., 462
Norman, Will, 245
North American Civil League for Immi-
grants, 45, *46
North Dakota: toured by BTW, 135-40,
141
North Louisiana Agricultural and In-
dustrial Institute, 206, 285
Northwestern University School of Phar-
macy, 320, 366, 404
Nott, Charles Cooper, Jr., 315, *324,
325

"The Oaks" (BTW's home), *5:27;
gets steam heat, 375-76
Oberlin College (Ohio), xxix
Occidental College (Calif.), 449
Ogden, Robert Curtis, *2:43; 417;
letter from, 104; letter to, 108-9; resigns from Tuskegee Board of Trustees, 104. *See also* Ogden Movement

Slavery: in Franklin County, Va., 240-41
Sloan Maternity Hospital, 119
Small, Maynard and Co., 340
Smalls, Robert, *6:600; letter to, 168; removed from office during Wilson administration, 270
Smallwood, John J., 159, *160
Smith, A. E., 438, *439
Smith, Harry C., *5:123-24; 11
Smith, Hoke, *6:465-66; 246, 482
Smith, Joseph, 150
Smith, Joseph H., 149, 151
Smith, Madison Roswell, *246
Smith, N. Clark, *184, 189; act accompanying band program criticized, 193; bad health prohibits work, 272, 280-81; challenges BTW's criticism of band program, 198-99; complimented on band tour, 255; criticized for student singing during band program, 194; ignores BTW's criticism of band program, 193; letters from, 198-99, 272, 280-81; letters to, 183-84, 193, 194, 255
Smith, Nick, 219
Smith, Robert Lloyd, *4:297-98; letter to, 388
Smith, Wilford H., *5:487; 147, 148; aids E. J. Scott in sale of New York Age stock, 274, 283-84, 383-84; letter from E. J. Scott, 274; letter to E. J. Scott, 283-84; receives eyewitness account of Ulrich incident, 205
Smith, William Alden: letter to, *369
Snow Hill Normal and Industrial Institute (Ala.), 128, 284; BTW criticizes appearance, 254
Social Service Conference of North Carolina, 296
The Souls of Black Folk, 6
South Africa: whites cause trouble, 330
Southern Education Board, 111
Southern Pacific Railroad, 458, 484-85
Southern Railway Co., 339, 462
Southern Sociological Congress, 163, 448, 449
Sparks, Kelly, 397
Spencer, Viola, *365; letter to S. H. Porter, 364-65

Speyer, James, 97
Spingarn, Joel Elias, *10:254-55; 85, 469, 472; letter from, 121; letter from E. J. Scott, 128-29; questions BTW's authorship of The Man Farthest Down, 121
Spokane Federation of Women's Clubs, 141
Sproule, William, 458
State Reformatory for Colored Youths (Mount Meigs, Ala.), 102
Stephens, Shadrack Smith, *376
Shephenson, Gilbert Thomas, *11:80; letter from, 296; letter to, 308-10
Stern, Laura J., *180; letter to, 179-80
Stetson, Francis Lynde, *10:126; 98
Stevens, George Walter, 255, *256; letter from, 381
Stevenson, John D., *189, 194, 198, 199; letter from, 453-56
Stewart, Gilchrist, *3:455-56; 31, 49, 295; claims loyalty to BTW, 89-90; investigates Jack Johnson case, 90; letter from, 89-90; letter to, 90-91
Stewart, Thomas McCants, 380
Stewart, Thomas McCants, Jr., 155
Stokes, Anson Phelps, Jr., *11:125; 40; interested in survey of Negro schools, 47-48, 52-53, 54; letters from, 47-48, 53-54; letters to, 44-45, 52-53, 83
Stokes, J. W., 243
Stokes, Olivia Egleston Phelps, *3:83; 301, 302
Stone, G. L., 98
Storey, Moorfield, *11:109; protests segregation of federal employees, 247
The Story of the Negro, 6
Strayer, Paul Moore, 449, *450
Streetcars: segregation in New Orleans, 327, 385-87
Sunday Evening Talk: notes for, 311
Sunset-Central Lines, 460
Swearingen, John Eldred, *11:533; 129
Swift, John L., 325, *326

Taft, William Howard, *7:530; 51, 99, 132, 133, 208; BTW's opinion of, 48; gains support of black newspapers, 298; loses presidential election, 48, 50; predicted to carry Ten-